The Last Blank Spaces

The Last
Blank Spaces

EXPLORING AFRICA AND AUSTRALIA

Dane Kennedy

Harvard University Press

Cambridge, Massachusetts · London, England

2013

"Hooray for Captain Spaulding": words and music by Bert Kalmar and Harry Ruby.
© 1936 Warner Bros. Inc. (renewed). All rights reserved. Used by permission of
Alfred Publishing Co., Inc.

Library of Congress Cataloging-in-Publication Data

Kennedy, Dane Keith.
The last blank spaces : exploring Africa and Australia / Dane Kennedy.
pages   cm
Includes bibliographical references and index.
ISBN 978-0-674-04847-8 (alk. paper)
1. Africa—Discovery and exploration—British.   2. Australia—Discovery and
exploration—British.   3. Explorers—Great Britain—History.   4. British—Africa—
History.   5. British—Australia—History.   I. Title.
DT3.K36   2013
916.0089'21—dc23   2012038239

For my family

Contents

Maps and Illustrations

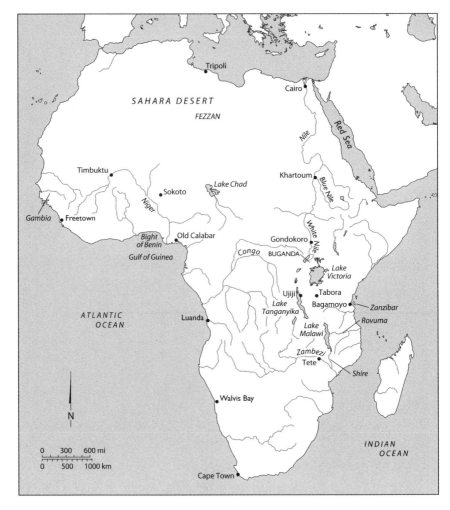

Africa

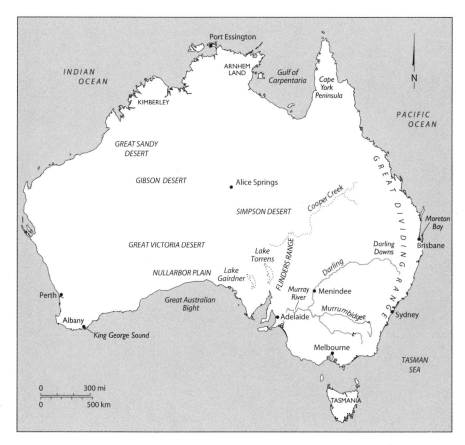

Australia

CHAPTER 1

Continents

He had bought a large map representing the sea,
    Without the least vestige of land:
And the crew were much pleased when they found it to be
    A map they could all understand.

"What's the good of Mercator's North Poles and Equators,
    Tropics, Zones, and Meridian Lines?"
So the Bellman would cry: and the crew would reply
    "They are merely conventional signs!

"Other maps are such shapes, with their islands and capes!
    But we've got our brave Captain to thank:
(So the crew would protest) "that he's bought *us* the best—
    A perfect and absolute blank!"

      —Lewis Carroll, "The Hunting of the Snark" (1874)

EXPLORATION IS A knowledge-producing enterprise. It can be under-taken for a range of reasons—to seek resources, to conquer territory, to promote trade, to convert heathens, to gain fame, and much more. There are, of course, plenty of other ways of achieving those objectives. What distinguishes exploration has less to do with its purposes than with its premises and practices, which derive from *how* it construes and acquires knowledge. For the Western societies that have given the main impetus to modern exploration, it has been understood since at least the eighteenth century to be an enterprise that seeks knowledge of other places and peoples in terms that can be broadly characterized as scientific in meaning and method.

1

This book is about how British explorers produced knowledge about Africa and Australia, and about how that knowledge was made problematic by the conditions of its production. Its point of departure is the proposition that explorers' efforts rested on the founding premise that the two continents were the conceptual equivalents of oceans, vast and empty spaces that could become truly knowable only through the application of scientific methods that seaborne explorers had pioneered. Over the course of the nineteenth century, hundreds of explorers who entered the interior of Africa and Australia emulated this approach by keeping journals and other written records of their observations and experiences; by using precision instruments to map their geographical locations and measure meteorological conditions; and by collecting and preserving large quantities of botanical, geological, and other specimens and artifacts. Local knowledge had little if any recognized place in this evidentiary system. Yet it proved essential to explorers' abilities to overcome the challenges they faced in the field. Where they went and how they got there was often predicated on what they learned from guides, go-betweens, and other indigenous peoples. So too was their access to food, water, shelter, and other necessities. Above all, their passage through unfamiliar societies and polities was made less fraught and less subject to failure as a result of the information and assistance they received from indigenous agents. This irreconcilable tension between exploration as experience and exploration as epistemology is the central theme of the book.

The focal point of this tension was the explorer and the expedition he commanded. The explorer was in certain respects a creation of the early nineteenth century. This was when the word "explorer" first came into general use in the English language, a linguistic innovation that reflected the way the explorer was coming to be seen as different from other kinds of travelers. The difference derived from the specialized skills the explorer was required to possess and put into practice during his journey. These skills ranged from charting an accurate route to recognizing a rare plant to acquiring an understanding of indigenous peoples' institutions, customs, and beliefs. The explorer shouldered heavy obligations, but he also acquired heightened status. He came to be seen as a proto-professional whose duties were carried out in the service of science, society, and the state. The organizational framework for his errand in the wilderness was the expedition, another key term in the construction of exploration as a specialized enterprise. Every expedition was unique, but all of them shared certain characteristics: they were supported by institutional sponsors, such as governmental agencies and learned societies; they were supplied with instructions that outlined their operations and objectives; and they were structured with clear lines of command and defined duties. The Royal Geographical Society even prepared a kind of template for organizing expeditions and establishing their purposes, a document that went through multiple editions.[1]

While British explorers ventured to virtually every corner of the globe in the nineteenth century, they devoted more prolonged attention to Africa and Australia than to any other large landmass. The systematic exploration of these two continents occurred in the same time frame, beginning in both cases near the start of the nineteenth century and concluding toward its end. Africa and Australia were seen to harbor some of the greatest geographical mysteries on earth, and many of the century's most famous explorers made their reputations by seeking answers to those mysteries. They provide what should be tempting targets for comparison. Yet Africa and Australia have rarely been placed in a comparative context.[2] While the entirety of Australia and large portions of Africa had been incorporated within Britain's imperial world system by the end of the nineteenth century, their patterns of incorporation seemed to accentuate rather than minimize the differences between them. The Australian colonies absorbed large numbers of British immigrants and adopted British institutions, while few of the African possessions claimed by Britain at century's end followed a similar trajectory. The main exception was the Cape Colony, which shared some intriguing similarities with the Australian colonies, reinforced by the fact that Cape Town served as the key refreshment station for travelers in transit between Britain and Australia. Otherwise, the two continents entered the twentieth century on very different terms, with consequences that endure to the present day.

These differences are reflected in the contrasting ways social scientists and other scholars have sought to make sense of Africa and Australia. Australia is commonly seen as an antipodal outpost of the "global

North," a "neo-Europe" or "white man's country" that has replicated Europe, and more particularly Britain, in its political structures, economic policies, and demographic character. Africa occupies a very different conceptual space, standing as the poster child of the political instability and economic underdevelopment that characterizes the global South, much of it traceable to the region's victimization by slavery, colonial conquest, and other forms of exploitation by imperial powers. The historical scholarship on Australia and Africa has helped to shape these separate analytical trajectories, which are evident in the very different sorts of questions and concerns that have informed their historiographies. Although one might expect historians of the British Empire to adopt a more integrative stance, they have been no less insistent on positing an analytical gulf between the two continents, classifying Australia as emblematic of white settler colonialism and Africa as the archetypal administrative colonial sphere.

The present study has been written in reaction against this long-standing view that little can be learned by comparing the African and Australian experiences. It seeks to show that important insights can be gained by viewing the exploration of these two continents within a shared frame. The first of these insights concerns the sociological, ideological, and institutional impetus of nineteenth-century exploration itself. The explorers themselves were motivated by a shared set of interests, which included professional advancement, public celebrity, and personal profit. The expeditions they led were informed in turn by a shared set of scientific protocols and practices. A similar array of institutional sponsors (government agencies, learned societies, etc.) drafted the expeditions' instructions, oversaw their preparations, and evaluated their outcomes. In Africa, where the British presence was limited to the Cape and a few entrepôts along the West African coast for much of the century and where other European and non-European parties had competing interests in the interior, the British imperial state took a more active and direct role in exploration than it did in Australia, where the rapidly expanding presence of settlers and the early elimination of any serious geopolitical challenge from other powers permitted London to adopt a lower profile, subcontracting much of the work of exploration to local agents. In both continents, however, the century-long process of exploration was inextricably bound up with the broader imperial interests and ambitions of Britain.

While empire and its vast network of agents and affiliates gave a common purpose to African and Australian explorers' contemporaneous efforts to penetrate the interiors of the two continents, it is equally important to stress that the quotidian conditions they confronted on the ground often complicated and even undermined that purpose. Too much of the literature on exploration is too quick to draw a causal connection between intentions and outcomes, presuming that empire's promotion of exploration meant exploration's advancement of empire. The triumphalist teleology that informs this view neglects the significance of events and experiences that cast a different light on efforts to investigate unfamiliar lands—the expeditions that failed ignominiously, the explorers whose loyalties proved ambivalent or divided, and, above all, the indigenous peoples and other non-Western parties who helped to shape exploration, often diverting it to their own purposes. Comparing the patterns of exploration in Africa and Australia provides a perspective that gives greater clarity to the distinctive influences that local forces—and local peoples in particular—exerted on their course and character. One of the book's key comparative conclusions is that African explorers were far more reliant on indigenous populations than their Australian counterparts. A second conclusion, however, is that the explorers of both continents were often weak and vulnerable. Far from demonstrating the great power of the British Empire, explorers in fact discovered its limits and learned that their success and, indeed, their very survival often depended on their ability to obtain local assistance and acquire local knowledge. Four decades ago the African historian Robert Rotberg made the case that explorers can best be seen "as precursors but not progenitors of imperialism."[3] It is a distinction that deserves more attention than it has received.

The Last Blank Spaces, then, is as much about the limits of empire as it is about empire's reach. It is about the need to distinguish between the ways exploration served an imperial society's panoply of purposes—political, economic, ideological, and more—and the ways it did not. It is about the gulf that arose between what expeditions were meant to achieve and what they actually accomplished. It is about the tension between explorers' public personas as agents of knowledge and power and their privately acknowledged confusion and vulnerability in the field. It is about the collision between British and indigenous values, interests, and ways of knowing the world, but it is also about their occasional convergences and signs of mutual appreciation. Above all, it is about the ways explorers' efforts to advance the West's universalist system of knowledge came face-to-face with their need to understand and accommodate local knowledges, which is to say it is about what the collision between epistemology and experience meant for exploration and for the societies it brought into contact with one another.

One of the great paradoxes of exploration as it came to be understood and practiced by the British and other Europeans from the late eighteenth century onward is that it was possible to explore and "discover" places that were already known—known not simply by the indigenous peoples of those places but also by Europeans themselves. Perhaps the most striking example of this paradox comes from Alexander von Humboldt's immensely influential travels through Latin America from 1799 to 1804, which he detailed in his thirty-volume *Voyage aux régions équinoxiales du Nouveau Continent.* While his meticulously documented journey came to be recognized as a model of scientific exploration, it traversed territory that the Spanish had for the most part occupied and colonized for several centuries. Humboldt was emblematic of how it became possible in the nineteenth century to explore territory that was not truly terra incognita to the explorers or their sponsors. Their aim was to discover the known anew.

This paradox derives in large measure from the transfer of maritime notions of space and methods of navigation and measurement to expeditions carried out across land. The great eighteenth-century voyages of discovery conducted by Louis-Antoine de Bougainville of France, James Cook of Britain, Alessandro Malaspina of Spain, and others had brought unprecedented prestige and authority to naval explorers, establishing them as heroes of national greatness and scientific progress. Not only did they sail across distant and dangerous seas, but they used the most sophisticated technologies available at the time to calculate and track their routes, measure and record meteorological and other environmental conditions, and collect and preserve an array of natural specimens from seas and shorelines, all the while meticulously recording their impressions and experiences in logbooks and journals. So successful were these endeavors that much of the mystery surrounding the Pacific and other great bodies of water had been solved by the end of the century, or so many contemporaries concluded. No one was a more influential proponent of this view than Joseph Banks, the naturalist on Cook's first voyage and subsequently Georgian Britain's most prominent and far-sighted proponent of scientific exploration. In 1788 he joined with some gentleman friends to found the Association for Promoting the Discovery of the Interior Parts of Africa, commonly known as the African Association. In its prospectus, they proclaimed that "nothing worthy of research by Sea, the Poles themselves excepted, remains to be examined; but by Land, the objects of discovery are still so vast, as to include at least a third of the habitable surface of the earth: for much of Asia, a still larger proportion of America, and almost the whole of Africa, are unvisited and unknown."[4]

This claim was not strictly true. By the late eighteenth century, the British and other Europeans had gleaned a great deal of information about the interiors of Africa, Asia, and the Americas (though not Australia). For Banks and his colleagues, however, the problem was that this information came from sources whose veracity could not be vouched for—from native informants, from foreign travelers, from random traders, trappers, and military adventurers, even from classical authorities such as Herodotus and Ptolemy, whose accounts still informed geographical commentary about the interior of Africa. The ambition of men such as Banks was to apply to land exploration the modes of investigation and discovery that had been developed and refined by seaborne explorers, deriving from them the kinds of scientific knowledge that could be measured, mapped, quantified, classified, catalogued, and compared. Although Humboldt's original ambition was to follow in the footsteps of his mentor Georg Forster by sailing on a British or French naval expedition as a naturalist, he became convinced that the new frontier for exploration lay "beyond the sterile coast" in remote mountains and forests. Whatever was already known about the interior of Latin

America was from Humboldt's perspective either scientifically unverified or irrelevant. "In the New World," he explained, "man and his productions disappear, so to speak, in the midst of a wild and outsized nature."[5] Much the same set of assumptions shaped the contemporaneous expeditions of Mungo Park in Africa, Alexander Mackenzie in Canada, and Meriwether Lewis and William Clark in the United States, and it would endure as an essential impetus of exploration as a European enterprise for many decades to come. The result was to make the nineteenth century what Joseph Conrad would term "the century of the landsmen investigators," who directed their attention to the interiors of continents.[6]

Spatial categories such as continents should never be taken as natural or given: they are abstractions that arise out of particular circumstances to serve particular agendas. As two historical geographers recently put it, "Spaces are produced, and are themselves productive of different social and material relationships."[7] Why did explorers turn their attention to continents as spatial categories? In their influential book *The Myth of Continents,* Martin Lewis and Kären Wigen have stated that "the division of the world into great continents became an increasingly important metageographical concept in the eighteenth and nineteenth centuries."[8] They argue that this was not simply the result of greater empirical knowledge about large landmasses, but rather the consequence of Europeans' discursive desire to set their homeland apart from Asia, Africa, and the like, differentiating it as a space imbued with civilizational superiority. The instrumentalist appeal of this "imaginative geography," as Edward Said famously phrased it, is apparent, but was it the reason continents assumed metageographical standing? I want to propose an alternative explanation for continents' newfound place in Europeans' mental map of the world.

In order to understand how continents assumed such importance as categories of geographical thought, we need to place them in the context of that other great metageographical concept, oceans. Europeans' familiarity with the world's oceans preceded their familiarity with the world's continents. Their evolving efforts to determine the legal and geopolitical status of these waters stand in interesting juxtaposition to their understanding of large landmasses. The early modern maritime empires of

Spain and Portugal sought to assert jurisdictional claims to the seas, insisting on exclusive control over particular navigational corridors and categories of shipping. Those claims came under challenge from the Dutch, the English, and other rivals, who pressed instead for freedom of the seas. The case for establishing a system of international law to govern traffic on the high seas was first laid out by the Dutch jurist Hugo Grotius in 1609. A nascent law of the seas gained purchase among European powers in the eighteenth century and soon thereafter achieved global predominance with the aid of British naval hegemony.[9] The oceans were thus established as spaces apart from the sovereign spheres of states.

Simultaneously, European states were consolidating their control over territorial possessions, both at home and abroad.[10] The main cartographic manifestation of this political project was the trigonometric survey, a methodical, labor-intensive, state-sponsored enterprise that relied on bulky tools such as the theodolite (a precision surveying instrument used to measure angles) and the Gunter's chain (a set of linked metal rods used to measure distance) and that resulted in detailed topographical maps of those lands the state claimed as its own. The famous Cassini surveys of the kingdom of France led the way, but the British were not far behind, mapping Scotland in 1745–1761, Quebec in 1760–1761, other North American colonies in 1764–1770, Ireland in 1778–1790, and England itself in the 1790s, followed by the great trigonometric survey of India, which lasted from 1802 to 1843.[11] Although these surveys drew on some of the same scientific principles and mathematical skills that were employed in contemporaneous efforts to chart the Pacific and other oceans by the British Admiralty and its European rivals, they had very different geopolitical implications and outcomes. Above all, they gave cartographic expression to political sovereignty, marking these mapped lands as the domains of the state. Such surveys were especially important to civil and military authorities, the former in determining land tenure and assessing taxes, the latter in suppressing revolts and repelling invasions. And because the same triangulating techniques could be applied to those narrow strips of sea within sight of land (though depth replaced height in such hydrographic surveys), it became possible for states to claim territorial waters as well, an extension of sovereignty that would become enshrined in modern international law.

There is no discernible correspondence, however, between this cartographic practice, with its emphasis on the assertion of political sovereignty, and the idea of continents as a metageographical space. That category appears instead to have come into play as a way to classify those boundless expanses of land around the globe that remained beyond the reach of trigonometric surveyors and their sponsoring states. At the end of the eighteenth century these regions included nearly all of Africa, Australia, and Asia, and the greater parts of North and South America (not to mention the entirety of Antarctica). If trigonometric surveys aided in the political imagining of nations and colonies, then their absence allowed for the geographical imagining of continents. Like oceans, continents came to designate empty space, inscribed in the abstract coordinates of longitude and latitude. Whatever polities and political divisions these spaces may have been seen to possess in the past were increasingly regarded as so incommensurate with Europeans' own cartographic conceptions of political sovereignty that their legitimacy as territorial units ran the risk of dissolving into thin air.

By emphasizing empty space, the category of continents clearly laid some of the ideological groundwork for the imperial ambitions of Britain and other European states.[12] These expansionist powers had cause to equate the absence of any cartographic surveys of continents such as Africa and Australia (or at least of any surveys that European cartographers recognized as such) with the absence of any valid claims by indigenous peoples and polities to the territories they inhabited. Indeed, a case can be made that insofar as continents came to be considered the counterparts of oceans, they were viewed in some sense as similarly empty of inhabitants, or at least of inhabitants with any sovereign claims to the land.[13]

Still, it would be a mistake to assume that explorers' efforts to map the interiors of continents simply made them the cartographic agents of European imperialism, extending to these distant lands the same notions of sovereign power that were produced by trigonometric surveys. The mapping practices carried out by explorers were quite different in character and consequence from trigonometric surveys, which presumed, and indeed as a practical matter required, that the lands being surveyed were already under the control of the state. Such conditions did not obtain in the places probed by explorers, nor were their cartographic practices meant to produce them. Most explorers engaged in traverse or transit surveys, maps made on the move that traced the route of an expedition and noted natural landmarks (rivers, mountains, lakes, etc.) that were sighted along the way. The difference between the traverse survey and the trigonometric survey has been aptly described by the historian of science D. Graham Burnett as the difference between boundary crossing and boundary making.[14]

The traverse survey resembled nothing so much as the mode of mapping practiced by maritime navigators. It served virtually the same purpose, using compass readings to determine direction and longitudinal and latitudinal readings to fix location. It relied on sextants, artificial horizons, chronometers, and other instruments designed for navigation at sea, not to mention naval almanacs, which were consulted to confirm the accuracy of chronometers and to independently establish longitude. Burnett, again, aptly explains the nature of such surveys: "By enabling the user to 'fix' points of a trajectory along the blank 'track chart' of terra incognita, navigational techniques constituted a superior way for an interior explorer to 'find himself' after he had succeeded in losing himself in unfamiliar terrain."[15]

This process of first losing and then finding oneself was constituted in terms made meaningful by maritime navigational methods. In order for it to achieve its intended outcome, preexisting conceptions of these spaces, which often accentuated their particularity as places imbued with meanings derived from the reports and rumors of local informants, had to be ignored or discredited. A striking illustration of this process of erasure can be found in the changes that took place in British cartographic representations of Africa at the start of the nineteenth century.

Most British-made maps of Africa in the eighteenth century presented the continent as a crazy quilt of political and ethnic units, their boundaries delineated by distinct lines and their territories colored in separate hues. This was how Africa was portrayed in the work of Herman Moll, a noted English mapmaker of German origin whose work appeared in the first third of the century. Emanuel Bowen's "A New and Accurate Map of Africa," published in London in 1747, characterized the continent in similar terms, as did Mathew Carey's maps of Africa from the end of the century. Maps such as these drew on a cartographic tradition—traceable to the sixteenth century, if not earlier—that presented Africa as a continent filled with distinct and identifiable states and peoples. Whether the territorial boundaries represented in these maps corresponded with any accuracy to the particular peoples and states they identified—whether, in fact, many of these boundaries and their designated inhabitants even existed outside the imagination of the mapmaker and his informants—is doubtful, but for our purposes the relevant point is this: British (and other European) cartographers of the period conceived of Africa as a place no less composed of territorially differentiated peoples and states than Europe itself.

After the turn of the century, however, Africa was transformed by British mapmakers into something resembling Lewis Carroll's "perfect and absolute blank." John Barrow, who used his long tenure as undersecretary of the Admiralty to promote the exploration of Africa, defended this difficult and costly enterprise by insisting that the "knowledge of the great continent of Africa . . . exhibits at this day, to the reproach of the state of geographical science in the nineteenth century, *almost a blank on our charts.* . . . So little indeed has our knowledge of this great continent kept pace with the increased knowledge of other parts of the world, that *it may rather be said to have retrograded.*"[16]

Barrow's view that British knowledge of Africa had "retrograded" to "almost a blank" was indicative of the new cartographical approach to the continent, an approach that emptied African space of prior political and ethnic identifications. Although the famed eighteenth-century French cartographer Jean-Baptiste d'Anville had initiated this process of erasure with a map of Africa produced in 1749, his precedent does not appear to have influenced cartographic practice in Britain until the African Association and its allies began to promote the exploration of the continent.[17] The first example of the new style appeared in the work of Thomas Kitchin, a prominent London-based cartographer who had apprenticed with Emanuel Bowen. His 1780 map of Africa had replicated the dense filigree of names and political boundaries characteristic of his predecessors' maps, but in 1794 he produced a new map that eliminated these details from much of the continent. The most influential example of the new cartographic approach, however, was Aaron Arrowsmith's

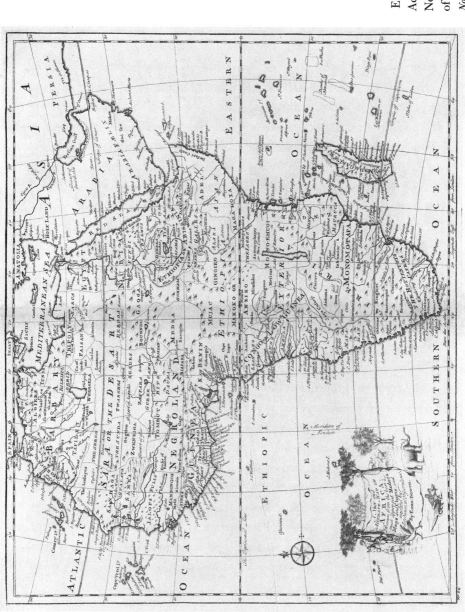

Emanuel Bowen, "A New and Accurate Map of Africa" (1747). Note the detailed delineation of political boundaries. *Source: Northwestern University Library.*

1802 map of Africa, tellingly produced for "the Committee and Members of the British Association for the Discovery of the Interior Parts of Africa." The only parts of Africa whose states it delineated by color and line included the northeast quadrant running from Egypt to Ethiopia, a strip stretching along the Mediterranean from Morocco to Tripoli, and a corridor of states south of the Sahara in West Africa, with slight indentations indicating where Europeans had come into contact with African polities in the Congo basin, Mozambique, and South Africa. The map of Africa included in John Cary's *New Universal Atlas* (1805) did not even acknowledge the West African states of the Sahel. Most of the continent was simply labeled "Unknown Parts." Sidney Hall's "Africa" (1829) identified North Africa's Barbary states, Egypt, and Ethiopia, but the only other political territories that interrupted the continent's blankness were the British colonies of Cape Colony and Natal. John Arrowsmith, probably the best known of Britain's nineteenth-century cartographers, published a map of Africa in 1844 that again included the North African states and Ethiopia, along with the West African state of Ashanti and its colonial neighbors, Senegambia and Liberia, but left the rest of the continent empty except in the far south, where "Hottentotia" and the Cape Colony were delineated. These and other nineteenth-century maps of Africa systematically erased those African political and ethnic units that could not be verified by European travelers.[18] The consequences of this cartographic heritage were aptly illustrated in Joseph Conrad's *Heart of Darkness,* which begins with his narrator Marlowe remarking that his fascination as a youth with those "many blank spaces" in maps of Africa was what eventually drew him to the continent.[19]

In order for this erasure to take place, the sort of information that had previously shaped European knowledge about the interior of Africa had to be relegated to the realm of hearsay. Arab reports, classical texts, African slaves' oral accounts, and various other sources came to be seen as little more than speculative placeholders for the scientific knowledge that could come only from specially trained European explorers. Direct observation was the sine qua non of their authority, though it was invariably supplemented and substantiated by other forms of evidence, especially the journal entries they made, the astronomical and meteorological readings they took, and the physical specimens they collected. All of

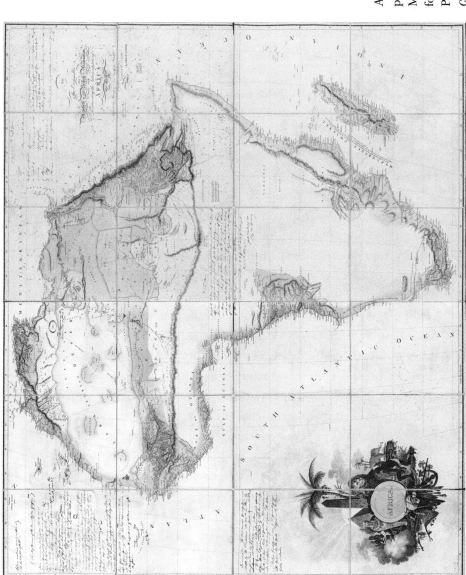

Aaron Arrowsmith, "Africa" (1802), prepared for "the Committee and Members of the British Association for the Discovery of the Interior Parts of Africa." *Source: Library of Congress.*

this information was subject in turn to review and analysis by experts at home. While the purported purpose of this new knowledge regime was to give greater scientific rigor to geographical inquiry, it did not prevent other sorts of cartographic fictions from shaping British perceptions of Africa. None was more notorious than the imaginary mountains of Kong in West Africa, first championed by the African Association's leading authority on Africa's geography, James Rennell, who extrapolated their existence from a fleeting remark made by Mungo Park and his own speculative assessment of the course of the Niger River. The mountains of Kong would endure as a prominent feature of most maps of the region until the end of the nineteenth century.[20] It was precisely because men such as Rennell, Banks, and Barrow considered the continent of Africa as "unvisited and unknown" that they and their successors felt so free to recast its cartography, rejecting prior modes of representation and introducing their own purportedly objective, but occasionally imaginative, geographies.

The same standards came to be applied to Australia, though the interior of this continent truly was terra incognita to the British and other Europeans. No prior sources of information about its interior were available to them. Hence Australia never experienced the same cartographic erasures as Africa. Until Matthew Flinders's circumnavigation of Australia in 1801–1803, Europeans lacked confirmation that it was a continent, much less an accurate appreciation of its shape and circumference. Eighteenth-century maps produced prior to Cook's voyage up Australia's east coast showed the outlines of the western half of the continent, which the Dutch had mapped, but delineated no boundary between land and sea on the other side. Some maps showed Tasmania as an extension of the mainland, while others rendered Australia and New Guinea as physically connected. Even after Flinders, the British had only the sketchiest sense of the shape of some portions of the coast, a deficiency that was not rectified until a series of hydrographic surveys were carried out over a number of years. As for the interior of the continent, British knowledge did not extend much beyond Sydney's immediate hinterland through the first two decades of the nineteenth century. John Arrowsmith's 1834 map was the first to give any inkling of what explorers had begun to learn about the interior. Apart from territory known to explorers and settlers in New South Wales and Perth's immediate environs, the continent remained emptier of identifying signs than the seas that surrounded it.[21]

Unlike African maps, Australian ones never gave any indication of the existence of indigenous polities and presence on the land. Cartographically, the continent was characterized as terra nullius from the start, a view that explorers' encounters with Aborigines did nothing to change. The physical environment itself seemed so far removed from British expectations and experience that they had difficulty making cartographic sense of it.[22] Explorers struggled to chart their course and fix their place in this flat, arid, seemingly featureless landscape. They puzzled over the few rivers they discovered, which seemed to flow away from the coast, dispersing into impassable marshlands or disappearing into desert sands. John Oxley, the former naval officer who became surveyor general of New South Wales and leader of several early expeditions into its hinterland, conjectured that these waters must eventually feed into a great inland sea. No less a feature of fictive geography than the mountains of Kong, this mirage gained a powerful purchase on the imaginations of explorers in the first half of the nineteenth century, inspiring a series of expeditions in search of its shores and adding strength to the view that Australia resembled an ocean.

Nothing, however, better illustrates how Australia came to be conceived in terms that suggest oceanic associations than the ambiguity surrounding its geographical designation. By the early nineteenth century, it was frequently referred to as an island continent, a hybrid classification that accentuated this ambiguity. The explorer Charles Sturt, a leading advocate of the existence of an inland sea, was also a prominent proponent of the notion of an island continent. "Australia," he declared, "is properly speaking an island, but it is so much larger than every other island on the face of the globe, that it is classed as a continent in order to convey to the mind a just idea of its magnitude."[23] To regard Australia as both an island and a continent was to view it as both part of the world of water and part of the world of land. This dual designation was reinforced in nineteenth-century maps by the widespread use of the term "Australasia," which stressed Australia's place within a larger region bound together by the seas of the South Pacific.[24] The duality of these

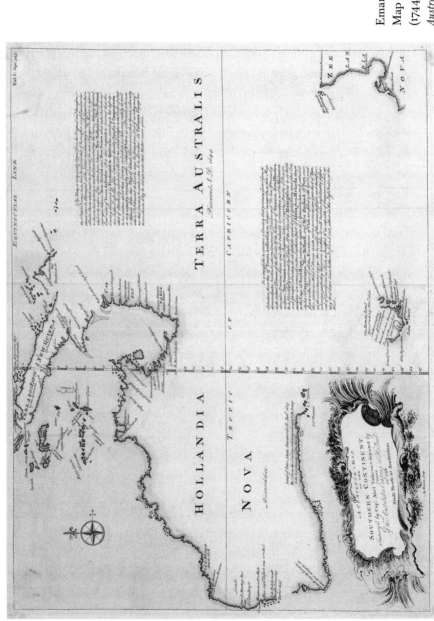

Emanuel Bowen, "A Complete Map of the Southern Continent" (1744). *Source: National Library of Australia.*

characterizations of Australia's geographical status provided a striking demonstration of how difficult it was to disentangle continents from oceans as metageographical categories.

The mental imbrication of these two great geographical spaces played out in various ways, perhaps most visibly in the maritime metaphors that Australian and African explorers often employed to describe their observations and experiences.[25] They frequently characterized their decision to travel in a particular direction as "navigating" a course and compared their movement through trackless territory to the passage of a ship at sea. Simon Ryan finds "the recurrence of the image of the desert as a sea" to be "one of the more surprising elements of the [Australian] explorers' descriptions of the interior," but it makes sense once one realizes how much they relied on maritime models for their conception of space, their modes of operation, and so much more.[26] Captain Cook was clearly a model for the explorer Thomas Livingstone Mitchell, who christened the two wagon boats he brought on his second expedition the *Discovery* and the *Resolution,* the names of Cook's vessels. He compared his "means of carrying provisions" to that of "a ship at sea" and found that the flat Australian landscape resembled an ocean insofar as "points conspicuous in the general horizon [are] few and far between."[27] Sturt also used maritime metaphors to describe his experiences: "We are like a ship riding at single anchor," he wrote when his party was trapped in Australia's arid interior, desperately ill from that classic scourge of sailors, scurvy.[28] Other allusions to ships, sailors, and the sea include the following comment by the member of a late nineteenth-century expedition in Western Australia: "Explorers, it seems, are not unlike sailors in some respects. When about to ship for a lengthy voyage the average sailor makes the most of his time on shore and has a real good jubilee."[29]

Maritime imagery also entered into the discourse on African exploration. It was common for explorers who ventured across the Sahara to equate their journey to a voyage across an ocean, often referring to camels as ships of the desert, but they were hardly the only African explorers to draw on this analogy. The instructions the South African explorer Dr. Andrew Smith received from his Cape Town sponsors included this arresting sentence: "The track of a caravan on land, as of a ship at sea, is defined as well by the less as the more remarkable points through which it passes."[30] "This terrestrial sea" is how David Livingstone referred to some of the African territory he passed through on his last expedition.[31] And an elated Joseph Thomson drew on the language of sailing to describe the final stage of his journey through East Africa: "Under these headwinds there was nothing for it but to 'down helm' and run before the wind with all sails set."[32]

The construction of cartographic knowledge is usually believed to derive from the empirical information gathered incrementally by explorers and other travelers specially trained to carry out geographical observations. Yet their efforts presupposed metageographical categories such as oceans and continents, which provided the epistemological premises that underwrote their understandings of the spaces they passed through. Those premises erased the presence of place from these categories of space, allowing explorers the opportunity to make them knowable in new terms that drew on the abstract, universalizing scientific methods refined and reified in the eighteenth-century seaborne expeditions of Cook and his counterparts. The exploration of Africa and Australia would occur in the context of these maritime models. They would permit explorers and their sponsors to conceive of continents, like oceans, as vast and seemingly empty spaces that could be truly known only after they had been made unknown.

It scarcely needs stating that Africa and Australia were far from empty spaces when the British sent expeditions into their interiors. Vast landmasses of varied environments, they were home to an immense array of plants and animals and long-established human communities with rich and complex cultures. Africa is much the larger of the two continents, with a total landmass of 18,860,400 square miles, four times more than Australia's 4,723,160 square miles. It sustained a far larger population as well, estimated at slightly more than 100 million at the beginning of the nineteenth century, compared to the 300,000 to 1 million indigenous people who inhabited Australia at this time.

Australia's far more modest population figures were a function not simply of less territory but also of the unique ecological constraints its inhabitants confronted. It is the oldest, flattest, driest continent on earth, with poor soils and erratic rainfall. A third of the land receives less than 10 inches of rain per annum, and nearly three-quarters of it is classified as arid or semiarid. Although Australia contains unique and diverse animal species, it has no large indigenous mammals suitable for domestication and pastoralism. Combined with its isolation from other large landmasses, these factors meant that the continent presented its indigenous inhabitants with little alternative but to pursue a hunter-gatherer existence, a mode of production that kept population densities low and separated peoples into small clan groupings.

Africa, by contrast, is a remarkably rich and varied environment that ranges from forest to savannah to desert. Although it is home to the Sahara, the largest desert in the world, it also has vast tracts of well-watered territory with rich soils, abundant woodlands, and great rivers and lakes. For millennia Africa's complex ecosystem has supported densely populated communities of agriculturalists, interspersed with large bands of pastoralists and smaller pockets of hunter-gatherers. These conditions have given rise to great cities, powerful states, and extensive trading networks that stretched across the continent and beyond, bringing Africans into contact with the peoples of South Asia, the Middle East, Europe, and elsewhere. The immense cultural diversity of the continent's inhabitants was manifested in its dizzying array of religious beliefs, social practices, political institutions, and linguistic traditions, which derived from four separate language families and led to the development of some 1,000 to 2,000 distinct languages.

While Australia nurtured nothing like the same degree of social diversity, Aborigines were far more varied in their linguistic and cultural traditions than one might suppose. They were divided into an estimated 400 distinct groups, each with its own lineage system, rules of affiliation, cosmological traditions, customary practices, and more. They spoke as many as 300 separate languages and dialects. Although they are sometimes characterized as nomadic, they occupied distinct territories and possessed a sense of land ownership as "custodians of constellations of sacred sites."[33] The greatest population densities probably existed in the region watered by the Murray River system in the southeast, but clans and bands occupied almost every corner of the continent, including some of its harshest and most challenging desert environments.

However appealing it may have been for explorers to approach Africa and Australia as empty spaces to be made known by means of maritime protocols and practices, it was a conceit that denied the complex particularities of these continents. Traveling across terra firma in Africa or Australia was profoundly different, both physically and emotionally, from sailing across the aquatic expanses of the Pacific and other oceans. One of the most obvious differences was that oceanic explorers had to rely on abstract coordinates to determine their routes and locations at sea, whereas land explorers were able to overlay that mode of mapping onto the far more empirical practice of locating themselves in relation to distinguishing features of the physical landscape. While some of these features—streams, hills, stands of trees, and the like—were natural, others, such as blazed trees and stone cairns, were man-made. This is a reminder that the most important difference distinguishing land from sea exploration is that the former's object of inquiry is the realm of human habitation. A variety of peoples had occupied Africa and Australia for millennia. They had marked and altered their landscapes in many dramatic and often irreversible ways, setting fires to clear brush, hunt game, and spur new growth, exterminating some species of flora and fauna and introducing others, reworking soils and reshaping waterways, fabricating dwellings and constructing cities, and so on. Explorers could hardly fail to notice their presence on the land, and the shrewder and more sensitive among them understood that these peoples' hard-won knowledge of their environments was well worth soliciting. Although maritime explorers had certainly done the same in those waters where indigenous pilots were available—Cook, for example, had benefited from the guidance of Tupaia as he sailed among the islands of the South Pacific—such opportunities were limited to those waters familiar to local pilots. Seaborne explorers had to rely on their own navigational skills and experience in oceanic environments for the greater part of their journeys. Many of Africa's and Australia's explorers certainly sought to emulate the self-sufficiency of such eminent models, but the conditions they confronted on the ground—both figuratively and literally—simply did not permit it. This is the story of how the universalist knowledge that gave the exploration of Africa and Australia its sanctioned aims and meanings came into collision with the local knowledge that placed its own stamp on what explorers did in the field.

In order to avoid two parallel but separate narrative histories of the exploration of Africa and Australia, the book is organized on thematic lines. The sequence of chapters is intended in some sense to emulate the characteristic trajectory of an expedition itself. It begins with the development of, and debates about, the scientific protocols and practices that provided the epistemological framework for exploration (Chapter 2), turns to the social backgrounds of the explorers and highlights their struggles to attain recognition as protoprofessionals (Chapter 3), analyzes the political agendas of the gateway states that gave expeditions access to the interior (Chapter 4), considers the logistical strategies that shaped the structures of expeditions and informed their relations with Africans and Aborigines (Chapter 5), examines the origins, roles, and contributions of the guides, translators, and other indigenous intermediaries who accompanied expeditions (Chapter 6), investigates the forces that determined the character and consequences of cultural encounters between explorers and local peoples (Chapter 7), and tracks the experiences of those explorers who returned to metropolitan centers as celebrities (Chapter 8). The book, in brief, traces the development of exploration from an idea to a practice, from a practice to an outcome, and from an outcome to a myth.

CHAPTER 2

Sciences

Astronomical pursuits, surveying, &c. have a peculiar attraction.
Let but one moderate draught be taken, fairly tasted, a species of
intoxication follows, "a scientific mania" ensues.

—Commander Edward Belcher, *A Treatise on Nautical Surveying* (1835)

I N 1774 the Scotsman James Bruce returned to Britain after having
spent the previous six years in Ethiopia and neighboring parts of Africa. During his lengthy sojourn in these distant lands he learned local languages, adopted local dress and customs, took part in local wars, and slept with local women. A physically imposing man whose personality was equally outsized, he quickly became a celebrity in London society, feted by the rich and famous. His tales of adventure enthralled dinner party guests and fed newspapers with gripping copy. But when he described his attendance at Ethiopian banquets where steaks were carved from the flanks of live cattle and served raw to guests, opinion began to turn against him. Some critics expressed disgust that Bruce had taken part in such a savage custom. Others wondered whether such an improbable story was even true. Their suspicions opened the door to doubts about his veracity more generally. Prominent public figures such as Samuel Johnson and Horace Walpole began to question other claims he had made. Bruce soon became a target of mockery, his stories even serving as scarcely disguised models for some of the tall tales in Rudolph Raspe's *Surprising Adventures of Baron Munchausen*.[1]

Bruce found himself the victim of shifting popular attitudes toward travelers' tales. The wondrous, highly embroidered accounts of exotic lands and peoples that had thrilled readers in the past were increasingly regarded with disdain and distrust. Jonathan Swift had mocked the genre as early as 1726 in *Gulliver's Travels,* which sought to show that such narratives often "impose[d] the grossest falsities on the unwary reader."[2] Samuel Johnson had turned such travel tales on their head in his novella *Rasselas* (1759), whose eponymous Ethiopian prince was a universal everyman, not an exotic stranger. Over the course of the eighteenth century, the public had come to expect new standards of evidence from those who reported on their journeys to distant lands, standards that the lone traveler telling undocumented and unverifiable tales could no longer meet.

These new standards were exemplified by the achievements of Bruce's contemporary, Captain James Cook. In 1768, the year that Bruce left for Ethiopia, Captain Cook set out on the first of his three great voyages of discovery. By the time Bruce was back in Britain, Cook had already made a triumphal return from his first expedition across the Pacific and departed on his second, which was then in its third year. John Hawkesworth's best-selling account of British exploration of the Pacific, based in part on Cook's own journals, had appeared in print the year prior to Bruce's return to England. Cook's reputation was further enhanced by the successful completion of his second expedition in 1775, followed by his departure on a third voyage of discovery the following year. In the course of these remarkable journeys, Cook charted vast tracts of the Pacific, discovered a number of islands hitherto unknown to Europeans, mapped the entire coastline of New Zealand and the eastern coast of Australia, probed the Bering Strait for a Northwest Passage, and put an end to speculation about the existence of a habitable southern continent. Cook's apotheosis as a national hero was ensured by his death at the hands of Hawaiians in 1779.[3]

What made Cook "paradigmatic for all voyagers to come" was the meticulous attention he gave to the production of accurate observations and verifiable reports.[4] His success derived above all from state-of-the-art navigational instruments, most famously the Harrison chronometers, which were specially designed to determine longitude at sea. Cook was able to chart courses and fix locations with unprecedented precision, locating any "place in a single, fixed grid of coordinates."[5] The ship itself served as a laboratory, even a scientific instrument in its own right, with temperatures, tides, winds, currents, water depth, and other natural forces regularly measured and recorded in logs. In addition, Cook was accompanied on his voyages by naturalists who collected botanical and zoological specimens, artists who produced visual records of the environments and peoples the expeditions encountered, and other specialists in the study of the natural world. To a greater degree than anyone who preceded him, Cook transformed exploration into an empirically verifiable enterprise and, in so doing, raised the evidentiary bar on those who made truth claims about their travels to distant corners of the globe.[6]

James Bruce was hardly unaware of the value his contemporaries had begun to place on exploration as a scientific endeavor. After falling out of favor in London, he returned to his Scottish estate to lick his wounds and restore his reputation. A decade and a half later, he published an encyclopedic account of his African experiences, *Travels to Discover the Source of the Nile* (1790), its five hefty volumes serving as a rebuttal to his critics. In his introduction he defiantly declared that to "see distinctly and accurately, to describe plainly, dispassionately and truly, is all that ought to be expected from one in my situation," a remark that assumed special meaning much later in his narrative when he reiterated the infamous story of the bloody banquets.[7] The main intent of his massive publication was to demonstrate his bona fides as a scientific observer. He listed the various instruments he had acquired in preparation for his journey, expressed his dismay at their loss in a shipwreck, and described his struggles to replace them. These instruments included a sextant, a timepiece, two telescopes, and a camera obscura, "a talismanic guarantee," Nigel Leask suggests, "of the veracity of his narrative."[8] Bruce ended one volume with the daily rainfall totals he had recorded in Ethiopia for five months in 1770 and another with his register of daily barometer, thermometer, and wind readings for a seventeen-month period in 1770–1771. Volume five was devoted to the botanical and zoological information he had gathered, offering detailed descriptions of indigenous plants, animals, and birds, each of them illustrated with handsome plates. At the end of the last volume were three large, fold-out African maps, including one of the Red Sea coast and Ethiopian interior that he claimed to have personally charted. The title of his tome advertised his principal geographical achievement, the tracing of the Blue Nile— secondary to the White Nile in length, but foremost in water volume—to its source, which "interested all scientific nations," he declared.[9] By portraying himself in the *Travels* as an agent of scientific inquiry and discovery, Bruce sought to reclaim his good name and reframe his accomplishments.

What the coinciding cases of Bruce and Cook demonstrate is that the truth claims of late eighteenth-century British (and other European) travelers were being held to a set of standards that demanded verification through quantitative measurements and other scientific methods. Travelers' authority rested first and foremost, of course, on their claims to have seen distant places and peoples with their own eyes. But could those claims be trusted? Without the corroborating evidence supplied by scientific measurements, natural specimens, and the like, this remained an open and troubling question. Although recent postcolonial scholarship on European exploration in the age of Enlightenment and romanticism has emphasized "the ocular authority of the traveler," this was precisely the period when that authority was no longer sufficient in and of itself.[10] Too many travelers had told too many tall tales for their assertions to be taken at face value.

At issue was the relationship between truth and trust. British philosophers and scientists had been agonizing over this issue for at least a century. Some of the leading figures of the scientific revolution of the seventeenth century had sought to resolve the problem by privileging a shared gentlemanly ethos and identity, which served as social validation for otherwise unverified experiments and observations. For the scientific revolution's heirs in the eighteenth and nineteenth centuries, gentility would persist as a criterion in the assessment of truth claims, with social status sometimes figuring prominently in late Georgian and Victorian assessments of the reliability of travelers' reports.[11]

Still, it is telling that the late eighteenth-century educated elite gave greater credence to Cook, the son of a farm laborer, than to Bruce, a landed gentleman. Cook, of course, was also a naval officer, an occupation that enjoyed a privileged reputation. Although social status continued to color assessments of trustworthiness, the traveler's veracity came increasingly to be measured in terms of his commitment to a rigorous set of scientific protocols and practices, the purpose of which was to generate quantitative and physical evidence that could provide independent verification for his or her claims.

The earliest and most commonplace of these protocols was a daily written record of events, observations, and instrument readings in logs, journals, and diaries, which served both as aide-mémoire and corroborating documents. Francis Bacon, the early seventeenth-century proponent of the empirical method, had recommended the use of a diary in his essay on travel. He had also noted "a strange thing, that in sea voyages, where there is nothing to be seen, but sky and sea, men should make diaries; but in land-travel, wherein so much is to be observed, for the most part they omit it."[12] Keeping a ship's log that recorded observations and readings in meticulous detail was deeply ingrained in maritime culture. In addition to written inscriptions, navigators' logbooks often included sketches of coastlines to assist in the identification of sites.[13] Proponents of the scientific method sought to instill some of the same habits of observation in territorial travelers. Robert Boyle wrote a manual to this end in 1692. But this advice was slow to be adopted, with field naturalists among the first to do so in the late eighteenth and early nineteenth centuries.[14]

A similar disparity informed a second key scientific practice—the use of precision instruments from the seventeenth century onward to obtain quantitative data concerning geographical location and climatic conditions. The compass had long been used by sailors to chart direction, and the effort that Edmond Halley had initiated in 1698 to map its magnetic deviations would be pursued across the globe by the Royal Navy over the next two centuries. The instrument known in its successive iterations as the quadrant, the octant, and the sextant, which determined latitude by measuring the angle between the horizon and the sun, the moon, or some other astronomical object, came into widespread use by mariners from the mid-seventeenth century onward. In addition, navigators were able to calculate longitude at sea with some degree of accuracy after the mid-1760s through the use of more accurate chronometers and the *Nautical Almanac*'s lunar tables, first published by Astronomer Royal Nevil Maskelyne in 1766 and recomputed and reissued annually thereafter.[15] The Admiralty fit out its naval expeditions from Cook onward with compasses, chronometers, sextants, barometers, thermometers, artificial horizons, and other scientific instruments. Such resources, however, were beyond the means of most land expeditions, which rarely received significant institutional support prior to the nineteenth century. Moreover, precision instruments were far more susceptible to breakage and calibration problems on territorial expeditions than they were on naval ones due to rougher handling and greater exposure to the elements. Ships provided a protective cocoon. As a result, "it was still more common and practical to carry instruments for great distances over sea than land."[16]

What purposes did the information obtained from these instruments serve? The positional data, of course, made it easier for others to follow the same course and reach the same destination as the pathfinder. The meteorological data helped to reveal predictive patterns in those natural forces that did so much to determine the success or failure of an expedition, forces that human senses could not discern with the same accuracy or consistency. Both categories of data provided an important check on the subjectivity of the individual observer, establishing a quantitative baseline for the determination of geographical position and meteorological patterns. The astronomical observations carried out by explorers helped "to prove beyond denial that we had been in a certain place of the earth[']s surface at a given second of time," noted John Kirk, a member of Livingstone's Zambezi expedition.[17] In a broader sense, these practices laid a conceptual framework for equivalency and comparison. They made the world comprehensible in a new way as a unified whole, inspiring a "planetary consciousness" that turned particular places into abstract spaces, quantified, collated, and condensed onto maps, graphs, and tables, their calculations and coordinates serving as the denominators of difference. Thus did these "instruments of precision . . . [become] a privileged means of bridging the gap between distant heterogeneous places."[18]

A third distinguishing feature of the scientific thrust of exploration was the collection and classification of botanical, zoological, geological, ethnographic, and other physical specimens and artifacts from those distant lands the explorers came in contact with. The intellectual roots of this endeavor derived largely from the upheaval caused by the discovery of the Americas, which introduced Europeans to a multiplicity of hitherto unknown plants, animals, and other living creatures, including peoples. Some of the strange wonders from this new world were collected in cabinets of curiosity, the precursors of modern museums. Botanical gardens proliferated as venues for cultivating, displaying, and analyzing exotic plants. In the eighteenth century, Carl Linnaeus and his rivals developed taxonomies for the scientific classification of plant species, as did others specializing in the study of animals, insects, minerals, and more. A coinciding impetus for the development of the botanical sciences came from proponents of agrarian improvement, mainly landed gentlemen eager to expand agricultural production through the introduction of new crops and the development of new cultivation and breeding techniques.[19]

The responsibility for making botany and other natural sciences integral elements of British exploration from the late eighteenth century onward rested largely with Joseph Banks, the precocious young gentleman naturalist who accompanied Cook on his first voyage. He returned with a treasure trove of botanical specimens and a much enlarged sense of the world. He soon established himself as the leading figure in the British scientific community, which elected him president of the Royal Society in 1778, and he served as that community's main conduit to the crown, the navy, and other institutions of state, advising on voyages of discovery and other matters. Perhaps his most lasting achievement was to persuade King George III to turn the royal gardens at Kew into a clearinghouse for botanical specimens from around the globe. Banks thereby managed to forge what has been referred to as "a new kind of alliance between agrarian wealth and the natural sciences, private initiative and Crown patronage."[20] Kew Gardens would henceforth become the institutional nerve center for a worldwide initiative to collect new plants, assess their economic value, and disseminate them to sites where they might be put to productive use.

By bringing back to Britain those botanical, zoological, and other specimens gathered in the course of their journeys, explorers and other travelers gave their own observations greater credence. Even if these items had no relevance to what made the journeys significant or sensational, they served as physical traces of strange places, enhancing the trustworthiness of the persons whose own sources of authority were based on their firsthand observations. Once again, oceanic expeditions figured more prominently than their territorial counterparts in institutionalizing these practices and establishing their importance to late eighteenth-century exploration as a scientific enterprise. The holds of ships were far more suitable than the backs of men or beasts for carrying the large quantities of supplies—paper, bottles, spirits, cases, and more— that were needed to pack and preserve organic specimens. Similarly, they were better suited for transporting bulky but fragile collections of potted and pressed plants, pinned insects, skinned birds, bottled fish, and the like. Ships provided a safer storage environment, where specimens were less susceptible to climatic spoilage or damage from the rough handling that so often characterized land transport. The logistics of scientific expeditions, like nearly all transport-dependent activities prior to the age of steam, favored the use of ships, and especially ships operating under the aegis of the Royal Navy.

The Admiralty would dominate British exploration as a scientific enterprise through the early nineteenth century. George Vancouver, Matthew Flinders, and various other naval officers won renown for their voyages of discovery, which enlarged British knowledge of distant seas and extended British influence to the littoral zones that bordered them. Typical of the scientific resources lavished on such ventures was the voyage of the *Investigator,* which sailed for the South Seas in 1801 with the latest precision instruments and a full contingent of specialists, including a botanist, astronomer, botanical draftsman, and landscape painter.[21] The Admiralty's Hydrographic Department, founded in 1795, sponsored a series of expeditions in the following decades that surveyed the coastlines of continents, the estuaries of rivers, and chains of islands.[22]

The heroic age of seaborne exploration was, however, coming to a close. Most nineteenth-century naval expeditions engaged in relatively mundane hydrographic surveys that retained little of their eighteenth-century predecessors' flair for drama and discovery. Only the polar regions provided naval explorers with any real opportunities for adventure and fame. In 1839–1845 James Clark Ross captained an important expedition that charted the Antarctic's Ross Sea and Ice Shelf. Various other naval explorers probed Arctic waters. Yet the disappearance of Sir John Franklin and his party during their search for the Northwest Passage in 1845–1846 served in some ways as an epilogue to the great era of naval exploration set in motion by Cook and his contemporaries. Search parties learned that Franklin's ships had been immobilized and crushed by Arctic ice, neatly symbolizing the geographical limits of seaborne exploration.

Expeditions into the interiors of continents increasingly adopted naval explorers' modes of mapping and methods of making sense of the natural world. Alexander Mackenzie prepared for his trek across Canada in 1793–1794 by traveling to London to acquire scientific instruments and learn how to use them. Around the same time, Joseph Banks began to recruit men with scientific skills to explore the interior of Africa. His most famous protégé was the Scottish doctor and naturalist Mungo Park, who had the rare good fortune to survive his journey, though he had to abandon his scientific instruments, survey data, and botanical specimens along the way.[23] Only a year before Park set out on his second expedition in 1805, President Thomas Jefferson dispatched the Lewis and Clark expedition to investigate the territory acquired by the United States in the Louisiana Purchase. In preparation for its journey, Meriwether Lewis had taken crash courses in botany, mineralogy, astronomy, natural history, and other subjects with scientists in Philadelphia, and the expedition returned in 1806 with a rich array of geographical information, meteorological data, botanical specimens (some of which found their way to Kew Gardens' massive herbarium), and other scientific findings.[24] What all of these initiatives, whether successful or not, put into play was the conviction that the scientific exploration of continents was feasible and necessary.

No one did more, however, to embrace what Commander Edward Belcher termed this "scientific mania" and apply its methods to land exploration than the great Prussian polymath Alexander von Humboldt. Tutored by Georg Forster, the naturalist on Captain Cook's second voyage, and Joachim Heinrich Campe, the German translator of *Robinson Crusoe,* Humboldt was attracted from the start to exploration as an experiential mode of knowledge, conceiving of it as an endeavor both scientific and romantic.[25] He spent five years (1799–1804) traveling through Spanish America, equipped with some fifty different scientific instruments that he used to chart his route, conduct astronomical observations, and measure a wide array of meteorological phenomena. "Humboldt saw his own traversal of physical space as incidental," a historian of science has pointed out. "What mattered was the traversal made by his measuring instruments."[26] He also collected large quantities of botanical specimens, geological samples, and other items. A year after his return to Europe in 1804, he published the first volume of what grew into a thirty-volume opus about his journey, *Voyage aux régions équinoxiales du Nouveau Continent* (1805–1834). Rich in romantic descriptions of exotic landscapes and astute observations about the natural environment, supplemented by mountains of data on meteorological patterns as well as an abundance of botanical drawings and other evidence concerning plant and animal species, geological formations, and social institutions (including a scathing critique of slavery), this exhaustive study established Humboldt's reputation as the prototypical scientific explorer, providing an unrivaled demonstration of how to carry out an expedition into the interior of a continent.

Humboldt served as a model and inspiration for some of the nineteenth century's leading natural scientists, encouraging them to carry out field research. Declaring Humboldt to be "the greatest scientific traveler who ever lived," Charles Darwin volunteered for the voyage of the *Beagle,* thereby setting in motion the series of observations and insights that led to the theory of natural selection.[27] Alfred Russel Wallace, the theory's co-originator, credited Humboldt with giving "me a desire to visit the tropics," where he spent decades collecting insects and other natural specimens in the jungles of the Amazon and Malaya.[28] The great Prussian ranked as one of the "Gods" in the pantheon of Joseph Hooker, who apprenticed as a botanist for Ross's Antarctic expedition and collected plants in the Himalayas before returning to succeed his father as the powerful director of Kew Gardens.[29] Countless others drew inspiration from Humboldt as well, not least a number of his countrymen who went abroad in pursuit of scientific careers. Ludwig Leichhardt, the German botanist who became one of Australia's best-known explorers, confided to a family member that Humboldt's "example has been and still is constantly with me—I strive to be like him."[30] When the famed Victorian geologist Charles Lyell advised young men who wanted to study geology to "travel—travel—travel," he was giving voice to a view that was directly traceable to Humboldt.[31]

The profound influence Humboldt exerted over so many nineteenth-century scientists speaks to the synergistic associations that developed in this period between the natural sciences as they gradually evolved into modern systems of knowledge and exploration as it set its sights on Africa, Australia, and other continents. Geography, botany, geology, zoology, and other scientific disciplines stressed observation and evidence acquired in the field, not the laboratory.[32] For many of those who specialized in these subjects, "traveling provided the basis for a scientific career."[33] Even as Darwin, Hooker, Lyell, and other prominent scientists settled into positions of power in Britain, they dispatched their apprentices into the colonies to serve as conduits of information. They also established close ties to amateur collectors in distant lands, relying on travelers, traders, missionaries, and military officers to collect the physical objects and meteorological and astronomical measurements necessary for their research. Above all, they drew on the wealth of new material gathered by explorers.

A network of organizations sprang up in the late eighteenth and early nineteenth centuries that provided institutional support and structure to this scientific enterprise. Foremost among those that sponsored expeditions to distant lands were the Association for Promoting the Discovery of the Interior Parts of Africa (commonly known as the African Association) and the Royal Geographical Society. The African Association was a society founded in 1788 by Joseph Banks and some of his gentleman friends for the purpose of improving "the science of Geography" through the exploration of Africa. It exemplified the importance given in the late eighteenth century to gentility as a criterion for conducting science and evaluating its findings, a stance that gradually would come under assault from less privileged proponents of scientific inquiry. Although the association often operated independently, especially in early expeditions such as Mungo Park's first journey, it also collaborated with the army, the Admiralty, and other official agencies in sponsoring a number of expeditions, including Park's disastrous second one.[34]

The Royal Geographical Society (RGS) came into existence as a result of a merger of the African Association and the Raleigh Travellers' Club in 1830. Far larger and more enduring than its predecessor, the RGS became inextricably associated with British exploration in the nineteenth century, establishing itself as the leading proponent of scientific expeditions and the principal source of disciplinary oversight of their operations. It sponsored the journeys of explorers, supplied them with maps and other information, loaned them scientific instruments, published their geographical findings in its journal, and brought their achievements to the attention of the public. And, like the African Association, it often worked in close association with the state, offering its advice on plans for government-funded expeditions and contributing its expertise to the evaluation of the geographical data and other information resulting from these endeavors. What above all made the RGS so successful, as the historical geographer Felix Driver has noted, was the fact that it was a hybrid institution, "part social club, part learned society, part imperial information exchange and part platform for the promotion of sensational feats of exploration."[35] Its multiple purposes were reflected in its diverse membership, which included army and navy officers, colonial officials, cartographers, travelers, natural scientists (including Darwin, Wallace, and Huxley), and an upper crust of peers and other members of the hereditary elite. By drawing these different constituencies together, the RGS made exploration an enterprise that merged scientific inquiry with social status, imperial interests, and much more.[36]

A variety of other scientific institutions, museums, and learned societies sprang up in the late eighteenth and early nineteenth centuries that benefited from the information and items obtained by explorers. In London alone, these organizations included the Linnaean Society (1788), the Royal Institution (1799), the Royal College of Surgeons (1800), the Geological Society (1807), the Astronomical Society (1820), the Asiatic Society (1823), the Athenaeum (1824), the Zoological Society (1826), and the British Association for the Advancement of Science (1831). In addition, the Royal Botanic Gardens at Kew and the British Museum assumed their modern forms in this period as research institutions and repositories of specimens collected from the far corners of the globe.

These metropolitan institutions had their provincial and colonial counterparts. Motivated by a strong sense of civic pride and desire for self-improvement, increasingly prosperous industrial and commercial elites in cities and towns across Britain organized scientific societies, libraries, museums, botanical gardens, mechanics institutes, and other organizations for the advancement of knowledge. Manchester, Liverpool, Edinburgh, and six other cities across the Midlands and Scotland had their own geographical societies by the late nineteenth century. Colonial metropolises including Cape Town, Sydney, Melbourne, Adelaide, Calcutta, and Bombay were equally active in establishing such organizations. As early as the 1840s, Cape Town had a natural history museum, an observatory, a library, a botanical garden, and a literary society. In Australia, state and municipal botanical gardens were established in Sydney, Adelaide, Melbourne, Brisbane, and other towns. Prominent citizens joined together to found learned societies such as the Adelaide Philosophical Society (1853), the Victoria Institute for the Advancement of Science (1854), the Victoria Philosophical Society (1854), the Brisbane Museum (1855), and the National Museum of Victoria (1858). The Bombay Geographical Society was founded in 1832, the Egyptian Geographical Society in 1875, and the Royal Geographical Society of South Australia in 1885.[37]

All of these institutions had an interest in the outcomes of expeditions. The Zoological Society was eager to acquire "reports, specimens, and live animals from all quarters of the empire."[38] It may have been the recipient of the various "specimens of Natural History" that Hugh Clapperton and Dixon Denham brought back from their journey across the Sahara into West Africa, which included a monkey, four ostriches, three parrots, and, strangely, a shark, which an official cautioned—unnecessarily, one would have thought—was "naturally savage & peculiarly dangerous."[39] Kew Gardens was the leading repository for the exotic plants and botanical specimens explorers brought back from their journeys. Their rocks and minerals went to the Geological Society and the Museum of Practical Geology (1835). The Royal College of Surgeons was keen to acquire any indigenous skulls they had gathered along the way. The British Museum welcomed items ranging from natural history specimens to archeological and ethnographic artifacts. While the RGS was exceptional in the scale of its involvement in exploration, other scientific institutions contributed their expertise and resources to expeditions. The Literary and Scientific Institution of Cape Town drafted the instructions and oversaw the preparations for the locally funded expedition that Dr. Andrew Smith led north across the colonial frontier in 1834–1836. The Bombay Geographical Society lent its support to the exploration of East Africa, supplying Richard Burton and John Hanning Speke with the scientific instruments they used during their expedition into the lakes region. The Philosophical Society of Adelaide supervised Benjamin Herschel Babbage's preparations for his 1858 expedition, funded by the colonial government, into the region around Lake Torrens. The Royal Society of Victoria, whose members were mocked by the *Melbourne Punch* as self-important "jolly philosophers," assumed a similar role for the ambitious and well-supplied expedition of Robert O'Hara Burke and William Wills.[40]

Explorers worked far more closely with scientific institutions than popular accounts of their exploits acknowledge. A recent study of David Livingstone's Zambezi expedition shows that it took its scientific agenda very seriously, supplying Kew Gardens and other depositories with a wealth of carefully labeled items.[41] When Burton and Speke returned from their East African expedition, they presented the botanical specimens they had collected to Kew Gardens, their field notes and maps to the Royal Geographical Society, their rock and soil samples to the School of Mines, their collection of shells to the Zoological Society, and twenty-four African skulls to the Royal College of Surgeons. They also distributed the snakes, insects, and other creatures they had preserved to various specialists for study. James Grant, who accompanied Speke on his second expedition, gave more than 700 species of plants—eighty of them previously unknown—to Kew Gardens and later prepared a catalogue of the collection that filled three volumes of the journal of the Linnean Society. Kew also was the beneficiary of the collection of 15,000 specimens amassed by Ferdinand von Mueller as botanist for the North Australian Expedition of 1855–1856. In appreciation, Joseph Hooker,

Kew's director, engineered Mueller's appointment as director of the botanical gardens in Melbourne, a position that permitted him to become the main conduit for the collection, distribution, and examination of botanical specimens brought back by other Australian expeditions.[42] Some explorers sought more direct compensation by selling the specimens they gathered to museums and private collectors. This is how the naturalist Ludwig Leichhardt got his start as an Australian explorer. But perhaps the most striking example of an explorer who turned the material he had collected to direct financial gain was Dr. Andrew Smith. Simply ignoring his letter of instructions, which stated that "every article collected by each individual belongs in property to the subscribers to the expedition collectively," Smith removed the expedition's 5,000 zoological specimens and 1,800 ethnographic artifacts from the South African Museum and shipped them back to London, where he placed them on commercial display at the Egyptian Hall for a time, then sold them for a handsome profit.[43]

It was more often the case, however, that the scientific and other learned societies held the upper hand in their dealings with explorers, employing various incentives and sanctions to impose their will. The Royal Geographical Society made itself the main "validating agency" for British exploration by awarding gold medals to those explorers whose accomplishments it deemed especially noteworthy.[44] Other societies and institutions honored explorers by naming newly discovered species after them, recognizing their work in publications and exhibitions, or recommending them for colonial posts. More important, they established the disciplinary ground rules that governed the practice of scientific exploration, controlled access to the scientific instruments and other resources that explorers required to carry out their tasks, and judged the outcomes of expeditions in their capacities as gatekeepers of scientific knowledge.

Natural history societies and museums oversaw the proliferation of scientific nomenclatures, taxonomic categories, and preservation methodologies, which were integral to the collecting, classifying, and cataloguing of botanical specimens, zoological species, geological samples, and the like. The nascent professionalization of the natural sciences grew out of these practices. Their disciplinary designs created barriers that placed explorers and other field workers in subordinate positions.

Although a recent study has shown that "colonial naturalists were active participants in the making of scientific knowledge" rather than merely its "inert recipients," metropolitan scientific authorities did their best to prevent colonials from overstepping their prescribed bounds. Joseph Hooker objected to colonial botanists naming new species they had found, insisting that this was a task for the experts at Kew. Even Ferdinand von Mueller roused Hooker's ire by presuming to name some plants on his own initiative. Hooker was even more protective of the classificatory role of Kew, which stood at the heart of botanical science. Similarly, Sir Roderick Murchison insisted that the Geological Society, not geologists in the field, was the proper body for resolving any interpretive issues that arose from the latter's findings.[45]

Scientific institutions also "carved out a niche for themselves as regulators of measurement," ensuring that the precision instruments and complex calculations so essential to astronomy, geography, meteorology, and other quantitative-heavy fields were reliable and accurate.[46] The sway these institutions exerted over explorers was twofold. First, they often controlled access to the scientific instruments required by explorers, who could rarely afford to purchase such expensive devices. The Royal Geographical Society loaned its instruments to more than 200 separate expeditions in the second half of the nineteenth century.[47] This beneficence made it possible for the society's officials to vet potential borrowers, deciding whether they were qualified to use the instruments and, by implication, to carry out scientific exploration. Francis Galton, who chaired the society's expeditions subcommittee for many years, opposed one request for the loan of instruments because the applicant "appeared wholly ignorant of their use . . . and seemed very doubtful of ever being in a position where instrument observation would be of value." Another applicant's request for instruments was rejected because it would be seen as "an implied approbation of his merits as a scientific traveller," which Galton considered unjustified.[48] In 1881 the RGS established its own program to train prospective explorers in the use of sextants, prismatic compasses, artificial horizons, and other surveying instruments. One of its earliest alumni was the explorer Joseph Thomson, whose first venture into East Africa was delayed a month so that he could improve his mapping skills.[49]

A second way the RGS and other scientific societies exerted leverage over the explorers was by insisting upon their return that they hand over their instruments and notebooks of readings and computations for review by metropolitan experts to confirm that they were properly calibrated and calculated. After his epic journey across the African continent from east to west in 1873–1875, Verney Lovett Cameron was obliged to give his maps to the society's curator of maps and submit his astronomical calculations to a "computer" at the Greenwich observatory.[50] When Joseph Thomson returned from Africa, he knew that his instruments would "have to go to Kew to be reexamined."[51] John Hanning Speke voiced his deep displeasure with the RGS "creatures" who requested that he hand over all of his "Photos, drawings, and lists of observations" from the Nile expedition, but he felt obliged to produce the material.[52] David Livingstone, however, bypassed some of this metropolitan scrutiny by submitting his observational computations for review and correction by his friend and mentor Thomas Maclear, a government astronomer in Cape Town.[53]

Lastly, the scientific societies led the way in addressing what was at once the most important *and* the most problematic form of knowledge that the explorer had to offer—direct observation. The Royal Geographical Society in particular took up the task of developing criteria for determining what an explorer should observe and how he should observe it. A related aim was to ensure those observations were recorded in a careful, standardized manner, producing what the novelist Patrick White aptly termed a "journal of acts and facts."[54] The most incisive analysis of this disciplinary project comes from Felix Driver, who states that a "whole methodology of observation was designed to ensure that reliable and unvarnished information could be collected, stored and eventually transmitted back to the centre."[55]

One of the earliest attempts to establish such a methodology was made by Julian Jackson, a former East India Company official who served as secretary of the Royal Geographical Society from 1841 to 1847.[56] Recognizing the need for a common language to describe topographical features, he proposed a standardized nomenclature in an early issue of the society's journal. The Australian explorer Thomas Mitchell, for one, took notice, applying it to his own exploration narrative.[57] In

1841, Jackson published *What to Observe; or, the Traveller's Remembrancer,* a 500-plus-page tome written in response to the frustration he felt at "the total absence of anything like solid information" in most travel accounts.[58] He wanted travelers to observe the territory they passed through in a systematic way, noting its topography, hydrography, meteorology, geology, and zoology, not to mention its native inhabitants and their agricultural products, manufactured goods, political institutions, social customs, and religious beliefs. He gave advice on how to map, how to collect and preserve plants and animals, how to use various scientific instruments, and much more. Jackson's book went through three editions, the third revised in 1861 by his successor as secretary of the society, Dr. Norton Shaw.

The Royal Geographical Society's "Hints to Travellers," first published in a special issue of its journal in 1854, quickly superseded *What to Observe* and expanded into a sizable book that went through multiple editions over the following decades. One of the key contributors to this multiauthor work was Francis Galton, who also published the popular *Art of Travel; or, Shifts and Contrivances Available in Wild Countries* (1855), which had appeared in eight editions by 1893.[59] Another volume intended for much the same audience was *A Manual of Scientific Enquiry,* originally edited by the famed astronomer John Herschel. With a subtitle announcing that it was "prepared for the use of officers in Her Majesty's navy, and travellers in general," the work went through at least five editions between 1849 and 1886.[60]

Many explorers turned to these manuals for guidance. William Balfour Baikie and David Livingstone took Herschel's volume on their respective midcentury expeditions up the Niger and Zambezi rivers. One member of an Australian expedition read Galton's *Art of Travel* aloud in camp. In preparation for his transcontinental journey, Henry Morton Stanley noted that he had acquired a book he identified as *How to Observe,* though he probably meant *What to Observe.* Richard Burton carried copies of Jackson's *What to Observe,* Herschel's *Manual,* and Galton's *Art of Travel* on his East African expedition, and he heavily annotated each of them, judging Galton's book, in particular, to be "excellent."[61]

All of these publications can be considered at their core as efforts to exorcise the ghost of James Bruce. Their primary aim was to mitigate doubts about the veracity of the explorer. Jackson, Galton, and Herschel understood that the explorers' truth claims would always ultimately rest on their ocular authority. The challenge, then, was to establish regulating practices and protocols that would improve the accuracy and objectivity of their response to unfamiliar and disorienting sights. They sought to train explorers' eyes and correct their refractions through the application of scientific methods—recording, measuring, collecting. They sought, in short, to impose new rigor on what explorers observed and how they observed it by giving guidance to their gaze.

There were limits, however, to what the specialists ensconced in their institutional citadels believed the explorers out in the field were capable of understanding and accomplishing as agents of science. Influential figures such as Hooker and Murchison sought to draw boundaries between their own metropolitan coterie of experts and those marginalized men on colonial frontiers who supplied them with the raw materials from which they manufactured their botanical, geographical, and other forms of scientific knowledge. For explorers, these issues assumed their most prominent and particularized form in the uneasy relations they had with the so-called armchair geographers. The rifts that occurred between these two groups reveal a great deal about the limits of exploration as a scientific project, exposing the fragility of its epistemological foundations.

The term "armchair geographer" implied a gentleman of leisure who passed judgment on the accomplishments of explorers without ever rousing himself from the comfort of his own club or study. This was the view of John Hanning Speke, who wrote disparagingly about "geographers who sup port, sit in carpet slippers, and criticize those who labour in the field."[62] Many explorers shared his disdain for those they considered an effete elite whose self-professed expertise about exploration was unearned and derived instead from a sense of social privilege. In point of fact, however, most armchair geographers were far less leisured and privileged than the term implies, and although class-based condescension did aggravate their disputes with explorers, real and serious epistemological issues lay at their core.[63]

If anyone personified the armchair geographer as leisured gentleman, it was Joseph Banks. A gout-ridden clubman in his later years, Banks wielded unrivaled influence as the impresario of scientific exploration until his death in 1820, using his connections to the court, the cabinet, the Admiralty, and the scientific societies to determine where to send expeditions, what to demand of them, and who to lead them. The small circle of men who collaborated with him as members of the African Association shared his preoccupation with gentility, which they saw as integral to scientific authority.[64] Yet Banks and other leading armchair geographers of his generation, most notably James Rennell and John Barrow, had not always operated from the comfort of their armchairs: they themselves had carried out arduous and risky expeditions in their youths. Moreover, by the early 1830s, Banks and his allies' model of a scientific structure that privileged their own socially derived authority had begun to crumble.

The men who came to prominence as armchair geographers in the Victorian era were with one exception a very different breed from Banks and his Georgian coterie of gentlemen. That exception was Sir Roderick Murchison, who pulled many of the institutional levers that determined the character and direction of mid-Victorian exploration. After a short and desultory career in the army, the independently wealthy Murchison took up the study of geology, achieving fame as the first person to identify the Silurian system or period of geological strata. He then turned his energies to the promotion of geography, casting it as an essential bridge between scientific and national interests. As a founder of the Royal Geographical Society and four times its president, as well as a central figure in the Royal Society, the Geological Society, the British Association for the Advancement of Science, and various other scientific organizations, Murchison came as close as anyone in the nineteenth century to inheriting Banks's mantle as the maestro of scientific exploration.[65]

The other leading armchair geographers were not so different from the explorers themselves in their social standing and professional ambitions. William Desborough Cooley, son of an Irish barrister, scratched out a living on London's Grub Street, writing articles on exploration for the *Edinburgh Review* and other periodicals as well as books. James MacQueen had managed a sugar plantation in Grenada and edited a newspaper in Glasgow prior to becoming a London journalist and self-taught African geographer. Charles Tilstone Beke, who had dabbled in business, the law, and archeology, made a name for himself as an explorer of Ethiopia, thereby laying the foundations for his subsequent reputation as an authority on the sources of the Nile. Francis Galton had abandoned medical studies upon the death of his Quaker banker father, using his inheritance to travel through Europe, Turkey, and Egypt, followed by an expedition into Namibia, after which he settled into a more sedentary, though far from lethargic, life as a leading member of London's scientific community and especially of the Royal Geographical Society.

The armchair geographers synthesized information about distant lands from a range of sources, using the evidence they gathered to ad-

Francis Galton, explorer, armchair geographer, and scientist. *Source: Library of Congress.*

vance broad speculative claims and to scrutinize individual travel reports for lies, distortions, and other errors. They assumed a disciplinary role that inevitably brought them into conflict with explorers. Cooley came to prominence when he exposed the Frenchman J. B. Douville's account of his Angolan expedition as an invention. Beke made similar charges against another French explorer, Antoine d'Abbadie. While attacks on agents of Britain's leading national rival were especially gratifying, armchair geographers targeted British explorers as well. In effect, they saw themselves as the guardians of geography as a scientific discipline, filling a role similar to the one played by Kew's William and Joseph Hooker in the field of botany and their counterparts in other natural sciences. They were aided in their efforts by the small army of cartographers, calculators, instrument makers, and other specialists who scrutinized explorers' maps, journals, and instruments, exposing errors in calibration, observation, and calculation.

Knowing that armchair geographers could ruin their reputations, most explorers did their best to be conciliatory. Writing from the interior of West Africa, an obsequious Heinrich Barth assured the notoriously quarrelsome Cooley that "You were *quite right in general* in all Your reasoning" about the region.[66] Even the combative Burton initially attempted to placate Cooley, referring to him as "the lynx-eyed detector of geographical frauds and fallacies" in the opening pages of the massive report he wrote for the Royal Geographical Society about his journey into the lakes region of East Africa.[67] Any hopes he may have had that these generous words would reconcile Cooley to the fact that the expedition had disproved his theory asserting the existence of a single great lake, the so-called Luta Nziga, were soon dispelled, however. Cooley challenged Burton's evidence and questioned his competence as an explorer, leaving Burton little choice but to respond in kind. He poured scorn on Cooley's theory as "one of the most ridiculous ever put forth by man . . . cobbled up in the map room of the Royal Geographical Society."[68]

Other well-known explorers faced critical scrutiny from domestic inquisitors as well. David Livingstone's self-proclaimed achievements during his Zambezi expedition were downplayed by Cooley and MacQueen, both of whom gave precedence to Portuguese explorers.[69] Some of his survey data, in turn, failed to satisfy cartographers. "I have taken lunars several times," a frustrated David Livingstone wrote in his journal, "measuring both sides of the moon about one hundred and ninety times, but a silly map-maker may alter the whole for the most idiotic of reasons."[70] The editor of his last journals refused to publish his astronomical readings because he feared they would be "picked to pieces by every tyro in Geography."[71] This is exactly what had happened to Speke a decade earlier: "Theorists are pulling my map to pieces," he wrote in anguish as doubts began to surface about his claim to have discovered the source of the Nile. It so happened they had much to pull apart: the map proved to be a forgery that Speke had foolishly if unwittingly borrowed to illustrate the region he had explored. Moreover, Speke's sloppy elevation readings seemed to show the Nile River flowing uphill for some 90 miles, a physical impossibility that his critics were quick to pounce on.[72]

Australian explorers largely escaped the rigorous scrutiny endured by African explorers. Armchair geographers in Britain had less access to Australian explorers' observational computations, field notes, and other evidence of scientific rigor, which were often retained by colonial institutions such as the Royal Society of Victoria and the Philosophical Society of Adelaide. In addition, Australian discoveries simply generated less interest in Britain and hence stirred less controversy. Still, Australian explorers' work was not immune to metropolitan review and reproof. For example, the surveying skills of Thomas Mitchell, the surveyor general of New South Wales and leader of four expeditions into the interior of the continent, were challenged by armchair geographers. "I well *know* that the scientific part of [Mitchell's] survey is not trustworthy," Cooley confided to a friend.[73] This view was reinforced by the stinging critique two reviewers gave to a manuscript Mitchell had submitted for publication in the *Journal of the Royal Geographical Society*. In the manuscript, Mitchell, who held his own abilities in high regard, declared that he had produced "the first map ever made by trigonometrical survey of a British colony." The first reviewer, the secretary of the RGS, dismissed what "the author calls *trigonometrical* surveys" as mere "*eye sketches.*" The second, the well-known cartographer John Arrowsmith, agreed: "The simple fact is, that his, so called Triangulation, is no Triangulation at all." Arrowsmith insisted that his longitudinal readings were flawed and his chain measurements could not be trusted, in part because they had been carried out by convicts. Mitchell no doubt helped to provoke these harsh assessments by taking a gratuitous swipe of his own at armchair geographers in the opening paragraph of his paper: "There are few enterprises attended with more difficulty . . . than the careful survey of new countries—yet nothing is more easy than for persons to say they are inaccurate—and, which is still more extraordinary, for persons to do so who have never seen such countries at all." Not surprisingly, the manuscript was rejected.[74]

Two explorers who endured especially harsh attacks from armchair geographers and their associates in the scientific community were Paul du Chaillu and Henry Morton Stanley. In 1861 du Chaillu arrived in London with the sensational news that he had discovered gorillas in the forests of West Africa. Largely because of the fierce debate swirling around Charles Darwin's recently published *On the Origin of Species,* which suggested an evolutionary link between humans and apes, du Chaillu's announcement attracted intense interest. Although he produced a gorilla skeleton that persuaded the prominent paleontologist Richard Owen, others questioned his veracity. Because "he took no observations, either astronomical, barometrical, meteorological, or thermometrical," his skills as a scientific observer were called into question. One of du Chaillu's leading critics, the keeper of zoological specimens at the British Museum, complained that his presumption in naming new species proved that he lacked appreciation of the protocols of science. Sneering speculation about his ancestry heightened suspicions that he was untrustworthy: one cruel critic commented that du Chaillu's "diminutive stature, his negroid face, and his swarthy complexion made him look somewhat akin to our simian relatives." Taken together, these ad hominem and arcane attacks raised enough doubts about his credibility that the existence of gorillas remained in doubt for some time to come.[75]

A decade later, Stanley met with a similarly skeptical response from the geographical cognoscenti following his dramatic announcement that he had found David Livingstone, long feared dead, on the shores of Lake Tanganyika. Although the press and public treated Stanley as a hero when he arrived in London in 1871, the Royal Geographical Society's reception was decidedly cooler. Stanley's success in upstaging two

RGS-sponsored expeditions sent in search of Livingstone certainly contributed to the society's antagonism. So did social snobbery, especially
when Francis Galton tried to humiliate Stanley by exposing his illegiti-
mate origins and childhood incarceration in a workhouse. The impact
this campaign had on some portions of the public can be discerned in a
crude bit of doggerel reportedly read at a medical banquet in Brighton:
"Gentleman? no such thing; / Shame on the vulgar thing! / Why must thy
meanness sting / Henry Stanley? / Where was thy honest pride? / Better
say, 'Sir, you lied,' / Than in a jeer to hide, / It would be more manly."[76]

The RGS, however, also had some serious methodological objections
to Stanley, which went to the heart of what was understood to be scientific exploration. Stanley had undertaken his journey as a journalist who
knew nothing about surveying and who carried no scientific instruments apart from a compass.[77] His deficiencies as "a practiced geographical observer," explained Clements Markham, the RGS secretary, was
why the society deemed his achievements unworthy of a gold medal: "A
medalist of the R.G.S. . . . is expected to fix his latitudes, longitudes,
heights above the sea &c with scientific precision, by observing meridian altitudes, lunar distances, &c &c."[78] The response from Stanley indicates that he did not fully appreciate what the fuss was about: "It is
true I did not lay my positions down by astronomical observations but
the means I adopted produced the same result."[79] The means he was
referring to was dead reckoning, a startling admission that simply strength-
ened opposition within the RGS. James Grant, the former explorer and
member of the society's council, questioned whether Stanley "has done
any real geography."[80] In the end, however, public pressure forced the
RGS to relent and grant him a gold medal in 1873. In his speech to the
RGS, Stanley conceded in turn that "I am not a man of science. I simply
went to find Livingstone." It was a concession he was determined never
to make again. Prior to setting out on his next expedition, he acquired
the requisite scientific instruments and learned how to take astronomical observations. The field notebooks for his subsequent expeditions are
replete with topographical and ethnographic observations, sketches, astronomical calculations, and transit maps.[81]

Lurking behind the snide remarks and social resentments that so often soured the relations between armchair geographers and explorers

were issues of substance. As the cases of du Chaillu and Stanley suggest, these entailed concerns about scientific protocols and evidence. At a deeper level, the two parties were at odds over the relative merits of their very different methods of asserting knowledge claims. The issue was whether the "theoretical" or "speculative" expertise possessed by armchair geographers trumped the "practical" or "ocular" authority asserted by explorers. Francis Galton explained to James Grant why theoretical knowledge was superior to field knowledge and why it should be left in the hands of armchair geographers such as himself:

> I should earnestly recommend your not burning your fingers with meteorological theorizings. Poor Speke's notions on these things were so crude and ignorant, that his frequent allusions to them did great harm to his reputation. What he could have done, and what you can do, is to state accurately what you *saw,* leaving it to stay-at-home men of science to collate the data of very many travelers, in order to form a theory. All that you two saw is a mere strip of land in the Equatorial Zone. The circumference of the Equ. Zone is 24,000 miles,—you have seen . . . say, of 100 miles at the utmost, or 1/240 the part of the whole. How is it possible to theorize on this? Recollect there is no novelty in the Enquiry. [A] number of the ablest heads among men of science (such as Herschel) have devoted serious attention to the subject and the *general theory is perfectly well understood*—far, far away better & deeper than Speke had the slightest conception of.[82]

It is clear from these remarks that Speke had attempted to assert knowledge claims on the basis of field experience that Galton insisted could be made only by means of the broader range of information collected by "stay-at-home men of science" such as himself. Although Galton's superciliousness in ridiculing Speke's "crude and ignorant" speculations was certainly off-putting, his central argument—that the explorer's narrow line of observation and experience did not permit sweeping conclusions about the nature of meteorological patterns or the like—was valid.

Some explorers dutifully deferred to the armchair geographers' views of their role. Edward Eyre, for example, prefaced his account of the famous expedition he made from Adelaide to King George's Sound with the announcement that his aim was "to record with accuracy [rather] than indulge in theory or conjecture." Others, however, rejected this distinction as one that armchair geographers had developed simply to defend their own privileged position. Richard Burton insisted in the opening pages of his *Lake Regions* book that he could not accept the premise that his role as an explorer was merely "to see and not to think." David Livingstone pointedly complained in his final journals, "I can not understand very well what a 'theoretical discoverer' is." By this time he had become so embittered toward the geographical community that Lt. Llewellyn Dawson, who led one of the RGS expeditions sent to search for him, feared that any "endeavour to procure from him copies of the geographical information he had obtained, would . . . cause him annoyance, and probably utterly prevent his disclosing what his movements had been or may be in the future."[83] Implicit in Livingstone's apparent determination to withhold the evidence he had collected was an appreciation that the "theoretical" geographers were reliant on it for their own work.

Another point of tension between the armchair geographers and the explorers concerned the credit they were prepared to give to information obtained from native peoples and other non-European sources. While both parties made extensive use of testimony from such sources, both also agreed that it had to be treated with caution and subjected where possible to verification. Where they parted ways was with regard to the weight explorers' evidence should be given relative to information from these other sources. For the armchair geographers, the reports supplied by explorers enriched the evidentiary pool from which they drew their conclusions, but did not negate the value of native testimony. For the explorers themselves, it *supplanted* that testimony, standing in an evidentiary class apart from indigenous informants.

The armchair geographers' working method was to accumulate, collate, and synthesize as much information from as many sources as they could obtain, including textual and oral evidence from non-Western sources. The dearth of such sources for Australia was one of the main reasons its explorers so often escaped the armchair geographers' scrutiny. Africa, on the other hand, was relatively rich in the range of information that could be collected about its interior. Cooley made extensive, innovative, and openly acknowledged use of Arab and other non-Western intelligence, an approach that would contribute over time to his marginalization within the geographical fraternity. He relied almost exclusively on written Arab sources to produce a sophisticated analysis of the political and economic geography and history of West Africa in *Negroland of the Arabs Examined* (1841). His speculative map of the East African interior, famous for the great lake that stood at its center, was the result of information provided by a Zanzibari merchant, Khamis bin Uthman, and his unnamed Yao slave, who were introduced to Cooley during their visit to London by Captain William Owen, the hydrographer of the African coastline. Cooley encouraged Uthman to explore the region, supplying him with "some good instruments" and requesting in return any "plants, minerals, [unclear], vocabularies, &c" he collected. Nothing seems to have come of this scheme, but it shows that Cooley saw no reason why an Arab could not carry out a scientific expedition of value to the British scientific community.[84]

Other armchair geographers made use of non-Western informants as well, though they were less likely to trumpet the fact. Charles Beke's speculative conclusion that two major lakes were located in central Africa was drawn largely on the basis of Arab and African sources. So was James MacQueen's assertion that the Niger River flowed into the Gulf of Guinea, subsequently confirmed by the Lander brothers' expedition. A recent study suggests that MacQueen relied in part on the unacknowledged testimony of a slave on the sugar estate he had earlier managed in Grenada.[85]

Explorers had a professional self-interest in discrediting or diminishing the value of these competing sources of information. David Livingstone insisted that "no dependence can be placed on the statements of these half Arabs," an allusion to bin Uthman, whom he mockingly called "Cooley's great geographical oracle!" Richard Burton also dismissed Cooley's Arab sources as unreliable.[86] The fact that Cooley's claims about the lakes region could be shown to be mistaken gave force to their complaints. Yet Burton and Livingstone themselves were deeply dependent on Arab and African informants, as indeed were almost all explorers of Africa. Similarly, Australian explorers commonly turned to Aborigines for intelligence about the territories they passed through. To admit how much they relied on such sources, however, was to erode the foundations of their own authority, which was predicated on the view that the scientific methods they employed necessarily surpassed and supplanted any information that derived from other sources. Hence they did their best to downplay the contributions made by local informants, often portraying them in narratives as nothing more than servants and other subordinates acting under their direction. In some instances they simply scrubbed these other sources of knowledge from their records. A careful study of Speke's maps from the East African expedition with Burton shows, for example, that he made extensive use of information supplied by Arab and African sources, but systematically sought to erase their traces.[87]

When Francis Galton inspected the on-site dispatches and transit surveys sent back by Burton and Speke, he realized "how much valuable matter is contained in these native reports," noting that "the filling in of [the] traveler map depends on native testimony." At the same time, he appreciated the dangers that this dependence on native informants posed for exploration's foundational premises. Not only did it undermine the position of an explorer as a privileged source of knowledge about distant lands, but it called into question whether an explorer could claim to have made a *discovery* at all. Galton grappled with this issue in reflections on what differentiated Livingstone's accomplishment in crossing the continent from that of Africans who almost certainly had done the same many times in the past. It was not "the *crossing of Africa*" that set Livingstone apart, he insisted, but rather the "Geographical exploration of his line of route . . . The one can be done & is done by uneducated negroes, the other can not." Galton's purpose here was to discount the significance of indigenous peoples' local knowledge, which might otherwise have given them an unassailable claim to precedence as transcontinental pioneers. The further, unspoken implication of this line of argument was that it was necessary to collude with explorers in minimizing the role and relevance of indigenous and other non-Western information in assessing the value of their expeditions.[88]

Faced with these threats to their special status, explorers embraced the idea and practice of science with a fierce determination. Here Speke describes some of the tasks he and his colleague James Grant carried out during his second expedition into Africa:

My first occupation was to map the country. This is done by timing
the rate of march with a watch, taking compass-bearings along the
road, or on any conspicuous marks . . . and by noting the water-
shed—in short, all topographical objects. On arrival in camp every
day came the ascertaining, by boiling a thermometer, of the altitude
of the station above the sea-level; of the latitude of the station by the
meridian altitude of a star taken with a sextant; and of the compass
variation by azimuth. Occasionally there was the fixing of certain
crucial stations, at intervals of sixty miles or so, by lunar observations, or distances of the moon either from the sun or from certain
given stars, for determining the longitude, by which the original-
timed course can be drawn out with certainty on the map by proportion. Should a date be lost, you can always discover it by taking a
lunar distance and comparing it with the Nautical Almanac, by noting the time when a star passes the meridian if your watch is right, or
by observing the phases of the moon, or her rising or setting, as
compared with the Nautical Almanac. The rest of my work, besides
sketching and keeping a diary, which was the most troublesome of
all, consisted in making geological and zoological collections. With
Captain Grant rested the botanical collections and thermometrical
registers. He also boiled one of the thermometers, kept the rain-
gauge, and undertook the photography; but after a time I sent the
instruments back, considering his work too severe for the climate,
and he tried instead sketching with water colours.[89]

Speke and Grant derived pride and a sense of purpose from conducting these time-consuming scientific activities. These feelings were shared
by most explorers, whose exploration narratives were often filled with
lengthy, detailed descriptions of plants, animals, topography, and other
topics that might have been of interest to scientific specialists but rarely
to the general reader. Thomas Mitchell peppered his book with foot-
notes, detailing *in Latin* the botanical characteristics of newly discovered plants.[90] Ludwig Leichhardt, whose daily routine was "to write
my log, and lay down my route, or make an excursion in the vicinity of
the camp to botanize, &c., or ride out reconnoitering," waxed enthusiastic about the unusual vegetation he came across.[91] A study of David

Livingstone's work as a field scientist notes that he was "an inveterate, even compulsive, measurer and recorder of almost everything in his path."[92] Few explorers, however, matched Verney Lovett Cameron's meticulous devotion to measurement: he doggedly recorded 195 latitude observations, 300 longitude observations, 593 lunar observations, and 3,900 altitude readings over the course of his arduous two-year journey across equatorial Africa, eliciting awe from the Greenwich computer who was commissioned to check his figures.[93]

Nothing was quite as emblematic of explorers' sense of themselves as avatars of scientific knowledge as the instruments of measurement they possessed and utilized. A list of the scientific instruments used on expeditions invariably appeared early in official reports, and explorers mentioned them repeatedly in their published journals. George Grey set out on his first expedition in western Australia with four compasses, a sextant, a pocket sextant, two artificial horizons, three mountain barometers, three thermometers, three pocket chronometers, and a pocket telescope. Government expeditions such as Grey's tended to be more generously supplied with instruments than private ventures, but even Ludwig Leichhardt's first expedition, which operated on a wing and a prayer, was equipped with a sextant, an artificial horizon, a chronometer, a thermometer, and a Kater's compass (though no barometer, much to Leichhardt's regret). The importance explorers attached to scientific instruments can be seen in a famous photographic portrait of Speke, taken upon his triumphant return to London after announcing that he had discovered the source of the Nile. He posed with a pocket chronometer in one hand and a sextant at his feet, fitting symbols of his self-fashioning as a field scientist.[94]

One of the most telling examples of the importance explorers attached to instruments as signs of their scientific intentions—and pretensions—comes from Hugh Clapperton's second expedition into West Africa under the auspices of the Colonial Office. In preparation for his journey, Clapperton charged the Treasury for the purchase of five chronometers at a cost of £139, along with a pedometer, a theodolite, three sextants, three artificial horizons, three camera lucidas, four barometers, three Kater's compasses, eight other compasses, and twenty thermometers, priced at £192.[95] When word of these purchases reached John Barrow, the Admiralty's permanent undersecretary and a leading authority on exploration, he was indignant. The barometers in particular were too fragile, he

John Hanning Speke, the explorer as field scientist, posing with key instruments of his profession—chronometer, sextant, and rifle—against a backdrop depicting Ripon Falls, where the White Nile flows from Lake Victoria. *Source: J. H. Speke, Journal of the Discovery of the Source of the Nile (1864), frontispiece.*

insisted, for such an expedition, the purpose of which in any case was not "to settle the boundary lines between the sovereigns of Africa or to watch the satellites of Jupiter or to do some nice and delicate matter of Science." Clapperton held his ground, arguing that cartographic accuracy made the instruments "absolutely necessary."[96] Some years later Barrow was equally dismayed when Charles Sturt submitted the list of instruments he required for his planned expedition to the center of Australia: the items included three sextants, seven thermometers, three mountain barometers, three prismatic compasses, six pocket compasses, a theodolite, two artificial horizons, a perambulator, and a Gunter's chain, along with six pounds of mercury to replenish the supply he anticipated would be lost through the relevant instruments' leakage—all at a cost of £3,900. Barrow rightly observed that some of these instruments, especially the theodolite, were intended for "stationary and continued observations" and hence were "not necessary" for the type of transit survey Sturt would be conducting. For his own survey of the Cape Colony's frontier in 1797, Barrow had taken a pocket sextant, pocket compass, artificial horizon, small telescope, watch, and Gunter's chain, and he did not see why his successors required much more. Indeed, he knew how difficult it was to make effective use of instruments of measurement in the field; for this reason he developed a formula for calculating distance in the desert by counting the pace of a camel. But the challenges that had limited the number and size of instruments available to land explorers of Barrow's generation diminished over time as the instruments became more compact and less expensive, while the expeditions themselves frequently became better funded.[97]

By the second half of the century, a new scientific device began to appear in the inventories of well-outfitted expeditions—the camera.[98] Photography gave explorers a potentially powerful tool to "bring back faithful representations of the country traversed," as the Australian explorer Benjamin Herschel Babbage put it. He equipped his 1858 expedition into the Lake Eyre basin with a camera, glass plates, and chemical emulsions.[99] In the same year, David Livingstone set out on his Zambezi expedition with similar supplies, which his brother Charles and John Kirk had been specially trained to use. These and other expeditions in the period employed the newly developed collodion wet plate process, a complicated and cumbersome technique that proved especially difficult to carry out in the harsh conditions explorers confronted. In 1860 James Grant took photography lessons in preparation for his expedition to East Africa with John Hanning Speke, but he found the process so troublesome that, as Speke stated above, the equipment was sent back in Zanzibar and Grant relied instead on his sketchbook. Other explorers were more persistent, however.[100] The real breakthrough in the use of photography by explorers came with the development in the early 1870s of the dry plate process, which required less preparation and shorter exposure times. Henry Morton Stanley took a number of dry plate photographs during his expedition across the African continent in 1874–1877.[101] On both continents, other explorers soon followed suit. Within a few years the value of photography to exploration was so widely acknowledged that Francis Galton recommended that the Royal Geographical Society establish a photographic studio and offer instruction in the dry plate method.[102]

The importance explorers attached to cameras, sextants, chronometers, and other instruments was indicative of the way they sought to cast themselves as agents of scientific progress and enlightenment. The South African explorer William Burchell insisted he had made his journey "solely for the purpose of acquiring knowledge."[103] A member of the 1844 Sturt expedition, hired to skin and preserve bird specimens, wrote on the eve of the party's departure that he had undertaken this risky venture for the benefit of the "scientific world."[104] Walter Oudney, who would die on the Bornu expedition in 1822, insisted that "we embarked for the sake of science and our country's honor—if we had other views, we enlisted in the wrong service."[105] The West African explorer Heinrich Barth eulogized his late colleague Adolf Overweg as "a martyr to science."[106] These men were not simply reciting a rhetorical formula that obscured their real motives. Were that the case, the zeal with which so many of them carried out their scientific duties even at the risk of injury and death would be difficult to explain. Such efforts held important emotional and ideological meanings for these men, providing a purpose for their sacrifices that transcended personal interest and contributed, as they saw it, to the advancement of knowledge and the improvement of humankind.

If explorers sought so eagerly to fashion themselves as men of science, this was due in no small part to their appreciation that the claims they made to such status were so tenuous and open to challenge. Nothing did more to expose the fragility of their scientific ambitions than the damage their instruments, records, and collections so often incurred during the course of expeditions.

The journals of explorers are replete with references to chronometers, barometers, and other scientific instruments that ceased to function during expeditions. Alexander Laing had been traveling less than two months when he reported that the Sahara's extreme temperatures and the camels' constant motion had broken his barometers, thermometers, and chronometer, while his hygrometers had been made useless by the evaporation of their measuring fluids and his artificial horizon rendered unreadable from sand's scouring effects on its glass.[107] His rival Hugh Clapperton, who was venturing into the same region from the south, complained that "most of the instruments are breaking and splitting" because of the climate.[108] Burton and Speke's chronometers and thermometers failed to withstand the "seasoning" trip the explorers had made along the East African coast even before setting out for the interior.[109] Australian explorers faced the same problems. "To carry Barometers and other delicately constructed Mathematical Instruments safely through such a journey at the present is impossible," complained John Oxley, the first of Australia's explorers to attempt to scientifically survey his route. Nearly all of his instruments had ceased to function, including a barometer broken when a horse bolted and threw off its load.[110] John McDouall Stuart and Ernest Favenc lost their sextants on their expeditions to precisely the same cause, while some of William Wills's instruments were ruined when a camel rolled over on them.[111] A Queensland explorer reported that his chronometer "declined to go unless held in the hand in a certain position and at intervals violently shaken," hardly a reassuring indication of its accuracy.[112]

Without instruments that worked, explorers could not conduct accurate astronomical or meteorological readings. William Hovell and Hamilton Hume discovered that their longitudinal calculations were in error by 30 to 40 miles because they relied on damaged instruments.[113] William Landsborough had "no confidence" in the sextant available to him during his expedition in search of Burke and Wills.[114] John McKinlay, who led another Burke and Wills search party, could not calculate the distances he traveled with any accuracy because his chronometer failed to keep time.[115] With the loss of one of his chronometers and "the other being much affected by the motion on horseback," John Septimus Roe, the explorer and surveyor general of Western Australia, conceded that "the Longitude deduced from it will probably be found not quite correct to a mile."[116] During his expedition to Lake Torrens, Edward Eyre discovered that the mercury had leaked out of his barometers, rendering his previous readings useless.[117] A malfunctioning chronometer forced John Kirk to resort to dead reckoning during one stage of the Zambezi expedition.[118] The technician who examined the aneroid barometers Verney Lovett Cameron had used on his expedition across Africa concluded that they were *"surprisingly bad instruments"* and warned: "How I am to make any results out of the observations I really cannot say at present."[119]

Other factors interfered with astronomical observations as well. Skies were often cloudy or otherwise obstructed, preventing regular sightings of stars or the moon. Explorers lost track of time, making a muddle of their calendrical calculations. One consequence of Livingstone's famous encounter with Stanley was that Livingstone found out he was "twenty-one days too fast in my reckoning," a discrepancy that threw all his astronomical calculations in disarray.[120] His mistake doubtless derived from frequent bouts of fever. Describing how malaria had affected him during his first expedition, Livingstone confessed: "I could not avoid confusion of time and distance, neither could I hold the instrument steady, nor perform a simple calculation. . . . I forgot even the days of the week and the names of my companions."[121] Plenty of other African explorers experienced debilitating and disorienting symptoms of this sort.[122] Australian explorers usually endured different afflictions, but they produced similarly disruptive effects on astronomical observations and other scientific practices. The leader of an expedition into the Lake Eyre region in 1874–1875 was too ill to hold his sextant steady enough to take readings.[123] Charles Sturt's eyesight deteriorated to such a degree during his central Australian expedition that he was unable to conduct astronomical readings, though in any case he had little confidence in longitude readings taken during "such hurried journeys as mine."[124] Sturt's onetime assistant, John McDouall Stuart, found that damage to his eyesight made it "useless to me for taking observations, for I can see two suns instead of one."[125]

These problems contributed to the surveying gaps and errors that the armchair geographers pounced on with such alacrity. They were exacerbated by other setbacks in the field, further undermining explorers' scientific standing. The various specimens and samples that explorers so assiduously collected during their journeys all too often were damaged or destroyed by water, heat, mildew, fire, and insects or had to be abandoned when pack animals died or porters fled. The inexorable disintegration of Edmund Kennedy's disastrous Cape York expedition obliged his botanist, William Carron, to leave behind "specimens of many beautiful trees, shrubs, and orchids."[126] John Kirk saw a good portion of the herbarium he had collected on the Zambezi expedition devoured by cockroaches.[127] And when three of Ludwig Leichhardt's horses drowned in a river, he had to abandon his precious botanical collection, which he decided with dramatic flair to burn: "Tears were in my eyes when I saw one of the most interesting results of my expedition vanish in smoke."[128] In countless other cases, explorers returned from their journeys with much of their collections lost or spoiled or otherwise made worthless as material affirmation of their scientific enterprise and achievement.

The British explored Africa and Australia for a number of reasons—to advance imperial agendas, to preempt political rivals, to inspire patriotic pride, to discover natural resources, to promote commercial interests, to further humanitarian objectives, and much more. Yet exploration as it was understood and manifested in the nineteenth century cannot be simply subsumed under categories such as imperialism, nationalism, capitalism, and the like. It was a distinct and rigorous enterprise with its own epistemological logic and codes of conduct. It was an integral part of the endeavor to establish science as an organized, consistent, universal mode of making sense of the natural world and its creatures. While multiple motives drove explorers to engage in their arduous and often foolhardy adventures, science supplied the essential framework that made their enterprise meaningful, giving it a structure and intent that differentiated it from travel undertaken for other purposes, such as trade, tourism, migration, or pilgrimage. Science, in short, supplied exploration with its ideological raison d'être.

It is misleading, however, to refer to Georgian and Victorian science in the singular. Historians of science have shown that various parties sought to claim the mantle of science in the nineteenth century, and these parties interpreted it in very different ways.[129] This struggle over the meaning and purpose of science was shaped by social and economic interests, ideological and professional agendas, and much more. Exploration was unavoidably enmeshed in these contestations. One of the most visible manifestations of its involvement in the conflict over the nature of science can be seen in explorers' clashes with armchair geographers and other agents of the increasingly distinct scientific disciplines that were then emerging in metropolitan centers. The physical challenges that confronted explorers as they sought to carry out precision measurements and other scientific practices produced additional causes for tension. These issues were harbingers of the marginalization of explorers from science as it came to assume a more uniform, standardized, institutionalized character from the late nineteenth century onward.

Although explorers were in many respects the victims of forces beyond their control, they bore some responsibility for their eventual marginalization. Their embrace of personal experiences that could not be replicated and that required what was often characterized as a special strength of will connoted a degree of subjectivity and romantic individualism that stood at odds with the premises and promises of modern science. Furthermore, their encounters with indigenous inhabitants whose ways of knowing the world differed markedly from their own generated unintended consequences, especially insofar as they depended on these peoples for information and assistance. While explorers were culturally conditioned to reject these alternative epistemologies as the superstitions of primitive peoples, force of necessity caused many of them to acquire greater appreciation for the skills and insights these peoples possessed, a stance that simply could not be reconciled to the standards of mainstream science. For various reasons, then, the relationship between explorers and science in the nineteenth century was intimate and generative, yet contingent and contested.

CHAPTER 3

Professionals

The Anglo-African traveller is an overworked professional. . . .
[He] is expected to survey and observe, to record meteorology and
trigonometry, to shoot and stuff birds and beasts, to collect geological specimens and theories, to gather political and commercial
information, beginning, of course, with cotton; to advance the infant study of anthropology; to keep accounts, to sketch, to indite a
copious, legible journal—notes are now not deemed sufficient—
and to forward long reports which shall prevent the Royal Geographical Society from napping through its evenings.

—Richard F. Burton, *Zanzibar: City, Island, and Coast* (1872)

C. H. COULTHURST, a man of "good descent & gentlemanly birth,"
set out in early 1832 to explore West Africa. Educated at Eton and
Brasenose College, Oxford, he had trained for the bar at Middle Temple
but "never really liked his profession." Coulthurst's father, a prosperous
businessman, explained in a poignant letter written after his son's death
that "so strongly has the bias of his mind [been] towards *African* discovery that I have *now* many of his Eton school books in which maps with
his *supposed* travels thro' the interior parts of that continent were traced."
His school papers also included a poem he had written, entitled "Solilo-
quy of Mungo Park." When it became clear that the dull routines of the
law had not dampened his desire to follow in Park's footsteps, Coulthurst's
father shipped him off to Barbados to live with an uncle. His hope was
that the "change of scene" would "eradicate the inclination . . . to attempt some further discoveries in the unknown parts of Africa." Instead,

his son used the opportunity to "exercise . . . in the heat of the day in order to season himself for the yet more torrid climate of Africa." When Coulthurst learned that Richard and John Lander had successfully traced the Niger to its mouth in the Gulf of Guinea, he "feared that another expedition would be fitted out on a great scale, and leave nothing which an individual could attempt." He approached the Colonial Office and the newly established Royal Geographical Society for assistance. The Colonial Office supplied him with letters of recommendation written in Arabic for "African Princes and Rulers," but declined to grant him free passage to Fernando Po. The RGS approved the loan of a chronometer but concluded that his preparations did not "warrant any very sanguine hopes of success." An acquaintance named Mr. Tyrwhitt initially agreed to accompany him but had second thoughts after falling ill soon after his arrival on the African coast. Undeterred, Coulthurst made his way to the trading port of Old Calabar in the Niger delta, where he hired a canoe, a crew, and a guide to take him upriver. Like so many wayward sons, he billed these expenses to his father. (The very fact that African merchants in Old Calabar accepted a promissory note for repayment by a third party in Britain who was unknown to them is a revealing indicator of their economic integration into the global capitalist system.) Coulthurst then set off into the interior. He did not get far: the Igbo people whose territory he hoped to pass through refused him transit, forcing him to return to Old Calabar. Here he contracted a fever and died. It was an ignominious end to this would-be explorer's lifelong obsession.[1]

While young Coulthurst's death undoubtedly broke his father's heart, it takes on a very different emotional register with the distance of time. It now reads as the inevitable denouement to a black comedy of the kind Evelyn Waugh might have written. However reckless most explorers might appear in retrospect, few of them matched the foolhardy naïveté of this devotee of Mungo Park. There is no evidence that he had ever taken part in an expedition before setting out for Africa, that he had any personal familiarity with the region and its peoples, that he had any institutional encouragement or patronage of his project, that he had made any serious logistical preparations for his journey, or that he had any experience taking observations, fixing his location, or carrying out the myriad other scientific tasks detailed by Richard Burton. In short, he was not prepared to be an explorer; he lacked the necessary professional qualifications. This is one of the reasons his tragicomic story is worth retelling: it reminds us that the success of explorers depended as much on their preparation, training, technical skills, and support as it did on their desire and strength of will. But Coulthurst is noteworthy as well because of the ways he resembled so many of the men who did become explorers. In his respectable origins and good education, his obsessive desire for fame and glory, and his evident willingness to suffer and even die in pursuit of those goals, Coulthurst was far from untypical.

Who were the explorers? We know a great deal about them as individuals, but surprisingly little about them as a cohort. The romantic conception of the explorer as a heroic figure whose personal struggles against harsh environments and hostile peoples set him apart from the common clay remains a popular motif in the literature on exploration. Biography has been its leading genre and hagiography its main mode of representation.[2] Even those biographers who have been critical of their subjects tend to stress what set them apart, not what they shared with other explorers. General histories of exploration are often little more than serial biographies, replicating many of the limitations of the genre.[3] Such studies leave important questions unanswered about explorers as a group, questions regarding their origins, motivations, qualifications, and rewards.

The *Oxford English Dictionary* indicates that the word "explorer" first came into common usage in the early nineteenth century. Its emergence signaled the advent of the explorer as a distinct type of traveler, different in crucial respects from others who ventured abroad. This development has been largely overlooked by recent scholarship, in spite of—but also because of—its attentiveness to discursive practices. Much of this work has been concerned with travel writing as a genre, focusing on the textual tropes and other rhetorical devices that travelers used to appeal to readers at home and advance the social and ideological agendas they shared, especially by indicating how their own society was superior to those they encountered in their travels.[4] While explorers certainly relied on conventional literary forms when they wrote their exploration narratives, they did not consider themselves merely travelers, nor were they regarded as such by their contemporaries. What set them apart most obviously was that their journeys took them to places that few if any of their countrymen had visited, and for good reason—they were usually distant, difficult to reach, and dangerous to enter. But other important distinctions existed as well. Explorers were much more likely than other travelers to possess specialized scientific training and skills, such as using precision instruments to fix location; to act as the official agents of institutional interests and organizations, especially learned societies and government agencies; to embrace an ethos of service, characterizing their endeavors as duties, not excursions; and to receive some form of compensation or reward, whether it be a cash payment, a land grant, a salaried position, a medal or knighthood, or simply public acclaim.

A prosopographical profile of nineteenth-century explorers permits us to identify their shared characteristics. The most obvious was gender: all were men. Although a growing number of financially independent women took up travel in this period, and some of them won respect and recognition for their arduous and often risky journeys into remote regions, contemporaries did not consider them explorers. This is partly because the term "explorer" evoked qualities of leadership, courage, and physical endurance that were inextricably associated at the time with masculinity. In addition, explorers had to possess scientific and other technical skills that few women ever had the opportunity to acquire. Toward the end of the century, the achievements of Mary Kingsley and other women travelers began to break down these gender distinctions. Not only did Kingsley, for example, venture alone into little-known regions of West Africa, but she wrote with such engaging aplomb about the challenges she faced there that the travel narratives of many male explorers seemed by comparison overwrought or—to use that highly gendered word—hysterical. Yet Kingsley opposed the election of adventurous women such as herself as fellows of the Royal Geographical Society. She accepted what one of her biographers has described as the "constructions of the overt masculinity of exploration and the more passive femininity of travel."[5] Her rationale for endorsing this distinction is revealing: "Though I have travelled further in West Africa than any of my countrymen still I have never fixed a point or taken an observation or in fact done any surveying work that entitles me to be called a Geographer."[6] For Kingsley, then, the defining difference between the explorer and the traveler was the ability to accurately map one's route and location.

This ability was one of the most important qualifications required of an explorer.[7] In Australia, where colonists' insatiable demand for land placed a particular premium on surveying skills, more explorers came from careers as land surveyors than any other occupation. Surveying was an activity, as the surveyor and explorer John McDouall Stuart pointed out, that took its practitioners "frequently into the Bush in all directions," preparing them for the challenges of exploration.[8] In addition to Stuart, the Australian explorers Alexander Forrest, John Forrest, William Gosse, Augustus Gregory, Frank Gregory, Edmund Kennedy, David Lindsay, Thomas Mitchell, John Oxley, John Septimus Roe, Charles Sturt, and William Tietkens had all worked as land surveyors, and indeed, several of them were surveyors general for their respective colonies. Oxley and Roe had originally acquired their surveying skills as naval officers, while Mitchell and Sturt had done so during their army careers, as, in all likelihood, had George Grey and Peter Warburton. Their experience as military officers also gave them useful logistical and command experience.

Many of the men who led expeditions into Africa had military backgrounds as well. William Allen, William Balfour Baikie, Verney Lovett Cameron, Hugh Clapperton, George Francis Lyon, and James Tuckey were naval officers. The Royal Navy's Surveying Service provided an important training ground for the scientific skills required of explorers.[9] Other African explorers were British Army officers: they included Dixon Denham, Alexander Laing, William Gray, and Andrew Smith. The East India Company's Bombay Army produced John Hanning Speke, James Grant, and Richard Burton, who had spent much of his Indian career seconded to the Sind Survey.[10] A military commission, it should be said, did not ensure expertise in navigational methods. Hugh Clapperton complained that his colleague Dixon Denham "could not read his sextant[,] knew not a star in the heavens and could not take the Altitude of the Sun."[11] Almost all naval and army officers, however, had at least a rudimentary knowledge of how to track their route and fix their location with the use of the compass and other instruments. Moreover, their appreciation of the information that derived from such skills can be discerned from the fact that military officers made up a large portion of the Royal Geographical Society's membership.[12]

When the Napoleonic Wars came to an end in 1815, many naval and army officers were placed on half pay, and even those who remained on active service had few prospects for promotion. These circumstances provided a powerful incentive for junior officers to seek other avenues of professional advancement. Exploration offered a high-risk, high-reward option for those who were especially restive and ambitious. Eric Leed has suggested that for the imperial state, the surge of scientific expeditions during the long peace of the nineteenth century served as an outlet for the energies of unemployed and underemployed military officers, operating in effect as "a substitute for war."[13]

Plenty of explorers, however, had never served in any officer corps, nor had they practiced land surveying. In Australia, the second-most common occupational background of explorers was pastoralism, especially "overlanding," a term that referred to the herding of stock across country to markets. This is how Edward Eyre, Alfred Howitt, William Landsborough, Duncan McIntyre, and John McKinlay acquired the bush skills they needed to venture into the interior. An essential aspect of those skills was the ability to determine one's direction, distance, and location. Most stockmen relied on dead reckoning, a rough-and-ready practice that required little more than a compass. For those whose only objective was to find new routes and fresh pastures for sheep and cattle, dead reckoning sufficed. But more was expected of those who sought to establish public reputations as explorers. While it is not entirely clear how stockmen who turned to exploration learned to use the sextant and other instruments of navigation, most of them did, and those who did not usually had the good sense to find partners with the proper qualifications. Though they subsequently had a bitter falling-out, the settler Hamilton Hume, who knew how to survive in the bush, joined forces with the former sea captain William Hovell, who knew how to map a route, resulting in the expedition that took them from Sydney's hinterland to Port Phillip. Robert O'Hara Burke, who served as both cavalry officer and police superintendent, lacked surveying skills, but he was able to draw on the expertise of William Wills, who had trained with Professor Georg Neumayer at his astronomical observatory in Melbourne. When the Victorian Exploring Expedition first set out, Wills was its third-ranking officer, but he soon became indispensable to Burke and eventually assumed informal standing as the expedition's co-leader, a status enshrined in its popular designation as the Burke and Wills expedition.

How did African explorers without military training learn how to map? Walter Oudney, a physician, prepared for his expedition to Bornu by acquiring the basics of astronomical observation at Greenwich. Some fifty years later, the geologist Joseph Thomson received training in the transit survey from Royal Geographical Society personnel. Others used long sea voyages to acquire such skills. Several scientific members of David Livingstone's Zambezi expedition took lessons in the use of the sextant and other surveying instruments while sailing from Britain to South Africa. Livingstone himself had learned to take observations from his friend Thomas Maclear, the government astronomer at the Cape Town Observatory. The poorly educated Richard Lander probably learned the rudiments of surveying from Hugh Clapperton, whom he assisted as a manservant on the expedition of 1825–1826. A rare African explorer who did not know how to map was James Richardson, who first ventured into the Sahara in 1845 on a fact-finding expedition for the Anti-Slavery Society. When he returned to the region to lead a government expedition in 1850, Heinrich Barth and Adolf Overweg were appointed as his companions because they possessed the astronomical and other scientific skills he so obviously lacked.[14]

While the ability to conduct a transit survey was commonly regarded as the explorer's most essential skill, expertise in medicine, botany, geology, zoology, or other natural sciences was prized as well. The South African explorer William Burchell, whose father was a botanist, had apprenticed as a botanical specialist at Kew. Allan Cunningham, another Kew-trained botanist, sailed for Australia on Banks's recommendation and made several expeditions into the interior of New South Wales in the 1820s, first under the command of John Oxley, then as the leader of his own parties. Most natural scientists, however, were appointed to supporting roles, serving as expeditions' second- or third-in-command: the botanist Charles Fraser on expeditions led by Oxley, Cunningham, and John Sterling; the botanist Richard Cunningham, Allan's brother, on Mitchell's second expedition; the taxidermist John Gilbert on Ludwig Leichhardt's expedition from Moreton Bay to Port Essington; the botanist William Carron on Edmund Kennedy's disastrous Cape York expedition.

When expeditions into the African and Australian interiors were especially large and well funded, they resembled naval expeditions in the number of scientific specialists that accompanied them. Captain James Tuckey's expedition up the Congo River in 1816 included the botanist Dr. Christen Smith, a University of Copenhagen–trained protégé of Banks, along with a geologist, a zoologist, an entomologist/ichthyologist, and a plant collector trained at Kew. The Niger expedition of 1841 had a botanist (Dr. Theodor Vogel), a mineralogist (Charles Gottfried Roscher), a geologist (Dr. William Stanger), a plant collector (John Ansell), a zoologist (Lewis Fraser), and an artist/draftsman (James Uwins). Among the members of Augustus Gregory's expedition to northern Australia in 1855–1856 were a geologist (J. S. Wilson), a botanist (Ferdinand von Mueller), a surgeon/naturalist (J. R. Elsey), a collector/preserver (J. Flood), and an artist (Thomas Baines). David Livingstone's Zambezi expedition of 1858–1864 included a medical officer/botanist (Dr. John Kirk), a geologist (Richard Thornton), an artist (Thomas Baines again), and, at a later stage in the expedition, another medical officer who carried out botanical duties (Dr. Charles Meller). Unlike military officers and government surveyors, naturalists and physicians had little command experience, which helps explain why they so rarely led expeditions. The only reason Livingstone himself was placed in charge of the Zambezi expedition was because his prior transcontinental journey in the company of Africans had proven his knowledge of the region and skills as an explorer—though the Zambezi experience would demonstrate in turn his unsuitability for the role. Most of the physicians and natural scientists who assumed command of expeditions did so when the original leaders died, an especially common occurrence in Africa's disease-rich environment. The German naturalist and linguist Heinrich

Barth might well have remained a footnote in the history of the exploration of West Africa had not James Richardson, the man appointed to
lead the expedition, died soon after it set out. The surgeon and naturalist William Balfour Baikie took command of the Niger expedition of
1854 only after its original leader, the British consul John Beecroft, was
felled by fever along the coast. Similarly, the death of Keith Johnston left
the inexperienced geologist Joseph Thomson in charge of the RGS-
sponsored expedition to Lake Nyasa in 1873.

Important patterns can also be discerned in the social and ethnic origins
of explorers. Because David Livingstone, the son of an impoverished
Scottish mill worker, and Henry Morton Stanley, whose childhood had
been spent in a Welsh workhouse, loom so large in the history and mythology of African exploration, it is tempting to assume that their hard-
scrabble backgrounds were typical. They were not. Most explorers
came from respectable middle- and upper-middle-class backgrounds.
Coulthurst was more representative in this respect than Livingstone and
Stanley. A surprising number of explorers—Verney Lovett Cameron,
Edward Eyre, James Grant, John Kirk, William Landsborough, John
Septimus Roe, and Peter Warburton—were the sons of clergymen. Oth-
ers, more predictably, came from military families, including William
Balfour Baikie, Robert O'Hara Burke, Richard Burton, George Grey,
Augustus and Frank Gregory, George Francis Lyon, and John McDouall
Stuart. The fathers of Hugh Clapperton, William Gosse, Joseph Ritchie,
and William Wills were physicians or surgeons. Samuel Baker, William
George Browne, John Davidson, Ernest Giles, and John McKinlay were
the sons of merchants or other businessmen. Francis Galton's father was
a banker, Alexander Laing's was a schoolmaster, Macgregor Laird's
was a shipbuilder, and William Tietkens's was a chemist. Benjamin
Herschel Babbage's father was the famous Cambridge mathematician
Charles Babbage, and John MacGillivray's was the well-known orni-
thologist and Aberdeen professor of natural history William MacGillivray. George Macleay, John Oxley, Mansfield Parkyns, and John
Hanning Speke came from landed families of long lineage. Ludwig
Leichhardt, Duncan McIntyre, and Mungo Park were the sons of farmers.

All of these men had received substantial schooling, and a number of them had attended university. Only a few explorers came from working-class origins: in addition to Livingstone and Stanley, they included the brothers Alexander and John Forrest, whose parents immigrated to Australia as servants; the brothers John and Richard Lander, whose father kept a small inn; and Andrew Smith, the son of a shepherd.

The ethnic and national identities of the explorers are also revealing. This study is concerned with what can be broadly construed as British exploration, and most of its participants can be broadly construed as British. Yet the United Kingdom's four constituent nations (England, Scotland, Wales, and Ireland) made strikingly different contributions to the pool of explorers. Given England's demographic dominance within the British Isles, it is to be expected that more African and Australian explorers were born there than anywhere else. These included such famous explorers as Richard Burton, Edward Eyre, Ernest Giles, John Oxley, John Hanning Speke, and William Wills. By contrast, the only notable explorer to come from Wales was Henry Morton Stanley, and he immigrated in his youth to the United States, worked as a journalist for an American newspaper, and carried an American flag on his first two expeditions into Africa. Ireland was equally arid soil for explorers: the only native sons of note were the unfortunate James Tuckey, who died of yellow fever during his probe of the Congo River in 1816, and the equally unfortunate Robert O'Hara Burke, who succumbed to starvation in central Australia. One distinguished Australian explorer was born in India: Charles Sturt was the son of an East India Company judge, though he regarded himself as English and retired to England. Only a few Australian explorers—Hamilton Hume, the Forrest brothers, and David Lindsay come to mind—were Australian-born, though plenty of others adopted the continent as their home.

What stands out most strikingly in any analysis of explorers' origins, however, is the prevalence of Scots. It is well known that Scots played a disproportionately large role in the empire as colonial officials, overseas traders, and the like, so it should perhaps come as no surprise that a number of them engaged in exploration as well. With widely accessible educational institutions of well-recognized quality, especially in medicine and the natural sciences, but with far too few opportunities for their graduates to practice their professions in Scotland itself, the place became an important recruiting ground for explorers, especially in Africa. The first British explorer after the Scotsman James Bruce to achieve celebrity for his African adventures was another Scot, Mungo Park. He had studied medicine and botany at Edinburgh University, making him an ideal candidate for the expeditionary designs of Joseph Banks and the African Association. Other African explorers of Scottish origins who had medical training were Walter Oudney, William Balfour Baikie, John Kirk, Andrew Smith, and, most famously, David Livingstone. Scots brought professional skills of other kinds to the exploration of Africa as well: Hugh Clapperton, James Augustus Grant, and Alexander Laing as military officers, Macgregor Laird as a shipbuilder, Keith Johnston as a cartographer, and Joseph Thomson as a geologist.

In Australia, where a rapidly growing settler population in boomtowns such as Melbourne created a strong demand for doctors and other specially trained professionals, those Scots who arrived with such skills had little incentive to take up the risky work of exploration. The most notable exception was Thomas Livingstone Mitchell, who came to New South Wales in 1828 as surveyor general after having served in the Peninsular Campaign during the Napoleonic Wars as one of Wellington's protégés, followed by a postwar stint as a surveying instructor at Sandhurst. He led four expeditions into the interior in hopes that he would be rewarded with a knighthood. Australia's other Scottish-born explorers tended to be men of more modest educational and occupational attainments, such as William Landsborough, Duncan McIntyre, John McKinlay, and John McDouall Stuart.

While British expeditions were composed mainly of Scotsmen, Englishmen, and other Britons, a surprising number of their scientific specialists were Germans. Their unusually prominent role in British exploration can be attributed to much the same range of factors as accounted for the striking Scottish contribution. The excellent scientific training provided by German universities produced far more botanists, geologists, and other scientists than the domestic economy could absorb, and many young German scientists looked in any case to emulate their heroes, fellow Germans such as the explorers Alexander von Humboldt and Georg Forster and the astronomer William Herschel, who had achieved their fame far from home. They recognized that they would have to go into "foreign service in order to fulfill their ambitions," and the foreign service that presented the greatest range of opportunities was Britain's.[15] Joseph Banks and the African Association tapped into this pool around the turn of the century by recruiting Friedrich Hornemann and Johann Ludwig Burckhardt (who was actually a Swiss national) as explorers. Both young men were recommended to Banks by Johann Blumenbach, the prominent University of Göttingen professor whose research into craniometry and racial ethnography drew heavily on explorers' observations and the skulls they gathered on their journeys.[16] Thereafter, Germans with scientific skills increasingly sought professional opportunities in Britain and the British imperial world in the nineteenth century.

"The Germans beat us hollow as observers of nature," declared the armchair geographer William Desborough Cooley in 1835.[17] It was hard not to notice how many of them obtained employment in domestic and colonial British museums, botanical gardens, and various other scientific and governmental institutions.[18] Their scientific expertise also made them attractive candidates for exploration. A well-known example was Ferdinand von Mueller, a University of Kiel–trained pharmacist who immigrated to Australia in 1847. By 1853 he was the Victorian government's official botanist, which led to his selection as the botanical collector for the North Australian Exploring Expedition under the command of Augustus Gregory. The reward for this service was his promotion to director of Melbourne's Botanical Garden, a position that made it possible for him to wield influence in various learned societies, including terms as president of the Philosophical Institute of Victoria (later the Royal Society of Victoria) and the Geographical Society, Victorian Branch, and to win a number of honors, not least a knighthood in 1879 and a gold medal from the Royal Society in 1888. He established a reputation as one of Australia's leading proponents of exploration.

A number of other German émigrés were involved in Australian exploration as well. The Burke and Wills party included three Germans. Hermann Beckler, a University of Munich–trained doctor and scientist who sought to emulate Humboldt's integrative analysis of the natural world, became the expedition's medical officer. Ludwig Becker, who reportedly had nearly completed a doctorate before the 1848 revolution forced him to flee Mainz, took on several roles—artist, naturalist, and geologist. The third German, William Brahe, commanded the base camp at Cooper's Creek when Burke and Wills made their dash to the Gulf of Carpentaria. He had joined the expedition on the recommendation of a fellow German, the astronomer Georg Neumayer, a member of the planning committee. Himself a protégé of Humboldt, Neumayer had explored the Australian Alps and conducted a magnetic survey of Victoria (and later offered to lead a scientific expedition across the continent).[19] Other Germans included Diedrich Henne, a botanist with one of the expeditions sent out in search of Burke and Wills, and D. D. Herrgott, a botanist and artist who took part in the South Australia–sponsored Babbage expedition of 1858.[20]

And then there was Ludwig Leichhardt, unquestionably the most famous Australian explorer of German origin. Leichhardt had studied the natural sciences at the universities of Berlin and Göttingen, but in order to avoid military service he fled Prussia before he could obtain a degree. After spending several years engaged in further coursework and field study in Britain, France, and elsewhere, he sailed for Australia in 1841, teaching himself how to carry out astronomical and meteorological readings using the sextant, the barometer, and other instruments during the long voyage out. Although Leichhardt sensed "good will" toward Germans in Australia, he was unable to find employment that made use of his scientific skills, so he began to undertake extended overland journeys on his own, living off the land, making field observations, and collecting plants, rocks, and other natural specimens, which he sold to a dealer in Britain. When the governor of New South Wales rejected a Legislative Council proposal that the government finance an expedition to find a land route from the colony to the military settlement of Port Essington on the north coast of Australia, Leichhardt decided that he would take on the challenge, soliciting funding from private subscribers and recruiting six volunteers to accompany him. The unexpected success of this expedition—he acknowledged that some doubters suspected he had "an intention of committing suicide"—brought him fame. Leichhardt now saw himself, and was seen by others, as a professional explorer. He would set out on two more expeditions, intending in both instances to cross the continent from east to west. Debilitating illness brought the first expedition to a premature end, while the second disappeared, leaving no trace of Leichhardt and his party.[21]

Germans also made significant contributions to the British exploration of Africa. None was more remarkable than Heinrich Barth, the great West African explorer. A student of Humboldt's at the University of Berlin, Barth had traveled across North Africa and become a university lecturer when he was asked to accompany James Richardson on a British-government-sponsored expedition into the western Sudan. He brought to his travels a genuinely Humboldtian spirit, displaying great learning, curiosity, and observational skill in his engagement with the natural world, as well as exceptional linguistic talent and cultural sensitivity in his dealings with the peoples who inhabited the region. His five-volume account of the expedition, *Travels and Discoveries in North and Central Africa,* was Humboldtian as well, not least in its length and detail.[22] Barth was accompanied by the Prussian astronomer and geologist Adolf Overweg, who died some two years after the expedition originally set out, while another German, the astronomer Edward Vogel, who worked at the Bishop Observatory in London, led a relief expedition to supply them with additional scientific instruments in 1854. Other Germans who contributed to British expeditions in Africa included Adolphus Kummer, a naturalist on an expedition the British dispatched into Guinea after the Napoleonic Wars; Theodor Vogel, a botanist, and Charles Gottfied Roscher, a mineralogist, on the 1841 Niger expedition; and William Bleek, an ethnologist on the 1854 Niger expedition.[23]

Admission to the fraternity of explorers was restricted to specific social and ethnic groups. Some European members of Australian and African expeditions were excluded from the category of explorer by reasons of their class status, which restricted them to the role of servants and assistants. Also excluded were indigenous and other non-European participants in expeditions, even though many of them had much more knowledge of the territory being explored and much more familiarity with the everyday operations of expeditions than did their European commanders. The definitional parameters of the explorer were determined, then, not simply by gender but by class and color as well.

The Africans who accompanied British-sponsored expeditions in Africa almost always outnumbered the European members of the parties by substantial ratios, yet it was always taken as a given that they could not be explorers, even when the regions they passed through were as unfamiliar to them as to the Europeans. The same was true of the smaller contingents of Aborigines who assisted Australian expeditions. Their roles as hired help was one of the factors that disqualified them. But so too did their indigeneity. How could Africans explore Africa or Aborigines Australia? Yet the fact that this question did not arise when Australian- or African-born whites engaged in exploration indicates the importance of race in determining who counted as an explorer. Even those nonwhite guides and go-betweens who played a far more instrumental role in the success of expeditions than their ostensible leaders, as many did, were never identified as explorers.

If race was one criterion for determining who was and was not an explorer, class was another. This was especially apparent in Australia in the first half of the nineteenth century. While expeditions were composed almost exclusively of white men, they were characterized by a rigid social hierarchy. The officers often had servants to see to their personal needs, and they kept their distance from the bullock drivers, blacksmiths, wheelwrights, baggage handlers, and other laboring men who made up the majority of their parties. Some of these men were convicts, some were soldiers, and still others were free wage laborers, but nearly all of them were members of the lower orders, often uneducated and illiterate. They did not write about their experiences, and they rarely received mention by those who did. The journals of Oxley, Mitchell, and Sturt, among others, are largely silent about the rank and file who accompanied them.[24] One of the few explorers from this era who does write about such men is George Grey, but his comments about the soldiers and sailors who took part in his two expeditions in Western Australia drip with disdain. He characterizes them as ignorant, improvident, uncouth, and incapable of acting with forethought. When his own incompetent leadership brings them to the brink of disaster, he interprets their growing sullenness and insubordination as evidence of their own mental and moral deficiencies: they simply cannot understand, as he sees it, that their own best interests were served by submitting to his orders. They are slaves to "superstition, which is so common amongst . . . Englishmen of the lower orders."[25]

Such men did not qualify as explorers for a multitude of reasons: they lacked the rationality, morality, autonomy, expertise, discipline, and sense of duty that those whose social standing was more elevated were presumed to possess. The botanist for the expedition that Augustus Gregory led into northern Australia in 1855 lamented "the extreme low-ness of moral tone among most classes in the colony," an outburst pro-voked by his discovery that the men assigned to assist him on his col-lecting ventures were drinking the alcoholic spirits intended to preserve specimens.[26] Their deficiencies extended even unto death. The com-mission of inquiry that investigated the unhappy outcome of the Burke and Wills expedition attributed several working-class members' deaths from scurvy to constitutions already weakened by their susceptibility to drink.[27] This effort to diminish the value of their sacrifice was echoed in one of the first publications to detail the expedition's fate, which drew a sharp distinction between its leaders, who were represented as heroic martyrs, and its other victims, for whom "there is no triumph connected with their deaths. They had not struggled and conquered for their duty's sake. All the fame which the colony will gain by this expedi-tion it owes BURKE and WILLS."[28] Neither in life nor in death, then, did the lower orders receive much if any recognition for their contributions to expeditions.

This was not the case for junior officers, scientific technicians, and other middle-class members of expeditions. Most of them joined these endeavors in the anticipation that their contributions would win them public notice and advance their careers. But their intermediate positions in the expeditionary party's social hierarchy also made them susceptible to status anxieties. They often felt underappreciated by the commander and undermined by the men. Granville Stapylton, an assistant surveyor and second-in-command of Thomas Mitchell's 1836 expedition, wrote bitterly in his private journal about being "bearded" by the party's con-victs and "insulted" by its commander. Proclaiming himself to be an "officer" and a "gentleman," he insisted: "I stand independant [*sic*] and would not stoop to abject servility" in his relations with Mitchell—in contrast, presumably, to the convicts.[29] Daniel Brock, who had been hired to skin birds and look after firearms for Charles Sturt's expedition of 1844, felt similarly insecure about his status. He complained continually about the convicts he had to work with, whose "depraved tastes," "obscene language," and "utter disregard . . . of a righteous God" stood in sharp distinction to his own determination to maintain Christian respectability. At the same time, he resented Sturt for failing to recognize and reward his superior social position and moral character.[30] Both men vented their resentments in their journals.

Australian expeditions were far less riven by class divisions and tensions in the second half of the nineteenth century. Convicts and soldiers, the mainstays of expeditions' labor force in the first half of the century, largely disappeared in later years, both because the transportation of convicts to Australia was coming to a close and because expeditions were increasingly organized at the behest of colonial legislatures and settler interest groups, who could not call on troops to carry out such endeavors. Plebeian types still played active roles in expeditions, but they were more often recruited and valued for the bush skills they possessed.[31] Expeditionary parties were also smaller and more tightly knit. They still maintained some social distinctions: John McDouall Stuart, for example, required that the men who took part in his 1862 expedition refer to him and his officers as "Mister."[32] Moreover, plaudits and prizes still went mainly to the expedition leaders. Yet their companions garnered a good deal more public recognition than had been the case in the past. The members of expeditions often appeared together at the banquets, parades, and fetes that followed their return from the outback and sat as a group for studio portraits. Even the expeditions' Aboriginal guides often appeared in these photographs. Such developments signaled a move toward a more collaborative, egalitarian conception of the enterprise of exploration in Australia.

African expeditionary parties tended to be much larger than their Australian counterparts and include many more indigenous participants. Race and class were often coterminous in these parties. Still, some African expeditions included lower-class whites. In West Africa, the naval expeditions that went up the Congo (1816) and Niger (1832–

Ernest Giles (seated, second from right) and the members of his 1875 expedition, including his Aboriginal guide, Tommy Oldham, and his South Asian cameleer, Saleh. *Source: State Library of South Australia (B1035).*

1834 and 1841) reflected the institutional structure of the Royal Navy, with an upper echelon of officers and scientists, who claimed explorer status, and a lower tier of sailors and marines, who did not. The same was true of expeditions that relied mainly on army manpower. Mungo Park's second expedition (1805–1806) included several officers and nearly fifty soldiers. A decade later, an even larger military expedition attempted to follow up on Park's failed effort. Now all but forgotten, this large expeditionary force consisted of some forty European and thirty African troops, along with thirty African laborers. The officers complained that the European soldiers were "men of bad character and drunkards" who were addicted to "*vice,* and *dissipation* of every kind." Their primary purpose was "to keep the Black men in check."[33]

Several South African expeditions also included socially marginal whites. The party that Andrew Smith led north from the Cape Colony in 1834–1836 consisted of himself and five other educated whites (an army captain, two scientific specialists, and two missionaries), six lower-class whites (three of whom were soldiers), and twenty-seven blacks (identified as "Hottentots" or Khoikhoi).[34] Francis Galton's expedition to Namibia in 1850–1851 had only one other middle-class participant, the naturalist Charles John Andersson, while the rest of his party consisted of Africans and several unnamed whites, convicts who had been recruited from Cape Town's prison.[35] Needless to say, only Smith, Galton, and their scientifically trained colleagues were characterized as explorers.

Perhaps the most intriguing case of an African explorer who recruited working-class white men to accompany his expeditions is Henry Morton Stanley. For his journey in search of Livingstone, Stanley hired William Farquhar and John Shaw, two footloose sailors who were stereotypically fond of drink. From the hundreds of individuals who deluged him with applications to join his subsequent transcontinental expedition, his improbable choices were Frederick Barker, a London hotel clerk, and two brothers, Francis and Edward Pocock, the sons of a fisherman.[36] Insecure about his own social standing, Stanley took care to select companions whose modest backgrounds made them unlikely threats to his own position. As it happened, all of these men died during their African journeys, but even if they had survived, their lowly status made it unlikely that they ever would have threatened Stanley's own claims to the mantle of discovery.

Most African expeditions relied on large retinues of African guides, translators, porters, soldiers, cooks, and hangers-on, leaving little need for working-class whites of the sort who carried out much of the manual labor on Australian expeditions. Indeed, it was feasible for a single white man to oversee an African expedition: Mungo Park, Friedrich Hornemann, Johann Ludwig Burckhardt, Alexander Laing, David Livingstone, Samuel Baker, Verney Lovett Cameron, and Joseph Thomson were among those who did so. Other African parties consisted of small teams of white men of similar social standing and educational attainments. Hugh Clapperton's second expedition into West Africa included three men—the hydrographer Robert Pearce and the surgeons Thomas

Dickson and Robert Morrison—who were presumed qualified to have assumed command of the expedition when Clapperton died if not for the fact that all of them had predeceased him. The only white survivor of the expedition was Clapperton's personal servant, the poorly educated John Lander, who was ordered by the dying Clapperton to retrace his steps to the coast. Although Lander managed to make his way back to England, where he delivered Clapperton's journals to governmental authorities, he was treated by them with great condescension. As he complained to the publisher John Murray, "because accident has thrown me into a humble sphere of life, my veracity is questioned & my promises treated with indifference & contempt."[37] In the end, however, his past experience in West Africa trumped his social disabilities, and he persuaded officials to send him on the expedition that succeeded in tracing the Niger to its outlet in the Gulf of Guinea.

When Britons of similar social status teamed together on expeditions, all of them could expect to receive some recognition for their contributions. Even so, every expedition had to have a commander, who invariably garnered the spotlight. This disparity in power and prestige often led to resentment and jealousy. One of the most notorious examples was the East African expedition commanded by Richard Burton, whose relations with his companion, fellow Bombay Army officer John Hanning Speke, had deteriorated by the end of the journey into mutual recriminations and lasting enmity. When Speke returned to East Africa as commander of his own expedition, he made a shrewder choice of companion to accompany him: James Grant, another Bombay Army officer, proved to be a loyal lieutenant. In still another case, John Kirk's private journals reveal that he became deeply disillusioned with the leadership of David Livingstone during their Zambezi expedition but kept his reservations to himself. While neither Grant nor Kirk ever commanded his own expedition or achieved the fame of Speke or Livingstone, both did become prominent authorities on African exploration, Grant as a leading member of the Royal Geographical Society and Kirk as the long-serving British consul in Zanzibar. Unlike men of lesser educations and occupations, they won entry into the fraternity of explorers because they possessed the training and expertise considered necessary to extract useful knowledge from the experience.

Most of these men saw themselves as members of a "service class," acting on behalf of interests greater than themselves.[38] They professed to be serving the needs of science, civilization, and Christianity. Yet they also pursued their own interests, exuberantly embracing the individualism so celebrated by Victorian bourgeois culture. Exploration provided them with the opportunity both to promote their own careers through service to society and to achieve that rare thing, the honor of being considered heroes.

The sense of professionalism that Richard Burton so acerbically declared a burdensome demand was remarked upon by other explorers as well. Charles John Andersson, the botanist who accompanied Francis Galton to Namibia, noted that the explorer "is now expected to be completely versed in many sciences. . . . He is supposed to understand meteorology, hygrometry, and hydrogeny; to collect geological specimens, to gather political and commercial information, to advance the infant study of ethology, to sketch, to write a copious journal, to shoot and stuff birds and beasts, to collect grammars and vocabularies, and frequently to forward long reports to the R.G.S."[39] To refer to exploration as a professional pursuit may seem anomalous: it was too risky and insecure an endeavor to qualify as a profession in any conventional sense. It did, however, demand a highly specialized set of skills, a criterion often associated with professionalization. This association was reinforced by the expectation that explorers meet certain social and educational standards and by the existence of a society, the RGS, that in certain respects established "best practices" and regulated entry to the craft and access to its resources. It also established a rewards system—most notably its annual gold medals—that conferred prestige and status. If not strictly a profession, then, exploration certainly offered "a means for professional advancement through alternative national service."[40] George Francis Lyon, the Royal Navy captain who agreed to accompany Joseph Ritchie on an expedition into the Sahara in 1819, did so "from a natural wish to rise in my profession."[41] Edmund Kennedy, the protégé of Thomas Mitchell, explained his decision to become an explorer this way: "Exploration appears to be one of the Roads to preferment in these days and although attended with many privations it is better than a quiet useless life."[42]

Exploration offered a potentially high-profile if risky career opportunity for ambitious men who were restive with conventional constraints. For military officers who had few if any prospects for glory and promotion in peacetime, exploration satisfied their craving for adventure and advancement on an expanding imperial frontier. For colonial surveyors who spent much of their time in the bush anyway, exploration promised them excitement, the likelihood of promotion, and the possibility of celebrity. For botanists, zoologists, and other men of science who struggled to obtain scarce positions, exploration provided useful apprenticeships in the field that could bring them recognition and a salaried appointment in a museum, botanical garden, or other scientific institution. African explorers often received government sinecures as rewards for their achievements. William Balfour Baikie, Richard Burton, Harry Johnston, John Kirk, Charles Livingstone (who accompanied his brother, David Livingstone, on the Zambezi expedition), and Henry Salt all received appointments in the British consular service. When the scramble for Africa began in the early 1880s, some explorers found lucrative work on behalf of competing imperial interests: Harry Johnston and Joseph Thomson as agents of Cecil Rhodes's British South Africa Company; Samuel Baker as the first governor-general of Equatoria, the southern Sudanese territory claimed by Egypt; and, most notoriously, Henry Morton Stanley and William Stairs in the Congo and Rwanda in the service of Belgium's King Leopold.

A few Australian explorers leveraged their accomplishments in the outback into imperial careers, most notably George Grey and Edward Eyre, both of whom became colonial governors. Others were rewarded by Australian authorities with administrative appointments: Alfred Howitt as police magistrate in Victoria, William Landsborough as police magistrate and commissioner of crown lands in the Northern Territory, William Gosse as deputy surveyor general of South Australia, Augustus Gregory as the commissioner of crown lands and surveyor general of Queensland. Still others received cash payments for their services. John McDouall Stuart's remarkable journey across the continent in 1861–1862 earned him a handsome reward of £2,000. Prize money more typically ranged from £250 to £1,000. The South Australian government paid Ernest Giles and William Tietkens the former amount for their respective expeditions of 1872–1874 and 1889, while John McKinlay and Peter Warburton got the latter for their 1861 and 1872 expeditions. Australian colonial governments also expressed their gratitude with land grants. Gregory Blaxland and his two companions were awarded 1,000 acres by Governor Lachlan Macquarie for their discovery of a route through the Blue Mountains in 1813. William Hovell and Hamilton Hume received grants of 1,200 acres from the government of New South Wales after their 1824 expedition. A few years later the same government gave 5,000 acres to the explorer Charles Sturt and 2,560 acres to his companion George Macleay. The South Australian government would soon take this kind of compensation to a new level of largesse as it pushed northward. In 1858 it promised the explorer Benjamin Herschel Babbage 990 square miles in leasehold (along with £1,000), which he apparently received despite being recalled by the governor for failing to make sufficient progress during his expedition. Peter Warburton, Babbage's successor as leader of the expedition, was granted an astonishing 2,287 square miles of land. Only marginally smaller was the 2,000-square-mile leasehold granted to Ernest Giles after his 1875–1876 expedition.[43]

In Africa, where Britain's territorial claims did not extend beyond the Cape Colony and Natal in South Africa and a few footholds along the coast of West Africa until the late nineteenth century, it was not feasible to offer land to explorers, nor would they have found such compensation lucrative. Cash payments were uncommon as well. Apart from appointments and promotions in various branches of government service, African explorers' main rewards came in the form of profit from the books they wrote about their journeys. The British public had an insatiable taste for travelers' tales, and Africa's mystery and exoticism made it especially compelling. As early as 1799 Mungo Park's *Travels in the Interior Districts of Africa* had shown the strength of this market: it sold out within weeks of publication and went through three editions within a year, generating well over £1,000 in royalties.[44] After Park, few of Africa's explorers were unaware of the potential profit they could make from telling tales of their adventures. When Alexander Laing, the first European explorer to reach the fabled West African city of

Timbuktu, was murdered soon after he set out to return to Britain, the letters and journal fragments he left behind provided so few revealing details about his journey that the editor of these documents speculated that Laing had deliberately withheld information so as to heighten interest in the book he intended to write.[45] The explorers who did survive rarely lost time turning their stories to print, though it is unlikely that any of them surpassed Park's success until the breakthrough appearance of David Livingstone's *Missionary Travels and Researches in South Africa* (1857). An unprecedented publishing phenomenon, this book sold more than 70,000 copies, producing a profit in excess of £12,000 for its author.[46] It also gave other explorers a powerful incentive, reinforced by publishers, to get their expedition narratives into print as soon as possible.

With so much at stake for such ambitious men—their careers, their earnings, their reputations—it is little wonder that competition among explorers was intense. Some explorers monitored their peers' activities and achievements with obsessive attention. According to Edmund Kennedy, second-in-command of Thomas Mitchell's 1846–1847 expedition, "Sir T was anxious to have *his* river explored" before Ludwig Leichhardt could "stumble upon it."[47] Leichhardt was equally preoccupied with Mitchell, sending a member of his own team back to the settled district they had left a week earlier to gather intelligence about his rival's progress.[48] When Ernest Giles set out on his 1873–1874 expedition into west-central Australia, he repeatedly crossed the tracks made by William Gosse's party, which was exploring the same region, causing him for a time to despair about whether his own endeavor had any purpose. Eventually he decided to "depart to some remoter spot, where none shall dispute my sway."[49] Alexander Laing's letters from West Africa show that he was obsessed with the concurrent expedition by Hugh Clapperton, "whose only object seems to be to forestall me in discovery."[50] When Livingstone's Zambezi expedition received word that Burton and Speke had returned from their journey into the East African interior with "splendid discoveries," John Kirk predicted that "this will pull us up to do something more."[51]

Explorers were acutely aware that their efforts were being measured against the accomplishments of others. Their letters, journals, and books were often peppered with disparaging comments about predecessors and competitors, revealing intense resentments and jealousies. Thomas Mitchell seldom resisted an opportunity to point out inconsistencies between what he observed in his journeys and what John Oxley had reported during his passage through the same area. He repeatedly sniped at his rival Charles Sturt as well.[52] Verney Lovett Cameron had nothing good to say about Stanley in his field journal, referring to several of Stanley's route sketches as "purely imaginary" and describing his reputation among the locals as that of a "merciless tyrant."[53] Stanley was no less critical of Cameron, charging that one of his geographical claims was fictitious.[54] The high-stakes competition to discover the source of the Nile generated some of the most famous examples of mutual animosity. During his final meandering expedition in search of this holy grail, Livingstone repeatedly expressed disdain for the character and claims of competitors such as Baker, Burton, Grant, and Speke, while each of these men was similarly disparaging in his judgments of the others.[55]

These rivalries and resentments occasionally escalated into full-fledged conflicts, some of which became public scandals. Relations between Hugh Clapperton and Dixon Denham deteriorated to such an extent during their 1922–1925 expedition in West Africa that Clapperton urged authorities to recall Denham, insisting that he was an incompetent who could not take astronomical readings. Denham, in turn, charged that Clapperton had besmirched "our respectability and National Character" by engaging in homosexual relations with an Arab servant, an accusation that caused Clapperton to demand an investigation by the British consul in Tripoli to clear his name.[56] The long-standing enmity between Thomas Mitchell and Charles Sturt had repercussions for Mitchell's reputation when Sturt charged that his hated rival had engaged in "the most fearful acts of cold blooded murder" against an Aboriginal tribe during his third expedition in 1836, an accusation that Mitchell and his friends believed responsible for delaying his long-expected knighthood.[57]

Perhaps the most notorious instance of open warfare between explorers occurred when Richard Burton and John Hanning Speke, erstwhile colleagues in the East African expedition of 1857–1859, fell out. Their bitter dispute about whether Speke had discovered the source of the Nile was aired publicly, with vituperative letters to the *Times,* disputatious articles and books, and the much-anticipated debate scheduled to take place between the two men at the annual meeting of the British Association for the Advancement of Science in 1864.[58] When on the day before the debate Speke died from a self-inflicted gunshot wound—which the coroner ruled a hunting accident, though many suspected suicide—this drama took on the character of a Greek tragedy. For years to come, passions would remain high among partisans of both parties. Although Speke's supporters proposed the erection of an obelisk in his memory in Hyde Park, the Royal Geographical Society had trouble raising funds for its construction, and it was unveiled in 1866 without public ceremony.[59] James Grant, whose loyalty to Speke and hatred of Burton never flagged, pursued a bizarre rumor in 1890 that Burton had tried to poison Speke during their joint expedition.[60] And when Burton passed away a few months later, Grant and the Speke family forcefully opposed the idea that a public memorial in his name be erected as a counterpart to Speke's.

What drove men such as Burton and Speke to such extremities of ill will toward one another was their determination to distinguish themselves from their counterparts, winning a place on the pedestal next to widely recognized giants of exploration such as James Cook and Mungo Park. Unlike conventional careerists, then, they were motivated not merely by material gain or professional status, but also by the desire for adventure and glory. We have already seen how powerfully these ambitions affected the unfortunate C. H. Coulthurst. For "men who make up their minds to these kinds of hazardous enterprises," wrote the Egyptian explorer Henry Salt, "it is not by a known rule, or road, that success can be ensured, and every man prefers his own route to the *Temple of Fame.*"[61] Australian explorers were no less susceptible to such inducements. "There are few undertakings more attractive to the votaries of fame or lovers of adventure," Thomas Mitchell declared, "than the exploration of unknown regions."[62] W. H. Tietkens agreed, explaining that he took up exploration in late nineteenth-century Australia because he felt the "desire for a life that seemed to me full of romance and adventure."[63] Even the supremely cerebral Francis Galton confessed that the main motive for his expedition into southwest Africa was "the love of adventure."[64]

Adventure, of course, entailed risks. A willingness to put one's life in jeopardy was an integral element of the explorer's unwritten job description. It was the route one took to glory. John Davidson, an explorer who aimed to reach the fabled city of Timbuktu, envisioned two possible outcomes to his journey: "I shall be wending my way over Africa's burning sands to a sort of fame, or the sad 'bourne from which no traveller returns.'" His fate was to be the latter outcome: he was killed by nomadic tribesmen soon after he set out from Morocco across the Sahara.[65] Although the British consul who had assisted him expressed the hope that "his name will be handed down to posterity," a sentiment seconded by the Royal Geographical Society in its annual report, Davidson had accomplished nothing worthy of note before he died, and hence his name left no posthumous mark.[66] Yet most explorers were prepared to gamble their lives in the pursuit of fame. And, like Davidson, many of them lost that gamble. In West Africa alone, the list of British-affiliated explorers who died before they had achieved their goals is a long one: Giovanni Belzoni, Friedrich Hornemann, Daniel Houghton, Alexander Laing, Henry Nicholls, Walter Oudney, Adolf Overweg, James Richardson, and Joseph Ritchie. Although a few of these men managed to travel far enough and survive long enough to garner the appreciation of geographers and others with a special interest in African exploration, none of them achieved the public recognition all craved.

On the other hand, there was no surer way to win the plaudits of the public and a place on the podium reserved for the nation's heroes than to carry out some great feat of exploration, then to die during a subsequent journey to a distant and savage land. Once again, Cook and Park were the models many sought to emulate. In 1833 the armchair geographer William Desborough Cooley noted "the rage for *Martyrdom* which seems to actuate European & particularly English travellers in Tropical Climates." This rage persisted through much of the nineteenth century, and it produced some of the most famous names in the history of exploration. No African explorer looms larger in popular memory in Britain than Livingstone, whose remains were entombed with great fanfare in Westminster Abbey. Similarly, Burke and Wills's deaths by starvation at Cooper's Creek after successfully crossing the continent made them venerated figures whose mythic importance to the Australian national imagination surpassed that of any other explorers. When a member of Charles Sturt's 1844 expedition into central Australia expressed concern that his leader seemed to "care nothing if he perished," he was sensing a self-destructive drive that more than a few explorers shared.[67]

While most explorers probably preferred to live, they certainly expected to suffer, and suffer they did. Physical privation and pain, not to mention psychological disorientation and distress, were almost inescapable aspects of exploration. What many of these men were able and willing to endure can beggar belief. It speaks to a quality we commonly call courage. Courage is, of course, a culturally defined category of behavior, and for the Victorians it was inextricably associated with notions of masculinity. The scholarship on Victorian masculinity has proliferated in recent years, and it has shown that the term referred to a wide range of values that varied by class and over time. Among the middle-class males from whom the pool of explorers was mainly drawn, masculinity entailed authority, independence, discipline, a sense of duty, the dignity of labor, and moral responsibility, which overlay deeper associations with vigor, virility, endurance, and, above all, courage.[68] While military men were the conventional embodiments of the latter virtues, war and warriors were viewed with considerable suspicion by Victorian liberals and evangelicals. Explorers filled the void produced by this suspicion, replacing soldiers as the archetypal embodiments of the courage that figured so prominently in Victorian conceptions of masculinity.

Africa and Australia presented rather different types of risks for explorers eager to demonstrate their courage and capacity for endurance. In Africa, the biggest danger came from infectious diseases. David Livingstone indicated that malaria and other illnesses had "reduced me to a mere skeleton" at the conclusion of his first expedition.[69] Similarly, John Kirk found that he had been "reduced to [a] skeleton" by fevers and dysentery by the time the Zambezi expedition had drawn to a close.[70] Other African explorers described their physical condition in similar terms.[71]

These skeletal allusions were hardly hyperbole, as the case of Henry Morton Stanley makes clear. His weight dropped from 180 to 134 pounds in the first month of his transcontinental expedition, then to 115 pounds several months later; even though he rarely went hungry, recurrent fevers and other infirmities ravaged his frame.[72] Richard Lander became so ill at one stage on the expedition led by Hugh Clapperton that he temporarily lost his sight and later wrote that he was "surprised I had lived so long." His surprise was understandable given how swiftly other members of the expedition had been carried off. Clapperton clinically described one of those deaths, detailing the victim's delirium, black tongue and mouth, "nervous twitching all over the face and body," and, finally, his death rattle.[73] Clapperton himself died of dysentery after arriving at the Emirate of Sokoto in what is now northern Nigeria, leaving Lander the only surviving European member of the party. Notwithstanding his horrific ordeal, Lander leapt at the chance to return to the region as leader of another expedition three years later, and he died there on a third expedition in 1832. Baker, Burton, Livingstone, Speke, Stanley, Thomson, and others kept coming back to Africa as well, returning with full knowledge of the terrible physical toll it was sure to inflict on them.

Although African explorers often played up in their books the perils posed by Africans, they were far less likely to face injury or death at the hands of indigenous peoples than they were as a result of disease. Still, deadly clashes occasionally occurred. Lander was killed by African middlemen along the Niger who wanted to prevent European traders from gaining entry to the interior. Burton and Speke were seriously injured and a colleague killed by Somalis who may have been motivated by similar concerns when these British officers appeared at the Berbera trading fair in 1855. Burton's face famously bore a scar from the spear thrust through his jaw in that near-fatal encounter. But perhaps the most striking case is that of Alexander Laing, who wrote the following letter to his father-in-law, the British consul in Tripoli, while recuperating from wounds suffered when Tuaregs attacked his caravan.

> To begin from the top, I have five saber cuts on the crown of the head & three on the left temple, all fractures from which much bone

has come away, one on my left cheek which fractured the Jaw bone &
has divided the ear, forming a very unsightly wound, one over the
right temple, and a dreadful gash on the back of the neck, which
slightly scratched the windpipe: a musket ball in the hip, which
made its way through my back, slightly grazing the back bone: five
saber cuts on my right arm & hand, three of the fingers broken, the
hand cut three fourths across, and the wrist bones cut through;
three cuts on the left arm, the bone of which has been broken, but is
again uniting. One slight wound on the right leg, and . . . one dreadful gash on the left, to say nothing of a cut across the fingers of my
left hand, now healed up. I am nevertheless, as I have already said,
doing well, and hope yet to return to England with much important
Geographical information.[74]

That Laing could survive such an assault seems improbable; that he
could inventory his multiple injuries with such clinical detachment gives
new meaning to the phrase "stiff upper lip." Even if Laing exaggerated
his injuries to impress his father-in-law and his wife, his stoicism and
determination were remarkable. He managed to haul his mangled body
to Timbuktu, thereby becoming the first European explorer to reach
that long-sought city. Several days after setting out on his return journey,
he was attacked once again, and this time his luck, such as it was, ran
out.

Australian explorers also ran the risk of attack by indigenous peoples,
and a few of them were killed. But most Aborigines either fled at first
sight of explorers or found them keen sources of interest. Some sought
trade and offered assistance, while those who did seek to harm these
strange interlopers used such simple weapons that the wounds they inflicted rarely proved fatal. More members of expeditions probably were
injured or killed as a result of the accidental discharge of their guns, falls
from their horses, and other mundane misfortunes than because of the
murderous designs of hostile natives.[75] Nor did infectious diseases pose
much of a risk. Malaria was limited to the tropical territories in the north
and east—and even there it was rarely fatal—while most of the other diseases that felled African explorers simply did not exist in Australia.
The principal challenge Australian explorers had to overcome was the

physical environment itself—the heat, the lack of water, and the scarcity of game and other food.

Australia's harsh environment required a remarkable capacity for endurance from the men who explored its remoter regions. They confronted temperatures in the interior that could drop below freezing in winter and spike above the century mark in summer. One expedition claimed to have recorded a temperature of 152 degrees Fahrenheit, another 164 degrees.[76] Searching for water and suffering from thirst became the recurrent themes of explorers' accounts. Nothing was more likely to spell disaster for an expedition than the failure to find water. Moreover, explorers lacked the Aborigines' skills at living off the land. When the supplies they carried ran low, they went hungry, and a few—such as Burke and Wills—starved to death. In Australia, as in Africa, one of the most visible signs of the suffering experienced by explorers was weight loss. John McKinlay's weight dropped from some 220 pounds at the start of his transcontinental expedition of 1861 to about 165 pounds at its end, and his diminished frame was hardly uncommon.[77] This was due not only to dietary deficiencies but also to the diarrhea and dysentery that came from drinking contaminated water. Two other afflictions plagued Australian explorers. One was ophthalmia, often referred to as sandy blight or fly blight, which temporarily blinded more than a few explorers and left some of them with permanently damaged sight. The other, strangely enough, was scurvy. Although Victorian medical experts understood the cause of this nutritional disease and knew how to prevent it, explorers were constrained by logistical considerations to carry much the same limited array of preserved foods that had contributed to scurvy among sailors in the past. Some explorers died of the disease and others suffered from debilitating pain and weakness. John McDouall Stuart, who contracted scurvy during his expedition to the center of Australia in 1860, gave a vivid account of its effects. It caused him "dreadful pain, & only about 2 hours of sleep . . . for the last 3 nights. This morning I observed the muscles of my limbs are changing from the yellow green colour to the black; my mouth is getting worse, it is with difficulty that I can swallow anything, but I am determined not to give in to it."[78]

This resolute response to such tribulations is indicative of the way explorers such as Stuart fashioned themselves as exemplars of the Victorian ideal of masculine courage. Even if we concede that much of what they wrote about their endeavors was cast within rhetorical conventions, the equanimity with which so many of them endured suffering and confronted death cannot be explained away as merely pretense. Consider Hugh Clapperton's icily unemotional advice to his servant Richard Lander after the deaths of the expedition's other members: "It is unmanly to repine at any trifling casualty."[79] He showed the same stoicism, according to Lander, when he confronted his own death a few months later. In a reprise of the familiar Victorian deathbed scene, Lander portrayed Clapperton, who was by now "little better than a skeleton," as a devout Christian and patriotic Englishman, stalwart and manly in the face of death: "Richard I am going to die. . . . it is the will of god it cant be helped, don't fret bear yourself up underall troubles like a man and a English man."[80]

What often worried explorers when they faced death during their journeys was whether the journals, charts, and other records that documented their achievements would survive. "Take care of my journal and papers after my death," Clapperton enjoined Lander, and "deposit them safely into the hands of the secretary" of the Colonial Office.[81] When Peter Warburton could "see no hope for life" during the direst stage of his 1872–1874 expedition in central Australia, he gave his second-in-command "written instructions to justify his leaving me . . . and have made such arrangement as I can for the preservation of my journal and maps." Perhaps the most famous account of an Australian explorer's death was the one Jackey Jackey, native guide for the tragic Cape York expedition of 1848, gave to his rescuers after hostile Aborigines speared the expedition's leader, Edmund Kennedy. According to Jackey, Kennedy told him: " 'I am very bad, Jackey; you take the books, Jackey, to the captain . . . —the governor will give anything for them.' " After struggling to write a few final words, he "fell back and died."[82] His dying words testified to his determination to attain some measure of immortality.

In the final analysis, what made the men who explored Africa and Australia so willing to embrace such daunting discomforts and dangers was that their own bodies and minds thereby became privileged sites of truth and knowledge. No armchair geographer or other domestic authority could challenge this aspect of their experience or belittle its significance. Physical ordeals supplied their own standards of measure, establishing the credibility of the explorer and the authenticity of his experience. "Contemporary accounts return repeatedly to the theme of the authentication of the explorer's travels by the trials of the body," observes Dorinda Outram, writing about late eighteenth-century explorers: "The body was the living proof of the otherwise unseen and unseeable vastness of the world."[83] What was true of the explorers Outram examines remained true of their nineteenth-century successors. The explorers of Africa and Australia were often "literally bearing the marks of an alien environment" on their bodies.[84] The physical effects of an extreme environment could in some cases become a scientific experiment in its own right. Alexander von Humboldt famously engaged in just such an experiment during his ascent of Ecuador's highest mountain, Chimborazo, meticulously recording how his own body was adversely affected by the high altitude.[85] The explorer's claim to be a trustworthy scientific observer of distant lands and peoples might rest as firmly on his own physical experiences as it did on his astronomical readings, his botanical specimens, and other conventional measures of his scrutiny of the material world.

The suffering endured by explorers also held a deeper spiritual meaning. Like saints of centuries past, they drew on "the Judeo-Christian tradition of self-renunciation in the wilderness."[86] They sacrificed their bodies for some purpose greater than themselves. It is surely no coincidence that David Livingstone, who supposedly died in a posture of prayer amid an attentive group of African disciples, attained a kind of canonization when his body was returned to Britain. Most explorers, to be sure, cast themselves as agents in the service of science and the state, not of God, but the physical sacrifices they made were rooted in the same determination to imbue their bodies with moral or spiritual value. To die on their journey or to return from it with some visible evidence of the ordeals they had endured—a skeletal frame, a pallid or yellowed complexion, a crippled limb, a disfiguring scar, a sightless eye—was to bear witness by means of the body to a transcendent truth that set them apart from their countrymen.

CHAPTER 4

Gateways

A race! a race! so great a one
The world ne'er saw before;
A race! a race! across this land
From south to northern shore.

—Nicholas Chevalier, "The Great Australian Exploration Race" (1860)

THE EXPEDITION that set out from Adelaide in early 1858 under the command of Benjamin Herschel Babbage was the first systematic effort to break through the barrier of salt lakes that had blocked South Australian settlers' expansion northward since Edward Eyre's unsuccessful attempt to do so nearly two decades earlier. Babbage was an engineer and assayer who had discovered a route around Lake Torrens during a gold-prospecting expedition a year and a half earlier. His official instructions, drafted by South Australia's commissioner of crown lands, were to survey the region between Lakes Torrens and Gairdner, then press northward in search of pastoral land. As one might expect from the son of Charles Babbage, the famous Cambridge mathematician and inventor of the first mechanical computer, Babbage was especially enthusiastic about the opportunity to bring to bear cutting-edge advances in science and technology during the expedition. He gave a paper to the Adelaide Philosophical Society that detailed the careful preparations he had made for the endeavor. In addition to equipping the expedition with all of the scientific instruments needed to map and measure the region, he had ordered a mobile borer, a still, and a set of six iron tanks to extract, purify, and store water from the region's salt lakes. To transport these bulky devices, he had designed drays specially fitted with iron wheels rather than conventional wooden wheels, which tended to shrink and fall apart in the dry climate. He planned to bring a camera to document the landscape, and he had prepared photographic plates with nine different iodized emulsions to combat the deteriorating effects of high temperatures. His party consisted of ten men, including a surveyor and a botanist, and was provisioned with eighteen months' worth of supplies. The cost to the South Australia government was a staggering £5,556.[1]

Two months after setting out, Babbage's expedition was stalled at its initial base camp. The heavy iron-wheeled drays sank in the spongy soil, making the transport of supplies more difficult than anticipated. Also hindering the expedition's advance was Babbage's overly conscientious survey of the arid terrain around the lakes. The press and public grew increasingly restive with the lack of progress. Their dissatisfaction reached the boiling point when John McDouall Stuart, who had set out several months after Babbage on a privately financed expedition in search of pasturage north of Lake Torrens, returned to Adelaide with the stunning news that he had discovered some 12,000–18,000 square miles of rich grasslands. Equipped with no scientific instruments other than a compass and accompanied by only two other men, one of them an Aboriginal guide, Stuart had managed to make "an immense circle round the contracted movements of Mr Babbage and his party," as South Australia's governor, Richard Macdonnell, pointedly put it. Relaying the news of Stuart's discovery to the Colonial Secretary in London, Macdonnell lauded Stuart's achievement as "a great monument of what can be achieved by the indomitable pluck of one man, imbued with a thorough spirit of self-reliance."[2] His subtext was a not so subtle dig at Babbage, who soon received word that he was being recalled and replaced by Major Peter Warburton, the colony's commissioner of police. In a comedic denouement to this decision, Babbage decided to throw caution to the wind and dash northward, traveling with such speed that Warburton had trouble chasing him down. The irony of the situation was not lost on the *South Australian Advertiser,* which mocked the fact that a man who was being recalled for having moved at a snail's pace now could not be caught by someone famed for his tracking skills. When Warburton finally overtook Babbage and sent him packing, he made a few desultory exploratory probes of his own and then disbanded the expedition.[3]

Preferring tales of triumph and tragedy to stories of failure and farce, historians of Australian exploration have largely ignored the Babbage expedition.[4] Yet it is worthy of our attention for several reason. First, it reminds us that science and technology were integral to how exploration was conceived and carried out by its proponents, whose confidence in their own ability to overcome nature harbored more than a modicum of hubris. When Babbage's failures eroded that confidence, those who turned against him and applauded instead the "pluck" and "self-reliance" of Stuart were drawing on another conception of exploration, one that placed emphasis on the explorer's inner resources of will, not the armature of technology. Governor Macdonnell, for one, seemed to embrace both of these seemingly contradictory stances, lavishing praise on Stuart for what he had achieved with so few resources while expressing dismay that his journals provided so little information on "subjects of general interest to the scientific world." He made the colonial government's co-sponsorship of Stuart's subsequent expedition conditional on the requirement that it "be accompanied by some person competent to observe and report on the botanical and geological character of the regions traversed."[5] Macdonnell was not alone in regarding the scientific and heroic aspects of exploration as complementary, not contradictory.

What makes the Babbage expedition and its aftermath especially noteworthy, however, is what it reveals about the political forces at play in Australian exploration at this time. The expedition was sponsored by a coalition that consisted of the colonial administration, the Philosophical Society (a key intellectual forum for Adelaide's urban elite), and South Australia's newly established House of Assembly (representing the broader settler community), which voted £2,000 in funding for the expedition. Each of these groups had its own particular reasons for supporting the costly endeavor, ranging from geopolitical to scientific to economic agendas. When Babbage bogged down, the coalition broke up. The land speculators who had placed their bets instead on Stuart were the big winners. Yet the political ramifications of the Babbage expedition extended far beyond what it tells us about local constituencies. By mobilizing such a range of interest groups and material resources on behalf of this project, South Australia signaled its expansionist ambitions in the interior of the continent to its colonial neighbors. The Babbage expedition set off a dramatic intercolonial scramble for unclaimed or disputed territory, leading to one of the most frenetic and concentrated periods of exploration in Australia's history.

Exploration is inextricably associated with empire. When Columbus launched the great age of seaborne discovery with his voyage across the Atlantic in 1492, he also set in motion the European conquest of the Americas and the projection of European imperial power across much of the rest of the globe. By the nineteenth century, the idea that exploration led naturally and inevitably to empire had become deeply imbedded in the imagination of the West, where it has remained to the present day. Modern historical interpretations of exploration have stressed their imperial agendas. Consider the titles of some notable recent works on the subject. A biography of Sir Roderick Murchison, the impresario of the Royal Geographical Society, characterizes him as a "scientist of empire." A study of Henry Morton Stanley's African expeditions highlights the "imperial footprints" they made. And one of the best books on British exploration in the nineteenth century is titled *Geography Militant: Cultures of Exploration and Empire.*[6] Explorers are invariably presented as men who helped make empire, blazing the trails that would be followed by conquering armies and mapping the terrain that would be claimed as colonial territories. But whose agendas did they actually advance? What parties benefited from their efforts? The answers to these questions are not quite as self-evident and straightforward as they seem.

Any consideration of the political forces at work in the exploration of Australia and Africa must first acknowledge and address the very different ways that Britain was engaged with these two continents in the nineteenth century. Australian and African territories followed two dramatically different trajectories of incorporation into the British Empire. In the first, settler colonialism predominated. The British established a penal colony at Sydney Cove in 1788, and a series of satellite colonies soon sprang up along the continent's southeast and southwest coastlines. While most of the early colonists were convicts, a growing number of independent immigrants arrived as well. South Australia became the first colony to be founded entirely for free settlers in 1836. The pastoralist and mining economies spurred colonists to push ever farther into the interior, subjugating and displacing the indigenous peoples they encountered along the way. After midcentury, the British government began granting "responsible government" to one Australian colony after another, transferring authority over domestic affairs to the settlers. The settlers, in turn, used their newly acquired political power to press for additional pastureland and any other untapped resources that might exist in central and northern Australia, encouraging their governments to compete for control of these still unclaimed territories. By the end of the century, Aborigines all across the continent had seen their lands alienated and their autonomy brought to an end by settler colonialism, which consolidated its triumph with federation in 1901.

The British imperial engagement with Africa assumed a very different character. Because of its extensive involvement in the slave trade, Britain had far greater interests in Africa and far more familiarity with Africans at the start of the century than was the case with Australia and its peoples. Whatever imperial ambitions these associations may have stirred, however, proved difficult to realize. The size and power of indigenous states and societies across much of the continent, combined with the deadly disease environments that confronted interlopers in many regions, made it difficult for the British to establish colonial beachheads in Africa. Apart from the Cape Colony, taken from the Dutch in 1806, and neighboring Natal, annexed in 1843, the only African territories under British control in the first half of the nineteenth century were a few coastal enclaves in West Africa. By midcentury a parliamentary commission was contemplating withdrawal from these locations. It was only in the late 1870s that conditions began to change as a conjuncture of geopolitical and economic pressures weakened African states and enticed European intervention. The result was the notorious scramble for Africa, which brought the British into competition for colonial territory with the French, Germans, and other European powers. When the dust cleared at the end of the nineteenth century, Britain had laid claim to immense tracts of territory across the continent, though it would take some time for it to establish effective control over the inhabitants. Only a few colonies ever attracted white settlers, and none of them saw settler numbers approach the size of the indigenous populations. Thus the terms of Africa's involvement with Britain were distinctly different from those that operated in Australia.

These differences made their mark on the intentions, modes of operation, and outcomes of British exploration in Africa and Australia. They were especially apparent in the forces that propelled penetration of the two continents. Except in the Cape, there were no local settler lobbies or colonial governments to press for the exploration of the African interior. The main impetus came instead from metropolitan pressure groups, a shifting alliance of scientific, commercial, humanitarian, and religious organizations, often acting in collaboration with agencies of the British state, above all the Admiralty, the War Office, and the Colonial Office, for whom geopolitical considerations predominated. These metropolitan forces played a far less prominent role in Australia. While there the geopolitical concerns of the imperial state provided some impetus for exploration in the first half of the century, its main drivers were local colonial officials and settler communities, especially after "responsible government" gave them greater control of finances and policy.

African and Australian expeditions did, however, depend in one crucial respect on a common political precondition: the presence of gateway states that supplied points of entry to the interior. In Australia, those gateway states were the creations of British colonists, whereas in Africa they were most often Muslim, Portuguese, and other non-British polities. Nevertheless, they resembled one another in that their interests and agendas were not simply subsumed within the ambit of the British imperial state. These regional parties provided assistance to expeditions for reasons that were often independent of—and occasionally at odds with—the interests of Britain itself. The central role they played in the exploration of Africa and Australia obliges us in turn to decenter our understanding of exploration as an imperial enterprise.

The British imperial government was actively involved in only a few expeditions into the Australian interior. It sponsored George Grey's two troubled probes of Western Australia in 1838 and 1839, Charles Sturt's futile effort to reach the center of the continent in 1844–1846, and Augustus Gregory's efficient investigation of northern Australia in 1855–1856. It also co-sponsored Frank Gregory's 1861 expedition in search of land suitable for cotton cultivation in Western Australia's northwestern corner. These expeditions constituted the sum total of the British government's direct contribution to Australian exploration. With the exception of the 1861 expedition, which was organized in response to the cotton shortage caused by the American Civil War, all of these expeditions were motivated mainly by geopolitical consideration. Grey's two expeditions were premised on the conviction that a large river must discharge its waters somewhere along Australia's northwest coast, offering a possible route into the interior that the French or Americans might benefit from if the British did not preempt them. Virtually the first thing Grey did when his party arrived on the shore was to raise the British flag and go "through the ceremony of taking possession of the territory in the name of Her Majesty and her heirs for ever."[7] Similar concerns motivated the expedition into northern Australia by Augustus Gregory, whose instructions were to seek navigable rivers, land suitable for settlement, and evidence of an inland sea. Above all, he was expected to assert British sovereignty over the region.[8] The Sturt expedition was driven both by an interest in learning whether the interior harbored any well-watered grasslands (along with that illusory inland sea) and by a desire to plant the British flag at the heart of the continent. Sturt was unable to break through the Simpson Desert and reach the center, but John McDouall Stuart, who served as an aide on that grueling journey, managed to do so fifteen years later in an expedition jointly financed by the South Australian government and private entrepreneurs, not the British government. He marked the event by fixing a British flag atop a cone of stones, which were almost the only things to be found in that bleak and arid landscape.[9]

As Stuart's expedition suggests, one reason the British imperial state so rarely involved itself directly in efforts to explore Australia was because it had no need to—settlers and local officials financed and launched most expeditions on their own initiative. They did so because they benefited the most from any land and mineral discoveries these expeditions made. For imperial authorities, the expanding frontier that derived from local initiatives created political and ethical complications, especially because of conflicts between settlers and indigenous peoples. Their interest in avoiding such conflicts provided another reason they played so little role in the exploration of Australia.

The first expedition to break through the Great Dividing Range and open up the interior of the continent is commonly credited to Gregory Blaxland, William Lawson, and William Charles Wentworth, independent settlers in search of pastureland. In 1813 they found a route from Sydney's coastal hinterland across the Blue Mountains, providing access to vast tracts of territory in the interior. The significance of their discovery, however, has been questioned. Other colonists had previously penetrated the Blue Mountains, but because the newly opened lands were remote from markets and colonial authorities needed to restrict the mobility of convicts, their breakthroughs were not exploited.[10] It was only after Blaxland and his companions completed their journey that the economic and political environment in New South Wales became more conducive to settler expansion. Thereafter, the relentless advance by drovers and other settlers across the continent became one of the central themes of Australian history. Although colonial authorities continued to worry about the clashes with indigenous inhabitants that resulted from this advance, their ethnic and ideological sympathies clearly resided with the settlers, whose gradual displacement and destruction of the Aborigines was considered by most of them to be inevitable. As Sir George Bowen, the first governor of Queensland, would put it: "There is something almost sublime in the steady, silent, flow of pastoral occupation over northern Queensland. It resembles an operation not of man, but of Nature. . . . The wandering tribes of aborigines retreat slowly before the march of the white man, as flocks of wild-fowl on the beach give way to the advancing waves."[11]

The government of New South Wales helped to open the floodgates for these advancing waves with the official expeditions it launched during the two decades following Blaxland's journey. Eager to learn more about the vast tracts of territory that lay on the other side of the Blue Mountains, Governor Macquarie and his successors sponsored expeditions by John Oxley, Allan Cunningham, Charles Sturt, Thomas Mitchell, and others. They searched for rivers that might grant access to these inland territories from the sea, lands suitable for pasturage and settlement, and commercially exploitable deposits of coal and other natural resources. As the oldest and most prosperous of the Australian colonies in the first half of the nineteenth century, New South Wales was able to second its own surveyors and other government employees as leaders of these expeditions, recruit skilled and reliable convicts to assist them, and provide the equipment and supplies needed to travel through uncharted territory for months at a time.

Once colonial settlements were established in Western Australia in 1829 and South Australia in 1836, officials there launched expeditions of their own. With fewer resources at the disposal of the nascent colonial administrations, these endeavors tended to be less ambitious and more reliant on the assistance of local settlers. The records of their early explorations reveal ad hoc, incremental efforts of modest dimensions and designs, especially in Western Australia.[12] The most notable exception was Edward Eyre's epic journey from Adelaide to Albany in 1840–1841, though it too relied on assistance from both public and private interest groups. The governor of South Australia contributed £100, fourteen horses, and a supply depot at Spencer's Gulf, while private citizens donated more than £500. Eyre spent £680 of his own money on the expedition.[13]

A critical turning point in the exploration of Australia came around mid-century with the granting of "responsible government" to settler constituencies in colonies across the continent, starting with Victoria in 1851, Tasmania in 1854, New South Wales in 1855, South Australia in 1856, and Queensland upon its founding as a separate colony in 1859. (The sole exception was Western Australia, which did not receive self-government until 1890.) These constitutional changes had important geopolitical consequences. As governments became more responsive to settlers' opinions and interests, they had more reason to ensure that boundaries with neighboring colonies were drawn to their advantage, permitting them to profit from whatever pasturelands, mineral deposits, and other resources might be discovered in those contested zones. Although boundary lines had already been drawn between Victoria, New South Wales, and South Australia, there was no reason they could not be redrawn. More important, much of central and northern Australia was still up for grabs. No one knew what the region might hold, and this very uncertainty encouraged colonists and their governments to organize expeditions to search for resources and lay claim to lands. Another incentive for exploration arose in 1860 when reports began to circulate that plans were afoot to run a submarine cable from Singapore to the northern coast of Australia. The first colony to find a feasible telegraph route across the continent would likely win the highly lucrative contract to serve as the hub for telecommunications for the continent's heavily populated southeast corridor. Some wealthy stockmen also hoped that the discovery of a cross-continental route would allow them to move horses to markets in India. For all these reasons, a colonial scramble for central and northern Australia soon ensued.[14]

South Australia's ambitions appear to have set off the scramble. Benjamin Herschel Babbage's 1856 gold-prospecting expedition in the Lake Torrens region precipitated four official expeditions the following year: one by Assistant Surveyor General G. W. Goyder, who announced the discovery of a freshwater lake in the region; the second by Surveyor General A. H. Freeling, who pronounced Goyder's sighting "illusory"; and the other two by Major Peter Warburton and Stephen Hack, who indicated that good pastoral land was likely to be found to the north.[15] As a result of these expeditions, South Australia consolidated its claim to the ill-defined territory separating it from Western Australia, extending its official boundary westward from 132 degrees to 129 degrees longitude.[16]

It was the Babbage and Stuart expeditions of 1858, however, that really put South Australia's neighbors on notice regarding its territorial ambitions. The sheer scale of the government's investment in Babbage's expedition demonstrated the importance it attached to this endeavor, while Stuart's discovery of thousands of miles of land suitable for sheep runs affirmed the promise made in earlier reports. In response, a Melbourne syndicate hired Alfred Howitt to search the region for land it could acquire for cattle grazing. The government of New South Wales, in turn, approved £4,158 to fund an expedition under the command of Augustus Gregory targeting much the same territory. Its announced purpose was to hunt for traces of Ludwig Leichhardt's expedition, which had disappeared a decade earlier, but its real aim was to consolidate the colony's claims to land that it feared, with some justice, South Australia aimed to annex. Gregory's efforts proved futile: South Australia persuaded the imperial government to transfer sovereignty over a sliver of territory from New South Wales to itself in 1861.[17]

Stuart's end run around Babbage may have discredited the expedition that South Australian authorities had poured so much money into, but his discoveries validated their original expectations by proving that significant tracts of usable land lay beyond Lake Torrens. Exactly how far these tracts might stretch remained unknown, so Stuart tried to find out by making two more expeditions into the region in 1859 and 1860, both financed by the land speculators James Chambers and William Finke. When Stuart prepared to set out on still another expedition near the end of 1860, news from Victoria radically altered both its purpose and its composition. What had been a small, privately financed party that sought to acquire new pastoral land was transformed into a large, government-financed project (though Finke and Chambers still paid Stuart's salary) with instructions to cross the continent and find a viable route for a transcontinental telegraph line.

The main reason the South Australian government sent Stuart on this expedition was that it had learned that the government of Victoria, acting in conjunction with the Royal Society of Victoria, had initiated its own ambitious effort to find a route across the continent, grandiloquently titling it the Victorian Exploring Expedition. This was the ill-fated enterprise better known as the Burke and Wills expedition. Governor Macdonnell frankly confessed in a letter to the RGS's Sir Roderick Murchison that his intent in promoting the efforts of Stuart was to take "the wind out of the sails of . . . [this] costly Victorian expedition."[18]

Those who organized the "costly" Burke and Wills expedition almost certainly saw it as Victoria's response to South Australia's earlier Babbage expedition, both in its scale and in its scientific ambition. Like the Babbage expedition, the Burke and Wills expedition was the product of a grand coalition, consisting of a colonial government with annexationist designs on northern territory, pastoralists, miners, and other settlers eager to acquire land and other resources, and an educated urban elite interested in advancing scientific knowledge and advertising its community's cosmopolitanism. Like the Babbage expedition, the Burke and Wills expedition was generously supplied with provisions and equipment, including ingenious new inventions such as pocket charcoal water filters. And like the Babbage expedition, the Burke and Wills expedition soon discovered that it lacked the logistical resources to move the 21 tons of supplies it had accumulated. In consequence, much of this matériel was sold or simply abandoned at the staging ground of Menindee, including the bulk of the scientific equipment. Robert O'Hara Burke, unlike Benjamin Herschel Babbage, had no interest in the scientific dimensions of his expedition, no sympathy for the scientists who were members of his party, and no desire to slow his progress by acceding to what he considered their collecting and measuring mania. Since he must have known that the well-stocked Babbage expedition had failed, its scientifically inclined leader recalled in disgrace, while the bare-bones Stuart expedition had triumphed and its "half childlike and . . . half idiotic" leader rewarded with public banquets and lavish praise, it seems reasonable to suspect that his decision to dispense with the expedition's scientific agenda was a result of the lesson he drew from Babbage's failure.[19]

What captured the Australian public's imagination, however, was not the way the Burke and Wills expedition resembled the earlier Babbage expedition but the way it challenged the corresponding Stuart expedition. The expansionist ambitions of Victoria and South Australia were portrayed in the press as a personal competition between the two expeditions' leaders. A famous cartoon in the *Melbourne Punch* showed Burke and Stuart galloping side by side, the former on a camel, the latter on a horse. This cartoon was accompanied by the poem "The Great Australian Exploration Race," whose opening stanza served as the epigraph to this chapter. The rest of the poem follows:

> A race between two colonies!
> Each has a stalwart band
> Sent out beyond the settled bounds,
> Into the unknown land . . .

No small concealments each from each,
    No shuffling knavish ways,
No petty jealousies and strifes
    No paltry peddling traits,

Will find a place in such a race,
    But honor, virtue, worth,
And all that can ennoble man
    Will brilliantly shine forth

A cheer then for each member, and
    A big one for the lot,
For it is known how all have shown
    These virtues.—Have they not?[20]

Neither party won the race. Stuart became the first explorer to arrive at the center of the continent, but he failed to reach its north coast. He tried again in 1861, and this time he got a glimpse of the Indian Ocean, returning to Adelaide a year later. Taken together, these two expeditions cost the South Australian government more than £9,000.[21] When Stuart returned from his first expedition with his goal unmet, Burke and Wills's whereabouts were still unknown, though not as yet a serious cause of concern. Soon, however, it became clear that Burke, Wills, and the two men selected to accompany them on their dash to the Gulf of Carpentaria had gone missing. Their failure to return to the base camp at Cooper's Creek before its beleaguered party abandoned it resulted in an even more frenzied scramble for the continent's unclaimed territories by Australian colonies.

The pretense for this scramble was the search for Burke and Wills. The relief expedition sent out by the Victorian government under the command of Alfred Howitt was the most sincere and single-minded in its effort to find the lost men, and it succeeded in rescuing John King, the only surviving member of the transcontinental team, and recovering the remains of Burke and Wills. South Australia organized what it characterized as a rescue party under the command of John McKinlay, but his instructions show that the search for Burke and Wills was little more than a pretense to open up new territory. Rather than returning to Adelaide after learning that Burke and Wills's bodies had been found, McKinlay pressed northward to the Gulf of Carpentaria, then east to the Queensland coast before returning to South Australia, where an enthusiastic public applauded his announcement of the discovery of large tracts of pastoral land.[22]

The newly created colony of Queensland lost no time making its presence felt in the scramble. Little more than a year after it had been founded in 1859, Queensland's governor had already dispatched an expedition to lay out what he insisted was "the only feasible route for the projected Indo-Australian telegraph."[23] Now he sent out *two* expeditions in search of Burke and Wills, one traveling westward from Brisbane under the direction of Frederick Walker, the other marching south from the northern coast, deposited there by ship, with William Landsborough in command. Both Walker and Landsborough had squatter backgrounds, and their main concern was to find promising tracts of territory for land-hungry settlers. Landsborough's reports in particular set off what has been described as "a frenzied rush into the gulf country" by Queensland settlers.[24]

These multiple expeditions established the framework for the territorial division of central and northern Australia. As soon as Victorian authorities learned from Wills's journals and King's testimony that the Burke and Wills expedition had reached the Gulf of Carpentaria, they lobbied the British government for the territory north of New South Wales between the 138th and 141st parallels, which they hoped to make into Northern Victoria.[25] Queensland made a competing case for the same territory, resting its claim on Landsborough's and Walker's expeditions and the subsequent influx of its settlers into the region. In the end, Britain sided with Queensland, granting it sovereignty over the region. The biggest beneficiary of the scramble, however, was South Australia. With Stuart's triumphant return from his transcontinental journey in late 1862, South Australia pressed its case for ruling northern Australia. As one South Australian newspaper editorial observed, "We look upon Stuart's new discoveries as practically giving South Australia another sea frontage."[26] In 1863, the British Parliament passed the Northern Territory Act, which made the region, for all intents and purposes, a colony of South Australia.

Buoyed by their victory, South Australian authorities launched several expeditions to consolidate control over the territory, survey choice tracts of land for investors, and develop a telegraph and stock route across the interior.[27] The first expedition did little more than establish a temporary foothold along the coast at the inauspiciously named Escape Cliffs, while members of the second expedition barely escaped with their lives after John McKinlay led them aimlessly through alligator-infested swamps, followed by a desperate sea voyage in a horsehide boat that nearly sank before reaching its destination.[28] A third expedition under the command of the shipping entrepreneur Francis Cadell also had little to show for its efforts.[29] In the short term, then, the Northern Territory failed to fulfill South Australia's expectations as a target of colonization and exploitation. But it did ensure that the transcontinental telegraph line, which began construction in 1870 with the anticipated arrival of a submarine cable in Darwin, would pass through territory that was entirely under the control of South Australia, giving it a power-ful advantage over its colonial neighbors in overcoming what Geoffrey Blainey famously referred to as "the tyranny of distance."[30]

Western Australia was the one mainland Australian colony that took no part in the scramble of the early 1860s. The vast expanse of arid wil-derness that ran from the Great Sandy Desert in the north through the Gibson Desert in the center to the Great Victorian Desert and Nullar-bor Plain in the south presented a seemingly impenetrable barrier to eastward expansion by Western Australia's settlers and a buffer against the annexationist ambitions of its South Australian neighbor. In the 1870s, however, explorers set out from both sides of the divide to cross this harsh region, the last major part of Australia still to be explored. Western Australia's governor, Frederick Weld, got the ball rolling when in 1870 he dispatched a party under the command of John Forrest to blaze a trail across the Nullarbor Plain from Perth to Adelaide.[31] Though the territory he passed through was virtually waterless and lacked any appeal to settlers, it would serve as a route for the telegraph line (and later the railway line) that linked the two colonies' capitals in 1877. The main focus of attention, however, was the region west of Alice Springs, which attracted a series of expeditions, most of them launched from the overland telegraph stations that now ran down the spine of the continent. Peter Warburton, William Gosse, and Ernest Giles led com-peting South Australian expeditions into this area in 1873–1874, while John Forrest soon followed suit from Western Australia. The failure of these expeditions to find any significant tracts of pastureland or mineral resources in the region mitigated whatever concerns Western Australia may have had about South Australia's territorial ambitions.

The boundaries between Australian colonies were now settled, leaving colonial governors and legislatures with less reason to finance expeditions. The government of Queensland sent an expedition in 1875 to search for pastoral land along its western border, and its Post and Telegraph Department organized an 1883 expedition to develop a telegraph route through the colony. The Western Australian government sponsored Alexander Forrest's expedition into the Kimberley region in 1879.[32] Official expeditions of this kind became increasingly rare, however. The main impetus for "the last phase in the history of the exploration of Australia" came instead from land speculators and other private entrepreneurs.[33] To be sure, these parties had played active roles in exploration in the past, with James Chambers, for example, exerting far more influence on Stuart than Governor Macdonnell considered healthy. But from the early 1870s onward they set the pace and determined the direction of exploration.

The dominant figure in South Australia was the squatter and businessman Thomas Elder. When the South Australian government selected William Gosse to lead its own expedition into the region west of Alice Springs in 1872, Elder and Walter Hughes, another wealthy landowner, financed a rival expedition led by Peter Warburton, whom the government had judged too old for the task. The Warburton expedition allowed Elder, the leading breeder of camels in Australia, to demonstrate the advantages of these beasts for travel through water-scarce regions. Warburton's party made the first successful crossing of the Great Sandy Desert. Elder's camels would become indispensable to a number of explorers in the late nineteenth century. Ernest Giles, whose first two expeditions were shoestring ventures that relied on horses, got funding and camels from Elder for his third expedition. This time he succeeded in crossing the Gibson Desert to Western Australia. Elder contributed camels to numerous other expeditions, including Tietkens's 1889 expedition and the self-named Elder Scientific Exploration Expedition of 1891–1892. Although Elder was described as a "public benefactor" in *The Australian Dictionary of Biography,* his motives were far from disinterested. As he chortled in a letter to a protégé, "What a pity you did not take out a slice of pastoral country in the Far North. . . . I have 17,000 sq. miles under lease now, and that ought to be enough—for one man."[34]

The acquisitive ambitions of private parties provided the impetus for various other late nineteenth-century expeditions. Ernest Favenc's expedition into the western reaches of Queensland in 1878–1879 was financed by investors searching for a potential railway route. The Victorian Squatting Company and several other commercial partnerships were responsible for a disastrous expedition sent into the Cambridge Gulf region of Western Australia in 1884–1885 to report on land they had acquired sight unseen. The Calvert Scientific Exploring Expedition of 1890 was funded by Albert F. Calvert, who hoped it would find a new stock route from Queensland to the Northern Territory. And David Carnegie conducted a lengthy self-funded expedition through central Western Australia in search of stock routes and gold deposits.[35]

The story of exploration would become an important element of the Australian mythos, supplying the colonial community with heroes and martyrs for its public pantheon. Because the colonists' nascent sense of nationalism developed within the cocoon of empire, the exploration of the continent has been seen as an enterprise that advanced British imperial and Australian colonial interests simultaneously. While the British Empire certainly counted the consolidation of control over the continent as beneficial to its interests, the principal impetus for exploration and expansion came from local parties, whose motives were distinct from those that existed in the imperial metropolis. It is difficult to imagine that the continent's remoter regions would have been probed and mapped with such speed and meticulousness if the initiative had been left entirely in the hands of British imperial authorities. The sheer multiplicity of colonial Australian interest groups, both public and private, acting both in collaboration and in competition, ensured that no large tracts of territory in the interior escaped investigation by the end of the century. In this sense, then, the exploration of Australia was a much more decentered enterprise than its associations with imperial expansion suggest.

British explorers confronted a vastly more complex and contested political terrain in Africa than they did in Australia. Nearly four times larger than Australia, Africa was also more ethnically, economically, and environmentally diverse, creating conditions that made the continent more accessible in some regions and respects but more impenetrable in others. With no colonial states and settler communities outside of South Africa to press for expansion across frontiers, the British imperial state assumed a more direct and active role in exploration. The Colonial Office, the Foreign Office, and the Admiralty all contributed at various stages in various ways to probes of the continent, as did the East India Company and its successor state, the Raj, in the region adjoining the Indian Ocean. Even the unofficial groups that sponsored expeditions—most notably the African Association and the Royal Geographical Society—generally did so in consultation or collaboration with government authorities. In Africa, then, the association between exploration and empire appears direct and unambiguous.

Yet Britain's greater involvement in the exploration of Africa did not mean that its efforts were unmediated by other agents and agendas. The British explorers who ventured into the African interior confronted a complex mosaic of polities and societies whose allegiances and rivalries they could scarcely understand. Insofar as they were able to negotiate passage through these fractious and often shifting social and political landscapes, their success usually had less to do with British imperial power and prestige than it did with assistance provided by Africans, Arabs, and other parties already present in the region. The logistics of African exploration required staging grounds where expeditions could obtain supplies, transportation, guides, and more. These staging grounds tended to be the coastal termini of regional trade routes, entrepôts that served as gateways to the interior. Unlike Australia's gateways, however, they were generally controlled by non-Western states and communities with interests of their own to protect and promote. If they permitted European explorers access to the interior, it was because they expected benefits for themselves. Those that were most likely to grant access to explorers had economic or political ambitions of their own in the interior, ambitions that they believed these outsiders could help them advance. In consequence, the British exploration of Africa often occurred in collusion with gateway states that were themselves expansionist in intent.

The first region to attract systematic and sustained attention was the interior of West Africa. Because of Britain's long involvement in the transatlantic slave trade, it already had an active presence along the West African coast from the Gambia to the Niger Delta. As the eighteenth century drew to a close, British authorities grew increasingly keen to establish direct contact with the great states and cities that were reported to exist in the Western Sudan, the savannah lands directly south of the Sahara Desert. Scientific curiosity, the prospects for trade, and geopolitical rivalry with revolutionary France all spurred British interest in exploring the region. But what route offered the best access?

The British tried to use their preexisting footholds along the West African coast to penetrate the interior. With an active presence at the mouth of the Gambia River, they viewed this slave caravan corridor as a promising avenue of entry to the upper Niger and the fabled emporium of Timbuktu. In 1790 Daniel Houghton, an army officer with knowledge of Arabic and experience in Africa, set out along this route on behalf of the African Association, but he soon disappeared. Five years later, the association sent the Scottish physician and botanist Mungo Park on the same route. His miraculous return after an arduous two years journey, which took him to the banks of the Niger and nearly within sight of Timbuktu, generated high hopes for the Gambian gateway. The British government lent its support to Park's much larger and better-equipped second expedition, which followed the same course up the Gambia in 1805. When Park and his entire party died on the journey, the prospects that this route would open up the interior dimmed. The fatal blow came with the ignominious failure of the large military expedition that was sent up the Rio Nuñez, just south of the Gambia, in 1816. Despite an enormous expenditure of resources, this expedition was unable over several years to penetrate more than a few hundred miles into the interior because of the obstructionist tactics of a local ruler.

The trading factories along the Gulf of Guinea proved to be no less problematic as gateways to the interior. The African states and merchants that supplied slaves to these factories sought to safeguard their own political and economic interests by sequestered Europeans along the coast. Their suspicions of British intentions were heightened when

Parliament voted to stop the slave trade in 1807. The explorer Henry Nicholls reported that a leading African trader in Old Calabar had warned him that "if I came from Wilberforce [the parliamentary leader of the British campaign to abolish the slave trade] they would kill me."[36] There was no need: Nicholls soon died of fever. His fate was a common one for explorers seeking to enter the West African interior from its coastline. Yellow fever, malaria, and dysentery presented a formidable barrier against penetration by outsiders, cutting a deadly swath through explorers' ranks. Nearly all of the forty-five men who took part in Park's second expedition succumbed to disease. The Royal Navy's expedition up the Congo River in 1816–1817 disintegrated when its captain and a majority of the crew were felled by yellow fever. Fevers defeated several attempts to journey up the Niger River, killing 40 of the 49 European participants in Macgregor Laird's privately financed expedition of 1832–1833 and 55 of the 159 Europeans in the government-sponsored Niger Expedition of 1841–1842.[37]

North Africa provided an alternative launching pad for expeditions into West Africa's interior. The disease barrier was less deadly at this end of the continent, and the Sahara Desert, for all its challenges, had been traversed by transhumant tribes and trade caravans for centuries. The shortest route to the savannah region where the kingdom of Bornu and the Hausa states held sway had its northern terminus in Tripoli on the Barbary Coast. This Muslim maritime state had been one of the main promoters and havens of the privateers that plagued Christian countries with raids on their coasts, the capture of their vessels, and the ransom of hostages, but its predations were brought to an end by European and American navies in the early nineteenth century. As a result, Tripoli's ambitious pasha, Yusuf Karamanli, redirected his state's energies toward commercial and political opportunities in the interior, asserting tributary claims to the crucial network of oases in Fezzan, exerting influence over the traders who controlled the routes across that part of the Sahara, and establishing his presence as a political force to be reckoned with among the states further south.[38] He was able to provide explorers with the escorts and assurance of safe passage that they so obviously lacked when setting out from the Gambia, the Gulf of Guinea, or elsewhere along the coast of West Africa.

The earliest attempts by the British to launch expeditions into the African interior from Tripoli were no less star-crossed than the efforts they made from the south and west, but their prospects improved as Tripoli projected its own power farther into the Sahara.[39] In 1788, the African Association recruited a longtime English resident of North Africa, Simon Lucas, to cross the Sahara from Tripoli, but reports of warfare along the caravan route convinced him that the undertaking was too risky. Friedrich Hornemann, another explorer sponsored by the African Association, retreated for a time to the safety of Tripoli when his efforts to reach the Western Sudan from Cairo in 1798 stalled in Fezzan. He left Tripoli for a second attempt in 1800 but soon died of dysentery. Once the Napoleonic Wars came to an end, Tripoli became the point of departure for several Colonial Office–sponsored expeditions. The first ended prematurely with the death of one of the two explorers. The second, however, was a great success. In 1822, Dixon Denham, Hugh Clapperton, and Walter Oudney set out on a three-year mission to establish diplomatic ties with Bornu and the Hausa states and supply intelligence about the region. They traveled under the protection of Yusuf Karamanli, and Denham found the route so secure that he claimed the journey from Tripoli to Bornu was no more dangerous than the one from London to Edinburgh.[40] Soon thereafter, Alexander Laing set off from Tripoli in search of the holy grail of West African explorers, Timbuktu, which he succeeded in entering in 1826. The loss of Fezzan to rebels in 1831 and the civil war that followed Karamanli's fall from power in 1832 closed the route from Tripoli for a time, though it did reopen after the Ottomans reestablished direct suzerainty in 1835. They permitted the British to launch an expedition south from Tripoli in 1850 under the original command of James Richardson, whose premature death opened the door to the remarkable journey by his scientific associate, Heinrich Barth.

Why did Yusuf Karamanli allow the British to launch these expeditions from Tripoli's shores? Self-interest. The British government paid him £25,000 to assist Denham and Clapperton. Colonel Hanmer Warrington, the British consul who negotiated the deal, explained to his superiors that the money would be used to help Karamanli conquer the interior states of Bornu and Sudan, which would in turn "enable Him to relinquish the Slave Trade."[41] Warrington wrote what he knew London wanted to hear, not what was true. Karamanli most certainly had imperial ambitions, but he had no intention of relinquishing the slave trade. He used the British funds to finance an army that accompanied Denham and Clapperton across the Sahara and conducted slave raids, sending captives to work in the fields of Fezzan and to sell in North African slave markets. Tripoli conducted this operation under the pretense of protecting the explorers from the very peoples who were its targets.[42] When Alexander Laing came to Tripoli in 1825 to launch his expedition in search of Timbuktu, Karamanli prevented him from setting off until the British government contributed 8,000 Spanish dollars, supplemented by a second "Secret Present" of 1,000 Spanish dollars.[43] In return for this payment, Karamanli supplied Laing with a letter of credit and a promise of safe passage across the Sahara. This was useful so far as it went. Unfortunately for Laing, Karamanli's influence did not extend to the environs of Timbuktu, where the explorer was murdered.[44]

Tripoli's imperial ambitions were reasserted under the Ottomans, who regained control of Fezzan in 1842, stationed garrisons at other oases, and sent an expedition to conquer the territory of Tibesti in 1859. Their aim was to protect the trans-Saharan caravan routes and guard against the expansionist ambitions of France, which had recently conquered northern Algeria and was advancing south through the desert.[45] By permitting the Richardson/Barth expedition access to the Western Sudan from Tripoli, the Ottomans no doubt hoped that the presence of these British agents would provide a counterweight to French imperial designs. It was in the interest of Ottoman authorities to do what they could to ensure that the British explorers met no harm during their journey, and to this end they issued a written promise of safe passage— known in Islamic discourse as *aman*—that was widely recognized and respected by Muslim states of the Western Sudan.[46] Heinrich Barth was able to travel through the region in relative freedom and safety for five years, during which time he gathered information for what became the most detailed and informed account of the region ever written by an explorer.[47] At one point he was arrested by the emir of Massina on suspicion of spying for the British, but Islamic legal authorities ruled that he had entered the *dar al-Islam* as a protected non-Muslim, who could not be detained nor have his property confiscated.[48] He was freed and permitted to continue on his way.

Dr. Thomas Dickson, one of the many short-lived explorers who sought to establish a route to the West African interior from the Gulf of Guinea, came to appreciate that the patronage of a ruler with influence in the region was invaluable to an explorer's success. A member of Hugh Clapperton's second expedition, he was sent to Dahomey, the powerful slave-trading state located in what is now Benin, to solicit permission to pass through its territory. Predictably, the king of Dahomey refused his request. Dickson observed that "without setting out at first under the protection of a powerful government whose very name is feared among its neighbours I feel convinced little or nothing can be accomplished in the way of discovery . . . the success of the former [Denham/Clapperton] mission was chiefly attributable to the respectable footing on which the Bashaw of Tripoli [Karamanli] placed it at the start."[49] During the half century that Britain invested so much energy and so many lives in the exploration of West Africa, the surety of safe passage that Tripoli granted explorers came to be recognized as a rare and valuable gift. What Tripoli received in return was less readily acknowledged.

Egypt provided a second important entry point to the African interior for British explorers. The beys who ruled Egypt prior to its invasion by Napoleon in 1798 had granted letters of protection to several British travelers seeking access to the West African interior, though the route from Tripoli proved shorter and safer.[50] A more attractive destination for expeditions originating in Cairo was up the Nile to Sudan and Ethiopia. In the aftermath of the French withdrawal from Egypt, Muhammed Ali came to power and transformed the country, giving an Islamic register to the modernizing processes that Napoleon had set in motion with his abortive occupation. Muhammed Ali began to reshape Egypt's state and society in emulation of western European countries, often drawing on their expertise and assistance. It was in this context that British explorers were given new freedom to probe the lands south and east of Egypt. The most famous and successful of these explorers was Johann Ludwig Burckhardt, whose travels from 1812 to 1816 under the sponsorship of the African Association took him up the Nile nearly as far as Khartoum, then overland to the Red Sea, followed by visits to Mecca and Medina and a voyage along the coast to Suez. Several Britons traveled up the Nile into unfamiliar territory during the following decade and a half, though Henry Salt was the only one who survived to tell the tale.

Like the European states it sought to emulate, Egypt under Muhammed Ali and his successors became an expansionist state with imperial ambitions.[51] Egypt gained control of the Red Sea's littoral zone, wrestled Mecca and Medina from the Wahhabis (who had previously driven out the Ottomans), and invaded Ottoman-ruled Syria (though it was pushed back when Britain and other European states intervened on the Ottomans' behalf). Its most successful and lasting effort at empire building took place along the upper Nile. Muhammed Ali conquered much of northern Sudan in 1821 and Egyptian forces soon pushed further south, establishing a base at Khartoum that became the political and economic capital of their Sudanese domain. Eve Troutt Powell has aptly characterized the Egyptian conquest of Sudan as "a different shade of colonialism."[52] Egyptian forces conducted large-scale campaigns to enslave indigenous inhabitants (who were impressed into the Egyptian army and employed on plantations and in other enterprises), expropriate their cattle, and obtain ivory, gold, and other natural resources. By the 1840s, Egypt's reach extended as far south along the White Nile as Gondokoro, the front line for an increasingly profitable ivory and slave trade.[53] This imperial enterprise received a mixed response from the British, some of whom objected to the slave raiding, while others insisted that the Egyptians were introducing civilization into a savage land.

Egyptian authorities launched two major expeditions that pushed further up the White Nile in 1839–1840 and 1840–1841. The armchair geographer James MacQueen judged them to be "the most remarkable and important & useful known in modern times."[54] These expeditions and the information they supplied assisted Europeans eager to explore the White Nile and Great Lakes. When in 1863 John Hanning Speke and James Grant left the shores of Lake Victoria to follow the Nile River north to Cairo, the route they took to Gondokoro had been pioneered at least in part by the Egyptians. At Gondokoro, Speke and Grant expected to rendezvous with John Petherick, a British consul, but Petherick was temporarily absent, conducting one of his own exploratory probes of the surrounding region. Instead, they found Samuel Baker and his Hungarian mistress preparing to set out for their own expedition up the White Nile. Baker carried a royal mandate or *firman* from the khedive that commanded Egyptian agents to assist his expedition. When they left Gondokoro for the lake region, they accompanied an Arab trade caravan for much of the way. Although Baker often complained about the caravan's delays and detours, it provided his party with vital protection. Conditions became far more precarious for Baker when he parted ways with the caravan. For a time, he and his party became virtual prisoners of the king of Bunyoro when they arrived at the shores of what he christened Lake Albert.[55]

The lesson Baker drew from his experience was that "the only means of commencing the civilization of Central African races . . . [is] by *annexing* to Egypt the equatorial Nile Basin." Egypt "might become a great power," he insisted, if it "could annex the entire country from Khartoum to the territory of the Imam of Muscat [meaning the Sultan of Zanzibar], and thus open up Central Africa."[56] Ismail Pasha, Egypt's ruler, shared those sentiments, and in 1869 he asserted Egyptian sovereignty over the upper Nile basin, naming the new province Equatoria and appointing Baker its first governor-general. Baker relished the task of imposing Egyptian imperial rule on the region's inhabitants. He had been granted "despotic powers," he stated, in order "to subdue to our authority the countries situated to the south of Gondokoro . . . to open to navigation the great lakes of the equator . . . [and] to establish a chain of military stations and commercial depots . . . throughout Central Africa."[57] He arrived with an armada of nearly sixty vessels, more than 1,600 Egyptian and Sudanese soldiers, and two artillery batteries. He proceeded to conduct a brutal military campaign that included scorched earth tactics against villagers who resisted the imposition of Egyptian rule.[58] While Baker characterized his purpose to the British public as the suppression of the slave trade and the advancement of civilization, his erstwhile friend and fellow explorer, James Grant, was unconvinced, charging that he "has perpetuated the evil he complains of" by annexing the region "for a Mahomedan power."[59] But Baker was not the only British adventurer to aid in the expansion of the Egyptian empire. He was succeeded as governor-general of the region by the highly regarded Charles "Chinese" Gordon, who would later lose his life when the Sudanese rebelled against their colonial subjugators. Until that setback, Egyptian imperial ambitions extended still farther south—to the benefit of British explorers. Verney Lovett Cameron carried a *firman* from Ismail Pasha during his transcontinental expedition across central Africa in 1873. It stated: "All officers of Egypt, all Kings and sheikhs are required to receive them [Cameron's party] with honor and give them protection and all hands to assist and help them on their journey as may be required. This is a public order."[60]

The very fact that Egypt's imperial designs on southern Sudan and the Great Lakes region preceded those of the European powers suggests that in this part of the continent, at least, the scramble for Africa was neither an unprecedented rupture nor an entirely European initiative. While many British explorers relied on an expansionist Egypt to gain access to unfamiliar territories, others found it counterproductive. The explorer Mansfield Parkyns was blocked by African authorities from venturing into the Sahara west of Sudan because he was suspected of spying on behalf of the Egyptians.[61] Similar suspicions forced Richard Burton to abandon his disguise as an Arab trader during his expedition to the Ethiopian city-state of Harar, whose peoples feared Egyptians more than Europeans.[62] And the principal reason why the ruler of Bunyoro detained Baker was that he was suspected of being an agent of Egyptian imperial designs on his kingdom. As it happened, this is exactly what he became. Time and again, explorers seeking to move beyond Egypt's imperial frontiers found that their passage was obstructed by peoples fearful that they were acting as the outliers of Egyptian expansionist ambitions.

A third important gateway for British explorers was Zanzibar, which proved to be a far more accessible avenue of entry to the Great Lakes region than Egypt. Like Tripoli, Zanzibar was originally a maritime state that provided an entrepôt for the exchange of goods between overseas traders and inhabitants of the interior. Like Egypt, it was a modernizing state of surprisingly cosmopolitan character. And like both, it was aggressively expansionist in its ambitions. In the 1830s the Omani ruler Sayyid Said shifted his capital from Muscat to the island of Zanzibar, making it the principal port along the East African coast. Ships from all over the world visited Zanzibar, disgorging cloth, beads, brass coil, and furniture for local markets and loading gum copal, cloves, ivory, hides, and slaves for markets abroad. Zanzibar was a major destination for cotton textiles from the United States, which signed a most-favored-nation treaty with this Afro-Arab state. Reaching its height under the reign of Sultan Barghash (1870–1888), Zanzibar had a fleet of six steamships and its capital city's residents enjoyed a public water system, electric lighting, and a "House of Wonder," a purpose-built museum that exhibited modern technologies and crafts.[63]

Zanzibar's exuberant enterprise was made possible by its skill in projecting power over a wide swath of East Africa. Its dominion soon stretched along the coast from Mogadishu in the north to Cape Delgado in the south. It also extended hundreds of miles inland. Zanzibari agents established trading stations at Tabora, Ujiji, and elsewhere in the interior, where they sought not only to expand commercial opportunities but to exert political influence. The sultan, in turn, supported them in their struggles against the Nyamwezi and other African competitors, even dispatching an army into the hinterland to defend the Arab traders on several occasions. When David Livingstone visited the region in the late 1860s, he reported that the Nyamwezi now "acknowledge Seyed Majid's authority."[64] One indication of how far the Zanzibari state's authority extended can be seen in its response to the murder of a German explorer on the northern shore of Lake Nyasaland in 1859. Zanzibari pressure forced the local chief to hand over the murderers, who were sent to Zanzibar, tried, and executed. Speke and Grant attended the execution, which no doubt helped to reassure them about their own safety.[65] Zanzibar, in brief, held sway over what its leading historian, Abdul Sheriff, has referred to as a "commercial empire" that stretched from Uganda in the northeast to eastern Zaire in the west and northern Zambia in the southwest.[66]

William Desborough Cooley, who was one of the first British observers to recognize the importance of Zanzibar's growing influence in East Africa, advised Heinrich Barth to seek the patronage of its sultan when he proposed journeying from Bornu to the port of Mombasa.[67] Richard

Burton and John Hanning Speke were the first British explorers to actually use Zanzibar as a staging ground for their expedition, setting out from its shores for their 1857–1859 expedition into the lakes region. The Zanzibari government appointed their caravan leader, supplied them with a military guard, and ensured that they had access to credit and other assistance from traders operating in the interior. It became common practice for expeditions to acquire letters of surety from the sultan. David Livingstone gratefully acknowledged the value of the letter he carried from Sultan Sayyid Majid during his final expedition, which more than once allowed him to obtain provisions and trade goods on credit from passing Arab caravans.[68]

Almost all British expeditions followed what Burton referred to as the "Arab line of traffic," the main caravan routes that carried ivory and other goods from the interior to Zanzibar.[69] When Speke returned in 1860 to prove that Lake Victoria was the source of the Nile, he and James Grant took the standard caravan route west to Tabora, where they turned north along another route pioneered by Arab traders to Lake Victoria. Several decades later, Henry Morton Stanley would sneer at the explorers who had preceded him in the region for following what he termed the "Arab parcel post," but he did much the same on his 1871–1872 expedition in search of Livingstone and again during the initial stages of his trans-African journey of 1874–1877.[70] In a striking echo of the remark Dixon Denham had made about the safety of the route from Tripoli to Bornu, John Kirk, Britain's long-serving consul in Zanzibar, insisted that travelers would face less danger on the "road" from Zanzibar to Ujiji (the Arab trading station on the shores of Lake Tanganyika) than they would "in the less frequented parts of Europe."[71]

What did Zanzibar hope to gain from permitting this steady stream of explorers to pass through its profitable trading hinterland? Historians of African exploration have not bothered to ask this question, simply assuming that Zanzibar was the puppet of British interests.[72] But this view both exaggerates the influence that Britain wielded over Zanzibar and underestimates the authority Zanzibar wielded over the interior, at least until the last decade and a half of the nineteenth century. Burton and Speke's caravan was led by a guide carrying the red flag of Zanzibar.[73] When Joseph Thomson wondered nearly twenty-five years later why his

Arab hosts at Tabora were so solicitous, he was told: "You are under the governor & we are under the governor"—meaning the sultan.[74] Thomson was seen, in other words, as an agent of the Zanzibari state. And in some sense he was. Zanzibar permitted British explorers to set out from its shores and provided them with assistance because it expected to benefit from the relationship. One benefit was the infusion of capital into the local economy as explorers hired porters and purchased supplies, trade goods, and other necessities. It cost Burton and Speke about £2,500 to outfit their expedition and hire a crew; by the early 1870s Verney Lovett Cameron's outlay was some £11,000, a sum that shocked his Royal Geographical Society backers. Beyond this, Zanzibar's rulers and merchants obtained intelligence from British explorers that helped them open new regions of the interior to trade. Explorers were well trained to carry out this task. Always on the lookout for commercially viable products, they were skilled in identifying botanical and geological specimens and careful about noting their location and collecting samples. Sultan Barghash even hired the explorer Joseph Thomson in 1882 to prospect the Ruvuma and Lugenda rivers for coal and other exploitable mineral resources. (At the same time Richard Burton was leading a gold-prospecting expedition into the Midian region of Arabia on behalf of the khedive of Egypt.)

Perhaps the most striking examples of the symbiotic relationship that was forged between explorers and the Zanzibari state came about during the trans-African expeditions of Cameron and Stanley. Once the two explorers had passed west of Lake Tanganyika, both of them turned for assistance to Tippu Tip (Hamid ibn Muhammad), an ambitious Zanzibari trader who had begun to push the frontier of Zanzibar's trading empire into the Congo basin. Tippu provided them with porters and protection, while they in turn supplied him with information about routes and trading opportunities. Stanley's discovery that the Lualaba River flowed into the Congo, for example, made it possible for Tippu to extend his own sway to Stanley Falls and its environs, where he traded for ivory and slaves. By the early 1880s Tippu had in effect established a state in the upper reaches of the Congo, one that Norman Bennett has described as "a vital component of the Zanzibar system."[75] When the Belgian king Leopold's Association Internationale Africaine set its sights on the same region, sending Stanley as its agent, Tippu responded to the association's overtures by declaring: "I am a subject of the Sultan Seyyid Barghash and the country . . . over which I rule, both it and I are under the authority of Seyyid. I can do nothing without his sanction."[76] Prior to the onset of the European scramble for Africa in the early 1880s, most of the British explorers who passed through this region were in some respects no less the subjects of the sultan than Tippu, collaborating either wittingly or unwittingly in the expansion of Zanzibar's commercial empire.

The only part of Africa where the political environment bore any resemblance to Australian conditions was South Africa, where the Cape's colonial officials and settlers had their own reasons and resources to launch expeditions into the interior. The first important expedition occurred a year after the British took the Cape Colony from the Dutch in

Tippu Tip, Zanzibari trader and facilitator of central African exploration. *Source: H. M. Stanley,* In Darkest Africa *(1890).*

1796. Feeling "shamefully ignorant even of the geography of the country," Lord Macartney, the newly appointed governor, sent his private
secretary, John Barrow, to conduct a scientific investigation of its hinterland, mapping the terrain, collecting botanical specimens, gathering
ethnographic information, and establishing political relations with Boer
and African communities.[77] Many of the probes of the northern and
eastern frontier that followed were carried out by cattle herders, petty
traders, gold prospectors, and big-game hunters, each in pursuit of personal profit. In 1834, however, two South African expeditions were
launched with wider sponsorship and broader ambitions. The RGS-
sponsored journey of Captain Alexander amounted in the end to little
more than a hunting safari, but Dr. Andrew Smith's expedition, initiated
under the auspices of the Literary and Scientific Institution of Cape Town,
was far more consequential, producing a wealth of scientific, political,
and commercial information about the interior. The Cape elite's enterprise in organizing and financing this expedition both resembles and
precedes by several decades the initiatives undertaken by the elites of
Melbourne and Adelaide through their respective institutions, the Royal
Society of Victoria and the Adelaide Philosophical Society.[78]

Rather than establishing a precedent for future initiatives, however,
the Smith expedition was a one-off enterprise. A major reason appears
to be the increasing violence and instability that afflicted the region. The
breakout by Boers opposed to British rule, the rise of an expansionist
Zulu state, the Cape's series of wars against the Xhosa, and the growing
firearms trade combined to cause the increasing militarization of southern African societies. As a result, it simply became too dangerous to
launch expeditions from the Cape. Francis Galton wanted to do so, but
when he arrived in Cape Town in 1850 he learned that the route north
was cut off by a Boer revolt. He had to hire a ship to take him to Walvis
Bay, which served as his alternative gateway to the interior.[79]

David Livingstone was the only notable explorer who started his career in southern Africa during those war-torn decades. He was dismayed
by the devastation caused by Boer expansion and must have realized
that the instability it caused posed a serious problem for conventional
exploration.[80] His own early exploratory ventures never relied on logistical support from the Cape; they were conducted with local mission and

African resources. When he made his great transcontinental journey across southern Africa, he relied on the assistance of Sekeletu, the chief of the Makololo people, who provided him with guides and porters. What accounted for this act of generosity is seldom considered, but the explanation offered by one of Livingstone's most recent biographers deserves to be taken seriously: that Livingstone was actually "leading an African expedition, as an African leader under the authority of Sekeletu."[81]

Livingstone's next expedition, the ambitious Zambezi enterprise, received most of its financial and logistical support from the British government. Its main purpose was to find a viable route into the central African highlands that would permit British missionaries, merchants, and others to bypass southern Africa's war-torn territories. It also needs to be noted, however, that the lower Zambezi was under Portuguese colonial control, which meant that this expedition, like so many others across Africa, relied on the cooperation of a gateway state with imperial interests and ambitions of its own.

The conventional view of British exploration in Africa and Australia attributes its political impetus almost exclusively to the imperial ambitions of Whitehall and its unofficial metropolitan allies, most notably the Royal Geographical Society. While it is indisputable that the British state's imperial influence extended across the globe in the nineteenth century, this should not be taken to mean that it always had an incentive to dispatch explorers into distant corners of continents, nor that it was always able to marshal the means to accomplish such goals. British imperial authorities were often reluctant to expend resources on risky expeditions into regions that promised little immediate strategic or economic return on their investment. And even when they were persuaded to do so, they frequently found that their influence did not extend very far into those distant lands. Most explorers acted only indirectly on behalf of British imperial interests, and they invariably operated in political environments that obliged them to bend to the will of other polities and peoples.

While the political environments that explorers confronted in the two continents were in most respects profoundly different, characterized above all by the contrast between settler colonialism's dominant influence in Australia and its relative absence in Africa, they shared several general characteristics that deserve greater attention. The first concerns the mediating role of gateway states. With rare exceptions, explorers of both continents relied on coastal entrepôts and the regimes that ruled them to gain access to the interior. In Australia, these gateway states were colonial creations, institutional offshoots of the British state whose immigrant populations retained strong emotional and economic ties to the home country. Even so, these communities acquired increasingly independent interests of their own, creating tensions with metropolitan authorities and bringing them into competition with one another. From midcentury onward, most of the expeditions launched into the Australian interior were informed by those interests, tensions, and rivalries. Gateway states were integral to the exploration of Africa as well, but they took a very different form. Apart from the Cape Colony, which ceased to serve as a major point of entry for explorers after the late 1830s, none of Africa's gateway states was the product of British colonialism. The three most important ones were in fact independent Muslim states with expansionist ambitions of their own. By drawing on these states' promises of safe passage and their trade and credit networks, British explorers, whether they admitted it or not, were serving more than one master.

The most dramatic manifestations of these gateway states' independent influence on the course and character of Australian and African exploration are evident in the efforts they made to exert economic or political control over neighboring regions and their inhabitants. Australian historians have devoted remarkable energy and intellectual resourcefulness in recent decades to the study of settler colonialism's devastating impact on Aborigines, but they have shown surprisingly little interest in how the continent was actually partitioned among competing settler states. A closer look at the remarkable flurry of expeditions that occurred in the decade or so after the Australian colonies were granted "responsible government" indicates that they were sent out by these colonies to claim possession of those central and northern territories that remained up for grabs. Given the competitive pressures that produced these efforts, it is hardly an exaggeration to refer to the consequences of Australian exploration in the third quarter of the nineteenth century as a scramble.

The role of exploration in the scramble for Africa is far more familiar to the historians of that continent, though it is invariably understood to mean the work of explorers such as Henry Morton Stanley and Pierre de Brazza in the final quarter century, when they led expeditions to claim colonial territory for competing European clients. However, British explorers were often pawns in the plans of other states to gain imperial influence in Africa, most notably the Muslim gateway states of Tripoli, Egypt, and Zanzibar. Insofar as those states' ambitions collided with one another (as they did for Egypt and Zanzibar in the Great Lakes region) or with other states (as they did for Ottoman Tripoli with respect to French Algeria), they can be described as scrambles for empire. Such an analysis suggests that Robinson and Gallagher's classic interpretation of the late nineteenth-century European scramble for Africa might be turned on its head.[82] Rather than regard this transformative sequence of events as the consequence of the political disintegration of Egypt, Zanzibar, and other local regimes, thereby forcing Britain and its European rivals to impose direct rule over regions they had previously influenced through informal means, it can be interpreted instead as a reaction to and extension of the imperial inroads already made by those regimes. Viewed from this perspective, Egypt and Zanzibar in particular can be said to have laid the groundwork for European states' subsequent conquest of large swaths of Africa, providing much of the competitive impetus that drove them to do so in the first place.

The broader implications of this insistence on seeing the gateway states of Africa and Australia as autonomous political actors in the scramble for the two continents is that it highlights the importance of decentering the way we conceive of the relationship between exploration and empire.[83] To attribute the expeditions that British parties made in these two continents to the imperial ambitions of the British state will only take us so far in understanding the political dynamics that underwrote exploration. Explorers were enmeshed in the political machinations of multiple parties, and whether or not they recognized this fact, their actions reflected the multilateral currents that carried them into some of the most remote regions of Africa and Australia.

CHAPTER 5

Logistics

O the oont, O the oont, O the floatin', bloatin' oont!
The late lamented camel in the water-cut 'e lies;
We keeps a mile be'ind 'im an' we keeps a mile in front,
But 'e gets into the drinkin'-casks, and then o' course we dies!

—Rudyard Kipling, "Oonts" (1890)

T HE NAPOLEONIC WARS were barely over when the British government launched one of the largest and most ambitious expeditions it
would undertake in West Africa in the period prior to colonial conquest.
The party consisted of 69 Royal African Corps troops (40 British, 29
African) and 32 African civilian laborers under the command of Major
John Peddie. A caravan of 46 horses, 116 asses, 8 mules, 8 bullocks, and
3 camels carried large quantities of provisions, arms and ammunition,
trade goods, and gifts. The purpose of the expedition was to establish
diplomatic relations with the kingdom of Sego and other African states,
block French traders in Senegal from access to the interior, and launch
vessels on the Niger in an effort to trace its course and establish economic relations with the peoples along the way. It set out from the Rio
Nuñez region of what is now Guinea, north of Sierra Leone. When the
expedition came to its sorry close some six years later, it had achieved
none of its objectives. Not only had it been unable to check the French,
forge an alliance with Sego, or establish a presence on the Niger, it had
not even been able to penetrate more than a few hundred miles into the
African interior. Indeed, this ambitious enterprise proved to be such a

spectacular failure that it has been all but written out of the historical record of British exploration in Africa.[1]

The expedition's failure can be attributed first and foremost to logistics. Its commander's strategy for moving such a large assemblage of men and matériel was the standard one for a British force on the march: a baggage train of draft and pack animals. But these animals quickly died off in the West African environment.[2] The journal of Captain Thomas Campbell, who assumed command of the expedition after the death of Major Peddie, detailed the mounting death toll of these beasts. Five asses, two horses, and one bullock died in a single day. It soon became clear that "without the assistance of the Carriers we cannot move one half our things." Two brass guns that Campbell had hoped "to mount upon some kind of Vessel or other on the Niger" had to be buried with their shot along the way. When the expedition entered a state known as Bondoo, Campbell appealed to its ruler, the Almamy, for porters. The Almamy complied, knowing that the expedition's dependence on his porters made it dependent on him. Convinced that the caravan carried large stores of gold and silver, he demanded gifts, and each present produced further demands. Whenever the British tried to march on, the Almamy simply withdrew his porters and cut off food supplies. "To advance without the King's permission," Campbell came to realize, "is not to be thought of." Eventually the expedition was obliged to retreat to the coast, having found it impossible to pass through Bondoo.[3]

In a scarcely believable display of dimwitted determination, the British decided to try again, doubling down on their bet by adopting the same route and mode of operation. Once again the expedition relied on large numbers of draft and pack animals, and once again this proved its undoing. Fourteen camels and countless horses died before the caravan even left its coastal base camp. The officers found that bleeding the ailing animals had "no effect," or none that could be considered beneficial.[4] By the time the expedition entered the Almamy's kingdom, it had to appeal to him once again for porters and provisions. Once again the Almamy used his leverage to demand gifts, especially guns, while repeatedly making, then breaking, promises to permit the expedition to continue on its way. It eventually dawned on Captain William Gray, the expedition's commander after Campbell succumbed to fever, that he and his men were virtual prisoners of the Almamy, who actually referred to them as "his tributaries."[5] In desperation, Gray appealed to the French for assistance, but even their surprisingly sympathetic response failed to extract his party from the Almamy's clutches. Eventually the expedition was left with no choice but to hand over most of its remaining goods and gifts and retreat to the coast, bringing its long ordeal to an ignominious end.

Logistics loomed large in any expedition. How explorers sought to make their way through unfamiliar territory, what they chose to take on their journey, and whom they selected to assist them in their efforts said much about their intentions and did much to determine their outcomes. While exploration was by its nature an uncertain and risky enterprise, explorers did their best to mitigate that uncertainty and its attendant risks by ensuring they were well stocked with supplies and well prepared to transport them. It was never easy to know, however, whether their logistical preparations were actually suited to the unfamiliar environments—climatic, topographical, social, political, and so forth—their expeditions intended to pass through. Logistical considerations had to be commensurate, then, not simply with the ambitions of the expedition but with the conditions it would confront on the ground.

The logistics of exploration involved three main factors. The first was transportation. Explorers preferred those modes of transportation that gave them the greatest independence and ease of movement, but their choices were constrained both by available technologies and by the suitability of those technologies to the conditions they confronted. The second key consideration was supplies. Explorers marshaled the provisions, medicines, weapons, and other matériel they regarded as necessary for their health and safety, but their assessments of needs were culturally informed and did not always correspond to the challenges that awaited them. Lastly, the logistics of exploration required a labor force to carry out the manifold menial tasks that came with moving people and supplies great distances. Explorers wanted workers they could trust and control, but those who were available often proved unruly and unpredictable.

The overriding goal governing explorers' logistical preparations was the quest for autonomy. They feared that the greater their dependence on local resources and local peoples, the greater their risk of becoming victims of forces beyond their control. They also feared that the truth claims they made as scientific observers would come into question if they were seen as too reliant on indigenous assistance. Their logistical decisions, then, were designed to make them as self-sufficient as possible. This was why the Peddie expedition was so large and well equipped. The irony is that it produced the very outcome it sought to prevent.

If Africa and Australia's explorers had a model for logistical self-sufficiency, it was the one provided by maritime exploration. The ship was its centerpiece. It could sail great distances, shelter large crews and a contingent of scientific personnel, safeguard them from attack, store the supplies they needed for a year or more at sea, and still have space for botanical and zoological specimens, ethnographic artifacts, and other items collected along the way. The ship's appeal was obvious; so too were its limitations as a vehicle for the exploration of continents. Nevertheless, one of the most striking and persistent features of the story of African and Australian exploration was its obsessive search for rivers and lakes. The alluring prospect of launching boats on these bodies of water and using them as highways through the interiors of the two continents gave hope that the logistical autonomy enjoyed by seaborne explorers could carry over to their land-bound counterparts.

Although Australia is the most arid continent on earth, many of the expeditions sent out in the first half of the nineteenth century set their sights on the discovery of navigable rivers or a great inland sea, that most seductive of explorers' mirages. In the first few decades of British occupation, when colonists were still clinging to a few coastal settlements along the southeastern corner of the continent, it was not unreasonable to suppose, as Joseph Banks did, that "a body of land, as large as all Europe, . . . [must] produce vast rivers, capable of being navigated into the heart of the interior."[6] Matthew Flinders, Phillip Parker King, and other naval explorers looked long and hard for such rivers during their hydrographic surveys of Australia's coastline, but without success.[7] George Grey's 1838 expedition set out in three whaleboats along Australia's barren northwest coast, hoping to find the estuary of a navigable river that would open up the interior. It failed miserably. Others took the opposite tack: they tried to travel down rivers from the interior to the sea. John Oxley's 1817 and 1818 expeditions included skilled boatbuilders who constructed vessels that followed stretches of the Lachlan and Macquarie rivers but stalled in swampy shallows. Charles Sturt took a boat on his 1828 expedition, which discovered what turned out to be Australia's largest river system, the Murray-Darling river basin of southeastern Australia. Returning to the same region the following year, he rowed a whaleboat down the Murrumbidgee and Murray rivers to Lake Alexandrina, which in turn gave access to the sea. This was the high-water mark for the exploration of Australia by boat. Thomas Mitchell took two portable boats and four sailors on his 1831–1832 expedition but found little use for them. During his next expedition, he carted two whaleboats across 1,600 miles of land without ever finding enough water to launch them.[8]

As reports accumulated that some rivers seemed to flow to the interior of the continent, speculation grew that there must be a great inland sea. John Oxley first proposed its existence to account for the puzzling course and character of the Lachlan and Macquarie rivers. The prospect of discovering an inland sea took a powerful hold on explorers' imaginations. Apart from the Indian Ocean, the only body of water George Grey saw during his disastrous journey along Australia's arid west coast turned out to be a mirage, yet he remained convinced that "there is hereabouts a communication with some large internal water."[9] Discovering the inland sea became Charles Sturt's grand obsession. His attempt to reach the center of Australia in 1844–1846 was premised on the conviction that he would find there a vast expanse of water. He brought along a 25-foot whaleboat and two ex-sailors to operate it, fully "prepared for a *voyage*."[10] As his party pulled the boat into an increasingly "barren waste," one member of the expedition wryly noted that Sturt remained "as sanguine as ever of falling in with a large body of water—if any body wants to please him they have only to tell him they heard swans."[11] Such hopes died hard. Partly at Sturt's instigation, the 1857–1858 expedition that the British government sent into northern Australia under Augustus Gregory's command was instructed to seek "an inland sea or river communication with the northwest coast." Gregory found neither, and thereafter few apart from Sturt would continue to believe that "the basin of the inland waters may yet be found."[12]

In the end, the only role ships played in the exploration of Australia's interior was to ferry parties to remote coastlines and resupply them. George Grey chartered a schooner to transport his first expeditionary party to the northwest coast of Australia, and the three whaleboats he used in his second expedition were towed to Shark Bay by an American whaler. Edward Eyre's expedition along the coastline of the Great Australian Bight was resupplied at one stage by a government cutter, and at another point a French whaling vessel provided fortuitous assistance. As attention turned to the remote northern reaches of the continent in the second half of the nineteenth century, ships were used to transport explorers, along with their mounts and matériel, to the coastlines of Arnhem Land, Kimberley, and the Cape York Peninsula. A series of expeditions—those of Edmund Kennedy (1848), Augustus Gregory (1857), William Landsborough (1861), John McKinlay (1865), and Francis Cadell (1867)—were deposited by ship along Australia's northern shores. Once these explorers left the coast, however, they lost these naval lifelines and confronted challenges that no maritime model prepared them for.

The prospects for the exploration of Africa by water seemed far more promising. After all, travelers had been sailing thousands of miles up the Nile River since ancient times, and classical and Arab sources had long reported that other great rivers snaked across the continent and that immense lakes sparkled in the interior. Mungo Park's second expedition was perhaps the earliest British attempt to put the nautical approach into practice. It sought not simply to trace the course of the Niger River but also to use the river itself as its means of transportation, thereby avoiding the depredations that Park had suffered at the hands of some of the region's inhabitants during his first expedition. What complicated matters was the fact that the British had a general idea of where the Niger started but not of where it ended. Park's plan was to lead his party to the river's upper reaches, build and launch boats onto its waters, stock them with supplies sufficient for their journey, and row downstream until they reached its terminus. What Park failed to reckon with was disease, which killed off most of his men, and rapids, which probably led to his own death by drowning. Still, Park's dream of building boats to launch on the Niger persisted in the Peddie expedition. Even the explorers who set out across the Sahara from Tripoli were prepared to travel by boat once they reached the Niger. The Denham/Clapperton/Oudney party included a shipbuilder from Malta. Alexander Laing brought two African boatbuilders on his expedition. And Heinrich Barth set out on his great journey across West Africa with a sailor *and* a boat.[13]

Seemingly a more straightforward strategy for exploring Africa by boat was to enter rivers from the sea, but a series of attempts demonstrated its difficulties. In 1816 the Royal Navy sent a ship up the Congo River under the command of Captain James Tuckey. This ambitious but now little-known expedition was organized by the Admiralty's John Barrow in consultation with Joseph Banks, and it was conceived as a counterpart to the Peddie expedition, both of them directed to determine whether the Congo and the Niger were the same river. In an intriguing preview of the importance future expeditions of this sort would place on steamship technology, Banks pressed the Admiralty to commission a specially designed steamship for the expedition's use. Once it was built, however, the steam engine manufacturers James Watt and Matthew Boulton concluded that the boiler's weight exceeded draft specifications and posed stability problems, so the engine was removed and the vessel refitted as a schooner. Its sails proved no match for the adverse currents and winds at the mouth of the Congo, so Tuckey had to hire local people to row his party upriver. By the time they reached the first of the Congo's great cataracts, yellow fever had struck: Captain Tuckey, all of the scientists, and twelve sailors were soon dead. A skeleton crew managed to sail the ship back to Britain, where the expedition was rightly deemed a disaster.[14]

Advances in steamship technology and Richard Lander's confirmation that the delta region known as the Oil Rivers was the mouth of the Niger River led to renewed efforts to penetrate the continent by boat. In the early 1830s a group of Liverpool merchants led by Macgregor Laird, scion of a Scottish shipbuilder, formed a company to establish direct trade with the peoples who inhabited the West African interior. It commissioned the Laird firm to build two steamships for use on the Niger. These vessels, 112-foot and 70-foot iron steamers, were engineered to navigate relatively shallow waters and equipped with an array of swivel guns and carriage cannons to repel anyone who tried to thwart their progress. Although the ships carried all the provisions their passengers required, the expedition's self-sufficiency was mitigated by the engines' voracious demand for fuel. A team of Krumen (a coastal African ethnic group that worked in the shipping trade from Sierra Leone to the Ivory Coast) was engaged to accompany the expedition and chop wood along the river's banks, a task that obliged the vessels to periodically pull to shore, where the locals' permission was often required to cut down trees. Soon a familiar foe began to strike: disease. Of the forty men who set out on the expedition, only four survived, including Laird and William Allen, a Royal Navy lieutenant who had been seconded to the expedition to survey the river's course.[15]

The same fate befell another Niger expedition a decade later. At a cost of nearly £80,000, the Niger expedition of 1841 was almost certainly the most expensive undertaking of its kind in nineteenth-century Africa.[16] The British government sponsored the expedition in association with antislavery campaigners led by Thomas Fowell Buxton. Its aims were to persuade African rulers to renounce the slave trade, encourage them to grow cotton, establish a model farm to disseminate cultivation methods, introduce missionaries to preach the benefits of Christianity, and demonstrate the marvels of British technology and, by extension, British civilization. Three purpose-built iron steamships, specially designed with interchangeable parts and an elaborate ventilation system intended to keep their crews healthy, steamed upriver in 1841. The commander of the expedition was William Allen, now a captain, and the party numbered more than 150 men, including scientists, missionaries, translators, Krumen woodcutters, and ex-slaves who had volunteered to staff the model farm. Yet once again the expedition's participants, especially the British members, quickly contracted fevers, and as the death toll mounted, the armada retreated to the sea and back to Britain.[17]

The first Niger expedition that contemporaries judged a success took place in 1854. The Admiralty dispatched another Laird-built iron steamer up the river, this time with "as few white men as possible," since they were believed to be more susceptible to the deadly environment than blacks. Yet all but one of this reduced contingent of whites did survive. They and the black members of the party—including Krumen to cut firewood—were kept alive by Dr. William Balfour Baikie's daily ministrations of quinine, proving beyond doubt that with proper use it provided protection against malaria.[18] The irony of the expedition is that its route took it past peoples and places already known to the British from previous probes up the Niger. Although it was the first expedition to venture some distance up the Benue River as well, its geographical discoveries proved modest.[19]

The Baikie expedition's apparent success in overcoming some of the most serious medical and technical challenges of steaming up the Niger River gave the British reason to believe that they could penetrate Africa's other river systems as well. Three years later, the Royal Geographical Society's president, Roderick Murchison, lobbied the government to launch another major expedition, this one targeting the Zambezi River with the now famous David Livingstone in command. Its aims were very similar to the Niger initiatives—to suppress the trade in slaves, encourage the growth of "legitimate" commerce, promote the cultivation of cotton, spread the word of Christ, advance the cause of science, and trumpet the benefits of technology. The British government commissioned a small iron steamer specially designed by Macgregor Laird to be broken into segments and shipped by the Royal Navy to the mouth of the Zambezi River, where it was reassembled and launched as the *Ma Roberts.* In addition to its half dozen or so white members, the expedition included a dozen Krumen recruited in Sierra Leone to serve as stevedores and woodcutters, as well as various other Africans recruited locally.[20] The original aim of the expedition was to steam up the Zambezi to the highland homeland of the Makololo people, who had assisted Livingstone on his previous expedition. Here he hoped to promote trade and establish a model Christian settlement. These plans were thrown into disarray, however, when it was discovered that cataracts blocked the steamship's passage above Tete. Faced with the prospect of failure, Livingstone shifted his attention to the Shire River, a tributary of the Zambezi, making exaggerated claims for its feasibility as a navigable route to Lake Malawi. The *Ma Roberts,* meanwhile, became so badly corroded it sank. The British government sent out a second steamship, the *Pioneer*, but its draft was too deep for the Zambezi and Shire, and Livingstone had no better luck using it to penetrate the Rovuma River. These setbacks were deeply embarrassing to nearly everyone involved in the expedition, demonstrating as they did the limits of British technological prowess. A further setback came with the collapse of the affiliated Universities Mission to Central Africa, a team of missionaries that entered the upper Shire on Livingstone's recommendation to establish a mission station, only to become entangled in the region's violent ethnic conflicts and fall victim to its fevers.[21] Meanwhile, personal relations among the members of Livingstone's own party had unraveled: the naval officer had resigned, the geologist and the artist had been dismissed, and the remaining participants had grown increasingly disenchanted with one another. Toward the end, John Kirk, the expedition's botanist, became convinced that "Dr. L[ivingstone] is out of his mind."[22] After five years of futility and the expenditure of some £30,000, British authorities finally pulled the plug on the expedition, recalling its remaining members in 1863.[23]

The ignominious failure of the Zambezi expedition brought an effective end to efforts by the British government and its various partners (missionaries, merchants, and the RGS) to marshal state-of-the-art steamship technologies and other resources to explore Africa by water. However tempting it must have been to conduct exploration in the relative comfort and security of a ship—"a British space" where "the explorers were 'at home'"—this proved all but impossible.[24] Few of Africa's rivers provided navigable access from the sea, and most of them presented further obstacles upstream. These ranged from fierce cataracts to shallow waters to shifting channels to the notorious Sudd, the floating masses of vegetation that clogged the upper reaches of the White Nile. And most of the continent was beyond the reach of rivers in any case. Expeditions required other strategies to reach their goals.

To say that travel by land posed its own distinct logistical challenges is, of course, to state the obvious, but the fact that so many African and Australian expeditions sought to circumvent those challenges through their search for navigable rivers and other waterways suggests that the obvious is still worth stating. However much they may have wished it otherwise, land explorers found that they had to cope with very different circumstances than did their water-bound counterparts. Both the physical and social environments they encountered were complex and varied, demanding their own distinctive logistical strategies.

The foremost logistical challenge facing Australian explorers was to carry all the provisions they needed for their journeys. They could not count on assistance from indigenous peoples, foragers who had little surplus to share with strangers and even less incentive to do so when those strangers seemed so dangerous. Nor could they count on the continent's wild plants or game to sustain them, though they did supplement their diets by hunting kangaroos, emus, opossums, ducks, and other animals when opportunities arose (often taking hunting dogs to assist them). The only way they were sure not to starve was to pack enough food to supply their needs. This made it necessary to move a large amount of dead weight across a vast expanse of rugged terrain. The strategies they employed to accomplish this feat of logistics varied with the conditions they confronted and the resources at their disposal.

Pack animals were scarce and expensive during the first decades of Australian colonization. Participants in early expeditions often had to shoulder their own supplies, placing severe limits on the time and distance they could travel.[25] Soon, however, parties venturing into the interior were able to obtain bullocks to pull carts, horses to carry packs, and sheep and goats to supply meat on the hoof, permitting them to go longer and farther than ever before. In 1824 William Hovell and Hamilton Hume had five men, five bullocks, three horses, two carts, and four months' worth of supplies for their private expedition from Sydney to Port Phillip.[26] With the increased availability of pack animals, expeditionary parties became larger, giving them greater security against attacks by Aborigines. When New South Wales's surveyor general, John Oxley, led the first major official expedition across the Blue Mountains in 1817, his party of 13 men was provisioned for five months. Charles Sturt and Allan Cunningham each had 11 men on their respective expeditions in 1828.[27] Two Western Australian expeditionary parties in the early 1830s numbered more than 20 men.[28] Thomas Mitchell's first expedition in 1831–1832 had 16 white men, his second in 1835 had 24, and his third in 1836 had 25, along with a large wagon (loaded with the pair of whaleboats), 7 carts, 15 horses, 75 bullocks, and 80 sheep. When he set out on his final expedition a decade later he took 28 white men, 17 horses, 112 bullocks, and 250 sheep.[29] These expeditions resembled armies on the march, which is hardly surprising given the fact that many of these early explorers had military backgrounds. Small reconnaissance patrols searched for viable routes while the main parties moved at a snail's pace set by plodding bullocks pulling wagons, accompanied by men trudging on foot, horses laden with supplies, and herds of sheep and goats. For Aborigines observing their passage, these cavalcades must have seemed analogous to swarms of locusts, a resemblance reinforced by their devastating impact on the surrounding vegetation and water supply.[30]

Another relevant feature of these expeditions is that their manpower consisted mainly of the coerced labor of soldiers and convicts. Soldiers probably had less say about their involvement than did the convicts, most of whom were volunteers hoping to receive reduced or rescinded sentences. Although some of these men brought valuable expertise and motivation to their tasks, most were unskilled laborers who herded sheep, drove bullocks, packed and unpacked saddlebags, and carried out other menial tasks, with little incentive to do more than the minimum necessary.

By the 1840s, explorers had begun to reduce the size of their parties and rely much more on the labor of free men, who often volunteered their services. Charles Sturt's 1844–1846 expedition to central Australia consisted of 16 free men selected from a pool of 300 eager applicants.[31] Each of Ludwig Leichhardt's privately funded expeditions in the 1840s numbered less than 10 men, all of them volunteers. Although Augustus Gregory's 1855–1856 expedition to northern Australia was generously funded and provisioned by the British government, it had only 17 participants, each of them eager for the adventure. Even the Burke and Wills expedition, which attracted an astonishing 700 applications, started out with only 19 men, and the number had dropped to 11 by the time the party reached its staging depot at Menindee.[32]

While expeditions may have reduced manpower in this period, they marshaled more animals and supplies. Sturt's 1844–1846 expedition had 11 horses, several dozen bullocks, 200 sheep, and 4 drays that held 7 tons of supplies, including 3½ tons of flour, 1,000 pounds of sugar, and 500 pounds of bacon. Leichhardt's 1846 expedition had 14 horses, 16 mules, 40 bullocks, and 300 goats, along with 1,000 pounds of flour and other supplies. Edmund Kennedy ventured into the Cape York Peninsula in 1848 with 13 men (two of whom were convicts), 28 horses, 100 sheep, and 1 ton of flour. Some 50 horses, 200 sheep, and 18 months' worth of supplies were landed on the north Australian coast for Gregory's expedition. The Burke and Wills behemoth had 18 horses, 26 camels, 7 large wagons, and 21 tons of supplies. The main purpose of these well-stocked expeditions was to permit explorers to push further into the interior and stay there longer.[33]

This strategy depended on finding sufficient water and fodder to sustain the horses that carried the explorers, the bullocks that pulled their supply wagons, and the sheep, goats, and other animals that provided them with fresh meat. The problem was that explorers repeatedly ran into territory that was simply too dry and devoid of edible grasses to support such large herds of stock. "I depend entirely on the existence of water," Leichhardt conceded, acknowledging a constraint that affected almost all the explorers of his generation.[34] Sturt's party was trapped for months at its base camp, unable to either advance or retreat, because it could not find sufficient water or fodder to keep its animals alive. For all the posthumous criticisms directed at Robert O'Hara Burke, who jettisoned the bulk of his supplies at Menindee and most of his party at Cooper's Creek, his instincts to travel light and rely on speed to reach his goal were right. The strategy got him across the continent to the Gulf of Carpentaria and back again to Cooper's Creek, though he had the famous misfortune to arrive a few hours after his base camp had been abandoned by its beleaguered occupants.

Another explorer who recognized the limits of the large supply train model of exploration and employed a more mobile method of travel was Burke's rival, John McDouall Stuart. He had been Charles Sturt's assistant on his failed expedition to reach the center of the continent, an ordeal that had vividly exposed the constraints that well-stocked wagons and herds of stock imposed on travel in arid zones. Stuart's own lightly equipped venture into the region beyond Lake Torrens in 1858—a small, privately financed expedition that consisted of himself, a white assistant, an Aboriginal tracker, a small team of horses, and a month's worth of provisions—demonstrated how much could be accomplished with such modest resources. By 1860 he was ready to vie with Burke for victory in what the *Melbourne Punch* aptly termed their "race" to cross the continent.

As *Punch*'s cartoon made clear, this was a race not merely between two men and their teams but between two contending modes of transportation—the horse and the camel. Stuart was a staunch advocate of horses. They were readily available, easily managed, and capable of being pushed to the limits of endurance. Their value as vehicles for small, mobile parties had been shown by the desperate journey Edward Eyre made across the Nullarbor Plain in 1840–1841, although the lessons of that experience were largely overlooked. Gregory made good use of a large team of horses when he conducted his reconnaissance of northern Australia's interior in 1855–1856. But it was Stuart's series of expeditions in the late 1850s and early 1860s, culminating in his transcontinental trek in 1861–1862, that demonstrated how much could be achieved by a mobile party moving at a rapid pace on horseback. He set out with 71 horses, pushing them to—and often beyond—the limits of their endurance: only 48 survived the journey.[35]

Camels, however, proved far better suited to the rigors of the arid regions that were the principal focus of Australian exploration in the second half of the nineteenth century. They could survive longer without water, carry larger loads, and eat a wider range of wild plants than horses.[36] David Lindsay, who had experience using both horses and camels in his expeditions, found that the former could only carry an average of 120 pounds and travel about 100 miles without water, while the latter could carry 400–700 pounds and go nearly 300 miles.[37] Ernest Giles also acknowledged their advantages, envying Peter Warburton and William Gosse, his rivals in the exploration of the arid region west of the MacDonnell Ranges in the early 1870s, because their parties had camels and his did not (until, that is, his third expedition, in 1875).[38] Similarly, John Forrest concluded that his 1874 expedition across west-

central Australia had labored under a greater burden than those of Warburton and Gosse because he was without camels, a complaint his brother
Alexander echoed a few years later in the course of his own expedition
across northwest Australia.[39]

How did the camel attain such an important role in Australian exploration? Several decades of trial and error and a shrewd investment decision by a wealthy businessman share the credit. The settler and explorer
John Horrocks appears to have imported the first camel to Australia,
using it in an expedition he made beyond the Flinders Range in 1846.
The animal proved difficult to manage and it was destroyed after Horrocks was fatally wounded during the journey in a firearms accident that
was blamed in part on the camel.[40] In 1853 the Royal Geographical Society received a proposal from a man named Ernest Haug to explore
Australia with camels, but his scheme was rejected as impractical, since
"no very long journey in the wilds of Australia can be accomplished
without bullock drays."[41] The organizers of the Burke and Wills expedition were more receptive to the idea: they purchased a herd of twenty-
four camels that George Landells had acquired in Peshawar, India, and
hired him to oversee their management.[42] When Burke and Wills made
their dash to the Gulf from Cooper's Creek, they relied entirely on camels to get them there and back, while those camels that were left at the
base camp subsequently saw service with at least two of the relief expeditions sent to search for the lost explorers.[43] The seven camels Duncan
McIntyre used in his 1865 expedition in search of the lost Leichhardt
party probably came from Landells's stock as well. The turning point,
however, came in 1866, when the land magnate Thomas Elder imported
124 camels from Karachi and began to breed them. Elder loaned animals from his growing herd to a series of South Australian expeditions,
starting with Peter Warburton's 1872–1873 expedition, which succeeded
in crossing the Great Sandy Desert for the first time.[44] Within a few
years, most knowledgeable observers recognized their value to Australian exploration.

The problem that camels presented for the first explorers who relied
on their services was that they did not know how to manage and care for
these exotic beasts, whose reputation for cantankerousness Rudyard
Kipling made memorable in his poem "Oonts." When Landells imported

his herd of camels to Australia, he also brought a team of cameleers, four of whom—identified as Dost Mahomet, Esau Khan, Samla, and Belooch—were attached to the Burke and Wills expedition. Dost Mahomet, along with another cameleer, reappeared as a member of Howitt's rescue party. Dost was identified as a Kashmiri and Belooch presumably came from Baluchistan, but it is uncertain where the other two cameleers hailed from.[45] Thomas Elder hired thirty-one cameleers from British India to manage his herd of camels. When he loaned camels for expeditions, he also supplied teams of cameleers. These men were commonly referred to as "Afghans," though most of them came from Rajasthan, Baluchistan, and other parts of British India.[46] Two of them accompanied Warburton's party; three went with Gosse. Another three took part in an 1874–1875 expedition to the Lake Eyre region. The camels that Elder lent to an 1874 expedition led by John Ross were managed by two men referred to as "Arabs." When Ernest Giles got several Elder camels for his 1875 expedition, he relied on the services of Saleh Mahomet, who had previously assisted Warburton, along with another so-called Afghan. Saleh joined Giles again on the journey he made a year later.[47]

While the cameleers certainly knew how to manage camels, they also provoked suspicion and resentment among the white members of expeditions. The dietary requirements of the cameleers were a frequent point for conflict. Samla, one of the Indians attached to the Burke and Wills expedition, quit a few days after the group had set out because his Hindu faith did not permit him to eat beef. The other three cameleers, all Muslims, were evidently "not so particular about their food," but their counterparts on other expeditions were often more demanding.[48] Gosse's camel men had an understanding with Thomas Elder that they would receive more generous rations than the rest of the party, an inequity that evidently caused complaints and compelled Gosse to offer the cameleers an additional five shillings a week if they would agree to regular rations. Two of the three cameleers on another expedition quit when their rations were reduced. Both Warburton and Giles noted that the camel men in their parties would only eat meat from animals killed according to Islamic precepts. Their insistence on stopping for prayers also caused tension: "although we did not object to their worshipping," a member of Giles's 1875 expedition claimed, "we disliked to have them wait so long."[49]

No expedition experienced as much turmoil due to the presence of South Asian cameleers as did the Elder Scientific Exploration Expedition of 1891–1892, a large and ambitious endeavor funded by Thomas Elder and commanded by David Lindsay. The party consisted of ten Europeans, including a surveyor, a geologist, a botanist, a doctor who doubled as photographer, and five men identified as Afghans, though probably Baluchis or Rajasthanis, who oversaw the expedition's forty-four camels. The recently published transcripts of a confidential inquiry into the collapse of the expedition reveal that its primary cause was the conflict between the so-called Afghans and the Europeans, especially the scientists. The Europeans resented the South Asians' refusal to eat the salt beef they had to consume and suspected that these outsiders received more generous water rations. They objected to the way Lindsay had allowed the cameleers to decorate his lead camel "with tinsel show, shells, Berlin wool, and all the extravagances of the Oriental mind," which they viewed as a garish display of "barbaric splendour" that "subjected the whole Expedition to contempt and ridicule." They charged that Lindsay treated Hadji, the head cameleer, who served as translator for the other South Asians, as his "pet." The botanist complained that Hadji handled his collection carelessly. The geologist nearly came to blows with another cameleer over the beating of a camel. In both instances, the scientists insisted that "they would refuse to go any further" unless Lindsay dismissed the offending cameleers from the party. In each case Lindsay did as they demanded but reinstated the cameleers the next day. The testimony of the scientists is filled with complaints that Lindsay "was unable to keep the Afghans in their places," that he "had no control over the Afghans," that his conduct encouraged "the insolence of the Afghans." Eventually the scientists simply refused to continue under Lindsay's command, bringing the expedition to a premature end.[50]

The collapse of the Elder expedition was an especially dramatic display of the racial antagonism that South Asian cameleers stirred among the white members of expeditionary parties. It was echoed and amplified in the resentment whites felt at cameleers' competition in the overland haulage trade.[51] David Carnegie refused to hire Asian cameleers for his privately funded expedition through the deserts of Western Australia in 1896–1897, complaining that "Indians or other black drivers"

Camels as transport for the Elder Scientific Exploration Expedition. Note the South Asian cameleer in the far left-hand corner of the photograph. *Source: State Library of South Australia (B10340).*

abused camels and made them unruly. Charles Winnecke and William Tietkens also did without such cameleers during their respective expeditions of 1883 and 1889. As commander of the Horn Scientific Exploring Expedition of 1894, however, Winnecke relied on a mixed team of cameleers—two Europeans and two "Afghans"—to manage the expedition's herd of twenty-three camels. And when Lawrence Wells, the leader of the 1896 Calvert Scientific Exploring Expedition, failed to recruit a qualified white cameleer to oversee his party's twenty camels, he reluctantly turned to Dervish Bejah, a Baluchi veteran of the Indian Army, whose skilled service during the journey so impressed Wells that he renounced his previous prejudice against Bejah's countrymen.[52]

African explorers generally faced different logistical challenges that demanded different solutions. Because most of the continent was populated by peasant societies that produced agricultural surpluses most of the time, it was rarely necessary for expeditions to carry much more than emergency provisions and specialty goods: they could usually count on acquiring basic foodstuffs from the local communities they passed through. Moreover, the vast herds of large mammals across the plains of southern and eastern Africa provided an additional source of nutrition, aptly referred to by John MacKenzie as a "meat subsidy." This helped to sustain expeditionary parties in areas of agricultural scarcity and provide "a 'sweetener' for relations with peoples through whose lands they travelled."[53] Villagers sometimes freely supplied explorers with food, but more often these interlopers were expected to pay for their meals with beads, textiles, and other trade goods. In addition, African rulers often imposed transit taxes (known in East Africa as *hongo*) on passing caravans and expected gifts in return for their hospitality. Hence the transportation requirements of African expeditions replaced one kind of dead weight, food, with another, mainly manufactured goods intended for exchange.

The modes of transportation that African expeditions relied on to move these goods also differed from those used by their Australian counterparts. Across the central swath of the continent, the presence of trypanosomiasis and its carrier, the tsetse fly, along with various other stock diseases, made it difficult if not impossible to use horses, oxen, donkeys, and other beasts of burden. Many expeditions relied instead on African porters to carry their supplies and trade goods. Taken together, this reliance on African labor and African food placed African explorers in much closer and more continuous contact with African peoples than Australian explorers were with Aborigines. It also made African explorers more susceptible to indigenous demands and constraints.

The early nineteenth-century expeditions that set out from the Cape Colony probably came closest to their counterparts in Australia in terms of their modes of transportation. Like Australian expeditions of the same period, they relied on oxen-pulled wagons, supplemented by horses for reconnaissance. But the ethnic composition of these parties tells a different story. In his tour of the Cape interior in 1797, John Barrow had three wagons, ten oxen, and two horses, which were managed by half a dozen Khoikhoi (commonly referred to as "Hottentots") and a "black boy." The only other white member of his party was a *landdrost* or local magistrate.[54] The caravan of wagons and oxen that transported Andrew Smith's expedition in 1834–1836 was staffed by thirteen Europeans and twenty or so Khoikhoi and mixed-race assistants. (It returned to the Cape with an Ndebele delegation intent on establishing official relations with the British.)[55] Francis Galton's expedition from Walvis Bay into southwest Africa's interior, which was organized in Cape Town, consisted of two wagons, seventy-five oxen, ten Europeans, and eighteen Khoikhoi and other Africans, including some women and children. At one stage in the journey, Galton's party joined forces with a Herero caravan numbering over a hundred people.[56] In each of these cases, the African members of the expedition substantially outnumbered the Europeans and supplied an essential source of labor.

At the opposite end of the continent, the early nineteenth-century explorers who set out across the Sahara from North Africa traveled by camel and horse, much as the explorers of Australia's desert regions would do in the second half of the century. Again, however, they operated in a very different social environment, one that obliged them to follow the routes of passage and rules of participation established by Berbers and Arabs. For Friedrich Hornemann, this meant attaching himself to a 120-man trade caravan from Egypt and traveling in the guise of a Muslim trader. Dixon Denham and Hugh Clapperton were able to cross the Sahara without concealing their true identities, but only because they traveled with a military escort supplied by Tripoli's ruler. Alexander Laing, who had no such escort when he followed the same route from Tripoli a few years later, adopted Hornemann's strategy of attaching himself to trade caravans and wearing a "Turkish costume" to avoid harassment, though he made no pretense of being a Muslim. Richard Lander did the same when he entered the interior of West Africa, as did Heinrich Barth. All of these men were constrained in their movement and conduct in ways their Australian counterparts could scarcely imagine.[57]

Nearly everywhere else across the continent, African explorers found that domesticated animals were simply too susceptible to parasites, predators, and other dangers to provide reliable means of transport. The Guinea expedition led by Major Peddie and his successors learned this lesson the hard way. So did Samuel Baker during his expedition up the Nile in the early 1860s. Soon after he set out from Gondokoro, the beasts of burden he depended on to carry his supplies began dying off in quick succession. Several months into the journey he had lost all of his horses and camels and twelve of his twenty donkeys; all the remaining donkeys died soon thereafter. In order to continue his journey, Baker had to join an Arab merchant caravan that was traveling south in search of ivory, cattle, and slaves. He repeatedly gave vent in his diaries to the frustration he felt at his reliance on "these robbers." "I being dependent on their movements am more like a donkey than an explorer," he tellingly complained.[58] On one occasion he had to cool his heels for a month while the traders he accompanied set out in a direction that was for him a detour. With few porters of his own, he was obliged to wait until they returned. Although he eventually managed to reach his goal, Lake Albert, he found himself trapped once again because of his dependence on the willingness of Kamrasi, ruler of Bunyoro, to supply him with porters. Only after Kamrasi was persuaded that he could acquire arms to use against his enemies by opening his kingdom to the ivory and slave trade did he provide Baker with an escort of 200 armed men and 700 ivory-laden porters to assist in his return to Gondokoro.[59]

Most African explorers relied upon the advice and experience of African and Arab traders regarding the system of transport best suited to the regions they sought to pass through. A vast web of trade routes across West Africa supported constant traffic by caravans moving goods from one region to another. Camels provided the principal means of trans-Saharan transport, while horses and donkeys did more of the freight work in the savannah south of the desert. Stock diseases largely precluded the use of animals in the more densely populated and heavily forested regions further south and west, so traders turned instead to porters, some of them slaves. Trade caravans in these regions often included 500 to 1,000 porters.[60] Explorers made use of all these systems of transport in their travels through the region.

For Denham and Clapperton, Laing, Barth, and others who crossed the Sahara and traveled through the savannah, camels and horses provided the principal means of locomotion, and wherever possible they sought the safety of large caravans, which often numbered into the thousands. Explorers seeking to penetrate the interior of West Africa from the south relied instead on porters. The party that accompanied Richard Burton on his journey to the kingdom of Dahomey consisted of about sixty porters and thirty "hammock men," who carried him and his three guides/interpreters. This was customary for dignitaries traveling through Dahomey, but further east explorers found that the Oyo people steadfastly refused to carry them in hammocks, regarding such work as demeaning.[61] In much of southern Nigeria, *caboceers* or headmen contributed carriers to help explorers cross the territories they controlled, transferring them to other *caboceers* and carriers in a reliable, well-established system of transport. It supplied Hugh Clapperton with roughly a hundred porters during each stage of his journey from the West African coast to Sokoto in 1825.[62]

Porters provided the main means of transportation in East Africa as well.[63] Much of the labor force was provided by Nyamwezi from the plains of central Tanzania, who worked for wages in experienced crews. From midcentury onward, they faced growing competition from coastal carriers known as Waungwana, many of them slaves owned and organized by Arab and Swahili merchants. Whatever their ethnic origins or legal status, however, all of these porters were part of a caravan system with its own customary codes regarding wages, workloads, rest days, and disciplinary practices.

Most expeditions seeking to enter the Great Lakes region set out from Bagamoyo, the main point of embarkation on the mainland for the trade caravans that moved goods and people between Zanzibar and much of east and central Africa. The explorers who gathered porters in Bagamoyo—including Burton, Speke, Stanley, and Thomson, among others—had little choice but to accommodate themselves to the customs of this caravan system, however baffling and frustrating they found it. Cameron supplies a vivid if racially offensive account of the process:

> The bargaining with pagazi [porters] was most dreadful work, I have been six hours amongst a crowd of odoriferous blacks, who smell of dried shark & other abominations and who all yelled and jabbered at the same time and was quite proud at the end of it having secured five [porters]. . . . The Arabs are not at all friendly and

altho' the two Jemadars [Zanzibari officials] are as civil as possible, all the others thwart us in every way, they bring out men who are halt, maimed & blind, they get hold of men we have engaged & swear they are their slaves or debtors and want more money from us and try all sorts of dodges to prevent our getting men.[64]

Once a caravan was organized and on the move, it assumed a life of its own, proceeding at a pace on a route in an order fixed by custom and experience. "Each party has a guide with a flag," reported David Livingstone, "and a drum is beaten, and Kudu's horn sounded. One party is headed by about a dozen leaders, dressed in fantastic head-gear of feathers and beads."[65] Disapproving of such display, Livingstone dismissed it as a peculiarity of Arab trade caravans. But most of the expedition caravans of his countrymen were similarly outfitted and ordered. As Joseph Thomson describes it, his own first expeditionary party was led by a man carrying a shield and spear who wore a feather headdress and raiment made of leopard, lemur, and monkey skins. He was followed by "the Band," presumably composed of drummers and horn blowers. Then came a boy carrying "the Flag," accompanied by three headmen, followed by most of the porters. Thomson and other headmen brought up the rear. "With such a turn out of barbaric splendor," Thomson observed, "you may be sure we made quite an impression."[66] That was precisely the point. The loud and colorful cavalcade was rather like a circus marching into town, proclaiming its arrival and enticing local people to view the show and prepare for trade.

These caravans were invariably composed of several distinct groups, each with its own identity, customs, duties, and lines of command. The party that accompanied John Hanning Speke and James Grant on their expedition provides a good example. It numbered around 220 people, with the largest contingent consisting of 115 or so porters. Many of the porters, Speke notes, came from the same villages or extended families, "so they cooked together, ate together, slept together, and sometimes mutinied together."[67] The second-largest group consisted of sixty-four Sidis or ex-slaves, who seem to have held somewhat higher status, though most of them evidently worked as porters as well. In addition, the sultan of Zanzibar had assigned twenty-five Baluchi troops to the expedition as military escorts and the governor of the Cape Colony had contributed ten Hottentot (Khoikhoi) soldiers, though not, it seems, to provide protection—one was a bugler and cook, another a butcher, a third a fiddler, and two others were valets for Speke and Grant. Half a dozen other men served in leadership or translator roles. Finally, the expedition also included several women, whom Grant describes as "quiet, decent, well-conducted, tidy creatures."[68]

The leading authority on the East African caravan trade indicates that these caravans usually numbered between 800 and 1,500 men. Explorers' parties were small by comparison. This was especially apparent in the case of the Burton-Speke expedition, which pioneered the use of the East African caravan route by explorers: it set out with only 36 porters, 5 men to manage the donkeys, 8 Baluchi soldiers, 2 headmen, and 2 Goan servants. Speke's subsequent expedition was substantially larger, though its 200-plus members still remained well below the norm. So did subsequent expedition caravans. Stanley's first expedition employed close to 200 porters. His second started with 230, though it grew to 270. Cam-

"Speke's Faithfuls," so characterized by John Hanning Speke because these headmen remained with his Nile expedition from its start in Zanzibar to its conclusion in Cairo, where the photograph from which this engraving is derived was taken. *Source: J. H. Speke,* Journal of the Discovery of the Source of the Nile *(1864).*

eron had about 200 porters when he set out. A decade later, Thomson had just 117 porters. None of these numbers, it should be stressed, included everyone who accompanied these parties. Caravan women and children, for example, were rarely counted, though Stanley did so for his transcontinental expedition of 1874–1877, noting that in addition to 270 porters, it included 36 women, 10 boys, and some 40 others.[69]

"As a general rule," Francis Galton observed, "small parties succeed much better than large ones; they excite less fear, do not eat up the country, and are less delayed by illness."[70] While the relatively modest size of explorers' parties was more likely due to their financial resources than to any advice Galton offered, he was correct in his assessment. Smaller caravans placed less pressure on local communities' stores of food and other resources and roused less anxiety about their safety. When Cameron joined forces with an Arab trade caravan in the latter stages of his transcontinental expedition, he estimated that the combined party numbered well over 2,000 men. It surpassed the capacity of most villages to supply it with food, leaving porters with the choice of starving or pillaging.[71] Charles "Chinese" Gordon made precisely this point, perhaps in connection with Cameron's conundrum, in an 1875 letter to Henry Morton Stanley: "Huge caravans mean large use of porters, large use of porters means pillage, pillage [unclear] soldiers, and hostility, & utter misery without gain."[72] Stanley ignored this advice when he organized his bloated Emin Pasha Relief Expedition of 1886, and as a result almost everyone impacted by this expedition would pay a terrible price. This was the largest party he led into Africa, consisting of 620 porters, 63 soldiers, and countless others. When it reached the upper reaches of the Congo River basin, it came in contact with indigenous communities that could not supply its voracious demands for food, a problem that became even more severe as it entered the Ituri forest. The result was the widespread looting of villages by starving porters and a string of bloody clashes with local people who were determined to drive away these marauding invaders.[73]

Stanley's Emin Pasha expedition is noteworthy too because its African recruits were drawn from such distant and diverse places. Most of his porters were hired in Zanzibar, shipped to West Africa, and sent up the Congo River. Others were engaged locally as the party advanced upriver, including a large number of men supplied by the Zanzibari trader Tippu Tip. The expedition's soldiers, meanwhile, were Nubians from the Sudan. Stanley was hardly the first explorer to draw his labor force from such geographically disparate locations. The African members of Livingstone's Zambezi expedition included twelve Krumen from Sierra Leone, nearly two dozen Makololo tribesmen from the Zambian highlands, ten Sena slaves from a village at the confluence of the Zambezi and Shire rivers, about thirty men from the Comoro Islands (off the coast of Mozambique), and occasional labor acquired from the communities the expedition came in contact with at various stages of the journey.[74] Other expeditions included disparate individuals from far-flung locations—the two Goans who served Burton and Speke, a Comoro man who acted as storekeeper and interpreter for Cameron, and more. Although these instances of the mobilization and movement of labor may not be as dramatic as the case of the South Asian cameleers recruited to assist Australian expeditions, they had similar consequences, causing unprecedented social and cultural collisions that had unpredictable outcomes.

Whatever logistical strategies explorers adopted, they invariably carried costs. These costs were contingent on the circumstances explorers faced and the choices they made, but several common patterns can be discerned. Recurring problems of transportation and supply reduced the speed and efficiency of expeditions and eroded the health and spirits of the explorers.

In Australia, where explorers relied on animal transport, one of the persistent challenges they faced was how to maintain the condition of their stock and prevent them from wandering away from camp. Expeditions that entered arid regions—and nearly all of them did so at some point in their journeys—soon saw the scarcity of water and fodder sap their animals' strength. Since the opportunities for animals to graze while they were on the move were limited, during nightly camps they had to forage for whatever fodder they could find. Sometimes they traveled great distances at night in search of food and water. Even when explorers hobbled their horses and camels, they might be nowhere to be seen in the morning.[75] Tracking down animals that had wandered away was one of the regular tasks of the Aboriginal guides who accompanied expeditions. It could take hours or even days to retrieve them, and in some cases they were never found, thereby eroding the expeditions' logistical capabilities. Moreover, explorers often had difficult decisions to make as their mounts' health deteriorated. If they could find sites where fodder and water were reasonably plentiful, they might halt their expeditions for a period of time to permit the animals to recover their strength, though this came at the cost of dwindling food supplies. If not, they might conclude that their only option was to drive their beasts to the breaking point, hoping to reach a water hole or pasture before the creatures collapsed and died. No one who is squeamish about the suffering of animals can read certain passages in Australian explorers' journals without dismay.

The human beings who provided the primary source of transport across much of Africa presented challenges of their own. One of the most common complaints of African explorers was the difficulty they had recruiting and retaining porters. We have already seen how this problem prevented the expedition commanded by Major Peddie and his successors from achieving any of its goals and how seriously it hampered Samuel Baker's progress. Nearly every explorer who relied on carriers for transport confronted similar problems at some point in his expedition. This was often due to the explorer's ignorance of the codes and customs governing the caravan trade and its labor force. Clashes occurred over workloads, levels of compensation, or lines of authority. Explorers who were too quick to resort to physical punishment often drove porters away. In other instances, carriers quit for reasons that had little or nothing to do with the behavior of the explorer. Porters might leave because they had to get in the harvest at home, because they heard rumors that the territory they were about to enter was populated by cannibals, or simply because they were bored or tired. Whatever the reason, explorers' inability to keep porters or find replacements could cause their expeditions to grind to a halt.

The health and welfare of the explorers themselves were often directly tied to logistical decisions. One of the most striking examples concerns scurvy, a nutritional disease caused by a vitamin C deficiency. By the early nineteenth century, the causes of scurvy were hardly a mystery, nor were its remedies in doubt. Yet scurvy became a serious scourge for explorers in Australia. They were obliged to bring along almost all the food they expected to consume during their journeys, which meant they had to have supplies that did not easily spoil. This usually resulted in a monotonous diet of salted meat and "damper" (soda bread), supplemented occasionally with fresh game and meat on the hoof.[76] For all intents and purposes, this was the same diet that had made sailors so susceptible to scurvy on long voyages. The salutary effects of anti-scorbutic agents such as fruits and vegetables were certainly not unknown to Australian explorers. The explorer and botanist Allan Cunningham kept an eye out for edible wild plants, feeding them to his party to stave off scurvy during his journeys in the 1820s. Thomas Mitchell treated members of his first expedition with lime juice and vegetable extract when they showed the first signs of scurvy.[77] And yet by midcentury, the incidence and severity of scurvy among explorers actually seems to have increased. Charles Sturt's expedition to central Australia in 1844–1846 was ravaged by the disease, which crippled Sturt himself and killed his second-in-command, James Poole.[78] Scurvy's effects were equally devastating to the competing expeditions led by Robert O'Hara Burke and John McDouall Stuart in the early 1860s. Three members of Burke's base camp party died of scurvy, and the disease almost certainly contributed to the deaths of Burke and Wills and their companion Gray.[79] Stuart's party suffered only one fatality, but Stuart was so ravaged by the malady's effects that he had to be carried back to Adelaide on a horse-drawn stretcher. Other cases occurred in expeditions over the next decade and more.[80] The prevalence of scurvy in this period can best be understood as a consequence of the logistical turn to lighter, more mobile parties. These parties were better suited to meeting the challenges of central Australia's waterless regions, but their strategy for doing so came at the cost of provisions, which were trimmed to a bare minimum. Antiscorbutic supplies were available but evidently viewed as dispensable. In effect, explorers appear to have taken the calculated risk that they could achieve their objectives before they succumbed to scurvy.

No similar dilemma confronted African explorers. Though they dealt with a far wider array of deadly diseases, they were blessedly free of the ravages of scurvy. Their heavy reliance on local foodstuffs tended to ensure plenty of vitamin C. This was not always the case for their labor forces, however. William Balfour Baikie reports that the Krumen who cut the firewood for his steamship's voyage up the Niger River in 1854–1855 showed signs of scurvy during the latter stages of the expedition.[81] Similarly, Samuel Baker indicates that the Egyptian troops he commanded during the conquest of southern Sudan in the early 1870s came down with scurvy.[82] The probable cause in each case is that insufficient attention was given to the dietary needs of these workers, whose status as strangers (and perhaps enemies) to local communities prevented them from supplementing their diets through informal exchange networks.

For nineteenth-century Europeans, and especially Britons, technology came to be seen as integral to their global dominance, granting them power over nature and setting them apart from other peoples.[83] Few enterprises seemed better suited to showcase its world-transforming effects than exploration. Here it could be brought to bear on places and peoples hitherto untouched by any awareness of its remarkable power. Explorers certainly saw themselves as agents of a technologically inspired modernity. Their books and journals were filled with anecdotes about how their chronometers, firearms, steamships, and other modern marvels inspired fear and awe in the indigenous peoples who observed the seemingly magical effects of these devices. They were attentive to technological strategies that could give them greater freedom and flexibility in their encounters with inhospitable environments. In 1858, the same year that Benjamin Herschel Babbage equipped his expeditionary party with devices to distill salt water and various other technologies designed to penetrate the salt lakes that blocked South Australia's northward expansion, a Mr. Brown proposed to explore Australia by balloon. Although the far-fetched scheme was an ideal target for *Melbourne Punch*'s mockery, it was reflective of an ongoing effort to marshal the resources of European modernity in response to the challenge that confronted every expedition: how to make it as free from constraints on the ground as possible.[84] What better way to achieve that aim, at least in theory, than to avoid the ground altogether?

Like Mr. Brown's balloon, most of the European technologies that promised greater logistical autonomy to African and Australian expeditions proved to be chimeras. None possessed more powerful appeal than the boat. Yet Australian explorers learned after their repeated failures to find navigable rivers or the great inland sea that it was entirely unsuited to the conditions they faced. The boat was only marginally more useful to African explorers. To be sure, state-of-the-art steamships did serve as vehicles for several expeditions up the Niger and Zambezi rivers, but they suffered so many setbacks that domestic sponsors could not but conclude that their costs outweighed their benefits. And as technologies intended to achieve autonomy, their appeal was mitigated by the fact that Krumen and other African stevedores and woodcutters had to be recruited to provide fuel for the ships' boilers. The vast majority of African expeditions were obliged in any case to travel on terra firma, where conditions conspired to contain them within indigenous systems of transport, supply, and labor. Those expeditions that achieved some success generally did so through their accommodation to local foods, local customs, and local power, not through their efforts to achieve logistical self-sufficiency.

Australian expeditions operated in an environment that made them far more self-sufficient than their African counterparts. Even if they had wished to do so, they could not rely on Aboriginal communities for sustenance, labor, or transport. Most of the food they consumed they carried with them. Most of the labor they employed came from their own people. They introduced modes of transportation unknown in precolonial Australia, including horses, camels, and wheeled carts and wagons pulled by bullocks, though these were hardly the cutting-edge technologies of their day: they had been available across Eurasia for thousands of years. Indeed, arguably the most important technology to advance the exploration of Australia in the nineteenth century was the Asian camel, which required in turn the recruitment of cameleers whose skills the British themselves did not possess.

While Australian explorers operated at greater remove from the logistical influence of indigenous peoples than did African explorers, they were no less reliant than their African colleagues on these peoples in at least one crucial respect: local knowledge. Such knowledge was essential to the success of any expedition, and how it was acquired and acted upon points to another way in which exploration was a far more collaborative enterprise than the explorers themselves were wont to acknowledge.

CHAPTER 6

Intermediaries

As soon as I had gotten this man, I said to my self, "Now I may certainly venture to the main land; for this fellow will serve me as a pilot, and will tell me what to do, and whither to go for provisions; and whither not to go for fear of being devoured, what places to venture into, and what to escape."

—Daniel Defoe, *Robinson Crusoe* (1719)

H ARRY BROWN and Charley Fisher were the English names given to the two Aboriginal guides who accompanied Ludwig Leichhardt on his first expedition into the Australian interior in 1844–1846. Apart from Leichhardt's passing references to Brown being a member of the "Newcastle tribe" and Fisher a member of the "Bathurst tribe," we know almost nothing about their backgrounds. They loom large, however, in the expedition journals written by Leichhardt and several of his British companions—so large, in fact, that they call into question standard assumptions about the roles such guides played in relation to the European explorers who were their self-described masters.[1]

The two Aborigines were hired to herd stock, hunt game, find water, and carry out various other tasks for the privately financed expedition that set out from Brisbane in search of a route to Port Essington, a military settlement on the north Australian coast. Charley Fisher figured most prominently in Leichhardt's account of the expedition. Leichhardt recognized from the start that Fisher possessed "wonderful power of sight" (a euphemism for his bush skills), but found that he would not adopt the submissive stance expected of Aborigines. Viewed as "insolent"

Charley Fisher and Harry Brown, Aboriginal guides for Ludwig Leichhardt's 1844–1846 expedition. *Source: L. Leichhardt,* Journal of an Overland Expedition in Australia *(1847).*

by the European members of the party, Fisher clashed with several of them. Tensions came to a head when he reportedly "threatened to shoot" a member of the party named Mr. Gilbert. Leichhardt promptly dismissed Fisher, but he returned to camp a day later, apologized for his conduct, and was reinstated. Soon thereafter his value to the expedition was demonstrated in dramatic fashion. Two white members of the party went missing and "would certainly have perished," Leichhardt wrote, "had not Charley been able to track them: it was indeed a providential circumstance that he had not left us." As the expedition pushed on, conditions deteriorated, bodies weakened, and nerves frayed. Leichhardt worried that Fisher was exhibiting renewed signs of what he characterized as "discontent, and . . . a spirit of disobedience."[2] Determined to show who was in charge, he provoked a confrontation with Fisher that took an unexpected and dramatic turn. John Murphy, one of the lost men saved by Fisher, described what happened. Fisher had spent the

day tracking down some horses that had wandered from camp, returning "much fatigued" late in the afternoon. Leichhardt "spoke rather
harshly to him" and, when Fisher failed to show proper deference, "very
menacingly showed his fist in Charley[']s face." Fisher responded by
striking Leichhardt in the jaw, dislodging several of his teeth and leaving
him, as Murphy quaintly put it, unable to "masticate his food."[3]

Given the racial structure of power relations in colonial Australia, an
act of this kind often carried a terrible penalty: black men who assaulted
white bosses could pay for their transgressions with their lives. In this
case, however, Leichhardt did little more than again expel Fisher from
the expedition, figuring that his prospects of survival were slim in such
an unfamiliar region where the local population was as likely to be hostile to strange Aborigines as to strange Europeans. What Leichhardt
failed to anticipate was the decision by Harry Brown to decamp in soli-
darity with his black brother: "One led the other astray, so that both resisted me."[4] Now the expedition was entirely bereft of a critical source of
labor and knowledge of the outback. Within two days, both men had
resumed their regular duties as if nothing had happened. A disapproving white member of the party, William Phillips, complained that Leichhardt had permitted Fisher and Brown to engage "in every species of
insolence towards the rest of the party," a remark that reveals just how
far race relations among members of the expedition had diverged from
the hierarchical pattern that conventionally governed dealings between
blacks and whites in Australia.[5]

When Ludwig Leichhardt organized his second expedition in 1847,
Charley Fisher was, unsurprisingly, not a member of the party, but
Harry Brown was. Leichhardt described Brown as "ill tempered" but
insisted: "I know well enough how to manage him." The other Aboriginal member of the party was Wommai, "a cheerful young fellow" known
to the Europeans as Jimmy.[6] The expedition went badly wrong very
quickly. Unusually heavy rains slowed its progress to a crawl and produced a bumper crop of mosquitoes, leaving everyone ill with what they
referred to as "ague," which usually meant malaria. When the white
members of the party learned that Leichhardt had failed to bring along a
medical kit, they nearly mutinied. It soon became clear that the expedition would have to turn back. Faced with failure, Leichhardt seems to

have suffered a nervous breakdown. John Mann, the expedition's botanist, believed Leichhardt was "going mad!"[7] No longer capable of making decisions, Leichhardt "put himself under the guidance of Brown," according to Hovenden Hely, another member of the party. From this point onward, the Aborigine Harry Brown was the de facto commander of the party, setting its course and measuring its progress. Hely's journal entries for this period are full of praise for Brown, remarking, for example, that "this man's knowledge and remembrance of locality are wonderful." As the expedition neared territory occupied by colonists, Leichhardt attempted to reclaim his authority, charging that Brown had led the party astray. Hely noted that "Brown denies it," adding: "I am inclined to believe him as he led us so well before."[8] And, indeed, Brown overcame Leichhardt's challenge and led the party to the safety of the Darling Downs soon thereafter. Four years later, when colonial officials approached Hely to organize an expedition in search of Leichhardt, whose third expedition had disappeared in the interior without a trace, the only person whose services he requested by name was Harry Brown, then an assistant to a government surveyor. Hely explained that Brown's "knowledge of all that country and his consummate skill as a bushman would much tend to the successful prosecution of the search."[9]

The multiple journals written by members of Leichhardt's first two expeditions offer an unusually rich body of evidence about the roles that Aboriginal guides played in the exploration of Australia. Although this evidence has its limitations, most notably the absence of any direct testimony by the guides themselves, it offers a rare and revealing glimpse into the ways that race, power, and knowledge intersected and informed relations between explorers and their guides. For all the constraints that Australian colonial society placed on Aborigines, what comes through most clearly in these accounts was the remarkable ability of Charley Fisher and Harry Brown to retain a real measure of autonomy, dignity, and even authority in their dealings with Leichhardt and the other white members of the expeditions. Their agency derived above all from their possession of specialized skills that the explorers found indispensable. While the ideal intermediary in the European imagination was Crusoe's Friday, the iconic example of the loyal and submissive native informant, a different reality generally confronted the explorers of Africa and Australia. If power was knowledge, then indigenous intermediaries often possessed far more power than explorers were prepared to admit, since it undermined their own reputations. In this sense, then, intermediaries' power derived from a secret knowledge, a knowledge that seldom surfaced in the public statements and publications produced by explorers and their sponsors.

Historians and other scholars have given increasing attention in recent years to the go-betweens who mediated between the European travelers who ventured to the far corners of the globe in the period after 1500 and the various peoples with whom they came in contact.[10] Given the unprecedented range and scale of these contacts, intermediaries played a crucial role in establishing lines of communication between peoples hitherto unknown to one another. Often elusive figures, they served as guides, agents, interpreters, emissaries, and, above all, cultural brokers. Among the questions that have been asked about these individuals and their role in cross-cultural encounters are the following: How did they acquire their specialized skills? Where did their loyalties lie? What were their agendas? How much agency did they possess? How did they shape the production and circulation of knowledge?

Like so many travelers in strange lands, the British explorers who entered the interiors of Africa and Australia sought the advice and assistance of individuals who were familiar with the terrain through which they intended to pass and who possessed the linguistic and cultural skills to serve as mediators with local inhabitants. Only a handful of these intermediaries have left us with firsthand accounts of their experiences.[11] The explorers, however, often had a great deal to say about the guides and go-betweens who assisted them. Much of that information is, to be sure, selective, self-serving, and coded in racial categories and cultural biases. The native assistants who received the greatest praise were those whose conduct could be construed as demonstrating a selfless loyalty to their "masters" under difficult and dangerous circumstances. David Livingstone's Susi and Chuma, Edward Eyre's Wylie, and Edmund Kennedy's Jackey Jackey are famous examples, and it is telling that their names are invariably invoked as they appear here, as objects of possession by the explorers they served. Apart from loyalty, the qualities that drew the most fulsome praise were physical characteristics such as keen eyesight, auditory acuity, and a hardy constitution. Explorers regarded those traits as evidence of their intermediaries' affinity with the animal world.

The contributions these intermediaries made as cultural brokers usually elicited a more ambivalent response. Rarely could explorers be certain that their go-betweens were actually speaking and acting on their behalf. This distrust was in some cases justified, but more often it derived from explorers' failure to understand the codes and customs that shaped negotiations with indigenous peoples. Although many explorers were little more than bystanders in these negotiations, it did their reputations no good to acknowledge this fact. They had reason instead to place themselves at the center of these encounters. What explorers had to say about the go-betweens who assisted them, then, needs to be viewed with caution. And yet, for all their biases and distortions, explorers' journals, books, and other records reveal a great deal about who these intermediaries were, what they did, and even in some instances why they did it.

For all the varied forces at work in the two continents and from region to region within them, most of the individuals who became intermediaries for explorers shared a common thread: they were deracinated figures, wrenched from their families, friends, communities, and localities by traumatic events such as war, slave raids, colonial conquest, and other forms of social violence. Thrust into subjugation to strange peoples in strange lands, they were resourceful enough to acquire linguistic and other skills that made them useful to explorers as cultural brokers.[12]

It is this condition of deracination that differentiates individuals who made a living as intermediaries from the local inhabitants who provided explorers with ad hoc information and assistance. Locals often greeted explorers with customary forms of hospitality, ranging from sustenance to shelter to sex. They traded goods for services, providing guides to pilot explorers through rough terrain, directing them to sources of water, and facilitating their reception by neighboring communities. But communication between the two parties tended to be crude and problematic, leading to miscommunication and confusion. Moreover, indigenes were known to deliberately misled explorers in order to get them to go away or, alternatively, to delay their departure in order to extract further gifts and other goods.

Explorers wanted intermediaries they could control. One way to do so was to kidnap local people and coerce them into aiding the expedition. Christopher Columbus had employed this strategy, as had Vasco da Gama and various other early European explorers. It was a common practice in cases of first contact, when neither party could communicate with the other. The first governor of the penal colony of New South Wales, Arthur Phillip, kidnapped four male Aborigines in hopes of teaching them English. He succeeded with Beneelon, who became accustomed to British food and habits, served intermittently as an intermediary with his own community, and even accompanied Phillip back to Britain in 1792, staying there for several years.[13] It was rare, however, for coercive measures of this sort to lead to lasting bonds. While many Australian explorers seized local people and forced them to reveal the locations of their precious wells and water holes, these incarcerations invariably intensified the captives' fear of—and hostility toward—those who captured them. David Carnegie, who explored the deserts of Western Australia in the 1890s, repeatedly rode down Aborigines, chained or tied them up, and denied them food and drink until they had guided his party to water.[14] Not surprisingly, his captives escaped or led him on wild-goose chases when they could. To kidnap an indigene was an act of desperation, and it rarely worked out as well as the kidnapper hoped it would. Moreover, it simply was not feasible in certain situations. For African explorers, who faced much larger and more powerful communities than their Australian counterparts, the very real risk of a violent backlash curbed this practice. In a rare exception, Francis Galton kidnapped two San people in the Namibian desert to "make them show us the water."[15] This incident is consistent with the circumstances in which kidnappings generally occurred in Australia: arid regions where indigenous people were usually few and far between. Even there, however, explorers could run into trouble, as Edward Eyre did when fifty to sixty armed Aborigines suddenly surrounded his camp to demand the return of a woman he had taken to lead him to water.[16]

Far more useful to explorers were guides and go-betweens who entered their service for reasons of their own. In Australia, some of these individuals were members of traditional Aboriginal communities, previously untouched by Europeans, whose curiosity, cupidity, or cognizance of the profound changes these outsiders were likely to bring to their societies caused them to collaborate with explorers. A notable example was Mokare, a Nyungar man from King George Sound who greeted British and French visitors when their ships began to anchor offshore in the early 1820s, spent considerable time in the company of the military garrison that soon set up camp near what would become Albany, and served as the guide for a series of expeditions that officials and settlers launched into the region's hinterlands.[17] In West Africa, the cosmopolitan communities of Africans along the coast that had traded with Europeans for generations occasionally contributed intermediaries to the interior. One such figure was Madiki Lemon, a prominent member of a Ouidah family that traced its ancestry to an Irish slave trader and his African wife. He served as interpreter and advisor for the explorer John Duncan and other British visitors to the kingdom of Dahomey in the 1840s and 1850s, though his proud claims to the status and privileges of a "white man" often irritated those he assisted.[18] Explorers much preferred more subservient guides and go-betweens, marginal men who had been separated from their birth communities and forced by the circumstances of their estrangement to forge a new niche for themselves at the intersection of cultures.

Not all of the intermediaries who assisted explorers in Africa and Australia, it should be stressed, were Africans or Australians: some were Europeans who had acquired the linguistic and cultural skills needed to navigate in indigenous societies in the two continents. In the early decades of Australian colonization, some convicts escaped from penal colonies and spent prolonged periods of time with Aboriginal communities. Those who were recaptured or willingly returned to British settlements possessed geographic, ethnographic, and linguistic knowledge that explorers often found useful. Three convicts who had been shipwrecked in 1823 near the future city of Brisbane and lived for seven months with local Aborigines provided the explorers John Oxley and Allan Cunningham with valuable information about the region and its inhabitants.[19] Expeditions often included convicts and other whites who had spent time in the company of Aborigines. One member of a Western Australian expe-

dition was a convicted cattle rustler who was known for his bush experience and "familiarity with the natives."[20] John Fahey, a member of
Augustus Gregory's 1855–1856 expedition into northern Australia, impressed other members of the party with his ability to construct "weath-
erproof cool & shady" dwellings from bark and other local materials, a
skill he had acquired as a result of having "long lived with the natives."[21]
The records remain silent about how he had come to live with Aborigines and what other indigenous skills and knowledge he contributed to
the expedition.

Many of the early nineteenth-century explorers who sought access to
sub-Saharan Africa via Arab-controlled caravan routes across the Sahara
found cultural brokers among countrymen who had been washed onto
North Africa's shores by war, slavery, or shipwreck. Friedrich Horne-
mann, who set out from Cairo for the West African interior on behalf of
the African Association, hired as his interpreter and advisor a fellow
German, Joseph Frendenburgh, who had been captured in battle by the
Ottomans and made a Mamluk slave soldier, winning his freedom only
after Napoleon invaded Egypt (which is where Hornemann met him).
Henry Salt's expedition to Ethiopia in 1809–1810 was assisted by Nathan
Pearce, a British sailor who had been shipwrecked on the shores of the
Red Sea and lived for some time among the local inhabitants, learning
Arabic, undergoing circumcision, and presumably converting to Islam.
Johann Ludwig Burckhardt was aided in his travels through Egypt and
Arabia by a Scottish soldier who had been captured in the British inva-
sion of Egypt, converted to Islam, and renamed Osman Effendi. North
Africa was in fact teeming with just the sort of deracinated Europeans
who were well suited to serve as cultural brokers in the Arab-dominated
parts of the continent.[22]

Elsewhere in Africa, however, the cultural brokers who accompanied
African explorers and guided their passage through unfamiliar territory
were almost always black Africans who had been torn from their families
and communities by slavery and war. In West Africa, the transatlantic
slave trade produced a plenitude of these individuals. Mungo Park was
accompanied on his first expedition to trace the course of the Niger by
two African interpreters whose lives had been wrenched apart by slavery: one was a Mandingo man named Johnson who had been sold in his

youth and shipped to Jamaica, where he eventually managed to reclaim his freedom and return to Africa in hopes of reconnecting with his family; the other was a youth named Demba, the slave of a British merchant in the Gambia who promised to free him at the conclusion of the expedition. The expeditionary party sent up the Congo River by the British government in 1816 was accompanied by two ex-slaves from the region, known by the names Benjamin Benjamin and Somme Simmons. John Davidson, who set his sights on reaching Timbuktu via Morocco, relied on the assistance of Abu Bekr, an African who claimed to have been born to a princely family in Timbuktu, enslaved in a succession struggle, then sold and sent to Jamaica. Freed after garnering notice for his knowledge of Arabic and the geography of the Western Sahara, he seemed to Davidson and the Royal Geographical Society exactly the sort of go-between they needed to penetrate the region.[23]

The establishment of the evangelical settlement for ex-slaves at Freetown and its transition in 1807 into the crown colony of Sierra Leone, where "recaptives" rescued from slaving vessels by the Royal Navy were deposited, created an environment ideally suited for the manufacture of Africans who possessed the multilingual skills and ideological loyalties to serve as reliable intermediaries for explorers in the West African interior. Most of the expeditions that set out from the Guinea and Windward coasts included Sierra Leoneans in their parties. The Niger expedition of 1841 had a team of translators recruited by a missionary in Sierra Leone. The expedition that William Balfour Baikie led up the Niger River in 1854 stopped at Sierra Leone to hire Igbo, Yoruba, Hausa, Nupe, and Bornu recaptives. An important member of both expeditions was Samuel Crowther, a recaptive who had been educated by Anglican missionaries in Sierra Leone and sent to spread the Christian gospel among his former Yoruba countrymen in Lagos. He took part in palavers with chiefs and other local dignitaries as the two expeditions steamed upriver, and he became such a prominent and respected member of the Baikie party that the surveyor taught him how to use a quadrant to take observations. He would later become the first Anglican bishop of southern Nigeria. Another member of the Baikie expedition was John Grant, an Igbo who served as an interpreter. He had been enslaved as a youth, sold to European traders at the Bonny slave market, liberated by a British naval vessel, and taken to Sierra Leone, where he had acquired a new name, faith, and identity. He had not forgotten his past, however. As the expedition steamed up the Niger, Grant was able to give Baikie the names of the villages along the way.[24]

Some of these individuals acquired reputations as skilled and reliable intermediaries whose services were sought by succeeding expeditions. Simon Jonas, another of the interpreters recruited for the Baikie expedition, had previously accompanied the disastrous 1841 Niger expedition. He was left to evangelize at the court of an *obi* (ruler) in Igbo country and rejoined the expedition when it returned downriver a few months later.[25] A member of Baikie's second expedition up the Niger in 1857 was Selim Aga, a Sudanese native who had been enslaved by Arabs, sold in Egypt, and redeemed by the British consul in Alexandria, who sent him to a Presbyterian school in Scotland. Aga then went to West Africa to engage in trade, but found employment first with Baikie, then with Richard Burton, whom he accompanied on journeys to Benin, Dahomey, and the mountains of Cameroon.[26] Perhaps the most ubiquitous of these West African go-betweens was a recaptive named William Pascoe. Born in the Hausa city-state of Gobir (now part of northern Nigeria), he was captured by slavers, sent to the coast, and sold to Portuguese merchants. The British Navy intercepted the slave ship that was transporting him across the Atlantic and he was freed, after which he worked for a time on British vessels, where he evidently learned English. He subsequently applied his skills as a translator and cultural broker in the service of Giovanni Belzoni in 1824, Hugh Clapperton in 1825–1827, Richard and John Lander in 1830–1831, and Richard Lander and Macgregor Laird in 1832–1834. His "sagacity and experience have proved of infinite value to us," averred the Landers, who referred to him affectionately as "old Pascoe." He succumbed to fever toward the conclusion of the Laird expedition.[27]

When British explorers began to enter central and eastern Africa in the mid- to late nineteenth century, here too they came in contact with a plethora of deracinated Africans who were well suited to serve as intermediaries. Donald Simpson has compiled brief biographical entries on more than a hundred Africans who held positions of note in these expeditions.[28] Many of them were fluent in trade languages such as Kiswahili and Arabic, familiar with one or more of the vernaculars of the regions they passed through, resourceful in recruiting porters and managing the operations of caravans, and experienced in negotiating with local rulers for food, shelter, and permission to pass through their territories. These skills made them valuable guides and go-betweens. Not surprisingly, certain individuals—Sidi Mubarak "Bombay," Baraka Wadi Ambari, James Chuma, Mabruki Speke, and Manua Sera, among others— reappeared time and again as headmen for expeditions.

Nearly all of these individuals had been previously displaced by the slave trade and its attendant warfare. Many of them were known as "Sidis," an Indian term for Muslims of African extraction, though commonly used in the East African context to refer to ex-slaves who had returned from South Asia. Noting the number of Sidis who played prominent and trusted roles in his expedition with John Hanning Speke, James Grant offered an insightful reflection on how their pasts may have shaped their psychological character: "Seedees [Sidis] have strong attachments. Separated from their parents in childhood by slavery, they are cast upon the world, and became devoted to some one—it may be their first master—whom they look upon as their protector and adviser for years, or even for life." Later he described an incident that highlighted the lasting emotional effects of enslavement and separation from family. The expedition was passing through a Bugandan village where a woman recognized one of the party's Sidis as her brother. Both of them had been enslaved and displaced as children. "The poor woman burst into tears . . . [and] fell at his feet," but the siblings were unable to communicate with each other, having lost any memory of their shared birth language. Grant does not indicate how the Sidi responded to this unexpected encounter with his sister, but it is telling that he continued with the expedition when it marched on. As someone who no doubt harbored an acute sense of vulnerability, he probably saw the caravan itself as a source of security and perhaps Grant and Speke as patrons who could offer some degree of protection.[29]

The most famous coterie of Africans to contribute to the British exploration of east and central Africa were those who came to prominence through their association with David Livingstone. James Chuma, John Wekotani, Abdullah Susi, and Jacob Wainwright, along with a number of others, had been sold into slavery as youths and then rescued— Chuma, Wekotani, and Susi by Livingstone himself and Wainwright by a British coastal squadron vessel. With no equivalent to Sierra Leone to provide refuge for recaptives in East Africa, many of them were sent to Bombay, where the British missionary institutions that congregated in the suburb of Nasik offered a refuge for young freed slaves. Livingstone enrolled Chuma and Wekotani in the Church of Scotland mission school in Nasik and got a job on the Bombay docks for Susi, who was judged too old for Christian schooling. Wainwright was sent to the Church Mission Society Asylum at Nasik. When Livingstone set out on his third expedition in 1866, he brought all four of these young men with him, along with several other so-called Nasik boys: still others joined him later.[30] The Livingstone Search and Relief Expedition of 1872 included six Nasik boys shipped over from Bombay. When the expedition disbanded upon learning that Stanley had already found Livingstone, they refused to return to Bombay, expressing "a strong dislike of that place," and decided instead to volunteer for Livingstone's party.[31] Their training and experiences made them well suited to serve as cultural brokers for explorers.

Livingstone also deposited several of the young boys he had freed from slavery during his Zambezi expedition with missionaries in South Africa. At least two of these boys—Chinsoro and Sinjeri—were subsequently recruited by E. D. Young to assist in his expedition to determine the accuracy of rumors that Livingstone had been murdered. When the expedition ended, they returned to South Africa, where they appear to have disappeared from the historical record.[32]

Livingstone was far from the only African explorer to collect stray boys displaced by the slave trade. Indeed, it is striking how many explorers picked up indigenous youths to assist them in their endeavors. Perhaps the most famous of these African boys was Kalulu, who entered Henry Morton Stanley's service during his expedition in search of Livingstone. Stanley brought Kalulu back with him to England, took him on a lecture tour, posed with him for a series of well-known photographs, and wrote a highly romanticized novel titled *My Kalulu* that purported to be an imaginative retelling of his early life.[33] In short, Stanley turned Kalulu into something of a celebrity whose exotic Africanness helped to authenticate Stanley's own experiences as an African explorer. In *How I Found Livingstone,* Stanley claims that Kalulu was placed in his care by an Arab trader, but his unpublished journal records that he purchased Kalulu for $20 "to carry one of my hunting guns."[34] Stanley proved to be a serial collector of African boys, though none of them made as visible a mark on the historical record as did Kalulu.[35] The precise nature of Stanley's relationship with Kalulu and other African boys is unknown, though sexual predation seems likely. Robert Aldrich observes that *My Kalulu* can be read "as an idealised homosexual love story in an exotic setting."[36]

Whatever intimacies may have arisen between explorers and the young Africans they attached to their parties—a subject about which the written records are predictably silent—these boys were valued above all because they were such tractable intermediaries. Their tractability derived from their vulnerability. Two slave boys named Dorugu and Abbega entered Heinrich Barth's service after the death of his colleague Adolf Overweg, who had hired them to care for his camels and subsequently purchased and freed them. "Freedom," however, was a relative term for children unattached to any kin networks in mid-nineteenth-century West Africa; for Barth's boys, it gave them no viable option other than remaining in the explorer's service. Dorugu referred to Barth as his "master" and accompanied him back to Britain, where he was placed in the care of a minister who had taken part in the 1841 Niger expedition. His memoirs offer a few hints of the emotional trauma he must have experienced in the company of Overweg and Barth. Having never seen a white man before he was hired out to Overweg, he confesses that he "was as afraid as if he [Overweg] were about to eat me." He also reveals that he tried without success to contact his father during his travels with Barth.[37] Another source that indicates how heavily the loss of family may have weighed on some of these youngsters comes from Francis Galton's account of his expedition into southwest Africa. One member of his party was "a young scamp" named Gabriel "who clung to my heels" during the early stages of the journey. Galton does not explain how Gabriel became attached to the expedition, where he came from, or what services he rendered. He does, however, make it clear that his apparent fondness for the "scamp" diminished when Gabriel "relapsed

Henry Morton Stanley and his young servant, Kalulu. *Source: Smithsonian Institution Libraries, Washington, D.C.*

into a timid frightened boy, and used to talk to the men in a piteous way about his mother."[38]

While we know nothing about Gabriel's subsequent fate, many of his young counterparts on other expeditions reappeared in the historical record, serving as intermediaries for other explorers, missionaries, and colonial officials. Several of Livingstone's Nasik boys became headmen and other prominent staff members of expeditions later in life. James Chuma oversaw African crews on a series of expeditions from the mid-1870s until his death in 1881. When Joseph Thomson returned to Zanzibar in 1883 to lead his third expedition into East Africa, he hoped again to hire "the well-known Chuma" as his headman, as he had done twice before. Chuma, however, had died, so Thomson turned instead to Manua Sera, an ex-slave who previously had taken part in the Speke/Grant expedition, Stanley's expedition in search for Livingstone, the latter stage of Livingstone's last expedition, and Stanley's great cross-continental journey.[39] A similar pattern shaped the subsequent careers of boys who had assisted explorers in other parts of Africa. Following several years of Christian education in Britain, Barth's Dorugu and Abbega returned to West Africa, where they became intermediaries in the service of Western interests in the region. Abbega became an assistant to the Anglican missionary Samuel Crowther, an interpreter to the explorer and British consul William Balfour Baikie, an employee of the Royal Niger Company, and a warrant chief for the newly established British colonial government in southern Nigeria. Dorugu slipped from public notice for several decades but resurfaced at the turn of the century as a schoolmaster and translator for the British in northern Nigeria.[40] Such Africans were able to turn the linguistic, cultural, and institutional knowledge they had acquired in their youths into opportunities for advancement in a world remade by European colonial rule.

In Australia, guides and go-betweens were the by-products of a rather different set of forces, though a common thread was the destabilizing effects these forces brought to bear on indigenous communities. Rather than being buffeted by the international slave trade and its attendant disorder, Aboriginal populations were instead overwhelmed by epidemic disease, land alienation, and settler violence.[41] One of the most characteristic features of the devastation wrought by Australia's new colonial dispensation was the collapse of families and clans and the consequent proliferation of orphans and other children severed from their traditional communities. They became easy prey for settlers seeking cheap and malleable sources of menial labor. Some were kidnapped; others were handed over by their parents, who were responding either to coercion or to promises of apprenticeship in the new colonial economy; and still others were supplied to settlers by so-called Protectors of Aborigines, as well as missionaries and other self-styled guardians. In colonial Australia's labor-scarce economy, considerable demand existed for these youths, who were put to work as stock herders, domestic servants, and more. They were often physically abused and sometimes sexually exploited.[42] Yet they also picked up the language and customs of their European employers, and some of them put these skills to use as cultural brokers.

It is possible to gain occasional glimpses of how these Aboriginal boys were transformed into intermediaries. When Henry Lefroy organized an expedition in Western Australia in 1863, his party included "the native Kowitch [whom] I had known from his childhood, he having accompanied Dr Lander and myself, when he was not more than Ten Years of Age, in an exploring expedition . . . made by us in 1842, and having in fact been brought up principally in Lander's house." Lefroy added that Kowitch had since "served many years as a Native Policeman and is well-known to all the settlers of the York district as an intelligent, sensible, courageous and trustworthy native."[43] While we are left to wonder how Kowitch came to be raised by Dr. Lander, the fact that he subsequently found work as a member of the native police force, notorious for its use of violence against Aborigines who were deemed hostile, marked him as someone who had tied his fortunes to the colonial regime and could be counted on to serve his employer's interests in an expedition.

Some explorers acquired the services of boys at remote sheep and cattle stations, where groups of Aborigines often congregated to pick up odd jobs and obtain food, liquor, and other goods. Edmund Kennedy "procured from the overseer [at Lady Jamison's station] an aboriginal youth, named Harry," for his 1847 expedition. Harry accompanied Kennedy on his reconnaissance for routes and water because he "has a very good idea of the 'lay' of a country." These prolonged periods together ahead of the main party gave Kennedy a fuller appreciation of Harry's personality and feelings:

> The boy is naturally brave and of a high and haughty spirit, accompanied . . . with a kind and affectionate disposition. He has often said of his mother, "b'lieve that fellow been boey," a quiet way of expressing his fear that his mother might be dead, and, whenever the [white] men mention his mother's name, he turns the subject or looks as black as thunder, knowing how little respect such men have for gins. He has picked up so much English on the journey that he can make himself understood whatever he wishes to say; and in addition to this, he has acquired an activity and obedience that would be no discredit to a white boy older than himself. His appearance has greatly improved. No longer a poor child, he has become a tall well-set lad, with a kind but bold expression of countenance.[44]

Kennedy clearly took pride in what he regarded as Harry's maturation under his care. He was consequently taken aback when Harry ran away from camp one night. Rather than attribute Harry's flight to unhappiness with his role in the expedition, however, Kennedy simply assumed that he was homesick.

Another explorer who gives us some sense of how young Aborigines were enlisted in expeditions is Edward Eyre. During his days as an Australian stock driver, Eyre came across two young Aboriginal boys, Cootachah and Joshuinig, both about eight years old, who had been left at a station by a stock driver from another region. "The overseer did not know what to do with them," Eyre writes, "so I at once attached them to my own party," using them to track stray sheep and cattle. During a subsequent drive along the Murray River, Eyre's party encountered a large band of Aborigines that included "the parents of my two boys who were greatly delighted to see their children again. . . . [and] shewed a great deal of feeling and tenderness." Eyre never explains how the two boys had been separated from their parents in the first place, but he makes sure they were not reunited: "By being very civil to the parents and making them sundry little presents they were however inclined to acquiesce in the children remaining with us."[45] Eyre acquired other Aboriginal boys during his overland drives and took three of them, including Cootachah, on his famous expedition from Adelaide to King George's Sound in 1840–1841. Not unlike Kennedy, Eyre had a misplaced confidence in his own ability to inspire loyalty. Cootachah was one of the two boys who killed Eyre's white overseer and fled into the bush during the expedition, leaving Eyre and the third Aboriginal boy, Wylie, in desperate circumstances.

Eyre's experience was exceptional, not least because he was perhaps the only explorer of note to have undertaken such an ambitious endeavor with such an odd party, consisting as it did of only two European adults and three Aboriginal youths. Whites invariably outnumbered blacks by a wide margin in most Australian expeditions, and adults were more common than juveniles in the latter group. But many expeditions did include Aboriginal boys, and their apprenticeships in these enterprises often led to subsequent employment as native policemen, surveyors' assistants, and other occupations integral to the advance of the colonial frontier. Moreover, many of the adult Aboriginal guides who took part in expeditions came from backgrounds that included periods of service in many of these same occupations.

Intermediaries carried out a range of duties that varied in accordance with the social and environmental circumstances confronted by explorers. The logistical demands of African exploration placed a premium on individuals who knew how to manage caravans and their crews of porters, whereas Australian expeditions' reliance on draft and pack animals meant that they needed men and boys who could track down strays and find water holes. The bush skills of Aboriginal guides were put to use in other ways as well—finding routes through rugged terrain, hunting small game to supplement the party's diet, and even saving the occasional Europeans who wandered off and got lost. African intermediaries had less need for bush skills since expeditions usually followed well-traveled trade routes with established camps and known water supplies.

Moreover, local people provided most of the food consumed by expeditions, transforming hunting from a necessity into a sport reserved for the European members of the parties.

Despite these differences, African and Australian intermediaries shared a common and crucial role as cultural brokers. Their ability to mediate between explorers and indigenous peoples was first and foremost a function of language skills. Communication was one of the greatest challenges that confronted explorers. They rarely stayed in any linguistic zone long enough to learn the local vernacular. "*Good interpreters* are very important," emphasized Francis Galton in *The Art of Travel*.[46] Without someone who could make each party's speech intelligible to the other, intentions became impossible to interpret, exacerbating suspicions and provoking conflict.

Aboriginal Australia at the time of British occupation consisted of some 400 distinct clan or tribal groups, most with their own dialects, occupying regions divided into mutually unintelligible language families. This posed a serious challenge to explorers. Indigenous guides could assist them in those regions where dialects were similar to their own, but as expeditions ventured ever farther afield they eventually crossed a linguistic point of no return that complicated communication immeasurably. A police trooper who was exploring the area northwest of the Spencer Gulf felt fortunate to find an interpreter who could speak English and the dialect of the region's inhabitants, since he knew that "without this assistance . . . I should be unable to ask them any questions as to the nature of the country and water."[47] More often, explorers relied on several layers of intermediaries—the regular guides who usually accompanied expeditions from beginning to end, providing a range of services that included translations when and where they could, and any local people they could find with a smattering of English or some other mutually intelligible language. Some sense of what was required to cope with the linguistic diversity of Aboriginal societies is supplied by Alfred Howitt, an explorer best known for his subsequent career as an anthropologist. He led the expedition that discovered the remains of Burke and Wills, along with the sole survivor, John King, at Cooper's Creek. Howitt initially communicated with the region's inhabitants "entirely by signs and gestures," but then he "obtained a black boy, Frank," who knew "something of the [local] Dieri language, which is near to the Yantruwunta tongue" Frank spoke. This permitted more meaningful exchanges with local people, and although Frank left the expedition after a short time, "he got me a Dieri boy," who helped Howitt "pick up a good deal of the language." As a result, Howitt was able to gain indigenous information about the fate of Burke and Wills and put to rest rumors that they had been killed and eaten by local tribesmen.[48]

It is perhaps unsurprising that explorers tended to devote more attention to those occasions when their go-betweens were unable to make sense of what native inhabitants said than when they managed to do so. After all, these failures of communication often had serious consequences, souring relations with indigenes, setting back efforts to find water, and causing an array of other problems for expeditions. Variations of the following remark were familiar refrains: "it is impossible for us to understand a word they say, nor could they understand us."[49] Explorers and their indigenous guides often turned to signs and gestures when the language barrier proved unbridgeable, but these modes of communication were haphazard at best. Edward Eyre claimed that he could make his meaning known to Aborigines by sign language, but he also described an incident when some indigenes responded to his efforts to communicate his party's desperate need for water by leading them to the ocean.[50] When John McDouall Stuart interpreted a gesture made by two Aborigines near the center of the continent as "one of the Masonic signs," he was surely either engaging in wishful thinking or suffering from overexposure to the sun.[51] Ludwig Leichhardt responded more pragmatically to the "pantomime" his party had conducted with some locals, concluding that it had "enabled us to form but very vague and hopeless guesses" as to their meaning.[52] Without intermediaries who could translate for them, guesswork was pretty much the only thing explorers had to go on when communicating with Aborigines in regions remote from European influence.

Africans, like Aborigines, spoke a wide range of languages, but long-established trade networks across various parts of the continent had given rise to lingua francas that facilitated communication between peoples. These trade languages, which included Arabic in the trans-Saharan trade, Krio among Guinea Coast traders, a Portuguese patois across a large swath of south-central Africa, and Kiswahili through much of east and central Africa, gave African go-betweens a far wider linguistic ambit than their Australian counterparts. This is not to say that communication was always simple or straightforward. William Balfour Baikie's conversation with one ruler along the Niger River required that his words be translated from English to Yoruba to Nupe to the chief's native tongue, identified as Igbira, and then back again. "This system of treble or quadruple rendering, is not only very tedious," Baikie noted, "but often quite alters the original meaning of the sentence."[53] Similarly, when John Hanning Speke met with Mutesa, the ruler of Buganda, he spoke in Hindustani to his headman, Sidi Mubarak "Bombay," who communicated his words, presumably in Kiswahili, to Nasib, another of his interpreters who knew Kigandan, who passed the message on to a fourth interpreter "before it was delivered to the King." Both Baikie and Speke insisted, however, that these multiple layers of translation had as much to do with customary practice in the two courts as it did with any linguistic necessity. In any case, the growth of trade and other forms of engagement between parties who lacked a common language encouraged efforts to forge an easier medium of communication. Speke's experience provides a good example. Although a poor linguist, Speke had acquired a basic grasp of Kiswahili by the time he reached Buganda, where he remained several months, and Mutesa used the opportunity to take lessons in the language. According to Speke, Mutesa did so in order for the two men to talk directly, but it is also likely that the Bugandan ruler recognized the value of Kiswahili in dealing with traders who could supply his kingdom with weapons and other goods.[54]

Speke's own knowledge of Kiswahili points to another feature of the linguistic environment encountered by Africa's explorers that sets it apart from the conditions Australian explorers confronted. The prevalence of trade languages across large parts of the continent gave explorers an incentive to learn the rudiments of these languages themselves. Nearly all of the explorers who entered the West African interior from North Africa studied Arabic before they set out, and some—Heinrich Barth may have been the best-known case—became fluent in the language. In East Africa, Richard Burton found his knowledge of Arabic very helpful in communicating with the many Arab traders who operated in the region. Kiswahili, however, was the region's real lingua franca, and most explorers learned at least the bare bones of this trade language. As Stanley observed, "There was . . . no mutual sympathy [between the explorer and his African staff], until the Englishman became a proficient in Swahili, and could express in words what he wished done—and then all at once—the Gulf between them was bridged, & Englishman & native looked in one another's eyes and knew one another."[55] This rosy endorsement of Kiswahili as the key to overcoming the cultural chasm between European and African was a bit rich coming from someone as brutal and ruthless as Stanley. Even so, such knowledge certainly enlarged an explorer's pool of informants and sharpened his awareness of the various agendas that were at work among his assistants and porters. Even those African explorers who became fluent in trade languages, however, could not count on the local rulers and peoples whose lands lay along their lines of march to share their skill. It was not possible, then, to entirely dispense with interpreters.

The task of translation was a means to the larger aim of mediating expeditions' encounters with indigenous communities. In Australia, Aboriginal guides helped to mitigate the shock and fear that so often swept through local populations when they first set eyes on white men and their domesticated animals. The very presence of these guides in the company of the pale strangers eased anxieties. They also served as emissaries to elders and other tribal leaders. With luck, they were able to speak some variant of the local people's vernacular and reassure them about the expedition's intentions. Even when the local language was unfamiliar to intermediaries, they were often able to draw on widely recognized codes and customs to establish lines of communication. The value of these efforts lay in assuaging any offense that the expedition's passage through the tribe's territory might otherwise cause, as well as eliciting its assistance in finding water and providing other forms of intelligence.

Experienced explorers understood how important it was for their guides to lead the way in these initial encounters. Charles Sturt's guides made "the very necessary ceremonies of an introduction" that "reconciled [the chief] at my presence," although Sturt observed that the chief continued to "cast many an anxious glance at the long train of animals that were approaching."[56] Thomas Mitchell's intermediary, Tackijally, "cooyed from a great distance" before the caravan approached a water hole so as to avoid startling or antagonizing the people who used it.[57] John Forrest had Jimmy, the Aboriginal member of his party, strip off his clothes before approaching a group of Aborigines so that he would appear less alien and threatening to them. Other explorers required their guides to do the same.[58] These precautions could place the intermediaries in jeopardy. A "lad" named Charley was sent into a native camp to prepare its inhabitants for the arrival of an expedition under the command of Peter Warburton. Although initially welcomed, he was speared in the back and arm and beaten over the head with a waddy when Warburton's camel-riding party came into view.[59]

Intermediaries used cultural protocols that the explorers themselves rarely comprehended in order to propitiate local peoples. This is evident, for example, from Charles Sturt's bemused description of the interactions between his guide Nadbuck and the elders of a large band that the expedition had just come in contact with: "These Natives have as many ceremonies as the Emperor of China and it was really amusing to see old Nadbuck play the Courtier. I found him in the midst of the Tribe noticing all of them by turns. He then took hold of the hands of two of the old Men and walked away with them in deep and earnest conversation."[60] At least Sturt had the patience to permit Nadbuck to do what he had to do to conciliate these people. Much the same was true of Sturt's great rival, Thomas Mitchell. In addition to using Aboriginal males as intermediaries on his expeditions, he may well have been the only Australian explorer to rely on the services of an Aboriginal woman as well. She was a widow named Turandurey who attached herself and her child to Mitchell's third expedition in 1836. Mitchell describes an occasion when she abruptly intervened in stalled negotiations between his male guides and some local leaders: "It was now, that we learnt the full value of this female, for it appeared that while some diffidence or ceremony always prevents the male natives, when strangers to each other, from speaking at first sight, no such restraint is imposed on the gins." Turandurey spoke "in a very animated and apparently eloquent manner" that seemed to resolve the difficulty. Mitchell "could not but consider our party fortunate in having met with such an interpreter."[61] One wonders what the male interlocutors in this parley thought about this unusual intervention by an Aboriginal woman.

Cultural brokers were crucial to the exploration of Africa as well, though explorers' narratives rarely acknowledge their contributions. In part, this may have been because they seemed too mundane to mention. Among the more commonplace tasks of intermediaries was the recruitment and oversight of the expedition's porters and other laborers, which required familiarity with their argots, customs, diets, and conditions of service. Given the hierarchical structure of expeditions, headmen and other indigenous intermediaries carried out these duties without much notice or understanding by explorers, who intervened only when some crisis forced them to do so.

Explorers' concerns about status and hierarchy may help to explain why they said so little about cultural brokers' other main contribution to expeditions—mediation with African rulers. While this role corresponded to the one Australian explorers' guides played in encounters with Aboriginal tribes, it occurred in a context in which both the explorers and the rulers they met brought their own distinctive social expectations into play. We get a revealing glimpse of these expectations from Richard Lander's account of how he and his party prepared for their appearance at the court of "King Obie" of the Igbo. Lander donned a general's uniform with cocked hat and dressed his entourage of Krumen in kilts and velvet hats, while his African guides, Pascoe and Jowdie, donned soldiers' jackets and caps. The party blew trumpets and beat drums as they marched off to meet the king.[62] Lander felt that it was important to make as grand an entrance as possible, believing that ceremony and status mattered to King Obie and made him more amenable to the expedition's aims. Prior to Lander's ceremonial appearance, Pascoe and Jowdie probably consulted with the king's advisors and they almost certainly counseled Lander on court etiquette, translated his words to the king, and conducted separate negotiations behind the scenes concerning shelter, provisions, and other matters. Many guides and go-betweens must have carried out these kinds of cultural mediations for their European employers, but because explorers such as Lander so often came in contact with powerful indigenous polities that shared their own sense of hierarchy and ceremony, they could not credit the contributions their intermediaries made to these encounters without undermining their own status and dignity.

Few intermediaries played as prominent and well documented a role in the exploration of Africa as Sidi Mubarak "Bombay." Because he took part in expeditions led by Richard Burton, John Hanning Speke, Henry Morton Stanley, Verney Lovett Cameron, and others, we know a good deal about his character, career, and contribution to exploration as a practical enterprise. Bombay was a Yao from modern Malawi or Mozambique who had been seized as a youth by slave traders, shipped to Bombay (hence his nickname), and freed upon his owner's death. Somewhere along the way, he became a Muslim and returned to Africa, taking up service with the Sultan of Zanzibar's Baluchi forces, so termed because the principal recruiting ground for this military unit was Baluchistan. He met Richard Burton and John Hanning Speke when they stopped during their "seasoning" foray along the Swahili coast at the Baluchi garrison on the Pangani River, where he was stationed.[63] He joined their expedition as an assistant to Speke and soon won the confidence and admiration of both men. Burton judged Bombay "the gem of the party," while Speke confessed to having "become much attached to Bombay," insisting that "I never saw any black man so thoroughly honest and conscientious as he was."[64]

"Tell Bombay I am swelling him all over the World and have created so much interest in him here, that the next time I must bring him home with me."[65] Speke wrote these words to Christopher Rigby, then the British consul in Zanzibar, while he was in London lobbying the Royal Geographical Society to return to Africa as leader of a second expedition to search for the source of the Nile. While Speke was no doubt sincere in his praise, he also had ulterior motives: he wanted both to get word to Bombay that he needed his services again and to persuade his prospective patrons that he had trained and trustworthy Africans to assist him in this difficult enterprise. (Simultaneously, Speke accused his rival, Burton, of having alienated the intermediaries any expedition would require by failing to properly pay those who had taken part in the first expedition.) When Speke won the RGS's support and returned to

East Africa in 1860, he hired Bombay and handed him the responsibility for recruiting translators and porters and overseeing the operations of the caravan. This position brought Bombay a great deal of power, which he wielded in ways that often escaped Speke's notice. On one occasion, a translator named Baraka, who appears to have been a rival for authority within the caravan, informed Speke that Bombay had stolen expedition stores to purchase a wife. When Speke confronted Bombay with this charge, he responded with what seems to have been a stereotypical performance of subservience, throwing himself on the ground, kissing Speke's feet, and begging his pardon. "I was his Ma Pap (father and mother)," Speke claims Bombay told him, swearing that "he owed all his prosperity to me." Speke forgave him on this occasion, but he was far less forgiving later in the journey when Bombay openly opposed Speke's order to move camp, thereby committing an act of insubordination that threatened to undermine his "command and respect." "It was the first and last time," Speke asserted, "I had ever occasion to lose my dignity by striking a blow with my own hands." The blow knocked out some of Bombay's teeth and he was demoted to a subordinate station. Although he subsequently regained Speke's confidence and his old position as headman, he did not accompany Speke back to Britain, as previously promised. He did, however, receive a silver medal from the Royal Geographical Society in recognition of his contribution to the expedition.[66]

Bombay's services were now sought out by almost everyone who launched an expedition from Zanzibar into the African interior. When Henry Morton Stanley set out in search of David Livingstone in 1871, he hired Bombay to organize and oversee his party. "Bombay is a man of great influence with the natives," observed James Grant, Speke's colleague on the Nile expedition, "and I do hope he will carry Stanley through to Livingstone."[67] It was a telling remark, one that reveals Grant's doubts about Stanley and his confidence in Bombay, making it clear which man he believed really ran the expedition. When Stanley published his best-selling book about the journey, he cast Bombay as a rather minor figure, and in his private journals dismissed him as a good servant but poor supervisor who "was neither very honest nor very dishonest."[68] This comment shows Stanley's awareness that Bombay was almost certainly engaging in private trade and probably drawing on the expedition's stores to do so. It also helps to explain David Livingstone's snappish aside in his journal that Bombay "could not hope to hoodwink me."[69]

Two years later Bombay resurfaced as the headman for Verney Lovett Cameron's transcontinental expedition. At first Cameron considered Bombay "a good old fellow" who is "as honest as the day." Over time, however, he grew less enamored with him, referring to Bombay at one point as "a drunken old devil" who failed to exert sufficient control over the porters. He complained on another occasion that Bombay was getting "lazier & more useless everyday." Yet the African members of the party almost certainly viewed Bombay as a man of great wealth and power: his private entourage included at least three wives and several boys, and he was for all practical purposes in charge of the caravan. It was precisely because he had acquired such standing that he could relax and drink to excess. However much his conduct may have aggravated Cameron, the explorer had enough sense not to provoke a crisis by challenging his leadership or abrogating his privileges.[70]

In 1876, the Royal Geographical Society granted Bombay an annual pension of £15 "for having served so faithfully as the leader of so many Expeditions into Africa." In the judgment of James Grant, who had pushed for the pension, Bombay was "rotten fond of drink—but a born man of honor & truth." John Kirk, the British consul in Zanzibar, who was charged with doling out the money, worried about the effect it might have on Bombay's "improvident habits." Improvident or not, he was still a figure who commanded respect. Even as the pension arrangements were being put in place, he agreed to lead a Church Missionary Society party into the interior. When Bombay died in Zanzibar a decade later, he was a well-known figure who left behind a number of wives, a telling measure of the wealth and status he had acquired during his remarkable life.[71]

Sidi Mubarak Bombay's career provides an especially rich and revealing example of the complex relationships these deracinated guides and go-betweens established with explorers, relationships that ranged from subservience to recalcitrance, abjection to autonomy, oppression to opportunity. Men such as Bombay often exerted considerable influence over an expedition's affairs, but they generally maintained an air of deference toward the white men who controlled the purse strings. Although members of Joseph Thomson's first expedition referred to him as "Chuma's white man," indicating who they considered to be in charge of the caravan, Chuma himself gave his ostensible boss no cause for concern about his standing.[72] The two parties engaged in an intimate and delicate dance that obscured as much as it revealed about their respective roles.

Occasionally toes got stepped on and quarrels arose over who was the lead partner in this dance. It happened when Speke struck Bombay. It happened when Charley Fisher struck Leichhardt. It happened when Jackey Jackey led a search party to find the surviving members of Edmund Kennedy's disastrous Cape York expedition, though the confrontation did not produce physical blows. Remembered as Kennedy's loyal and subservient Aboriginal guide, Jackey showed a very different side of his character when his directions were challenged by a white member of the search team. His testy response—"Do you think I am stupid[?]"— shut up the challenger, and Jackey soon became the party's "head & leading man in every sense of the word."[73]

In most cases, however, power remained firmly in European hands, forcing Aboriginal and African intermediaries to express their discontent in other ways. Explorers constantly complained about assistants who displayed "impudent and sulky" attitudes, classic weapons of the weak.[74] Desertion was another option. It occurred with considerable frequency, especially among the otherwise powerless young boys who accompanied so many expeditions. Edmund Kennedy's Harry, Edward Eyre's Cootachah, and Henry Morton Stanley's Kalulu were just a few of these runaways. We do not know what drove the boys to such drastic actions, but we can assume that they were acts of desperation. Passages suppressed from David Livingstone's journals reveal that his Nasik boys were less faithful than subsequent mythology sought to portray them, and Livingstone's behavior helps explain why. He docked their pay, flogged several of them, and threatened to shoot others. As a result, six of the original nine Nasik boys who took part in Livingstone's final expedition deserted before his death.[75]

One of the most tragic and troubling cases of resistance by desertion was that of "a Cape York blackboy" named Tommy, who in 1867 accompanied a South Australian expedition to Arnhem Land under the command of Francis Cadell. We do not know how Cadell obtained Tommy's services, nor do we know what his duties were or why he became so disaffected. His name did not appear in official reports until he slipped out of camp one night with a double-barreled gun. Eight days later he returned, "poor and miserable, without a vestige of clothing" or the gun. His punishment was a "taste of a rope's end." That night he deserted again, taking a carbine with him. An angry Cadell insisted that he "will assuredly be shot by any of our men who come across him, and as certainly will be speared by the blackfellows on that side." His prediction proved wrong on both counts. Three days later Tommy was discovered in an Aboriginal camp, captured, and confined on the expedition's ship, which was anchored offshore. That night he escaped a third time by slipping overboard and swimming to land. The following day some local Aborigines who were trading with members of the expedition reported that Tommy had come to their camp. They were told in no uncertain terms that all trade would cease unless they returned the runaway, which they did later that afternoon. Tommy was again imprisoned on the ship, probably after a severe flogging. Two and a half weeks later he reportedly drowned while making another escape attempt, though Cadell confessed in a separate report that his death "was not, strictly speaking, one of drowning." How this wayward "blackboy" actually died is not revealed, but Cadell claimed that Tommy "had confided to one of the men his intention of shooting me before he got back to Cape York," supplying a rationale for what must have been his murder.[76]

The story of Tommy reminds us again that almost all the information available to us about indigenous intermediaries comes from the explorers who employed them. We should keep this caveat in mind as we turn our attention to those instances when bonds of affection and respect were said to have been forged between explorers and their guides and go-betweens. Explorers usually found it in their interest to cast their relations with intermediaries in a rosy light: it enhanced their own standing as experts whose insights into strange societies derived from their close personal ties to such reliable informants, and it appealed to the public's romantic conception of the relationships between explorers and guides as variants of the famous one between Crusoe and Friday. Still, explorers' claims of friendship cannot be entirely discounted. They spent prolonged periods of time in close contact with their guides, an enforced intimacy in conditions of great stress that gave rise to fierce feuds, to be sure, but also to strong and enduring bonds. Moreover, they often expressed their appreciation for the guides' services in terms that did nothing to advance their own reputation or play to popular stereotypes.

More than a few explorers referred to their indigenous guides and go-betweens as friends. Ernest Giles fondly called his guide, "old Jimmy," a "philosopher, and friend."[77] George Grey portrayed the relationship between himself and his guide, "my friend Kaiber," as akin to a squabbling but affectionate couple. The two men were constantly together during the expedition, conducting reconnaissance ahead of the rest of the party by day and sleeping apart from its other members at night, huddling around their own personal fire.[78] For Grey, camaraderie with Kaiber was clearly more appealing than association with the British soldiers who constituted the rest of his crew. In this context, class trumped race as a category of difference. Thomas Mitchell, another army officer turned explorer, drew a similar social distinction. Most of the white members of his 1837 expedition were convicts, and he considered them inferior in many respects to his Aboriginal guides, John Piper and two youths, both named Tommy. "The intelligence and skill of our sable friends," he declared, "made the 'white-fellows' appear rather stupid." Mitchell considered Piper "the most accomplished man in the camp" when it came to bush skills. Moreover, "in authority he [Piper] was allowed to consider himself almost next to me," adding approvingly: "The men he despised."[79]

Although African expeditions rarely employed convicts or other working-class whites for menial labor, the African porters, Krumen, and other nonwhite laborers they relied on were even further removed from European explorers in social and cultural terms. With few if any of their own countrymen present to provide companionship, explorers frequently turned to headmen and other high-ranking African members of their parties. The praise that Speke and Grant gave to Bombay, Stanley to Manua Sera, and other African explorers to their own headmen and guides may have been couched in the patronizing terms that Victorians commonly used in reference to those categorized as social and racial inferiors, but such conventions of speech should not prevent us from considering the possibility that they gave publicly sanctioned expression to much deeper and more nuanced feelings of appreciation and affection. In private, at least one explorer was far franker in acknowledging how grateful he was for the expertise and leadership of his African intermediaries. Joseph Thomson, who assumed command of an expedition to the Great Lakes region after the death of its original leader, Keith Johnston, repeatedly praised his headmen in letters to the secretary of the RGS, the expedition's sponsor: "A headman like [James] Chumah is a treasure that cannot be valued to[o] highly. . . . Chumah and my 2nd headman Makatubu have worked like heroes. . . . [T]he success of the expedition has been to a large extent due to them. Indeed I can claim but little merit as the men were all imbued with the idea that I was put specially under their care by . . . Dr Kirk [British consul in Zanzibar] to be taken carefully & safely round and shown the sights of Central African [*sic*] and then safely returned to Dr Kirk."[80] No wonder Thomson was so saddened a few years later when he learned that Chuma, whom he was counting on to lead his next expedition, had passed away.

What makes Thomson's remarks so striking is that they portrayed Chuma and his African associates as the ones who really ran the expedition and ensured its success. Such a frank confession stood starkly at odds with British exploration's foundational racial premise—that white men were in charge. Most of the indigenous intermediaries whose contributions garnered public praise were portrayed as "highly sentimentalized emblems of fidelity, loyalty, and obedience."[81] These were the terms of recognition attached to the medals the Royal Geographical Society awarded to Bombay and other East African guides and the brass plates Australian colonial authorities presented to Aboriginal guides such as Jackey Jackey. It required someone like Thomson, then a novice at African exploration, to dispense with the pretense of power and acknowledge the determinative role played by Chuma. He did so, of course, in a private letter, not a public pronouncement. There is at least one instance, however, of just such a pronouncement. When John Forrest's second expedition arrived in Adelaide after traveling from Perth across the barren Nullarbor Plain in 1870, he and his party were feted at a public banquet. Among those present at the head table was Tommy Windich, who was already "well-known" as a "reliable" guide to explorers when Forrest hired him to accompany his own expeditions. The speech made by Mr. Barlee, the colonial secretary, on this celebratory occasion included the following statement: Forrest's "friend Windich," he declared, "was the man who had done everything; he was the man who had brought Mr. Forrest to Adelaide, and not Mr. Forrest him." He almost certainly made this remark with the knowledge and approval of Forrest, whose journals make clear how heavily he relied upon Windich. When Windich died of pneumonia several years later, John and Alexander Forrest had a tombstone placed on his grave, its inscription praising him in the rhetorical conventions of the period for his "great intelligence and fidelity."[82]

Whether intermediaries such as Windich and Chuma felt affection for the explorers they served is more difficult to say. All we know for sure is that they found some sort of satisfaction from these challenging enterprises, most likely in terms of material reward but perhaps because they too enjoyed the adventure and the applause. John Piper, the guide whom Thomas Mitchell praised so fulsomely, demanded a horse, food, and clothing in compensation for his contribution to the expedition, and upon its return he also received a red coat, a cocked hat, and a brass plate engraved with the ironic words "Conqueror of the Interior."[83] Other early nineteenth-century Aboriginal guides were paid for their services with knives, guns, blankets, and other material goods. In later years, cash payments became more common. The expedition that Alfred Howitt led in search of Burke and Wills paid its two Aboriginal guides ten shillings per week; a decade later Peter Warburton paid his guide £10.[84] In the more monetized economy of Africa, headmen, guides, and other intermediaries usually expected cash payments. Men such as Bombay also made a profit from the private trade they conducted on the side. In both continents, moreover, intermediaries were quick to realize that their roles as expeditions' cultural gatekeepers gave them the power to extract sexual favors and other benefits from local peoples.[85] In Africa in particular, they often used their privileged positions to accumulate wives, slaves, and other dependents, thereby enhancing their own social standing.

It must be kept in mind that the deracinated status of these intermediaries made them fairly fluid in their loyalties. Most of them had no reason to embrace an identity that derived from claims of indigeneity; they were open to various modes of self-fashioning, including those offered by their explorer employers. While the brass plate that proclaimed John Piper a "Conqueror of the Interior" spoke to British preoccupations, there is no reason to assume that he disdained the designation. The clans whose territory the Mitchell expedition passed through were often as hostile to Piper as they were to the white members of the party, and he responded to them in kind. When a local man tried to spear Piper, he shot the attacker and "hammered out the fellow[']s brains with the Butt end of his piece."[86] Other intermediaries expressed their alienation from indigenous societies in other ways. Jacob Wainwright, one of the Nasik boys who carried Livingstone's body to the coast, kept a diary that resembled those written by British explorers, providing ethnographic commentary on "the character of the Wabisa Tribe," among others, and expressing moral condemnation of "wicked natives."[87] Like many of his counterparts, the Christian-educated Wainwright sought in some respects to emulate his British teachers and masters. At the same time, he was open to alternative models, spending several years, for example, as advisor and interpreter to Buganda's charismatic ruler, Mutesa. Some of the Aborigines who took part in expeditions were clearly drawn to the strength and dynamism exhibited by colonial culture in Australia. One Aboriginal guide, who had the rare privilege of being referred to as *Mr. Brown*, announced to the European members of his party that it was "his intention of becoming . . . 'a white fellow.' "[88] For many deracinated intermediaries who had lost their connections to kin and community, aspirations of this sort must have figured among the calculations that caused them to contribute to the exploration of Africa and Australia.

It should hardly be surprising to learn that the indigenous intermediaries who were commonly characterized in their time as loyal and simple servants—or, alternatively, as irascible scoundrels—were in fact far more complex figures whose relations with explorers were marked by conflict and co-dependency and whose lives were shaped by struggles to achieve some measure of autonomy and choice. The fact that historians have been trained to attend to agency, however, makes it all the more necessary that we seek to understand who the indigenous intermediaries involved in African and Australian expeditions actually were, where they came from, why they participated in these enterprises, and how they responded to their challenges and constraints. While written records rarely retain traces of these intermediaries' voices, the evidence these records do supply is sufficiently rich and varied to permit us to draw some general conclusions about how these individuals influenced the course and character of British exploration in Africa and Australia. In the broadest terms, we can say that these were men (rarely women) who had been deracinated by slavery, war, and colonialism; that they crafted careers for themselves that required much skill and provided them with material compensation; and that they helped to make expeditions much more complex and culturally hybrid enterprises than conventional accounts of exploration suggest.

Acknowledging and illuminating the integral role that these intermediaries played in the exploration of Africa and Australia obliges us in turn to reexamine the central epistemological premise that informed nineteenth-century exploration as a scientific enterprise. This premise held that the explorer's unmediated encounter with the places and peoples under investigation was the sole legitimating source of knowledge about their nature. Only information that derived directly from the explorer's own observations, enhanced by instruments of measurement, merited consideration as scientifically valid knowledge, and even then, it existed as a qualified knowledge, subject to review and reexamination by metropolitan experts. Not only was there no place in this evidentiary system for the local knowledge possessed by indigenous peoples, but for the most part their understanding of the environment they inhabited did not even merit the label "knowledge." Indigenous peoples came to be seen as the passive objects of scientific inquiry whose languages, customs, and other ethnographic characteristics were considered subject to the same classifying impulses that shaped botany, geology, and other fields of science.

Yet the abler explorers quickly learned that their prospects for success— indeed, their prospects for survival—depended in large measure on their ability to acquire access to local knowledge. And it was the intermediaries who for the most part provided that access. Their contributions to expeditions were commonly characterized in purely functional terms— that is to say, as a function of their ability to manage porters, track horses, find water, or pacify locals. This representation of their roles was in some sense true, but also inadequate and misleading. It failed to allow for the fact that the functions they carried out had epistemological underpinnings too, drawing on distinct and hard-earned bodies of knowledge. Unable to reconcile this system of knowledge with the one they were trained to utilize and promote, explorers either dismissed it as a set of instrumental practices or understood it as a secret knowledge, necessary but not suitable for acknowledgment. Insofar as they adopted the latter stance, explorers were confronted with an epistemological rupture between exploration as it was understood in principle and as it was experienced in practice. The only way they could cope with this intellectual dissonance was to adopt a dual set of criteria for determining what counted as knowledge: one criterion for application in the field, the other for dissemination at home. We may go further, in fact, and suggest that one consequence of this uneasy duality was that it turned some explorers themselves into culturally deracinated figures.

CHAPTER 7

Encounters

It is insufferable nonsense to talk of the right of an Englishman to travel unmolested wherever he may choose to go. Show us that travelling among these wild borderlands and through these disorganized tribes is reason; show it to be common sense and the means of attaining useful ends; but in heaven's name spare us all talk about the right.

—John Morley, *Fortnightly Review* (1876)

I N   T H E   C O U R S E of his famous expedition in search of the source of the White Nile, John Hanning Speke spent four and a half months in residence at the court of Mutesa, the *kabaka*, or king, of Buganda. The ostensible reason for this lengthy layover was to await the arrival of his companion, James Grant, who had been left to recuperate from a leg injury in the kingdom of Karagwe farther south. In an offer of hospitality, Buganda's queen mother sent Speke two girls, both probably slaves, to help him while away his time.[1] One of them was twelve, the other a few years older and "in the prime of youth and beauty." In his book *Journal of the Discovery of the Source of the Nile,* Speke claims that he "would rather have had princes, that I might have taken them home to be instructed in England," but he graciously accepted the queen mother's offer. He named the younger of the two girls Kahala, which simply meant "girl," and the older one Meri, "plantain." The three of them, he says, "became great friends." However, he also alludes to "a series of domestic difficulties" that led the queen mother to advise him to put the girls in irons until they had been "tamed." Instead, he insists that he was able to resolve the unstated difficulties by creating "cords of love, the only in-strument white men know the use of."[2] It requires little reading between the lines to infer that Speke had sexual relations with these girls. The armchair geographer James MacQueen certainly drew this inference. As part of his excoriating campaign to discredit Speke's claim to have dis-covered the source of the Nile, MacQueen did his best to destroy the explorer's personal reputation by accusing him of having bedded women and fathered children during his African adventure.[3]

Unpublished passages from Speke's journal both confirm and compli-cate the inferences MacQueen drew about the Ganda girls. Speke, it should be noted, refused to hand over his journal to the Royal Geo-graphical Society when he returned from Africa, and its subsequent fate is unknown. But the archives of Speke's publisher, Blackwood, contain a preliminary set of page proofs that the typesetters evidently transcribed directly from the original journal manuscript.[4] Various passages in these proofs were marked by editors for revision and deletion, including some especially revealing sections on Speke's troubled relations with Kahala and Meri.

A mere adolescent, Kahala figured less frequently in Speke's journal entries than Meri, but she clearly caused some of the domestic difficulties he alluded to in his book. She ran away from Speke at one point, though he does not say why. Sometime after her return, Speke threw her out of his residence because "she prefers to play with dirty little children." He was particularly put out with her because she had not "tended to me whilst sick" and had "caught the itch"—most likely scabies—which no doubt made her an undesirable bed partner. In consequence, he handed her "over to [Sidi] Bombay [his headman] as a wife." So much for the cords of love.[5]

Those cords were established, however, in Speke's relationship with Meri—though it was Speke, not Meri, who became entangled by them. This is evident from the drama that began to unfold on April 30, 1862, when Speke noted in his journal that Meri had been vomiting. Since she showed no other symptoms of illness, Speke suspected her of "sham-ming." That same day, Speke reports that one of Sidi Bombay's wives gave birth to a stillborn child soon after taking a dose of quinine. This incident may help to explain why Meri, who still felt unwell the following day, refused the "strengthening medicines" Speke prescribed for her. Was she pregnant? Did she fear the medicine would make her miscarry? Meri asked Speke instead to sacrifice a goat on her behalf, telling him that it "would prove that I loved her and her health would be restored to her at once." His reaction is revealing: "Oh God was I then a henpecked husband!" When he refused her request, Meri went behind his back, personally soliciting the services of a Ganda healer to sacrifice the goat. Speke was furious when he learned what had happened, and he ordered the man to receive fifty lashes. This action in turn outraged Meri, who insisted that if anyone deserved to be lashed, it was she. The couple had reached a point of no return, and Speke's syntactically clumsy but emotionally honest account of what transpired next and how it affected him deserves to be quoted at length:

> Meri would neither talk, walk nor do anything she was bid, aiming as it appeared at supremacy in the house, and in consequence showed neither love nor attachment for me, which broke my sleep and destroyed my rest[.] I divorced her on the spot. . . . I rushed out of the house with an overflowing heart and walked hurriedly about till after dark, when returning to my desolate abode, turned supperless into bed but slept not a wink that night, reflecting over the apparent cruelty of abandoning one who showed so much maidenly modesty when first she came to me. . . . Haunted all night by my fancied cruelty the first thing in the morning in symbolical language after Uganda fashion I sent Meri a goat in token I ever loved her and could do so now . . . , a black blanket as a sign of mourning that I never could win her heart[,] a bunch of gundu [?] in remembrance of her having once asked for them though . . . I thought they would ill become her pretty ankles. Lastly there was a packet of tobacco in proof of my forgiveness, though she had nearly broken my heart and for the future I only hoped she might live a life of happiness with people of her own color as she did not like the man because she did not know his language to understand him.[6]

This passage, along with others marked for deletion in the page proofs, leaves no doubt that Speke loved Meri and considered her something like a spouse. Meri made several visits to Speke after this incident—he described her on one of these occasions as being more "beautiful than ever"—but the couple never reconciled.[7] Their relationship, of course, was doomed in any case. Once Grant arrived in Buganda, Speke had no choice but to move on, and so he did. It is probable that Meri was pregnant when he departed. According to Roy Bridges, local Church Missionary Society records indicate that Speke fathered a daughter in Buganda.[8]

The tale Speke told in his journal could be read, depending on one's inclinations and purposes, as a touching love story, a maudlin soap opera, or a case of sexual slavery, but the more relevant point is that it could not be read at all by the British public. What placed it beyond the bounds of Victorian taste and rectitude was not merely the fact that Speke revealed he had had sexual liaisons with native women, which was, after all, an unspoken but hardly uncommon practice among British men in foreign lands, but also the fact that he confessed he had become emotionally attached to one of these women, which was much more troubling to his countrymen's confidence in their superiority, be it measured in religious or cultural or technological or racial terms. To succumb to the power of the heart in such a context was to betray the social values and ideological commitments the explorer was expected to embody. It posed the prospect of going native.

It is rare for explorers to allude to emotional relationships of the sort Speke acknowledges in his journal. Whether this was a rarity of commission rather than a rarity of confession is difficult to know for sure. Many explorers no doubt sought to maintain an emotional and physical distance from indigenous peoples, but the demand for discretion usually prevented those who did not from acknowledging the fact. There were plenty of opportunities for intimate encounters for those who were so inclined: explorers often interacted with native peoples on a daily basis over a period of weeks or months, relying on them for food, water, shelter, and—surely—sex, companionship, and other forms of sociability. What exactly transpired in the course of these quotidian encounters is often unrecorded, but its influence on explorers' understandings of these peoples and their environments, not to mention its effects on their own emotional well-being, should not be underestimated. It was another manifestation of the secret knowledge that proved so essential to their success in the field, but irrelevant if not subversive to the truth claims they made when they returned from their journeys.

One of the principal tasks of explorers was to gather information about the peoples with whom they came in contact. As agents of scientific inquiry, they were expected to give meticulous scrutiny to indigenous populations, describing their physical features, observing their social practices and customs, inspecting their modes of production and exchange, detailing their systems of governance, gathering lexical and grammatical information about the languages they spoke, and more. In short, they were expected to act as ethnographers. Yet they rarely spent a sufficient length of time among any one group of people to acquire much more than a superficial grasp of the societies with which they came in contact. As John and Richard Landers frankly confessed, "It would require a long residence in this country, and a perfect acquaintance with its language, to enable a foreigner to form a correct judgment of its laws, manners, customs, and institutions, as well as its religion and the form and nature of its government. . . . We can only answer for what we *see*."[9]

Inevitably, explorers filtered what they saw through interpretive lenses that were shaped by ethnocentric assumptions and expectations. British (and, more broadly, European) ideas of difference informed how they made sense of African and Aboriginal character and capabilities. As these ideas altered over time, so too did explorers' understanding of the indigenes with whom they interacted.

Much of the commentary on Africans and Aborigines by early nineteenth-century explorers drew in varying degrees on Enlightenment ideas about racial categories, romantic tropes of noble savages, and evangelical notions of moral redemption. An important contributor to the Enlightenment's understanding of race was the German scientist Johann Blumenbach, whose influential classificatory schema divided humans into five distinct racial groups. Not only did he lay some of the intellectual foundations for nineteenth-century scientific racism, but he also had a more direct impact on African exploration by mentoring several of the young men—notably Friedrich Hornemann and Johann Ludwig Burckhardt—who entered the continent on behalf of the African Association. Enlightenment thought, it should be stressed, was hardly monolithic in its attitudes toward race. It also produced a more sympathetic tradition of inquiry into other cultures, evident, for example, in Blumenbach's fellow German, Alexander von Humboldt, who was a sharp critic of New World slavery. He too had acolytes who explored Africa and Australia, including Heinrich Barth and Ludwig Leichhardt.

A number of early explorers, especially in Australia, drew on romantic rhetoric that extolled the virtues of noble savages. Captain Cook voiced such sentiments in a key journal entry about the Aborigines he observed during the days his ship was beached for repair along the Queensland coast. "They are far happier than we Europeans," he asserted: "They live in a Tranquillity which is not disturb'd by the Inequality of Condition."[10] Similarly, Thomas Mitchell expressed a "feeling of regret, that civilized man, enervated by luxury and all its concomitant diseases, should ever disturb the haunts of these rude but happy beings." Mitchell's sincerity can be questioned, however. Elsewhere in his narrative he wrote about the "hideous . . . fiendish . . . savages" who threatened him at one stage in his expedition. According to one of his lieutenants, he referred to Aborigines as "the *Devil*[']*s people.*"[11] Mitchell's feelings may have fluctuated in response to the ways indigenous people reacted to him and his party, or he may simply have sought to appeal to more than one audience. The result, however, was rhetorical dissonance about whether Aborigines were noble or wicked savages.

Perhaps the most important intellectual influence on early nineteenth-century explorers' views of Africans and Aborigines was evangelicalism, which preached that all peoples shared a common humanity as children of God. While the Australian explorers Edward Eyre and George Grey would institute notoriously ruthless policies toward colonized peoples during their subsequent careers as colonial governors, both of them expressed decidedly humanitarian sentiments about Aborigines in the expedition narratives that originally brought them public acclaim. Eyre in particular sought to show that the continent's native peoples were the innocent victims of violence by predatory settlers, not the savage perpetrators of unprovoked attacks on his countrymen. Virtually the entire second volume of his book is given over to a knowledgeable and sympathetic study of the "Manners and Customs of the Aborigines of Australia." So too is a substantial portion of the second volume of Grey's expedition narrative.[12]

In light of Africa's associations with the British slave trade and the abolitionist campaign against it, it is hardly surprising that evangelical humanitarian sentiments were particularly prevalent among early nineteenth-century Africa explorers. Such sentiments assumed a central place in many West African expedition narratives, especially those written by Macgregor Laird, William Balfour Baikie, and the survivors of the Niger expedition of 1841. All of them placed great faith in the capacity of Africans to achieve moral and material improvement. No one, however, did more to establish an association between evangelical humanitarianism and African exploration than David Livingstone, who characterized Africans as the victims of Arab and Portuguese slave traders and called for their redemption through commerce and Christianity. He cast such a long shadow over those African explorers who came after him that they felt obligated to give at least rhetorical obeisance to his views, despite a shift in the latter part of the century toward a much harsher, more racialist stance, one that cast doubt on the ability of Africans to advance to anything resembling civilization as Europeans defined it.

Not even Livingstone, of course, was immune to racism, especially regarding those he referred to as "half-castes."[13] Such sentiments were even more pronounced in the private journals of his principal assistant on the Zambezi expedition, John Kirk. Kirk considered the mixed-race children of Portuguese colonists to be "abortions both in mind and body" and believed "it would be a charity to twist their necks and keep down such things which are a disgrace to the European name." He was not especially enamored with Livingstone's Makololo allies either, believing there was no point in making "fools of them by supposing they are equal to ourselves." Kirk, it should be added, held in contempt almost everyone other than his fellow Britons: "We would not call a Frenchman a brother and it is not likely we shall begin with niggers," even if "they are decent fellows for savages."[14]

As Livingstone's protégé, Kirk took care not to air such opinions publicly, but they were indicative of the turn toward a much harsher assessment of non-Western peoples. Pronouncements about the innate inferiority and eventual disappearance of other races became increasingly commonplace in the second half of the century. Among explorers of Africa, Richard Burton led the way, establishing himself as a leading proponent of the polygenist view that Africans were a separate and degraded species of humankind, unfit for anything other than brute labor. Speke, his erstwhile companion, began his book by proclaiming that Africans were the cursed descendants of Ham, condemned to a state of backwardness by their banishment from God's providence. Francis Galton's narrative of his expedition into Namibia offered a preview of his ideas about the immutability of heredity, which led him to develop eugenics. He observed, for example, that "the Hottentots about me had that peculiar set of features which is so characteristic of bad characters in England . . . known by the name of 'felon face.' "[15] Inspired in part by Darwinian theory, other explorers took to comparing Africans' physiognomies to those of monkeys and other apes.

Similar racist rhetoric appeared in the writings of late nineteenth-century Australian explorers. David Carnegie claimed to have been reminded of "the monkey-house at the 'Zoo' " by the gestures of a hostile band of Aborigines who opposed his entry into their territory.[16] Ernest Giles aimed to amuse his readers by offering a description of an elderly Aborigine who "was so monkey-like he would have charmed the heart of Professor Darwin, and I had some thoughts of preserving him, but I had not a bottle large enough."[17] Like many explorers of his generation, Giles subscribed to the social Darwinist conviction that Aborigines were a dying race who would soon disappear from the face of the earth.

Explorers' commentaries about indigenous peoples invariably reflected the ideas of difference prevalent in their own society at the time they wrote their travel narratives. These commentaries were intended in most instances to appeal to the domestic audiences who attended their lectures and read their books. What influence such views may have had on explorers' encounters with Africans and Aborigines is more difficult to determine. Conditions on the ground created their own dynamic, obliging explorers to modify their assumptions and expectations in response to the circumstances they faced. A prolonged period of close contact with indigenes could cause the erosion of the sense of superiority that racialist doctrines rested on. So too could the influence that local peoples and polities often exerted over expeditions, exposing these intruders' vulnerabilities. How explorers engaged with the inhabitants of the territories through which they passed often had far less to do with whatever ethnocentric beliefs they may have shared with their countrymen than they did with the balance of power in these quotidian encounters.

Buganda, the kingdom where Speke made his abortive bid for domestic bliss, was one of a number of notable states that could be found across the African continent. These states had sizable populations, substantial resources, and significant power. Explorers were often impressed and even cowed by their might. Until the late nineteenth-century European scramble for colonies transformed the political landscape of Africa, most of the explorers who came in contact with indigenous rulers took care to treat them with respect, recognizing their legitimacy as sovereigns and requesting permission to travel through their territory. They even found it necessary in many instances to acknowledge the jurisdiction of lesser chiefs and headmen, who wielded sufficient power to demand gifts, transit fees, and other levies from merchants and wayfarers. Even highly decentralized acephalous societies, which lacked any discernible political institutions or hierarchies, were capable of mobilizing their populations to prevent expeditions from taking particular routes or influencing them in other ways. Across Africa, explorers' reliance on local communities for food, shelter, labor, and other resources gave these people considerable sway over expeditions.

A very different sociopolitical environment confronted Australian explorers. Although Aboriginal communities were culturally complex, they were demographically dispersed, politically fragmented, and economically limited by their hunter-gatherer mode of production. Organized in relatively small clan and tribal groups, they had limited power to prevent or manage the passage of explorers through their territories. Lacking the food surpluses and other resources available to agricultural societies, they could not draw these alien intruders into positions of dependency. Nor did their political economy give them the motives or means to impose tolls or other regulatory demands on explorers. While they were certainly capable of organizing sustained and potent opposition to European incursions, their numbers and weaponry placed limits on the scale and form of their resistance.

Explorers were well aware that the balance of power generally favored them, and they behaved accordingly. In consequence, relations between Australian explorers and Aborigines took a strikingly different trajectory than they did between explorers and indigenes in Africa. The contrast needs to be contextualized and qualified, of course: conditions and responses varied from place to place, as well as over time. But the general patterns are sufficiently striking and pervasive to confirm that explorers confronted very different power dynamics in the two continents, causing them to adopt very different strategies of engagement with indigenous peoples.

The official instructions drafted for Australian explorers by their sponsors invariably included passages that stressed the importance of avoiding violent clashes with Aborigines. "The greatest forbearance & discretion in treating with the Aborigines, is strongly impressed & urged upon the traveller," the Royal Geographical Society informed George Grey in the instructions for his 1837 expedition. "As all exploring expeditions in this country are sent out with a view to future colonization, it is of the utmost importance to make friends with the natives; to avoid familiarity with the females, a common sources of quarrels; never to allow a fancied insult to provoke retaliation, rather submit to trifling vexations than risk creating ill will & perhaps bloodshed." The document added an enlightened flourish: "it should be remembered theirs is the right of the soil—we are the intruders."[18] Augustus Gregory was similarly instructed by the colonial authorities who sponsored his 1848 expedition from Perth that "it is no less impolitic than cruel to come into actual collision . . . with the natives," explaining that settlers might suffer the consequences of any ill-will caused by such an event.[19] And John Septimus Roe, the surveyor general of Western Australia, penned the following advice to John Forrest in preparation for his 1869 expedition: "In your intercourse with the aborigines of the interior, many of whom will have no previous personal knowledge of the white man, I need scarcely commend to you a policy of kindness and forbearance mixed with watchfulness and firmness, as their future bearing towards our remote colonists may be chiefly moulded by early impressions."[20]

It is scarcely surprising that authorities did not want indigenous peoples to come away from their encounters with explorers with a hostile view of the white settlers who were likely to follow. At the same time, it is evident that circumstances often made conflict between explorers and indigenes hard to avoid. The intractable history of violence between colonists and natives in Australia provides the backdrop and impetus for these instructions. More than thirty years before Roe advised Forrest of the value of self-restraint, for example, he himself had led an expedition that can best be described as punitive in intent. Composed of four mounted police and ten soldiers, it killed between fifteen and twenty Aboriginal men and captured eight women and several children.[21]

If settler colonization provided the violent backdrop to explorers' encounters with Aborigines, mutual incomprehension and suspicion informed its immediate context. Even explorers who sincerely sought to avoid clashes with the peoples they encountered on their journeys were sorely tempted to use force. Shortly before his departure as second-in-command of Mitchell's 1845–1846 expedition, Edmund Kennedy reported that the governor "gave me a long lecture about [not] shooting the Blacks." After leading his own expedition a few years later, he proudly announced upon his return "that we had to shoot none [of the Aborigines] . . . although . . . twice I allowed them to throw at me with impunity and on one occasion suffered a man to whiz a boomerang across my face . . . and yet did not give him the contents of a pistol I had."[22] His journal of this expedition also reveals, however, that his party often drove hostile Aborigines away by firing shots over their heads and he came close to aiming lower: "The kindness and forbearance, it is our duty to shew towards such savages, create in them a degree of boldness and daring, not at all times to be checked, I fear, without a severe example."[23] As it happened, Kennedy's final expedition did eventuate in a "severe example," though not quite the kind he had in mind: Cape York Aborigines speared him to death.

Because "we were rather unceremonious invaders of their country," acknowledged Kennedy's mentor, Thomas Mitchell, "it was certainly my duty to conciliate them [the Aborigines] by every possible means." Yet he was sure that "these people cannot be so obtuse as not to anticipate in the advance of such a powerful race, the extirpation of their own," and he consequently assumed that they would feel motivated to strike out against the agents of their destruction. Thus, "notwithstanding all our gifts and endeavours to be on friendly terms," he was not surprised when "a state of warfare" occasionally broke out with local peoples.[24] For all his protestations of friendly intentions, however, Mitchell and his men almost certainly caused some of the hostility they encountered. According to one rumor, several members of his party lured an Aboriginal woman to camp with the offer of a kettle, then raped and killed her, along with her child.[25] On another occasion, Mitchell admitted launching a preemptive strike against a group of Aborigines whom he suspected of scheming to massacre his party. His rival Charles Sturt, who subsequently passed through the same region, accused Mitchell of having committed "the most fearful acts of cold blooded murder." Sturt's account of the incident suggests he may have interviewed some of its survivors. Not only was the attack unprovoked, he insisted, but it concluded with Mitchell and his men systematically killing "the wounded both of men and women laying on the Ground."[26]

Expedition journals, especially unpublished ones, are replete with reports of bloody encounters with local peoples. Frederick Walker, founder of the notoriously violent Queensland native police force, led an expedition in search of Burke and Wills that "had many difficulties with the blacks and was obliged to kill many."[27] Angered by some Aborigines who had attempted to sneak up on his camp one night, William Landsborough announced that he "fully intended to shoot at them if we had a chance," and when that chance arose, he acted on his intentions.[28] John McKinlay led a surprise attack on a camp of some 200 Aborigines after one of his men was killed in the Northern Territory in 1865.[29] John Forrest detailed at least three occasions when his party fired on Aborigines during his third expedition, insisting that it was "the only way of saving our lives."[30] James Ricketson, the member of a private expedition financed by some pastoral companies, made no excuses for the murders he and his party committed. These included one member of an Aboriginal family, an old man, who was judged a threat because he carried a boomerang.[31]

Is it any wonder, then, that so many Aborigines either fled or froze in fright at the first sight of explorers? This was especially true of those individuals who happened to be hunting or foraging alone in the bush when expeditionary parties surprised them. John McDouall Stuart describes encountering one man whose initial response was to stand "riveted to the spot, with his mouth wide open, and his eyes staring." After gathering his wits, he climbed to the top of a tree, where the "poor fellow trembled from head to foot and could not utter a word."[32] Similar accounts of fear and flight appear repeatedly in explorers' journals. Some of these terrified individuals may have been catching their first glimpse of white men (not to mention the horses and camels that accompanied them), while others were undoubtedly responding to what they already had heard or knew from firsthand experience about how dangerous these intruders could be. A British sailor who had been shipwrecked and lived among Aborigines for seventeen years reported that they were "in great dread of the whites, from an incurable notion of their cruelty and murderous intentions toward them."[33]

Other Aborigines, however, were remarkably friendly and helpful to explorers. During Alexander Forrest's 1879 expedition into northwest Australia he received frequent visits from locals, who advised him on where to find water along his route: he gratefully acknowledged "following the natives' guidance."[34] One "extremely well made and good looking" group of Aborigines assisted Ludwig Leichhardt and his men in a hunt for wild honey.[35] Aborigines were often eager to trade, exchanging wild game, opossum cloaks, and dilly bags for tomahawks, knives, and blankets. Sometimes they simply appeared at explorers' camps for curiosity's sake. They would "collect around us," wrote an early explorer in Western Australia, "burst into roars of laughter, eye us from head to foot, pull our clothes and seem anxious to touch every thing we possessed excepting our guns, which they much dreaded."[36] (As that concluding clause indicates, even friendly Aborigines were well aware that these strangers could turn deadly.) When McKinlay's expedition in northern Australia was not engaged in punitive raids against hostile

Aborigines, it was encountering others who were "very affectionate," throwing their arms around the reluctant explorers.[37] According to a member of Edmund Kennedy's first expedition, Aborigines who visited their camp "were of most lively disposition and were excellent mimics and any little peculiarity of any of our party they imitated exactly."[38] Other explorers noted Aborigines' skill at mimicking their manners and expressions as well. Were these instances of mimicry evidence of what Homi Bhabha has identified as a subversive strategy of the weak?[39]

These seemingly genial encounters often came to an abrupt end as explorers or indigenes crossed some line that offended or frightened the other party. Each group had codes of sociability and reciprocity that the other either failed to understand or chose to ignore. This was especially true when Aborigines offered their women to members of expeditions. "Our Sable friends were very generous offering the Dr. [Leichhardt] the services of a gin," reported a member of his party in one such incident.[40] In another case, "the women commenced pelting the party [of Augustus Gregory] with stones, apparently in revenge for the refusal of certain courteous invitations" of a similar sort.[41] Such offers were common expressions of hospitality by Aborigines, but they also carried expectations of social obligations by the recipients of these sexual favors, since they entailed kinship bonds.[42] Most explorers knew that this was the case, and many of them took care to keep native women out of their camps. Sturt, who was convinced that Mitchell's troubles with Aborigines could be traced to his permissiveness in this matter, announced at the start of his own central Australian expedition that he opposed "all communication with the Natives, particularly with the Women, and assured the party that any breach of this order would be visited by me with the very utmost severity."[43] The temptation, however, was too much for many men, especially after many lonely months in the outback. Inevitably, Aborigines who anticipated gifts or expressions of reciprocity in return for their generosity were disappointed, becoming confused and angry.

Explorers also caused antagonism when they hunted game, drank water, and exploited other resources relied upon by indigenous communities without obtaining those communities' permission or offering them compensation. In some cases, Aboriginal guides no doubt sought through customary means to gain the approval of the local inhabitants, but ex-

plorers either did not know what they were doing or chose not to acknowledge it, especially since it ran directly at odds with the foundational premise of the colonial regime—that the native peoples had no
claim to the land and its resources. A rare exception can be found in the
journal of Alfred Turner, a member of Kennedy's first expedition, who
notes that a particular group of Aborigines *"gave us permission* to en-
camp" in their territory, and that Kennedy decided to move camp the
next day so as not to "inconvenience our Black friends."[44]

It was more often the case that explorers pushed through territories
with little consideration for the sensitivities or needs of the indigenous
inhabitants. They usually killed any game they could find, and their
large herds of horses, camels, oxen, and sheep placed enormous pressures on water resources in arid regions. Sturt estimated that his party
consumed 1,200 gallons of water per day.[45] Water became one of the
primary causes of conflict between explorers and indigenes. Kennedy,
who showed such admirable consideration for indigenous rights at one
stage in his expedition, drove off a group of Aborigines at another when
his party reached one of the area's scarce water holes, where the "horses
made an end of the water at this camp."[46] The ruthless David Carnegie
drained more than one well "of almost every drop it contained" during
his expedition through the Western Australian desert.[47] No wonder explorers so often encountered such fierce resistance from native peoples.
Ernest Giles, whose journey across the deserts of central Australia in
1873–1874 provoked repeated attacks from Aborigines, probably was not
too far off the mark when he speculated that the angry Aborigines who
so often harangued him and his companions in languages they did not
understand were probably calling them

> a vile and useless set of lazy crawling wretches, that came on hid-
> eous brutes of animals, being too lazy to walk like black men, and
> took upon ourselves the right to occupy any country or water we
> might chance to find; that we killed and ate any wallabies we hap-
> pened to see, thereby depriving him and his friends of their natural
> and lawful game, and that our conduct had so incensed himself and
> his noble friends . . . that he begged us to take warning that [they
> meant] . . . to drive us from the face of the earth.[48]

Giles, of course, was unmoved by these objections, as were his fellow explorers. But they were not unfazed by the acts of resistance that frequently followed. Firearms gave explorers some technological advantage over Aborigines in clashes, though not as much as might be supposed in the first half of the century, when guns had limited range and reliability.[49] While this advantage increased over time, they continued to fear surprise attacks by indigenes. As a result, Australian explorers were acutely susceptible to rumor-mongering and panic.

It was Mitchell's "fear of the natives" that led him to commit his terrible crimes, according to Sturt.[50] Elsewhere, Sturt observed that the commander of an expedition had an obligation

> not to mistake natural alarm for hostility. He will find his men ready enough to fly to their arms, for their fears are easily raised, but the Leader . . . should on no account allow a shot to be fired, excepting on his express command for let a collision once take place between a party and the natives, no matter how strong the former may be, and the utility of the Expedition is at once destroyed. No individual will thenceforth be certain at what moment he may not have a spear through his body.[51]

Sturt certainly knew whereof he spoke. During his 1844–1846 expedition he received a false report that Aborigines had murdered fifteen Europeans in a region he was passing through, and he prepared for a possible attack: "I fear we shall have some bloody work with these fellows," he wrote in his journal, adding that "I should not have much hesitation in giving them [the supposed perpetrators] a wholesome lesson." After several days of "perpetual watching and anxiety," he and his men were impatient for a confrontation. Fortunately, no Aborigines had the misfortune to cross their path during this period of panic.[52]

Anxieties about Aborigines' intentions were widespread among explorers. All of them knew of pastoralists, prospectors, and other frontiersmen who had been killed or wounded by Aborigines, and they too had faced attacks and experienced losses. George Grey was speared by an Aborigine during his first expedition. Richard Cunningham, the botanist for Mitchell's second expedition, got lost while collecting plants, and although he was initially welcomed by the Aborigines who found him, they reportedly grew suspicious when he got up repeatedly during the night, so they decided to kill him. Two of Ernest Giles's traveling companions during his early years in Australia had lost their lives in attacks by Aborigines.[53] Like Giles, many of the men who took up exploration had clashed with Aborigines in the past.

Any large congregation of Aborigines aroused explorers' suspicions. All too often, they simply could not discern the intentions of these groups. Mitchell describes an occasion during his first expedition when he was not sure whether the hundred or so Aborigines who appeared near his camp intended to attack his party or invite them to a corroboree.[54] Explorers took care to avoid regions they knew to be heavily populated. William Landsborough "travelled longer than usual" at one point in his expedition "as I wished to get out of the neighbourhood of some blacks." Four days later he stopped for a day's rest because "we did not think the blacks in the neighbourhood were numerous or dangerous."[55] Ludwig Leichhardt's party took the trouble to pack up and move on at one stage in its journey because, according to one member, the "blacks [are] getting very troublesome, could not keep them out of camp."[56] Expeditions generally kept armed watches through the night when passing through areas with large and potentially hostile Aboriginal populations. The members of John McDouall Stuart's 1862 expedition, who had been instructed from the start to sleep with their guns at the ready, had to maintain nightly watches when they ran into resistance in the Northern Territory. John Forrest's party did so during the entirety of its expedition in 1874.[57] For men who were already worn down by the physical demands of their arduous journeys, the loss of sleep these night watches required taxed them to the limit. During one particularly tense stage in an expedition commanded by John McKinlay, he and his men rotated nightly watches and slept in their clothes with firearms at their side. When at last they went several days without seeing any Aborigines, "we shall have no watch to keep to-night, the first time for some months."[58]

Some clans waged well-organized campaigns of resistance against explorers who entered their land. Ludwig Leichhardt's first expedition was nearing its goal of Port Essington when a number of Aborigines suddenly descended on his camp, spearing to death one member of his party and severely wounding two others, one of whom was riddled with five spears. (A participant in the expedition who escaped injury judged Leichhardt guilty of "culpable negligence" for failing to require regular watches.)[59] Aborigines used a range of tactics to stymie explorers and thwart their firepower. They set fire to the surrounding brush to drive the explorers away. They launched hit-and-run attacks to avoid direct assaults. The members of the Burke and Wills base camp came under a prolonged siege from a hundred or so Aborigines, during which time several of them died of scurvy.[60] Burke and Wills's competitor, John McDouall Stuart, was prevented from reaching the Gulf of Carpentaria by a contingent of warriors who organized a shrewd and determined military campaign to prevent his passage through their territory. Stuart concluded that his party was "far too small, to cope with such wily determined natives . . . their arrangements & manner of attack were well conducted & planned as well as Europeans could."[61]

In cases like these, Aborigines' encounters with explorers seemed all but indistinguishable from their encounters with pastoralists, prospectors, and other agents of settler colonialism. While engagement between the two parties on grounds of mutual interest were not impossible, it was not common. The circumstances that structured the conditions of exploration in Australia meant that most explorers maintained their distance from indigenous peoples, regarding them with suspicion and benefiting from their experience and knowledge only in periods of desperation.

African explorers and their sponsors gave far less attention than their Australian counterparts to the need to avoid acts of violence against indigenous peoples. This was not because violence was more acceptable in the African context. Rather, it was because violence was less viable for African explorers. The balance of power tended to favor Africans until the late nineteenth century, which meant that explorers were more likely to come out on the losing end of any conflicts that might arise. Sponsors consequently saw less need to caution explorers to avoid conflict and seek conciliation.

This was one of the principal lessons to be drawn from Mungo Park's two expeditions into West Africa. The memorable account he gave of his first journey from the Gambia to the upper reaches of the Niger River stressed his vulnerability.[62] Robbed, beaten, and abused in countless other ways, Park was by his own telling fortunate to have survived the ordeal. He aimed in his second expedition to avoid a similar outcome by traveling in the company of armed troops. This resulted in violent clashes with local peoples and, according to some reports, the murder of Park and those members of his party who did not die of disease. What his two expeditions demonstrated was how difficult it was to pass through African territory without the cooperation of native peoples.

Almost every explorer who entered the continent thereafter learned that Africans usually held the upper hand in encounters between the two parties. One of the most striking examples was Major Peddie's disastrous military-style expedition into the interior of Guinea, trapped for years in the web spun by the Almamy of Bondoo. Other cases abound. During his expedition up the Niger River, Macgregor Laird and his party were unable to escape from the clutches of the ruler of Fundah until they fired off rockets and frightened him into releasing them.[63] In the course of their march to Lake Victoria, Speke and Grant were so often detained by local rulers demanding *hongo* and gifts that "the wonder is they did not take everything from us."[64] Samuel Baker voiced a very similar complaint about the relentless demands of Africans he encountered during his journey up the Nile. Matters only got worse when he reached the interlacustrine state of Bunyoro, where he and his party were held hostage in an apparent attempt to prevent raids by Arab slave traders. Still stinging from the experience a decade later, he told Charles "Chinese" Gordon that the people of Bunyoro "had me at all times in their power."[65] Joseph Thomson felt similarly helpless during his encounter with the Warua people in 1880. These "outrageous scoundrels & thieves" showed "no respect for the white man," demanding "exorbitant mhongo," threatening the expedition with violence, and sending it back the way it had come. "How we ever escaped with our lives," Thomson concluded, "I cannot comprehend."[66]

African explorers' sense of vulnerability was made manifest in more mundane ways as well. When they passed through villages and towns they frequently attracted large crowds of people, who were eager to see these strange men with their white skins, sharp features, and peculiar dress. Once again, Mungo Park was one of the first explorers to highlight what became an enduring motif of narratives of African exploration. Local peoples considered his appearance "unsightly and unnatural," some of them responding with revulsion, while others were fascinated by his freakishness. The residents of one town speculated that when he was a child his skin must have been dipped in milk to whiten it and his nose pinched to make it longer. Park claims that women were particularly eager to get a glimpse of him. On one occasion, some Muslim women wanted to inspect his penis to see if he had been circumcised. Everywhere he went he found himself the object of relentless scrutiny.[67]

Africans' intrusive curiosity became a common refrain among explorers. According to John Hanning Speke, he and Richard Burton passed through villages so thick with Africans eager to catch a glimpse of them "that nothing short of a stick could keep them from jostling me."[68] The "hundreds of curious niggers" who stared at the European members of David Livingstone's Zambezi expedition made John Kirk feel as though he and his companions were "wild beasts in a show."[69] Livingstone himself wearied of the "unlimited staring" he endured, writing in his journal during his last expedition that "it is as much as I can stand when a crowd will follow me wherever I move."[70] James Grant found that there "was not the slightest privacy even inside our tents; they were certain to peer in."[71] Similarly, "a mob of natives came and squatted close to me to stare," complained Verney Lovett Cameron, who found them especially curious about his shoes and socks, his glasses, and his writing instruments: "I shifted 3 or 4 times in the vain hope of getting clear of them but it was no good."[72] Not only could Joseph Thomson not keep inquisitive Africans out of his tent, but he had to submit to their physical examination: they "touch me on the face, feel my hair, push up the sleeve of my coat, and examine with intense curiosity my boots."[73]

Where possible, explorers sought to escape this type of intrusive gaze by traveling in disguise. This stratagem was feasible in those regions inhabited or frequented by Arabs, Berbers, and other lighter-skinned Muslim peoples. Europeans living in North Africa often adopted so-called Turkish dress, both for reasons of comfort and to escape undue notice. In light of the unwelcome attention Mungo Park received during his first expedition, Joseph Banks concluded that it might be wise for future explorers to adopt disguises.[74] As a result, Friedrich Hornemann, the next explorer sent out by the African Association, prepared himself by adopting Turkish dress and learning Arabic in Cairo. "Pray, Sir," he wrote to Banks shortly before his departure for sub-Saharan Africa, "do not look on me as a European but as a real African." This bravado proved premature. When doubts about his identity were raised by members of the caravan he accompanied, he retreated to Tripoli and reinvented himself as a European convert to Islam.[75] The association's strategy met with greater success when Johann Ludwig Burckhardt, the great Swiss explorer, traveled up the Nile, across the Red Sea, and into Arabia and Syria in the guise of Shaykh Ibrahim ibn Abdallah. When Heinrich Barth carried out his equally remarkable journey through West Africa at midcentury, he donned a "half-Sudanic, half-Arab garb," assumed an Arab identity and sobriquet, and even stained his skin. Although his Muslim friends evidently knew he was a European Christian, he did adopt an Islamic persona during the month he spent in Timbuktu, where it was considered too risky to reveal his true identity.[76]

Even in those parts of Africa frequently by Arabs, however, some explorers learned that this masquerade had its limits. Richard Burton, who famously made the hajj to Mecca in the guise of a Pathan Muslim, was unable to replicate this feat during his subsequent journey to the closed Somali city of Harar (now in Ethiopia). A rumor spread that he was actually a European or a Turk, forcing him to give up the disguise before he reached the city gates. The pasha of Tripoli advised Dixon Denham and his companions Hugh Clapperton and Walter Oudney to travel openly as Englishmen and Christians, insisting that "do what you will, no living creature will take you for a Mahometan."[77] When Alexander Laing followed much the same route from Tripoli across the Sahara a few years later, he adopted "Turkish" dress but made no effort to deny his identity to the inhabitants of the towns he passed through. At one point,

> upwards of a thousand people of both sexes came out to meet me, and
> so surrounded my Camel that I had much difficulty in proceeding. . . .

As nothing but my eyes were yesterday visible the curiosity of the
multitude was not gratified, and my poor attendants were beleagued
with a thousand questions—Is he white? Is his hair like a Turk's?
Has he a beard? . . . I was glad to get into my quarters where I
hoped for a little repose, but even there the curious made their way,
and absolutely dragged me from the dark chamber . . . into the open
air that they might see me better; this however did not suffice, and
they requested I wou'd oblige them by mounting upon the terraced
roof, with which request although reluctantly I complied, and to my
surprise found on an adjoining Terrace an assemblage of nearly a
hundred women waiting in eager expectation to see me, staring with
outstretched neck.

In order to prevent some of these inquisitive residents from barging into
his quarters, Laing eventually resorted to nailing his door shut.[78]

It was not Africans' curiosity per se that demands attention here, but
rather the confident, assertive way they sought to satisfy it. Apart from
children and others who occasionally fled at the first sight of these pale-
skinned strangers, Africans felt no fear in their presence. They scrutinized explorers with a frank and relentless determination that stands in
challenging contradistinction to the "imperial gaze" that so many scholars in recent years have attributed to the explorers themselves. The imperial gaze refers in this analysis to the discursive power explorers held
over Africans and other non-Western peoples, a power derived from
their claims to scientific objectivity and supposed freedom from the constraints of place or particularity, permitting them to scrutinize with an
authority that mirrored and manifested imperialism itself.[79] Explorers'
written accounts of what they observed on their journeys did, to be sure,
include stereotypical statements about the innate primitiveness of Africans, the untapped potential of Africa, and so forth, assertions that certainly would serve to rationalize imperial conquest. But what was at
work here was the way explorers represented Africa and Africans in the
accounts they wrote for British readers. Insofar as the actual gaze itself
can be characterized as a manifestation of power, it appears to have been
vested far more fully in the attention Africans directed toward explorers
than vice versa.

Richard Lander, posing in the "Oriental" garb that aided passage through the interior of West Africa. *Source: Library of Congress.*

Furthermore, Africans were no less inclined than Europeans to characterize those who were the objects of their gaze in terms that mocked or demonized them. A few examples should suffice. When Hugh Clapperton arrived at the court of the king of Yoruba during his second expedition, he was treated to a theatrical performance that included a humorous caricature of the white man—not so different, perhaps, from the mimicry Aborigines engaged in. Later in the same journey, his assistant, Richard Lander, encountered a group of Tuaregs who asked him if his countrymen "had tails like monkeys."[80] And explorers encountered

Africans all across the continent who believed that Europeans ate human flesh. Mungo Park heard this charge from West Africans, David Livingstone from southern Africans, and Richard Burton from East Africans.[81] We even have firsthand testimony from James Dorugu, the Hausa camel boy who was placed in the service of the explorer Adolf Overweg. Frightened by this man whose "face and hands were all white like paper," Dorugu wondered "if he were about to eat me."[82] Such a response supplies an ironic counterpoint to the widespread suspicion among explorers themselves that certain African tribes were cannibals.

Other Africans had a more realistic appreciation of the dangers explorers posed. For many traders, there was an understandable suspicion that these interlopers intended to break into markets they controlled. John Davidson found that Moroccan merchants in the town where he waited for a caravan to cross the Sahara expressed "fear lest I should divert a most lucrative trade into another channel."[83] His murder soon thereafter may have been carried out to forestall this possibility. An Arab trader in Sokoto voiced his concern to Hugh Clapperton that British merchants would follow in his footsteps and undercut the caravan trade from Fezzan and Tripoli. Clapperton also was closely questioned by Mohammed Bello, the emir of Sokoto, who had been warned by the ruler of Bornu that the explorer was a spy, gathering information the British intended to use to conquer Bello's country.[84] When Alexander Laing arrived in Timbuktu soon thereafter, Bello passed this warning on to Seku Amadu, ruler of the neighboring Massina empire, who evidently ordered Laing's assassination.[85] West Africa's Muslim emirs were well informed about British imperial expansion in India and elsewhere, and they were understandably apprehensive about what might happen to their own lands. One of them told Dixon Denham that the British "eat the whole country—they are no friends."[86] Nor were they the only ones to harbor such suspicions. When Samuel Baker arrived at the outpost of Gondokoro on the upper Nile, some of the Arabs there regarded him as a spy. So did some of the Herero chiefs with whom Francis Galton came in contact during his expedition in Namibia.[87]

As the fates of Davidson and Laing demonstrated, suspicions about explorers' intentions could turn deadly. West African travelers did what they could to guard against attacks, but the resources at their disposal were limited. Heinrich Barth, for example, traveled through the region with a double-barreled gun and two pistols, weapons that might ward off attack by bandits but provided scant protection against more substantial threats. The only expeditions that were prepared to repel organized assaults from West African peoples and polities were those that steamed up the Niger River under the command of Laird in 1832–1834, Allen in 1841, and Baikie in 1854–1855. Their vessels were equipped with swivel and carriage guns and other weapons to drive off attacks by any estuarial communities of African traders that sought to prevent their passage upriver. Even these waterborne parties, however, became vulnerable when they pulled ashore to confer with chiefs and cut wood for their boilers.[88]

Explorers in Africa quickly learned how essential it was that they seek accommodation with local inhabitants. The use of force to gain access to unexplored territories was rarely an option. Until the late nineteenth century, European weaponry was not intimidating enough to overcome Africans' superior manpower, knowledge of the terrain, and other sources of strength. Moreover, explorers who used violence to achieve their ends ran the risk of drying up supplies of food, labor, and other resources. Although some expeditions had military escorts, such as the Baluchi forces supplied by the sultan of Zanzibar, these units were intended for defensive purposes, guarding caravans against unprovoked attacks. Sometimes, of course, clashes did occur. John Kirk cites two instances during David Livingstone's five-year-long Zambezi expedition when it directed deadly force against Africans. In the first case, a skirmish with some Ajawa slave raiders resulted in six of them being shot and their village being burned down. In the second, Kirk and the coxswain of their vessel responded to a shower of arrows from hostile Rovuma River people by shooting two of them. It was far more common, however, for Livingstone's expedition to passively endure subtler forms of resistance, such as villages that refused to sell it food and guides who deliberately led it astray. A frustrated Kirk attributed this lack of cooperation to a belief "that because we don[']t take things by force, that we are weak and in their power." His comment begs the question of whether they were in fact in a position to "take things by force." For the most part, they were not.[89]

African explorers, then, were less inclined than their Australian counterparts to resort to violence during encounters with indigenous peoples, if only because their position relative to those peoples was far weaker. This began to change, however, in the final quarter of the century, and no one exemplified that change more dramatically than Henry Morton Stanley. In the dispatches he wrote to the newspapers sponsoring his transcontinental expedition of 1875–1877, Stanley gave dramatic accounts of a series of bloody clashes between his party and various African tribes. As Samuel Baker described them, these reports told of "burning villages and plundering cattle &c through whole districts, and shooting great numbers of natives." Baker joined a chorus of critics in Britain who objected to Stanley's methods. Coming from a man who had only recently conducted a brutal war of conquest against the peoples of southern Sudan on behalf of Egyptian imperial interests, Baker's criticisms of Stanley might be considered hypocritical. Yet he drew a subtle but important distinction between the violence he had perpetrated as an agent of the Egyptian government and the violence that Stanley had perpetrated on his own behalf: "If a government finds it necessary to make war, it is a matter of course; but if an *individual* traveller begins this sort of thing I fear he will close the road for all future explorers. Neither Livingstone nor Speke & Grant, nor myself ever pulled a trigger when exploring, but suffered hunger and delay with patience."[90] Baker's point was no doubt self-serving, not to say misleading: it ignored the fact that he and other explorers showed "patience" because they had no other choice. But that was precisely why his contrast between "an *individual*" and the state was an important one: it pointed to a crucial disparity of power between the two.[91]

The question posed by the destruction Stanley left in the wake of his transcontinental expedition is whether that disparity was breaking down. Stanley himself insisted that he was no more violent than previous explorers, just more "indiscreet," which he attributed to the fact that he was a journalist whose stories of derring-do were designed to sell papers.[92] Stanley's most recent biographer, Tim Jeal, has taken this defense a step further, arguing that Stanley actually exaggerated how many Africans he killed in order to make his story more sensational.[93] While this claim cannot be entirely discounted—there were some discrepancies between his public and private figures of how many Africans he had killed—it fails to acknowledge that he resorted to violence with a frequency and lethality that far exceeded the actions of his predecessors. As the *Pall Mall Gazette* pointedly observed, Verney Lovett Cameron was able to complete his own transcontinental journey two years prior to Stanley "under sore trials and grievous provocation, [but] without violence or bloodshed and almost without the loss of a single life taken in self-defense."[94]

Stanley *was* different. Not only did he set out on his journey across the continent with "the most heavily armed European-led exploration of Africa's interior ever put together," but he contracted with the Zanzibari trader and state builder Tippu Tip for an additional military escort as he entered the region west of the Great Lakes. He had already established a reputation as "a merciless tyrant," according to Cameron, who found that "no one had a good word for him" in territories he had passed through on his first expedition.[95] The African nicknames he acquired on his subsequent expeditions—"breaker of rocks" *(bula mutari)* and "vicious white man" *(wazungu wakali)*—show that this reputation gathered strength over time.[96]

A. G. Hopkins points out that Stanley was "both a symptom and a cause" of increasing pressure on central Africa from slave and ivory traders and other interlopers, producing widespread violence and instability in the final decades of the nineteenth century.[97] The greater significance of Stanley's transcontinental expedition is that it marked a transition to a new mode of exploration in the late nineteenth century, one in which larger parties equipped with more powerful armaments (including Maxim guns and repeater rifles) and more abundant supplies (such as tinned foods) moved through territories with less reliance on indigenous peoples and therefore less need to consider their concerns or objections.[98] Stanley himself would make further contributions to this new, militarized approach to exploration with his work to establish King Leopold's rule over the Congo River basin in the late 1870s and his notorious Emin Pasha Relief Expedition in 1886–1890.[99] In effect, exploration in the aftermath of Stanley became more militarized and less distinguishable from the imperial agendas that eventuated in the scramble for Africa.

It is hardly surprising that encounters between explorers and indigenes were often marked by suspicion, anxiety, antagonism, and occasional outbreaks of violence. After all, the two parties were strangers to each other, with different languages, customs, beliefs, dress, appearance, and more, all of which placed roadblocks in the path to familiarity and fraternization. The gulf that separated them made it easier for each party to believe rumors of cannibalism and other charges of deviance about the other. And all too often the gulf between them was widened by contending interests, ambitions, and expectations. Especially when it came to access to markets, claims to territory, or control of resources such as water, wildlife, and grasslands, explorers' interests were bound to collide with those of native peoples.

Despite these fissiparous pressures, the two parties were not always at odds. Common ground could be—and was—found, often on the basis of mutual self-interest, occasionally through affective intimacies. Africans' and Aborigines' curiosity about the strangers who passed through their territories often overcame suspicion, and in these instances they extended the hospitality that was so deeply ingrained in their cultures. By welcoming explorers, they also gained access to manufactured goods such as tools, weapons, and textiles, as well as medicines and other products and services that were otherwise unavailable in their societies. The explorers, in turn, obtained food, shelter, and labor in Africa, access to water in Australia, and information and assistance of various other kinds in both continents. It is important to remember how many weeks, months, even years explorers spent in continuous interaction with indigenous peoples. What impact this interaction may have had on explorers' sensibilities regarding difference—and, perhaps more important, their own sense of self—is difficult to measure, since any variance from normative perceptions and practices rarely found its way into written records. But enough trace evidence exists to suspect that such shifts in attitudes and sympathies could and did occur.

The form of fraternization most frequently acknowledged by African explorers was the relationship they established with a king, chief, or other official or dignitary. As products of a hierarchical society that privileged hereditary status, explorers were culturally conditioned to respect rulers and admire the ceremony and pageantry that so often characterized their courts. Even if they viewed the peoples over whom these kings ruled as uncivilized, they tended to treat the rulers them-

selves with a certain respect, acknowledging their rank as a category that
to some degree trumped their race.[100] A rare exception was Francis Galton, who mocked the very idea of African monarchy by buying a crown
from a theatrical shop in London, "which I vowed to place on the head
of the greatest or most distant potentate I should meet with in Africa,"
which he did when he met Nangoro, king of the Ovambo.[101] While many
explorers shared Galton's smug sense of racial superiority, they also
were drawn to if not cowed by the presence and power that these African
rulers so often embodied and displayed. Verney Lovett Cameron insisted that "the more European types prevail chiefly among the chiefs &
their relations," thereby accounting in his own mind for their dignity
and authority by attributing these qualities to their supposed racial superiority over the people they ruled.[102] As commander of the 1841 antislavery expedition up the Niger River, Captain William Allen drew a
very different conclusion: his interactions with rulers such as the king of
the "Filatahs," who was "one of the most courtly men I had ever seen,"
convinced him that "the supposition that [Africans] were savage or uncivilized" was simply wrong.[103] Henry Morton Stanley wrote an admir-
ing essay titled "African Royalties I Have Known" (though it is unclear
whether he published it).[104] He was especially impressed by Mutesa, the
kabaka of Buganda, declaring him to be "an extraordinary monarch. . . .
a generous prince and a frank and intelligent man."[105] John Hanning
Speke, James Grant, and Samuel Baker also had high praise for Mutesa,
in large part because he was so hospitable and showed such interest in
their customs, their Christian beliefs, and their firearms.[106] Other explorers established relationships with rulers as well. David Livingstone
famously forged a close and fruitful association with Sekeletu, the Makololo chief whose support made possible the transcontinental journey
that turned him into a British celebrity.

Fraternization of a more intimate sort also took place during expeditions. Speke was hardly the only explorer to have had sexual relations
with native women. For the first generation of African explorers, the
amorous activities of Banks and other visitors to the South Pacific served
as an alluring model that many of them hoped to emulate. Despite the
Admiralty's warning to the crew of the Congo River expedition of 1816
that liaisons with local women were a "great cause of the disputes of

Speke and Grant at the court of Mutesa, Buganda's charismatic ruler. *Source: J. H. Speke,* Journal of the Discovery of the Source of the Nile *(1864).*

navigators with uncivilized people," members of the party found it hard to resist the offers, some expressed in terms that Captain Tuckey found "most disgusting and obscene," that came their way as they sailed up the Congo. He described the local women as "perfect Otaheitans [Tahitians] in their manner," and the expedition's head scientific officer detailed an incident when a "little black Venus" arrived in camp, stirring "an amorous flame in the breasts of several of our gentlemen" and provoking a bidding war for her affections.[107] No less enthused by the erotic opportunities opened up by exploration in Africa was Dixon Denham, whose narrative was filled with coy references to the many pretty and attentive women he met during his journey across the Sahara to West Africa. He made it clear that race meant little in these circumstances: "Man naturally longs for attentions and support from female hands, of whatever colour or country."[108] Both Friedrich Hornemann, who had preceded Dixon in attempting to cross the Sahara by camel caravan, and Alexander Laing, who did so soon after Dixon, noted with appreciation the "wanton manners and public freedoms" of female residents of certain oasis towns.[109] After Hugh Clapperton's death in Sokoto, his servant Richard Lander accepted an enslaved woman from a chief during his return journey, "as I knew she would be serviceable to me." He justified his conduct by indicating that he intended to free her once he arrived on the coast.[110]

As Victorian values acquired greater force toward midcentury, explorers wrote about interracial dalliances with greater discretion. One exception was the iconoclastic Richard Burton, who embedded a sly remark in his report to the Royal Geographical Society about the women of the Wagogo being "well disposed towards strangers of fair complexion, apparently with the permission of their husbands."[111] Most of his contemporaries limited their public comments to occasional observations about the physical beauty of certain women and accompanying reminders that few of these women wore much in the way of clothing. Though they (or their editors, as the case of Speke indicates) addressed this issue more circumspectly, Burton was almost certainly not alone in enjoying the physical charms of the women encountered en route.

The key question, however, is whether these "tense and tender ties" altered explorers' understanding or appreciation of the African societies they encountered during their journeys.[112] Here we enter a realm of inquiry that is difficult to document and open to competing interpretations. On the one hand, there is little reason to believe that Dixon and his ilk would have been any more likely to experience an emotional or intellectual epiphany as a result of their brief dalliances with African women than we might expect of modern truckers who hire prostitutes at stops along their routes. On the other hand, the social opprobrium that such conduct elicited from an increasing segment of nineteenth-century opinion suggests not simply a shift in the moral climate in Britain but a heightened anxiety that such affective encounters could alter the explorer's outlook and loyalties in profoundly subversive ways. The colloquial expression for this anxiety was "going native," and more than a few explorers themselves worried about the erosion of their status and identity as "white men" during their long sojourns in the continent. "I never expect to become white again," John Davidson bemoaned, pointing to changes in his physical appearance. "My beard is very long, my hair is

cut close to the head . . . my bare legs and arms are covered with the
bites of vermin," and, lastly, "[my] teeth [are] very sharp from having
little or nothing to do," a strange comment that alludes, perhaps, to the
fear that he might be acquiring cannibalistic proclivities.[113] Samuel
Baker found to his dismay that the peoples he encountered on his expedition up the Nile could not discern any difference between himself and
his Arab assistants, causing him to repeatedly "take off my shirt to exhibit the difference in colour between myself and my men."[114] If men
such as Davidson and Baker feared the loss of their identity as Englishmen, other explorers embraced the opportunity to experiment with
alternative identities. This was certainly the case for Richard Burton,
whose views and conduct caused some contemporaries to charge that he
had become, as he himself put it, a "white Nigger." An even more striking example is Mansfield Parkyns, who set out to explore Ethiopia and
neighboring territories in 1843 and did not return to Britain until 1849.
During his long sojourn in Africa, he adopted indigenous customs and
dress, plaited and greased his hair, spoke Tigrinya and other local languages, married an Ethiopian woman, and declared himself to be "an
Abyssinian gentleman." "Anyone who has tasted the sweets of savage
life," he declared, "will always look back with longing to them."[115] Having gone native, as his British critics saw it, he had discredited himself
and diminished the value of his accomplishments. It is impossible to say
how many other explorers might have suppressed evidence that they too
had been enchanted by the "sweets of savage life" for fear of condemnation at home, but the case of Speke suggests that there may have been
more of them than contemporaries could have imagined.

Australian circumstances conspired against cross-cultural interactions
of the sort that might have permitted explorers to acquire indigenous
perspectives and knowledge. The logistical autonomy of Australian expeditions, which relied so rarely on local inhabitants for food or shelter
or other resources, limited the opportunities for sustained and intimate
encounters. These opportunities were further inhibited by the absence
of a lingua franca such as Kiswahili to facilitate communication, which
was related in turn to the limited scale and importance of Aboriginal

trade networks. Additionally, the fact that Aborigines had no kings or other hereditary rulers and their societies no structures of hierarchy and privilege discernible to Australian explorers meant that they had no readily recognizable figures or institutions the explorers could turn to as points of contact and interaction. Even the availability of Aboriginal women as sexual partners, which was both an occasional function of indigenous hospitality and a frequent feature of settler exploitation on the colonial frontier, proved problematic to explorers, since it so often created obligations and antagonisms. By keeping women out of their camps, they sequestered themselves from a potential source of affective knowledge.

Only occasionally did individuals involved in expeditions break through the barriers of difference between themselves and Aborigines. Those who did often ran the risk of being dismissed as social deviants who had gone native. This was the case when a member of Kennedy's Cape York expedition—a man named Carpenter, probably a convict— slipped away from camp and was found a day later sharing food with some Aborigines. Although he rejoined the expedition, the botanist William Carron judged him to be "little better than an Idiot."[116] Perhaps, but his evident ease in interacting with native peoples may have proved helpful later on. When the expedition fell into disarray, its horses dying off, its supplies running low, and its men falling victim to dysentery and malaria, someone—was it perhaps Carpenter?—persuaded previously hostile Aborigines to supply the starving men with fish and other foodstuffs.

Desperation served as the main solvent of distance and disdain for Australian explorers. The most famous demonstration of its effects occurred after Robert O'Hara Burke and William Wills, along with their companion John King, returned to Cooper's Creek, only to discover that their base camp had been abandoned. They had little choice but to turn for assistance to the Yandruwandha people who inhabited the area, which required, as Burke reluctantly acknowledged, that "[we] live the best way we can like the blacks." Although the "blacks" supplied them with fish and taught them how to gather and prepare nardoo seeds, they also exhibited a physical familiarity with the explorers that Burke found unnerving. "Lest they should be always at our camp," he decided to drive them away by firing his gun over their heads. Needless to say, his action had disastrous consequences for himself and his companions, who were left to fend for themselves. Wills, recognizing that their survival depended on restoring friendly relations with the Yandruwandha, set out in search of them, intending, as he put it, "to test the practicability of living with them and to see what I could learn as to their ways and manners."[117] He failed, and in consequence both he and Burke starved to death. King, however, survived until he was able to reestablish contact with, and attach himself to, the Yandruwandha. When Alfred Howitt's search party found King several months later, he seemed "a complete blackfellow in almost everything but the colour."[118]

The idea that desperate circumstances could force white men to live with Aborigines and adopt their way of life served as an essential underpinning for the myth of the lost explorer. Its power was especially evident in the case of Ludwig Leichhardt, whose third expedition had disappeared without a trace in 1848. Exploratory parties were sent out in search of Leichhardt and his men in 1851–1852, 1858, 1866, 1869, and 1871. Ferdinand von Mueller, who led the campaign to finance the 1866 expedition, argued that survivors might still be found in some remote part of the interior, citing by way of example the case of a white man named James Morrill, who had recently reappeared in a settler district after having spent the previous seventeen years in the company of Aborigines. When the search party set out, it showed particular interest in rumors of mixed-race children in the outback, figuring that any members of Leichhardt's party who remained alive were likely to have been taken in by Aborigines and fathered children with them.[119] Five years later, Andrew Hume, "a man who from boyhood had lived much amongst the aborigines" and who was regarded "in instincts and habits as a 'blackfellow,'" reported that he had come across Leichhardt's second-in-command, a German named Glassen, while wandering in the interior. He claimed that Glassen had three mixed-race children with whom he spoke a language unfamiliar to Hume, who believed it to be German. A private entrepreneur hired Hume to lead an expedition to find Glassen and recover "relics" of the Leichhardt expedition (with the apparent intent of selling them for a profit), but Hume and one of his companions succumbed to heat and thirst during the journey and his story died with him.[120]

While close contact with Aborigines was considered for the most part either an act of desperation by lost explorers or an act of deviance by random "Idiots," some highly successful explorers appear to have understood that they had much to gain from indigenous peoples' knowledge of their environments and that they had to forge relations of familiarity and respect in order to access that knowledge. Edward Eyre, for one, showed that he was amenable to what Aborigines could teach him and made it clear in his expedition narrative how much he owed his survival during the journey from Adelaide to King George Sound to local inhabitants' bush skills. A more ambiguous and intriguing case is that of Ernest Giles. One of Australia's most determined and accomplished explorers in the second half of the nineteenth century, as well as one of the most gifted travel writers of his generation, Giles was also one of the most forceful advocates of the view that Aborigines were a savage people who were destined to die out. Such views certainly did not prevent him from having sex with Aboriginal women; in all likelihood, he fathered several children with them. Nor did they preclude him from engaging in the empathetic leap of imagination needed to appreciate why indigenous peoples might object to his appearance in their country, as the passage quoted earlier demonstrates. But perhaps the most revealing evidence that his relationship with Aborigines may have been more complicated than the racist pronouncements he issued in print suggest takes the form of a stray anecdote that appears near the end of one of his expedition journals. When Aborigines visited his camp, he states that he "amused them greatly by passing a stick through my nose (having formerly gone through an excruciating operation for that purpose), and telling them I had formerly been a blackfellow."[121] Had he really undergone that "excruciating operation" simply to amuse random Aboriginal visitors? Or had he done so during an Aboriginal body ritual that was intended to establish bonds of kinship with a particular clan? And if Giles had trespassed across the boundaries between cultures in this fashion, what other explorers might have committed similar trespasses that they failed to acknowledge to their countrymen?

The journals and books written by explorers provide a troublingly rich reservoir of ethnocentric and racist remarks about the peoples of Africa and Australia. Historians, literary scholars, and other students of cultural encounters in the age of British imperial expansion have mined these sources for decades, making telling use of them to expose the arrogance, ignorance, and intolerance that characterized so many Britons' stance toward other peoples. Some explorers believed that Africans and Aborigines could attain the abstract promise of a shared humanity only if they embraced Western values, customs, and practices. Others made portentous pronouncements about the innate and unalterable inferiority of Africans or Aborigines, and warned of the latter's bleak future as a "dying race." These discourses of difference derived their patina of authority from explorers' claims that their observations and insights sprang from the privileged stance of firsthand experience.

This experience was in fact far more varied, complex, and subversive to explorers' discursive claims than most scholars have recognized. While explorers in both continents invariably saw themselves as agents of a superior civilization, their actual agency on the ground was often limited and insecure. Through most of the nineteenth century, the explorers who entered Africa came to realize that whatever sense of superiority they might possess in their own minds was difficult to exercise in the field: most of them found that they wielded remarkably little power or prestige in their encounters with indigenous peoples. Their very weakness and dependence on the range of services provided by Africans drew them into intimate relations with their hosts, resulting in impressions and assessments that often ran at odds with the glib generalizations and classificatory categories they were expected to confirm. The Australian explorers operated in a very different physical and social environment, one that gave them far greater autonomy of action, far fewer opportunities for engagement with indigenous inhabitants, and far more occasions when encounters with those inhabitants turned violent. Yet even in Australia, explorers were afflicted with feelings of anxiety and vulnerability that stood at odds with their presumptive sense of power and superiority.

What explorers wrote about their expeditions was meant to be read by their countrymen, which required that it conform to public tastes and sentiments. When explorers put pen to paper, then, they self-consciously selected their words and censored their accounts in order to enhance their reputations. One of the methodological challenges this practice poses for the historian is how to discern the disjuncture between public pronouncements and private thoughts and actions, a disjuncture that was particularly acute with regard to what explorers had to say about their encounters with indigenous peoples. Unpublished letters, logbooks, and journals take us some distance toward a fuller appreciation of those encounters. But even some ostensibly private logbooks and journals were written with the public in mind. After all, they were often scrutinized by specialists at sponsoring agencies and occasionally published verbatim in newspapers. As a result, it is difficult to know whether Speke, who wrote about his affection for Meri in such frank and touching terms, was exceptional in his feelings or merely in the honesty with which he expressed them. What is clear, however, is that many explorers engaged with indigenes in more intriguing and intimate ways than they acknowledged openly.

The secret knowledge that resulted from these cross-cultural encounters is by its nature difficult to excavate, but occasional traces of its presence can be uncovered. It has become increasingly apparent, for example, that explorers relied heavily on local informants for geographical knowledge about the regions through which they passed. A member of Ludwig Leichhardt's second expedition noted that "a black fellow . . . drew a kind of chart on the ground" that delineated rivers and other features of the lands ahead.[122] During his transcontinental expedition, Livingstone "employed the natives to draw a map embodying their ideas" about the upper reaches of the Zambezi River.[123] These were in most cases ephemeral maps drawn in the dirt, which left no traces in the archival records apart from the random statements made by explorers themselves.[124] In some instances, however, African and Arab rulers and merchants produced maps on paper, the most famous being the one that Mohammed Bello, the emir of Sokoto, drew of the Niger River's course at the request of Hugh Clapperton.[125] Even the maps produced by explorers were in some instances co-productions. Adrian Wisnicki's meticulous examination of Burton and Speke's maps of their East African expedition reveals that early iterations of these maps acknowledged "the Arab-African basis of their cartographic statements," an acknowledgment erased from subsequent versions.[126]

The contributions Africans and Aborigines made to the knowledge (geographical and otherwise) that explorers obtained on their journeys should not be taken to mean that these peoples shared their sense of purpose. Snatches of conversations occasionally appear in explorers' accounts of their interactions with individual Africans or Aborigines, brief and no doubt distorted dialogues that nevertheless remind us that these encounters often consisted of two human beings from different cultures who were trying to understand each other's motivations. Two reported conversations dealt with an issue that must have puzzled most indigenous peoples: why these strangers from a distant land were traveling through their territory. Recalling an exchange with an Aborigine named Imbat who queried him on this subject, George Grey complained that "it is impossible to make a native understand our love of travel,—I therefore replied—'Imbat, you comprehend nothing—you know nothing.'—'I know nothing!' answered he; 'I know how to keep myself fat; the young women look at me and say, Imbat is very handsome, he is fat!'"[127] Grey, who was emaciated by this stage in his journey, does not indicate if or how he responded. He takes it for granted that his readers will understand his motives and he shifts the focus instead to Imbat's comment, which he presents as an amusing anecdote illustrating the naive simplicity of the Aborigines. Samuel Baker had a similar exchange with a local chief as he traveled up the Nile in search of Lake Albert. The chief asked, "'Suppose you get to the great lake, what will you do with it? What will be the good of it? If you find that the large river does flow from it, what then? What's the good of it?'" Rather than respond with an explanation of his own motives, Baker resorts instead to what might be considered the "company line": "I could only assure him, that in England we had an intimate knowledge of the whole world, except the interior of Africa, and that our object in exploring was to benefit the hitherto unknown countries by instituting legitimate trade, and introducing manufactures from England in exchange for ivory and other productions."[128] Neither Baker nor Grey offered honest answers to their interlocutors' questions. Perhaps they did not want to alarm their hosts by frankly acknowledging who would likely benefit from their explorations. Or perhaps they simply did not want to confess either to their indigenous questioners or to their metropolitan readers how hungry they were for the fame and honors that likely awaited them at home.

CHAPTER 8

Celebrities

At last we are to meet him,
The famous Captain Spaulding,
From climates hot and scalding,
The Captain has arrived.

Most heartily we'll greet him,
With plain and fancy cheering.
Until he's hard of hearing
The Captain has arrived. . . .

Hooray for Captain Spaulding,
The African explorer.
He brought his name undying fame
And that is why we say, Hooray, Hooray, Hooray.

—Bert Kalmar and Harry Ruby, "Hooray
for Captain Spaulding," *Animal Crackers* (1936)

ON SEPTEMBER 15, 1861, a relief expedition led by Alfred Howitt found John King, the sole surviving member of the Burke and Wills advance party. King, a veteran of the campaign to suppress the Indian Mutiny, had been recruited by George Landells to assist in the purchase and shipment of camels from Karachi to Melbourne for use by the Victorian Exploring Expedition. His camel skills led to his selection to accompany Burke and Wills in their push across the continent from the base camp at Cooper's Creek. Following the expedition leaders' deaths from starvation, he had lived among the Yandruwandha people for two and a half months. When Edwin Welch, the Howitt party's surveyor, discovered him, he was physically emaciated and emotionally fragile. After several weeks spent regaining weight and strength, he set off for Melbourne under Welch's care. By this time, news of the expedition's fate had spread and public interest in the sole survivor was intense. The circuslike atmosphere that confronted King as he made his way back to Melbourne aptly illustrates how explorers' exploits and travails could turn them into celebrities.[1]

The first indication of what was in store for King came at the Murray River trading port, Swan Hill, where most of the residents came out to meet him. They treated him that evening to a series of dinners, with speeches, toasts, and songs.[2] The reception was even more fervid when King reached the mining town of Bendigo. Welch reports that they were greeted at the outskirts of the town by "crowds of diggers . . . blowing horns, firing guns & pistols, cheering, & waving flags &c &c as much as if it were a triumphal entry of blood royal." A brass band and a theatrical troupe led "a procession of enormous length" that accompanied the carriage supplied to bring the aptly named King into town, where local dignitaries awaited his arrival amid "flags, garlands, bouquets & other nonsense." Residents eager to catch a glimpse of the expedition's survivor mobbed the hotel he was staying in and pressed him to speak at a local theater, where an overflow crowd spilled into the street. Emotionally overwrought and unprepared for this frenzy of attention, King collapsed in what Welch describes as "a state of semi-stupidity." When Welch intervened, leading him off the stage, the audience responded with "hisses, groans & curses." The following morning, Welch found himself "besieged with applications from Photographers to allow King to sit for his likeness." After breakfast, he entered King's room to find it "full of ladies, sitting on the beds, hanging round him." Clearly, celebrity had rewards that even King could appreciate. The following day, however, his arrival at Castlemaine was met with the same overwhelming enthusiasm from local residents as he had encountered in Bendigo: "Every man, woman, & child . . . turned out as we passed, throwing bouquets, firing guns, and . . . displaying an intensity of hero-worship, little short of mono mania."

This mania was even more intense when King reached Melbourne. A cheering throng awaited his train when it pulled into the North Melbourne station. Dr. William Wills, the self-promoting father of the ill-fated expedition's second-in-command, barged into his carriage and tried to take custody of King. When Welch opposed this effort, he was "met with a volley of abuse" from Wills, and the two men battled over the bewildered object of everyone's attention all the way to the main station. Here an even larger assemblage of excited colonists awaited King's arrival. Welch was able to extract King from Wills's clutches, shepherd him through the crush of the crowd, and hire a carriage to take them to Government House, where he gladly relinquished responsibility for his vulnerable ward. King, however, would continue to endure the frenzied attentions of his countrymen for some time to come, culminating in his testimony to a royal commission of inquiry. Eventually, however, he was able to escape to the obscurity from whence he had come.

While King was a reluctant celebrity, many explorers were Captain Spauldings, happy for hoorays. They were willing participants in the celebrity culture of the nineteenth century, feeding the public's hunger for heroes who could be seen to embody some of the country or colony's

A crowd greeting John McDouall Stuart and his party upon their return to Adelaide in 1863. *Source: State Library of South Australia (B9382).*

ideals and ambitions. Their collaborators in this enterprise were politicians and government officials, leaders of learned and scientific societies, newspaper editors and book publishers, lecture and exhibition hall impresarios, manufacturers of travel kits and memorabilia, and many others who had their own commercial, political, and institutional reasons to promote explorers and their exploits.

But celebrity and its sponsors also placed demands and constraints on explorers, pressures that extended well beyond the relentless attention the public gave to poor King. Explorers had to speak and write about what they had seen and done and felt in ways that did not diverge too markedly from prevailing norms and popular representations. They had to assert intentions and express ideals that gave social validation to their actions, providing rhetorical endorsement to civilization, Christianity, commerce, and progress. They had to present the peoples and places they visited in terms of need and negation, using charged adjectives such as "primitive," "savage," "empty," and "dark." They had to edit their journals and massage their memories in ways that accentuated their drive, insight, and courage while minimizing their fears, doubts, and confusion. They had to avoid acknowledging how dependent they had been on the information and assistance of local intermediaries and indigenous peoples. In short, they had to craft accounts of their adventures that conformed to the expectations of their sponsors and their public, requiring varying degrees of divergence from what they had actually experienced and observed in the course of their journeys through the interior of Africa or Australia.

The existence of a public was integral to the creation of the explorer as a celebrity. Over the course of the nineteenth century the size and shape of that public would be transformed by various forces, including increased prosperity, greater literacy, and a more vigorous print culture.[3] The public that explorers sought to engage in the early decades of the century was much smaller and more socially select than it would become later on. As a result, the pressures and profits that accompanied celebrity status were considerably different for, say, Mungo Park than for a late nineteenth-century counterpart such as Henry Morton Stanley. Moreover, the public that followed the adventures of African explorers was not quite the same as the one that applauded Australian explorers. These differences were reflected in the strategies explorers employed to gain recognition and fame.

Patronage played a prominent role in African explorers' engagement with the public early in the century. This reflected the influence that the gentlemanly elite exerted over exploration through their leadership roles in learned and scientific societies and their access to the corridors of power in Whitehall. They arranged for explorers to meet with governmental and other institutional sponsors and hosted soirees for them with supporters and dignitaries. Joseph Banks and his associates in the African Association proved particularly adept at promoting—and controlling—explorers' public appearances. One of the attendees at a London party in honor of Mungo Park observed, for example, that he was "very much protected by Sir Joseph Banks."[4]

With the death of Banks in 1820, the gentlemanly elite's influence waned and the exploration of Africa attracted the interest of a much larger public, composed mainly of an increasingly prosperous, educated, and politically mobilized middle class. Having succeeded in their efforts to outlaw the British slave trade in 1807, middle-class evangelicals and their free trade allies subsequently turned their attention not only to the abolition of slavery in British territories but also to the suppression of the international slave trade, targeting its source in Africa, in large part by pressuring African polities to shift their economies to what was termed "legitimate commerce" with British traders.[5] Explorers were able to tap into the energy and enthusiasm of the antislavery campaigners by casting themselves as contributors to their cause, gathering the knowledge of African places and peoples needed to shut off the slave trade at its source and open the interior of the continent to British producers. The anti-slavery lobby and its allies in government and the business community began to lend their considerable moral, institutional, and monetary support to African exploration. Soon, nearly every explorer who ventured into the West African interior was expected to exhort African rulers to renounce the slave trade. Moreover, abolitionists and the British government joined forces in 1841 to carry out what was perhaps the most expensive African expedition of the century, the ambitious effort to send a flotilla of steamships up the Niger River to establish diplomatic relations with African rulers along the way and introduce them to the benefits of trade with Britain.[6] The dismal failure of that effort dampened the antislavery movement's enthusiasm for African exploration for more than a decade, but David Livingstone's triumphant arrival on the national scene in the 1850s showed that explorers could still inspire the public by connecting their efforts to the abolition of slavery and the slave trade.

Early nineteenth-century Australian explorers attracted far less interest from the British public, which had little ideological or emotional investment in the outcomes of their expeditions, and the Australian public was initially limited to colonial officials and a small but increasingly powerful network of large landholders known as squatters. By the 1840s, however, Sydney, Melbourne, Adelaide, and other cities and towns had begun to boom, and as they grew larger and more prosperous, their residents acquired a civic consciousness and created a public sphere, consisting of friendly societies, learned institutions, newspapers, and more. They began to view the exploration of the interior as an investment in their future and an expression of their character as a community. Adding impetus to action was their inexorable land hunger.

Colonists became enthusiastic advocates of exploration, exhibiting their support in economic and emotional terms. All three of Ludwig Leichhardt's expeditions were privately financed by Sydney merchants, land speculators, and other local investors, who anticipated that he would return with information that would bring them financial rewards; they organized banquets and other public events in his honor as he prepared to depart. Even expeditions that had the official imprimaturs of colonial governments usually relied on contributions from private parties, frequently in kind (stock, saddles, and other supplies) but occasionally in currency. Take, for example, Edward Eyre's expedition of 1840–1841. The governor of South Australia provided £100, plus men, horses, instruments, and a ship to transport supplies to Spencer's Gulf, while the citizens of Adelaide contributed £500 in subscriptions during a public meeting at the local Mechanics Institute.[7] The ceremonies that preceded Eyre's departure revealed the public's emotional as well as financial investment in his endeavor. The governor hosted a farewell breakfast attended by "60 gentlemen," followed by prayers, speeches, and the presentation of a Union Jack stitched from silk by the local ladies.[8] The expeditionary party then rode out of town to the "cheering of the people, the waving of hats, and the rush of so many horses" that Eyre was touched, he wrote, by such "a heart-stirring and inspiriting scene."[9]

Public ceremonies of this sort soon became a common feature of Australian explorers' departures. Just a few years after Eyre's expedition, Charles Sturt and his companions were honored by the governor and prominent citizens at a similar farewell breakfast, characterized by "many fine speeches," and the road that led them out of town was lined with "people taking leave of us."[10] Even a more modest expedition, such as the one that left York, Western Australia, in 1863, was treated to a farewell dinner by the town's dignitaries, and "a large gathering of the population of York . . . gave us three very hearty cheers" as they set off.[11] Few expeditions, however, were bid farewell with as much fanfare and ceremony as was the Burke and Wills party. The governor of Victoria and other dignitaries visited the members of the expedition at their encampment in Melbourne's Royal Park a few days before their departure. A special service was held on their behalf at the Anglican cathedral, and they were feted at a dinner hosted by the German Association. The mayor, the chief justice, and some 10,000–15,000 residents gathered at Royal Park to see the expedition off, the men cheering and the women waving handkerchiefs.[12]

However much attention was lavished on explorers when they set out on their journeys, it paled by comparison to the excitement they generated upon their return. The frenzy surrounding John King's homecoming was exceptional, to be sure, but nearly all of the leading names in late nineteenth-century Australian exploration received large and enthusiastic receptions from citizens eager to honor their accomplishments. Augustus Gregory got a hero's welcome from the governor and citizens of South Australia after blazing a trail from Brisbane to Adelaide in 1858. Some 3,000 people attended a public meeting in Melbourne to celebrate the achievements of William Landsborough and John McKinlay, whose contemporaneous expeditions in 1861–1862 had begun in search of Burke and Wills, but ended by announcing their discovery of important new tracts of territory. To celebrate his success in crossing the Great

Sandy Desert in 1872–1873, Peter Warburton was the guest of honor at public dinners hosted by local dignitaries in Roebourne, Fremantle, Perth, and Albany, followed by a great banquet in Adelaide upon his return to South Australia.[13]

These celebrations were expressions of the growing sense of community and civic consciousness among the immigrant populations of Australia's colonies. Insights into the social and ideological functions such events served can be seen by looking more closely at two of them—the reception that John Forrest received in Adelaide in 1874 and the welcome that Perth's residents gave to Ernest Giles a year later. When Forrest reached Adelaide after crossing the central Australian desert from Perth, an estimated 20,000 people turned out to greet him, lining a route that was decorated with flags, streamers, and "arches adorned with large pictures representing incidences of bush life." Bands, horsemen, carriages, and members of various friendly societies (including Odd Fellows, Foresters, Druids, the German Club, and Good Templars) paraded along the route, as did the explorers Ernest Giles and William Gosse, along with two horses that were said to have accompanied Charles Sturt and Robert O'Hara Burke on their expeditions. Forrest and the members of his expedition were greeted by the mayor, members of parliament, and other public officials at the town hall, where they were honored at an evening banquet. Speakers placed Forrest in a pantheon of "exploring heroes" that included Ludwig Leichhardt, Burke and Wills, and John McDouall Stuart, and he was asked to lay the first stone for a monument in Gawler to commemorate the achievements of the explorer John McKinlay, who had died two years earlier.[14]

Ernest Giles received a similar welcome from the citizens of Perth after crossing Gibson's Desert from South Australia in 1875. Cheering crowds lined the route, which was "decorated with flags and scrolls, while streamers stretched across the street." Once again, members of the Odd Fellows, Good Templars, Freemasons, and other friendly societies led Giles and his companions in a parade to the town hall, where officers gave welcoming addresses. More than a week of banquets, balls, and other social events followed, the festivities in no way diminished by Giles's admission that "no areas of country available for settlement were found."[15]

The public celebrations that accompanied the arrival of Forrest in Adelaide and Giles in Perth are revealing for several reasons. If the estimate of the numbers that greeted Forrest is accurate, the crowd comprised nearly a quarter of Adelaide's total population, which is a remarkable turnout.[16] We do not know the size of the crowd at Perth, though Giles says it was large. The public parades, the decorative displays, the involvement of the friendly societies, and the culminating ceremonies at the city halls all signaled the civic importance of these events. Why they held such importance is suggested by the memorializing attention the Adelaide celebration paid to past explorers, along with its banners extolling "bush life." The citizens of Adelaide used the arrival of Forrest as an opportunity to celebrate a series of heroic explorers whose endeavors exemplified in turn a pioneering spirit that could be characterized as the community's shared heritage. Much the same meaning must have informed the greeting Giles received from Perth's residents. By honoring Forrest and Giles and their predecessors, Australian colonists were embracing an identity as rugged frontiersmen.

To characterize these public events as nascent expressions of Australian nationalism is surely anachronistic, but they did give voice to two closely related forms of allegiance to political community. One was civic pride in the colony that had become their home, a sensibility that grew stronger after midcentury as a result of the establishment of "responsible government." Given greater control over their own affairs, colonial legislatures and interest groups spurred the intracolonial scramble that led to the partition of previously unclaimed territory in central and northern Australia. The other form of political identity that found expression in the celebrations of explorers' achievements was a transcolonial commitment to the British imperial project. Colonists embraced the idea that their labors were advancing the cause of commerce and civilization by bringing the hitherto unexploited riches of the continent into productive use for the greater benefit of mankind. Explorers were seen as essential agents of these endeavors, and the cheering crowds that applauded the explorers' achievements were simultaneously expressing their own emotional attachments to colony and empire.

The power that explorers exerted over the imaginations of the Australian public in the latter part of the nineteenth century was exhibited in other ways as well. Explorers who had died or disappeared during their journeys stirred especially strong passions in settler communities. They became public martyrs in the colonial struggle to conquer a harsh and intractable continent. Potent myths accrued around them.[17] This was certainly the case for Ludwig Leichhardt after he and his party vanished in the Australian outback in 1848. Multiple expeditions were sent out in search of Leichhardt, including the Ladies' Leichhardt Relief Expedition, which was organized nearly two decades after the famed explorer's disappearance. This belated endeavor was the result of a campaign in 1866 by a committee of sixteen prominent women, each representing a major Sydney church. They raised £1,000 in private contributions, inspired women in other Australian colonies to establish affiliated committees, and lobbied colonial and imperial authorities to support the expedition, extracting financial commitments from the governments of New South Wales, Victoria, Queensland, and South Australia. Ferdinand von Mueller, director of the Melbourne Botanical Gardens and tireless advocate of exploration, served as spokesman and advisor for the women, whose efforts he believed "will prove for the first time in the world's history, that Ladies may well step out of the circle which hitherto has narrowed their sphere of action." By assuming a role in the public sphere on behalf of a lost explorer, they were promoting a cause that exerted strong emotional appeal, especially with men who might otherwise have considered such activism by women disturbing and objectionable.[18]

The ladies' campaign to solve the mystery surrounding Leichhardt came only a few years after the greatest outpouring of public emotion ever exhibited in connection with Australian exploration—the memorialization of the deaths of Burke and Wills. The frenzy surrounding King's return was merely the opening act of this cathartic drama. Burke and Wills's remains were placed in state at the Royal Society, where nearly all of Melbourne's 120,000 residents reportedly paid their respects. The first state funeral in Australia's history followed, an elaborate procession that attracted an estimated 40,000–100,000 mourners, making it "one of the great spectacles of colonial Australia."[19] The explorers' hair and other relics of the expedition were put on public display and assumed a status similar to saints' reliquaries. Artists painted posthumous portraits of the two men and canvases portraying important incidents from the expedition. Entrepreneurs produced waxworks and dioramas that dramatized Burke and Wills's dying days. A monumental bronze statue of the two men was commissioned at a cost of £4,000 and unveiled in central Melbourne with great fanfare in 1865. Nothing did more to demonstrate how much meaning Australia's colonists attached to explorers as symbols of their identity as a pioneering people than the apotheosis of Burke and Wills.

The memorialization of men who had died while exploring unknown territory proved a potent means of mobilizing the public's sympathies and sense of allegiance to the colonial state and the imperial enterprise. Even otherwise obscure members of minor expeditions could be made into martyrs by their deaths. When C. F. Wells and George Jones, two members of the privately financed Calvert Scientific

Melbourne's vast funeral procession for Robert O'Hara Burke and William Wills, January 21, 1863. *Source: State Library of Victoria (IMP 24/01/63/8–9).*

Exploring Expedition of 1890, got separated from the main party and died of thirst, they were mourned in an elaborately choreographed public ceremony in Adelaide. The funeral procession was a mile long, with the gun carriage carrying their Union Jack–draped coffins accompanied by an entourage of military forces, members of friendly societies, civil servants, and men who had taken part in previous expeditions. The dead men were described in patriotic terms as "true sons of Britain—eager, adventurous, bold." The eulogist who spoke those words went on to explain the significance of their loss: "Britain is what she is to-day, mistress of the seas, Queen ruler of one-fourth of the children of men, because of the noble army of martyrs who have laid down their lives for their country."[20]

While colonists in Australia found meaning in the deaths of men such as Wells and Jones, seeing their sacrifice as contributing to the greater glory of the British Empire, few people in Britain paid much notice. Even the dramatic story of Burke and Wills's tragic deaths barely registered on the consciousness of the domestic British public. Australian explorers certainly won their share of gold medals from the Royal Geographical Society and honors from other specialist societies, but these plaudits seldom translated into popular acclaim.[21] When one speaker at an Adelaide reception honoring John Forrest compared him to Samuel Baker, John Franklin, David Livingstone, John Hanning Speke, and Henry Morton Stanley, Forrest responded by insisting that "exploration in other parts of the world, as in Africa, was carried out in a very different style to the exploration of Australia."[22] He saw no need to elaborate on what he meant by a different style: it was clear that Australian explorers could not match the appeal of their African counterparts with the British public. Ernest Giles's explanation for this disparity of interest was that he and his fellow Australian explorers "have no Victoria and Albert Nyanzas, no Tanganikas, Suatabas, or Chambizes like the great African travelers, to honor with Her Majesty's name." This remark served as the preface to an apology for having nothing more dramatic than a drab desert and a simple spring to name in the queen's honor.[23] Australia's landscape may have been less arresting to Victorians than Africa's, but the British public's greater interest in African exploration probably had far more to do with Britain's long and vexed relationship with Africa and the slave trade, its educated elite's classically inspired curiosity about the source of the Nile and other African geographical mysteries, and Britain's status as the initial point of departure for most African expeditions.

Unlike Australia, Africa had no British-affiliated public of its own to embrace exploration apart from the citizens of Cape Town and its environs. The elites of this entrepôt certainly encouraged the exploration of the interior in order to promote economic growth and civic pride, with Andrew Smith's expedition perhaps the most notable initiative associated with their aims.[24] Yet even Smith was quick to return to England, exhibiting the African artifacts and curiosities he had collected to a paying public in London's Egyptian Hall. Any British explorer of Africa who hoped to achieve celebrity had to look to a metropolitan audience for public acclaim. Mungo Park led the way with the publication of his *Travels in the Interior Districts of Africa* (1799), a best-selling account of his first expedition. Park's sensitive account of his ordeal inspired the Duchess of Devonshire and others (including the unfortunate Mr. Coulthurst) to write poems about him, and it stirred an interest in African exploration among the Romantics, including Wordsworth, Shelley, and Keats.[25] His reputation was subsequently secured as a result of his death during a second expedition in West Africa. He provided a model that men such as Hugh Clapperton, Alexander Laing, and other early nineteenth-century explorers sought to emulate, although none of them rivaled Park in capturing the public's imagination.

All that changed with David Livingstone's entry onto the public stage. This missionary-explorer received a rapturous reception when he arrived in London after his journey across the African continent in the mid-1850s. He was awarded a gold medal from the RGS, an honorary degree from Oxford University, a private audience with the queen, and countless other honors. His public lectures drew large crowds across the country. Thousands attended his address to the British Association for the Advancement of Science in 1864, many of whom were women. Livingstone's visage appeared in newspapers and magazines and on matchboxes and other products, making him one of the most widely recognized men in Britain. He was mobbed by admirers on London's streets, and one biographer reports that his appearance at church services could cause "chaos, with people clambering over the pews to try and shake his hand."[26]

Livingstone attained "a new kind of fame," observes Clare Pettitt.[27] It derived from a distinct convergence of forces. As a missionary, he held a special attraction for the largest single constituency in mid-Victorian society, the millions of devout Christians who learned about the man and his achievements in Sunday sermons, church newsletters, and a plethora of other religious publications and platforms. An overlapping source of Livingstone's appeal was his antislavery message, which resonated with the same constituency while broadening its reach by arguing that the key to the destruction of slavery was the spread of "legitimate" commerce. Livingstone also benefited from the shrewd public relations campaign conducted by Sir Roderick Murchison, the president of the RGS, who sought to recast this rough-hewn Scot as a paragon of scientific exploration and avatar of the progress and prosperity his geographic discoveries would bring to the world. Finally, Livingstone's arrival on the British stage occurred in conjunction with the emergence of a cheaper, freer, and more popular press, whose editors understood that celebrities sold newspapers.

The African explorers who followed in Livingstone's wake were beneficiaries of his breakthrough. Richard Burton, John Hanning Speke, Samuel Baker, Verney Lovett Cameron, and others achieved far greater fame or public recognition than did the men who had led expeditions into Africa in the first half of the century. These ambitious men wrote best-selling books about their adventures, corresponded with individuals of prominence and power, gave well-attended public lectures, conducted spirited debates in the press and on the stage, and confidently pronounced their opinions on matters of public policy. Their use of lantern slides, maps, and other visual aids "lent an air of theatricality" to their presentations, even those ostensibly directed to geographers and other scientists at meetings of the RGS and the British Association for the Advancement of Science.[28] They were lionized by members of the social elite, receiving invitations to London parties and weekends at country estates. Burton had his portrait painted by Lord Leighton. Speke went one better, sitting both for a portrait and for "a marble bust [that] is to be struck up at Taunton."[29] When Murchison arranged for the two men to debate at the annual meeting of the British Society for the Advancement of Science in 1864, nearly 1,500 tickets were sold to members of the public eager to attend this "gladiatorial exhibition," as the *Times* aptly called it.[30] The tragic denouement of the much-anticipated event—Speke's death the day before the debate—merely intensified this cult of celebrity.

No African explorer's demise, however, generated the outpouring of grief and gratitude that took place when David Livingstone died. His state funeral in 1874 was one of the great public events of the Victorian era, attracting widespread media attention and a huge crowd of mourners. Like the funeral for Burke and Wills a decade earlier, it showed how much importance the public attached to the martyred explorer as the embodiment of the imagined community and its ideals, whether characterized in terms of the achievements of the colony of Victoria or the advancement of British civilization in Africa. Laying Livingstone to rest in an elaborate ceremony at Westminster Abbey, his coffin draped with a Union Jack, served as an official affirmation of his standing as a national hero, a symbol of those values the Victorians cherished.

Henry Morton Stanley had sought to portray himself as the sainted hero's heir from the moment he returned from his first expedition with the announcement that he had found Livingstone on the shores of Lake Tanganyika. Stanley proved in fact to be a far more controversial figure than Livingstone, but no less famous for that. He put firmly to rest the fears voiced in the early 1870s by Richard Burton and Francis Galton that exploration had lost its popular appeal. According to Burton, the "public [was] glutted with adventure," while Galton warned that the "career of the explorer . . . is inevitably coming to an end."[31] Stanley showed how wrong they were. A journalist by trade, he had an unerring eye for a sensational story. The accounts he gave of his expeditions included hair-raising clashes with bloodthirsty savages and herculean marches through deadly jungles, all the while preaching the promise of Christian redemption for "darkest Africa." He devised a unique and highly successful strategy for promoting himself and his adventures, arousing the public's interest with his field dispatches to the *New York Herald* and other newspapers, bringing it to a fever pitch with the publication of his books, and sustaining it with lecture tours, exhibitions, and paraphernalia such as stereographic images and commemorative plates. He even marketed his name with endorsements for products such as Wellcome tropical medical chests.[32] While some critics condemned him for crass commercialism and crude pandering to a thrill-seeking public, Stanley understood more clearly than most that exploration had become integrally connected to commerce and celebrity. He used this knowledge to become the first explorer whose fame extended to the United States and much of continental Europe, making him a genuinely "global media celebrity."[33]

Stanley confirmed near the end of the century what Park had demonstrated at its start—that there were few surer ways for explorers to achieve fame than to write popular books about their expeditions. These books were rarely if ever the direct and unmediated expressions of explorers' observations and experiences. They were self-consciously crafted works that marshaled literary techniques already well established within the genre of travel writing.[34] They often went through multiple revisions as the explorers' original texts were reworked by publishers, officials, and other parties with vested interests in the outcome. One of the main objectives of these revisions was to make the texts more appealing to readers, which usually required the development of strong narrative arcs that accentuated dramatic events and eliminated mundane or redundant ones. At the same time, explorers and their amanuenses and editors took care to excise unpleasant or embarrassing remarks and revelations. All of these emendations were informed in turn by assumptions about readers and their expectations that were rooted in shared cultural values and convictions. No wonder the published accounts of expeditions diverged in so many ways—some of them minor, others far more significant—from the explorers' quotidian experiences in the field.[35]

Explorers usually kept several different types of written records of their journeys. Small pocket notebooks were used to jot down compass bearings, sketch topographical landmarks, record weather conditions, and add other bits of information as they were obtained and observed. In the evenings, explorers often summarized the day's events and recorded data from their scientific measurements in more substantive diary or journal entries. When time allowed, they also prepared longer, more self-consciously crafted narratives of their experiences and observations. Although structured as day-to-day records of events, these entries were often written at least in part some time after the fact. Good examples of all three kinds of record keeping can be found in the papers of Verney Lovett Cameron, who maintained separate notebooks, diaries, and journals during his journey across Africa in 1873–1875.[36]

In the course of an expedition, days and even weeks might go by with little or nothing of interest to report. "Unless the niggers attack us, there is hardly anything to put down in a journal," complained John Davis, a member of John McKinlay's 1861–1862 expedition. McKinlay's own journal, he noted, had entries on little "save the state of the weather and the range of the thermometer."[37] Lord Bathurst conceded in his introduction to Hugh Clapperton's journal of his 1827 expedition to Sokoto that "the same thing [was] repeated over and over again."[38] Most of the diaries and journals that recorded expeditions' day-by-day activities were similarly mundane and repetitious.

Those journals that possessed the narrative drive and drama that would appeal to the general reader required reflection, selection, and revision. Explorers in the field rarely had the time to turn their attention to such matters: they were either too busy with more pressing matters or too debilitated by exhaustion or illness. The time needed for this task could be found only during an expedition's periodic stages of stasis or after it had come to an end. Yet most explorers were reticent about revealing that their journals were often "written up sporadically," as Richard Davis indicates was the case for Charles Sturt, who worked "both from memory and from field notes."[39] To acknowledge this fact was to unsettle the explorer's truth claims, which rested first and foremost on a promptly registered record of direct observations and experiences, not a belated account drawn from often faulty recollections. John Forrest's parenthetical aside that he was "sitting down writing this journal" about his third expedition "months after the time" was a rarity.[40] Few of his counterparts were quite so revealing about how or when they wrote the most fully rendered versions of their journals.

It was well understood by most explorers that the writing of those journals was as crucial to the public acclaim they hoped to attract as were the journeys themselves. Edmund Kennedy, the ambitious protégé of Thomas Mitchell, took note of the fact that "[Charles] Sturt, [George] Grey, Sir Thomas [Mitchell] & [John] Stokes gained more by writing themselves into notice than their labors would have done for them." Intending to do the same, he kept two journals, the first for the purposes of his sponsors, the second with an eye to publication.[41] No doubt he did the same during his disastrous expedition into the Cape York region the following year. Kennedy's final request to his guide Jackey Jackey before succumbing to the spear wounds inflicted by hostile Aborigines was to "give me paper and I will write."[42] He died with pencil and paper in hand. Jackey Jackey, who understood the importance his master attached to these written records, took care to bury them in hopes that they could be recovered later, though subsequent efforts to find them proved futile.

One of the greatest calamities that could befall an explorer was to lose his journals. It happened to Mansfield Parkyns, whose efforts to rewrite the lost material entirely from memory did his reputation no good. John Kirk lost his scientific notebooks near the end of the Zambezi expedition, which could help to account for his failure to publish his botanical findings after his return.[43] Yet such misfortunes were remarkably rare. Knowing the value of their notebooks and journals, explorers usually kept them close at hand. George Grey, for example, "never trusted [them] out of my possession, however heavy my labours," since they were "precious documents."[44] Hugh Clapperton's dying request to his servant Richard Lander was to "take great care of my journals." When Lander delivered them to the Colonial Office, he was rewarded for his "fidelity and zeal," then dispatched on another mission into West Africa, one purpose of which was to recover the long-lost papers of another dead explorer, Mungo Park.[45]

While explorers were intent on "writing themselves into notice"—even from the grave—many of them were equally determined to prevent their lieutenants from doing the same. Sharing the spotlight with subordinates or running the risk of being cast in a negative light by them was hardly in their interest. As Simon Ryan points out, "the univocal official journal never has to contend with other voices presenting their opinions."[46] For Australian explorers, this univocality was relatively easy to maintain so long as their parties consisted of unschooled convicts and soldiers. But it became more challenging as more educated and ambitious men began to volunteer for expeditions from the late 1830s onward. These men, who understood the value of keeping written records of their experiences, were also less likely to submit unquestioningly to the decisions made by their commanders. Expeditions led by both Thomas Mitchell and Ludwig Leichhardt included members who wrote highly critical accounts of their leadership, though these journals did not appear in print during their lifetimes.[47] Charles Sturt sought to prevent the members of his 1844 expedition from undermining his own reports about their progress by requiring them to submit their outgoing letters for his scrutiny. Although Daniel Brock, the expedition's collector of bird specimens, kept a journal during the expedition, he had to do so secretly, not least because he was so critical of Sturt. When John McDouall Stuart, another member of Sturt's party, assumed command of his own large-scale expedition, he issued rules prohibiting his men from keeping journals or even taking notes.[48]

The same problem confronted African explorers. Some commanders took the view that any notebooks and journals written by members of their parties were official records to be handed over as evidence of the expedition's knowledge-gathering activities, much like botanical specimens and other material artifacts. This was how Richard Burton appears to have justified publishing a portion of John Hanning Speke's diary without his consent as an appendix to Burton's book about their Somali expedition. Speke would harbor a lasting grudge about what Burton had done.[49] Yet Speke was scarcely more generous when he led his own expedition in 1860. He required James Grant, his second-in-command, to sign a contract agreeing to "renounce all right to publishing in collections of any sort on my own account until approved of by Capt. Speke."[50] When Grant's modestly titled *A Walk across Africa* appeared a year after Speke's book, Sir Roderick Murchison confided to him: "Everyone says your name should have been printed with that of Speke in the title page of his book."[51] This suggestion that Grant deserved recognition as Speke's co-author was no doubt hyperbolic, but Speke's own success in supplanting Burton as the hero of their joint expedition and the leader of the subsequent expedition pointed to the very real threat an ambitious subordinate could pose to a commander. By restricting Grant's right to publish his own account of their expedition, Speke was doing what he could to make sure his companion would not nudge him off the public stage. Other explorers took similar precautions. Henry Morton Stanley, for example, required the British officers who accompanied him on the high-profile, high-risk expedition to rescue Emin Pasha to sign a contract promising not to bring into print any account of their experiences until six months after Stanley's own book on the subject had been published.[52]

Explorers who intended to write themselves into notice had to decide whose notice they wanted and how they meant to get it. It has been argued that travel writing was "shorn of its scientific pretension" in the early nineteenth century, turning instead to a discursive style designed to appeal to the general public. This may have been true for other forms of travel writing, but exploration narratives continued for the most part to fall "between the stools of scientific and literary discourse" for much of the nineteenth century.[53] While many explorers were certainly keen to reach a wide audience, they were also acutely aware of the need to establish their trustworthiness as observers. They often took pains to preface their narratives with declarations that what they had written was the raw and simple truth, unadorned by literary embellishments. Mungo Park proclaimed his book to be "a plain, unvarnished tale."[54] Edward Eyre reassured his readers that he had employed "the language [of] . . . plainness and fidelity."[55] The Lander brothers promised to provide "a faithful account . . . [that] adhered religiously to the truth."[56] Some explorers adopted a dry, largely drama-less mode of scientific discourse that made few if any concessions to popular taste. Both Heinrich Barth and Ludwig Leichhardt wrote books that were intended to emulate the sober, rigorous style of their fellow German and role model, Alexander von Humboldt. Others drafted different texts for different audiences, preparing scientific reports for the *Journal of the Royal Geographical Society* and other specialized publications while writing more engaging narratives for commercial publishers.

The last third of the nineteenth century saw some explorers openly embrace the highly charged prose style of sensationalist journalism and adventure fiction in their expedition narratives. Among Australian explorers of this period, Ernest Giles was the most skilled and successful practitioner of the new approach. He complained that most expedition reports were "too dry even for mental digestion," so he spiced up his own narratives with what he modestly referred to as the "odd anecdote or imaginative idea."[57] A contemporary reviewer praised him as "a clever word painter" of "very great descriptive power."[58] Late nineteenth-century African explorers were under even greater pressure to inject drama into their narratives. Joseph Thomson declared in the introduction to his *Through Masai Land* (1887) that he had "resolved to clothe the dry bones of a mere report in the flesh and blood of a narrative."[59] He also tried his hand at adventure fiction, as did Samuel Baker and Verney Lovett Cameron. Drawing on their African experiences and reputations, they sought to cater to the same audience that made H. Rider Haggard's *King Solomon's Mines* (1885) such a huge commercial success.

No one, however, matched Henry Morton Stanley in crafting narratives about his expeditions that attracted a mass readership. His books straddled the line between journal and journalism and arguably between nonfiction and fiction.[60] Yet even Stanley found it hard to turn his back entirely on the geographical community and the scientific standards it used to assess explorers' accomplishments. Still stinging from the Royal Geographical Society's criticisms of his previous expedition in search of Livingstone, Stanley proposed a third volume of *Through the Darkest Continent*, one that would have detailed the scientific findings of his transcontinental expedition of 1874–1877. His publisher, Edward Marston, talked him out of it, gently arguing: "I am sure you could make an interesting volume—but are you not committed rather to the scientific line? . . . after all the scientific readers will be *few*."[61]

As Marston's advice to Stanley indicates, publishers played an important role in explorers' efforts to come to public notice. Scholars have given increasing attention in recent years to the "redactive practices" publishers brought to bear on explorers' texts.[62] Their editorial interventions reshaped those texts in important ways—altering passages, condensing events, modifying meanings, and otherwise transforming what the explorers had written about their experiences. The purpose of these changes was, of course, to sell books, and publishers understood what this required in terms of public tastes and expectations.

Both publishers and their markets were concentrated in Britain. Because travel literature was already a well-established genre at the start of the nineteenth century, a number of firms specialized in the publication of books about exploration. This was especially the case for accounts of Africa, which attracted strong interest among British readers. Mungo Park's *Travels in the Interior Districts of Africa* was an immediate best seller, bringing its author a profit of £1,050 from the first edition and a further £2,000 from the three editions that quickly followed.[63] African explorers' narratives became a mainstay of the London publishing house John Murray, which specialized in travel literature. Murray published works by William Balfour Baikie, Hugh Clapperton, Francis Galton, and others. David Livingstone's *Missionary Travels* in particular was a huge success for Murray, selling 70,000 copies and bringing Livingstone a profit in excess of £12,000.[64]

The market for books about Australian exploration was considerably smaller. John Murray published one of the first books about the exploration of Australia's frontier, John Oxley's *Two Expeditions into the Interior of New South Wales* (1820), but few others. William Hovell and Hamilton Hume's account of their important 1824 journey was published in Sydney, not London, and then only after a long delay caused by a scarcity of paper in the colony.[65] By the late 1830s, however, the London firm T. & W. Boone had found a niche for Australian exploration narratives, becoming the main outlet for the works of explorers such as George Grey, Edward Eyre, Ludwig Leichhardt, and Thomas Mitchell.

Australia's colonies began to develop profitable print markets of their own from the midcentury on. The dispatches that explorers wrote during their journeys were often published verbatim by the local newspapers that proliferated in Sydney, Melbourne, Adelaide, and other Australian cities. The reports that explorers submitted to authorities after they had returned from their expeditions also appeared in print as official publications issued by colonial governments. Commercial presses fed settlers' curiosity about the fate of Burke and Wills and other explorers with a stream of pamphlets and books.[66] All of these publications helped to generate the popular interest in explorers' exploits and ordeals that found expression in civic ceremonies such as those organized in honor of Forrest and Giles. Even so, most Australian explorers likely preferred the prestige of a British imprint.

Meanwhile, the market for African exploration narratives continued to grow, attracting more and more publishers. John Murray faced competition from Blackwood, Longman, Tinsley Brothers, Macmillan, and other publishing houses. Blackwood outbid Murray for the right to publish John Hanning Speke's *Journal of the Discovery of the Source of the Nile* (1864). Its initial run of 7,500 copies quickly sold out, and an additional 2,500 copies had to be printed on short notice, with further runs soon to follow. Macmillan, anticipating brisk sales for Samuel Baker's *The Albert Nyanza* (1866), offered him a £2,500 advance and printed 25,000 copies. Henry Morton Stanley, however, overshadowed everyone else. Sampson, Low sold 150,000 copies of *In Darkest Africa* (1890), making it an unprecedented blockbuster for a book about exploration.[67]

African explorers' accounts of their travels and adventures attracted the interest of reading publics in other countries as well, especially the United States. The exploration narratives of Park, Clapperton, Lander, and others had appeared in American editions, and Livingstone's *Missionary Travels* was a commercial success for its Philadelphia publisher. And after the Welsh-American journalist Stanley appeared on the scene as the man who had found Livingstone, Americans acquired an insatiable appetite for African stories of exploration.

Stanley and the American publishing industry also contributed to print culture's promotion of exploration through their newspaper innovations. The American penny press, which preceded its British counterpart by several decades, pioneered the use of sensationalist stories to expand sales. Expeditions, especially those that went badly, were well suited for such coverage. The *New York Herald*'s innovative owner and editor, James Gordon Bennett Jr., took the public's interest in the ordeals of explorers a step further by manufacturing his own sensational news: he sponsored Stanley's expedition in search of Livingstone, which gave him proprietary control over the story itself. Making innovative use of newly laid transatlantic telegraph cables, the *Herald* printed dramatic and timely dispatches from Stanley about his perils and progress. These gripping stories attracted readers, sold papers, and pushed competitors to adopt similar strategies. When Stanley set out on his subsequent transcontinental journey, the expedition was jointly financed by the *Herald* and a leading English newspaper, the *Daily Telegraph.*[68]

While a sensationalist press made a celebrity of Stanley, his own journalistic skills contributed mightily to his fame. Stanley's ability to craft a thrilling narrative was unmatched by other explorers. Many wrote stolid, uninspired prose, and a few were scarcely capable of writing at all. Quite apart from their deficiencies as writers, they often were not well attuned to the themes and topics that appealed to popular tastes. How many of them relied on friends and family to help them prepare their journals for publication is impossible to say, and scholars have barely begun to undertake a systematic study of the editorial interventions by publishers. But research into the process by which some well-known African explorers struggled to make their prose fit for publication indicates that the transition from the original text to the final product involved multiple intermediaries.

Mungo Park returned from West Africa in 1797 with little more than the fragmentary notes he had famously stuffed into his hat. Joseph Banks asked fellow African Association member James Rennell to prepare a report on Park's geographical findings, and urged Park, who lacked experience as a writer, to turn to another association member, Bryan Edwards, for assistance when he sat down to write a narrative account of what he had seen and done. Exactly how extensive that assistance proved to be is unclear: some portions of Edwards's own narrative reappeared in Park's book, but Edwards himself assured Banks that Park grew more skilled and self-confident as the writing progressed. What is clear, however, is that Park's best-selling book was not entirely his own work.[69]

As the only white man to survive Hugh Clapperton's second expedition into West Africa, Richard Lander had hoped to publish a book about his experiences. He used his "leisure time in writing about the laws, Customs, trade," and other features of the African territories he had visited, as well as recounting "my own personal adventures." He intended to "offer it [the manuscript] to Mr. Murr[a]y for sale," but he recognized that his deficiencies as a writer required the assistance of someone capable of "putting [his prose] together grammatically." He turned to his brother, a compositor at the *Cornwall Gazette*. Their efforts failed to impress John Murray, and the only account of the expedition to appear in print was the one drawn from Clapperton's journals, where portions of Lander's journal, its spelling and grammar corrected, appeared as an addendum.[70] When Richard and his brother John made their triumphant return from the expedition that traced the Niger River to its outlet in the Gulf of Guinea, there was little doubt that a narrative of their journey would appear in print. Its principal author, however, was not Richard, the expedition's leader, but John, who "in point of education and literary attainments . . . has the advantage of his brother."[71]

The missionary and abolitionist Horace Waller played an important role in preparing several expedition journals for publication, most notably the journals David Livingstone left at his death. A champion of Livingstone and his memory, Waller had previously assisted E. D. Young in transforming the monotonous journal that detailed his 1866 expedition in search of Livingstone into a marginally readable book. When Livingstone's journals from his final expedition were brought back to Britain, John Murray hired Waller to prepare them for publication. Waller has been shown to have suppressed or minimized passages that placed Livingstone in an unflattering light, including those that revealed his racist disdain for the Portuguese and their mixed-race offspring, his troubling collaboration with slave traders, his dismissive remarks about other explorers and geographers, and his harsh treatment of the Nasik boys. Waller worked to ensure that the journals presented Livingstone as the saintly martyr the public expected him to be.[72]

And then there is the case of John Hanning Speke. "I hate writing," Speke informed his publisher, William Blackwood, who later learned to his dismay how true that statement was.[73] At the time, Speke was trying to write an account of his two expeditions in the company of Richard Burton, but he had a problem: "I never kept diaries with a view to writing and never should have written had it not been required of me." In consequence, he was unable to provide "precise verbatim accounts of the various circumstances as they took place; and I have had to extract nearly as much matter from letters which I wrote to my brother . . . as from the diaries themselves."[74] This was a damning confession, and it may help to explain why the book that resulted from this unpromising material, *What Led to the Discovery of the Source of the Nile* (1864), was not published until the year after Speke's more famous *Journal of the Discovery of the Source of the Nile* (1863). Moreover, a recent study has revealed that the latter work required extensive editorial revision before it became suitable for publication.[75] Although Speke kept a journal during his expedition to find the source of the Nile, his efforts to transform the journal into a book manuscript exposed his serious deficiencies as a writer. Blackwood found that Speke "writes in such an abominable, childish, unintelligible way" that he had to hire a ghostwriter to revise the text.[76] In addition to correcting grammar and spelling, changing words, and tightening the narrative structure, the ghostwriter deleted passages that seemed likely to shock or offend readers, including Speke's entries about his romantic relationship with Meri. The result was a book that differed in important ways from the original manuscript, presenting a far more forceful and confident narrative that stressed "the triumph of Speke over nature and inferior races."[77]

How many other explorers had their manuscripts massaged and reworked by publishers in order to make them more palatable to the public is uncertain, but there is no reason to suppose that the experiences of Park, Lander, Livingstone, and Speke were exceptional. Many of the books advertised as explorers' unmediated records of their observations and adventures must have gone through multiple emendations as they were prepared for publication. Nor were publishers the only mediating forces involved in the effort to shape the reputations of explorers and their representations of alien lands and peoples. Newspaper owners such as James Gordon Bennett Jr., scientific impresarios such as Sir Roderick Murchison, and a great many other individuals and institutions contributed to this enterprise, creating a popular conception of explorers and exploration than served their own social, cultural, political, and commercial interests.

Explorers who sought celebrity were in many respects subject to the desires and expectations of the societies that sponsored their endeavors and sanctioned their achievements. They were all too often obliged to cast themselves, their experiences, and their observations in terms that accorded with what the public wanted to hear. And what the public wanted to hear could be characterized in its essence as confirmation of the moral purpose they attributed to themselves as a people. Explorers were meant to manifest this purpose in various ways: by exemplifying the enterprise and resourcefulness that were considered integral to what made their colony, their country, and their civilization great; by exposing the sloth and savagery that explained why the peoples whose territories they penetrated were degraded and in desperate need of the Britons' improving presence; and by imbuing the challenges they overcame and the sufferings they endured with a spiritual significance, a sacrifice for some greater good that transcended the self.

Many explorers embraced these understandings of their purpose with alacrity and conviction. Yet even those who exhibited the greatest skill and success in winning the public's plaudits often seemed strangely alienated from the society they served. What Edwin Welch unsympathetically described as John King's "state of semi-stupidity" may have been a more common affliction than we realize. Richard Burton acknowledged that he often lapsed into depression and avoided the company of his countrymen for as long as possible once his expeditions had come to an end. Henry Morton Stanley felt listless and depressed at the conclusion of his triumphant trek across the African continent, and he had little desire to bask in the adulation that awaited him in Britain. Charles Sturt repeatedly sought escape from his unhappy personal and professional life by undertaking the expeditions that brought him fame. John McDouall Stuart went on prolonged drinking bouts when he returned from his travels and dried out only when he set off for the interior once again. David Livingstone spent the last seven years of his life in what can best be described as self-imposed exile from his country and his family, seeking refuge in a long, meandering, futile search for the Nile. The fact that so many explorers were so determined to set out time and again to distant and dangerous lands despite the travails they had endured during previous journeys suggests that they did not find it easy to adjust to the demands of a place conventionally characterized as their "home." For many of them, it seems, it resembled a prison.

This was the paradox that plagued explorers: on one hand, they were hungry for the acclaim of their countrymen; on the other hand, they were uneasy in their company, an unease that extended to their country as well. The constraints that celebrity imposed on them account for this paradox. It necessitated discretion if not deception about what they had seen and done and felt. To act otherwise was to run the risk, as Speke aptly put it, of "getting abused when disclosing disagreeable truths."[78] They were obliged, in effect, to distort, diminish, and deny much of what they had experienced in the field—their doubts, their fears, their desires, their confusions, and more. The mediations and alterations required to bring their expedition journals into print were indicative of this process, and it extended to almost every venue that brought them into the public eye. It ensured that much of the knowledge they acquired through their quotidian experiences in the field—a knowledge that often challenged their expectations and convictions, causing them to reconsider the nature of normative behavior and the sources of personal satisfaction—would remain a private knowledge, a secret knowledge stored discreetly out of sight.

Epilogue

This book has advanced two linked arguments about the exploration of Africa and Australia in the nineteenth century. The first is that this endeavor was informed by a new scientific spirit that drew much of its inspiration from the eighteenth-century naval expeditions of Captain Cook and his counterparts. The continents of Africa and Australia came to be conceived as analogous to oceans, essentially blank spaces that could be made truly knowable as physical places only through the application of those scientific practices that seaborne explorers had done so much to pioneer: recording observations in logbooks and journals, measuring geographical locations and meteorological conditions with precision instruments, and collecting and preserving botanical, zoological, and other specimens. The men who adopted these practices and employed them on their journeys came to be known as explorers, whose skills and status set them apart from other travelers. With rare exceptions, the expeditions they commanded received financing, instructions, and oversight from sponsoring organizations whose demands and rewards enhanced explorers' reputations even more. Although their efforts to claim greater autonomy as scientific observers collided with the regulatory regime overseen by scientific specialists at home, they were recognized as the lead agents in the process by which Africa and Australia were revealed as objects of Western knowledge.

The second argument is that this new way of knowing Africa and Australia was of little practical value to explorers as they entered these unfamiliar environments and engaged with their inhabitants. They confronted strange places, plants, animals, diseases, and more, and their success in coping with these challenges was often contingent on their access to local knowledge. But local knowledge derived from local peoples. These peoples were among an array of mediating forces that shaped the character and outcome of expeditions. Gateway states gave explorers access to the interior, but often on their terms, which were not necessarily coterminous with those of Britain. The technological hubris that inspired many expeditions collided with the constraints of climates, topographies, political economies, and more, requiring logistical accommodations to the targeted region's conditions and established practices. Explorers had to rely on the expertise and experience of guides and go-betweens, whose own agendas often had a far greater influence on the operations of the enterprise than their reputations as selfless servants or petty subordinates suggest. And no expedition could progress very far without encountering indigenous peoples and polities, whose receptivity to this strange party often determined the course and even the outcome of its journey. Explorers' success in coping with these forces necessitated a very different knowledge from the kind they were expected to acquire for their domestic sponsors and publics. It was a quotidian knowledge of tangible places, not an abstract knowledge of empty spaces. It was a hard-won knowledge, the product of dislocation, danger, and desire. It was an intimate knowledge, derived from long periods of close contact with other peoples. It was perforce a secret knowledge, incommunicable to countrymen back home.

As the nineteenth century came toward its close, Africa and Australia ceased to serve as sites for exploration, at least as this enterprise has been characterized in this book. The most straightforward explanation is that almost every corner of the two continents had been probed by the end of the century, leaving little for explorers to discover. Members of the Elder Scientific Exploration Expedition, which ventured into west-central Australia in 1891–1892, complained about being "twittered by everyone that we were not the explorers of old" and that "we were simply travelling over settled and known country."[1] A self-serving Henry Morton Stanley declared after his own exploring days were over that "Geographical Novelties have already become scarce even from Darkest Africa."[2]

It would be simplistic, however, to attribute the end of the era of exploration in Africa and Australia entirely to its own success. A much broader array of political, social, and ideological forces contributed to its cessation. These forces were especially evident in Africa, where the onset of the European scramble for colonial possessions in the 1880s overturned the balance of power among Europeans, Africans, and Arabs. A common characteristic of expeditions prior to this point was their relative weakness, evidenced by explorers' frequent capitulation to the demands of local rulers and their sometimes willing, sometimes unwitting contributions to the ambitions of Muslim gateway states. With the scramble, however, self-styled explorers became increasingly indistinguishable from conquerors, leading heavily armed columns into the African interior as agents of metropolitan imperial interests. Stanley's transition from explorer to empire builder began when King Leopold of Belgium hired him to claim the vast Congo River basin as the monarch's personal fiefdom. He followed up with the ruthless Emin Pasha Relief Expedition, which resembled nothing so much in its organization and conduct as an invading army, its implicit intent being the opening of central Africa to imperial ambitions. Like Stanley, most of his late nineteenth-century contemporaries—Pierre de Brazza, Jean-Baptiste Marchand, Carl Peters, William Stairs, Harry Johnston, and Joseph Thomson among them—were involved in the transition from exploration to conquest, acting as agents for European parties eager to claim colonial territory.[3]

The violence most of these men perpetrated during their marches through Africa eroded the popular perception of exploration as the heroic endeavor of a lone explorer exhibiting moral and physical courage in the face of great danger. No event proved more disillusioning in this regard than the scandal caused by the conduct of the officers who commanded the Rear Column during Stanley's Emin Pasha expedition. Left on the banks of the Congo to await porters needed to move the expedition's mountain of military supplies, the column soon ran short of food and descended into starvation and savagery, its British officers ordering raids on local villages, brutalizing their own forces, and abetting an act of cannibalism. When the officers' conduct came to light, the British public began to wonder who were the more uncivilized, the Africans or the Europeans. Samuel Baker called the story of the Rear Column "the most horrible and indecent exposure that I have ever heard or seen in print."[4] Stanley's own unrestrained use of violence during the expedition provoked further dismay, reviving criticisms that he was a "sham explorer" and stirring doubts about whether the narrative of British exploration in Africa as a humanitarian endeavor still obtained.[5]

A more subtle but perhaps more significant indicator of the structural shifts that were bringing the era of exploration to an end in Africa was the turn from the traverse survey to the trigonometric survey. Several generations of African explorers had relied on the traverse survey to track their routes across space, much in the manner of navigators at sea. The new mode of mapping African territory had its impetus instead in the needs of imperial states to assert sovereignty over territory. As European powers partitioned Africa, they had to delineate the boundaries of their new colonies, lay out the routes for railways and telegraph lines, and establish the parameters of property for the purposes of taxation, alienation, and exploitation. Stanley endorsed this shift in surveying strategy, acknowledging that the trigonometric survey was better suited to the new imperial geography in Africa. Even within the Royal Geographical Society, which had been the leading proponent of the transit survey, an increasingly powerful group of army officers and new geographers such as Halford Mackinder lobbied for it to promote trigonometric surveys instead.[6]

Australian exploration underwent a more incremental and prosaic process of closure. The colonial conquest of the interior began in the early decades of the nineteenth century, and as it progressed, settlers continually clashed with indigenes along a moving frontier. The scramble of the 1860s brought about the territorial apportionment of the continent among the mainland colonial states, although much of central and northern Australia remained terra incognita to settlers and other Europeans for decades to come. By the end of the century, however, expeditions had crisscrossed nearly all of this territory, leaving little doubt about its topography, hydrography, and prospects for development. Where those prospects appeared promising, colonial governments sent out surveyors to conduct the trigonometric surveys necessary to establish land titles and property markets.[7] Where commercial opportunities seemed slight or too difficult to develop, as was the case across much of the Northern Territory, Aborigines enjoyed some respite from the settler advance.

As the century drew to a close, the boundaries between explorers and other travelers began to blur in both Australia and Africa. The realm explorers had once regarded as entirely their own was now increasingly crowded with others, undermining their special status. Intrepid female travelers posed a particular challenge. Their journeys into remote regions called into question the very idea of exploration as an exclusively masculine sphere, requiring a man's special strength, skill, and courage. Two of the women who helped to overturn these gender distinctions were the African travelers May French Sheldon and Mary Kingsley. Sheldon, an American-born admirer of Henry Morton Stanley, organized and led her own expedition into East Africa in 1891, which she recounted in her book *Sultan to Sultan* (1892). She was soon overshadowed by Kingsley, whose two journeys through West Africa in the 1890s and engaging accounts of her experiences in the best-selling *Travels in West Africa* (1897) and *West African Studies* (1899) made her a prominent public figure whose policy recommendations about Africa were widely respected. Similar challenges occurred in Australia, where women such as the botanical painter Marianne North traveled into parts of the outback hitherto regarded as the preserve of pioneering men. And no wonder Ernest Favenc's biographer characterized him as "the last explorer" of Australia: he contributed to the collapse of exploration's masculinist identity by bringing his wife with him on his 1878–1879 expedition and inviting another married couple to accompany them on a subsequent expedition.[8] Moreover, as roads, railways, steamships, and other modes of transportation spread their tentacles across the two continents, growing numbers of tourists and other curiosity seekers of both sexes made their way into hitherto remote regions in search of picturesque landscapes, exotic peoples, big game, and other hitherto inaccessible attractions.

British explorers in the twentieth century turned their attention to other frontiers. Some sought lost civilizations in Yucatan's jungles, the Peruvian highlands, and the deserts of Central Asia. Others pursued lost tribes in the Amazon and New Guinea. None attracted as much attention, however, as did the explorers who entered Antarctica's frigid wastelands in search of the South Pole. Here was an environment without human inhabitants, a harsh and empty continent that came closer than any large landmass to replicating the vast emptiness of the oceanic realm. Here too was an objective of supreme scientific abstraction for explorers to pursue, a geographical location indistinguishable from its surroundings and identifiable only by its longitudinal and latitudinal coordinates. The Antarctic permitted Robert Falcon Scott and Ernest Shackleton, both naval men, to launch expeditions that resembled those of the seaborne explorers they revered, especially in terms of their manpower, logistical arrangements, and navigational practices. Above all, it permitted them to test their physical and mental mettle against an unforgiving environment without indigenous mediation or interference.[9]

Mount Everest held a similar allure for George Mallory and the various others who sought to reach its peak. But Everest proved to be the last hurrah for the heroic mode of exploration that had so long stirred British national pride. When mountaineers finally reached its summit in 1953, it was the Australian Edmund Hillary and his Sherpa partner, Tenzing Norgay, who shared the achievement, a striking collaboration that stretched claims of Britishness to its limits and simultaneously exposed the vital role that local Sherpas had long played in efforts to ascend the mountain. And soon thereafter, the frontier of exploration shifted to outer space, a realm that was beyond the reach of Britain with its much-diminished postwar resources. It was the two superpowers, the United States and the Soviet Union, who vied for supremacy in this competition. As Stephen Pyne has observed, the expeditions they sent into space entered "worlds inoculated against life, where no natives can guide and enlighten explorers, where no explorer can possibly live off the land, and where colonization is a fantasy."[10]

For all intents and purposes, the era of exploration in Africa and Australia came to an end more than a century ago. Yet it retains a powerful hold on the cultural imaginations of the British and their colonial cousins. Nostalgia has been its principal mode of expression. Consider a few examples. A few years ago the History Channel broadcast a reality show, *Expedition Africa: Stanley and Livingstone,* which dispatched four "elite explorers" on Stanley's route in search of Livingstone, accompanied by Tanzanian porters to carry their luggage and, anomalously, Masai warriors to provide "protection."[11] In Denbigh, the Welsh town where Henry Morton Stanley was born, a statue was recently unveiled honoring its famous son. For Stanley's most recent biographer, Tim Jeal, the statue was a courageous challenge to what he characterized as "post-imperial guilt."[12] And in late 2010, Hendrik Coetzee, a South African "explorer" who had earlier conducted journeys in the footsteps of Stanley and Mungo Park, was killed by a crocodile while kayaking near the headwaters of the Nile, a place that one of his obituaries could not resist referring to as "the darkest heart of the continent's dark heart."[13]

Similar echoes of exploration's past can be heard in the Australian context. The Royal Society of Victoria, the Burke and Wills Historical Society, and other groups recently organized a series of events to commemorate the 150th anniversary of the Burke and Wills expedition. The president of the Burke and Wills Society retraced the entire route taken by his heroes. John McDouall Stuart received reverential attention in *Ray Mears Goes Walkabout,* a four-part BBC series by the eponymous British survivalist and TV personality. Substantial numbers of white Australians have participated in "footsteps" expeditions, which follow the routes of various explorers. A recent study has shown that the "footsteps" treks initially arose in response to Aboriginal challenges to white land claims in the 1970s and 1980s and were intended to advance "a counter-claim," one that involved the "removal of Aborigines from the nation's past" by portraying the places the explorers passed through as empty of indigenous inhabitants.[14]

This book can be read as a rebuttal to the nostalgic view of African and Australian exploration so prevalent in certain circles today. The analysis that has been advanced in these pages challenges key aspects of exploration's appeal as nostalgia. First, it has shown that the expeditions that ventured into the interiors of Africa and Australia can be characterized as the instruments of a triumphalist British civilization exerting its influence and bestowing its benefits on these continents only if we willfully ignore the fact that many of these expeditions were abject failures and most were swayed in their operations, channeled in their movements, and checked in their objectives by local forces. Second, it has shown that the explorers who made these journeys through the two continents can be cast as autonomous agents whose achievements derived from their personal reservoirs of will and courage only if we minimize the fear, bafflement, and helplessness they experienced and ignore the evidence of their dependence on indigenous intermediaries. While rosy notions of the resolute hero overcoming all odds in pursuing his quest and advancing the cause of civilization may stir a sense of nostalgic pride in some breasts, such sentiments fail to communicate the complex realities that confronted explorers and shaped their expeditions. Those realities offer us a far richer and more compelling story, one that involves emotional dissonance and desire, cultural misunderstanding and communication, social conflict and conciliation, political rivalry and collaboration, and more. It is the story, above all, of the intersection of contending ways of knowing the world, and as such, it is a story that retains its relevance in our own increasingly interdependent world.

Comparative Timeline of African and Australian Expeditions

Year	Africa	Region	Australia	Region
1795	Park (1)	west		
1796	Park (1)	west		
1797	Park (1)	west		
	Barrow	south		
1798	Hornemann	north		
1799	Hornemann	north		
1800	Hornemann	north		
1801	Hornemann	north		
1802				
1803				
1804				
1805	Park (2)	west (Niger)		
1806	Park (2)	west (Niger)		
1807				
1808				
1809	Salt	northeast		
1810	Salt	northeast		
1811	Burchell	south		
1812	Burchell	south		
1813	Burchell	south	Blaxland et al.	southeast
	Burckhardt	northeast		
1814	Burchell	south		
	Burckhardt	northeast		
1815	Burchell	south		
	Burckhardt	northeast		

(continued)

Year	Africa	Region	Australia	Region
1816	Burckhardt	northeast		
	Tuckey	central (Congo)		
1817	Burckhardt	northeast	Oxley (1)	southeast
1818	Peddie et al.	west	Oxley (2)	southeast
			Hume (1)	southeast
1819	Peddie et al.	west	Oxley (3)	southeast
1820	Peddie et al.	west		
1821	Peddie et al.	west		
1822	Denham & Clapperton	west	Hume (2)	southeast
1823	Denham & Clapperton	west	Oxley (4)	southeast
			Cunningham (1)	southeast
1824	Denham & Clapperton	west	Hume & Hovell	southeast
1825	Denham & Clapperton	west		
	Laing	west		
1826	Clapperton	west	Hovell	east
	Laing	west		
1827	Clapperton	west	Cunningham (2)	southeast
1828			Sturt (1)	southeast
1829			Sturt (1, 2)	southeast
			Cunningham (3)	southeast
1830	R. & J. Lander	west (Niger)	Sturt (2)	southeast
1831	R. & J. Lander	west (Niger)	Mitchell (1)	southeast
1832	Lander & Laird	west (Niger)	Mitchell (1)	southeast
1833	Lander & Laird	west (Niger)		
1834	Lander & Laird	west (Niger)		
	A Smith	south		
1835	A. Smith	south	Mitchell (2)	southeast
1836	A. Smith	south	Mitchell (3)	southeast
1837				
1838			Grey (1)	northwest
1839			Grey (2)	northwest
1840			Eyre	southwest
1841	Allen	west (Niger)	Eyre	southwest
1842				
1843				
1844			Sturt (3)	central
			Leichhardt (1)	central
1845			Sturt (3)	central
			Leichhardt (1)	central
			Mitchell (4)	central
1846			Sturt (3)	central
			Leichhardt (1)	central
			A. Gregory (1)	west
			Mitchell (4)	central
1847			Leichhardt (2)	central
			Kennedy (1)	east

Year	Africa	Region	Australia	Region
1848			Kennedy (2)	northeast
			Leichhardt (3)	central
1849				
1850	Barth	west		
	Galton	southwest		
1851	Barth	west		
	Galton	southwest		
1852	Barth	west		
1853	Barth	west		
1854	Barth	west		
	Livingstone (1)	transcont.		
	Baikie (1)	west (Niger)		
1855	Barth	west	A. Gregory (2)	north
	Livingstone (1)	transcont		.
	Baikie (1)	west (Niger)		
	Burton (1)	northeast		
1856	Livingstone (1)	transcont.	A. Gregory (2)	north
			Babbage (1)	south-central
1857	Baikie (2)	west (Niger)	Hack	south-central
	Burton & Speke	east (lakes)		
1858	Baikie (2)	west (Niger)	Babbage (2)	south-central
	Burton & Speke	east (lakes)	A. Gregory (3)	southeast
	Livingstone (2)	central (Zambezi)	Stuart (1)	south-central
1859	Baikie (2)	west (Niger)	Stuart (2)	central
	Burton & Speke	east (lakes)		
	Livingstone (2)	central (Zambezi)		
1860	Baikie (2)	west (Niger)	Burke/Wills	transcont.
	Speke & Grant	east (lakes)	Stuart (3)	central
	Livingstone (2)	central (Zambezi)	Howitt	southeast
1861	Baikie (2)	west (Niger)	Burke/Wills	transcont.
	Speke & Grant	east (lakes)	McKinlay (1)	transcont.
	Livingstone (2)	central (Zambezi)	Stuart (4)	transcont.
	Baker	east (Nile)	F. Gregory	northwest
			Howitt (2)	central
			Landsborough	transcont.
1862	Baikie (2)	west (Niger)	Stuart (4)	transcont.
	Speke & Grant	east (lakes)	McKinlay (1)	transcont.
	Livingstone (2)	central (Zambezi)	Landsborough	transcont.
	Baker	east (Nile)		
1863	Baikie (2)	west (Nile)		
	Speke & Grant	east (lakes)		
	Livingstone (2)	central (Zambezi)		
	Baker	east (Nile)		
1864	Baikie (2)	west (Niger)	Jardine	northeast
	Baker	east (Nile)		
1865	Baker	east (Nile)	McKinlay (2)	north

(continued)

Year	Africa	Region	Australia	Region
			Jardine	northeast
			McIntyre	central
1866	Livingstone (3)	central (lakes)	McKinlay (2)	north
			McIntyre	central
1867	Livingstone (3)	central (lakes)	Cadell	north
1868	Livingstone (3)	central (lakes)		
1869	Livingstone (3)	central (lakes)	J. Forrest (1)	west
	Baker (2)	east (Nile)		
1870	Livingstone (3)	central (lakes)	J. Forrest (2)	southwest
	Baker (2)	east (Nile)		
1871	Livingstone (3)	central (lakes)	A. Forrest (1)	southwest
	Stanley (1)	east (lakes)		
	Baker (2)	east (Nile)		
1872	Livingstone (3)	central (lakes)	Gosse (1)	west-central
	Baker (2)	east (Nile)	Warburton	west-central
			Giles (1)	west-central
1873	Livingstone (3)	central (lakes)	Warburton	west-central
	Cameron	transcont.	Giles (2)	west-central
	Baker (2)	east (Nile)	Gosse (1)	west-central
1874	Cameron	transcont.	J. Forrest (3)	transcont.
	Stanley (2)	transcont.	Giles (2)	central
1875	Cameron	transcont.	Giles (3)	west
	Stanley (2)	transcont.	Gosse (2)	central
1876	Stanley (2)	transcont.	Giles (4)	west
1877	Stanley (2)	transcont.		
1878			Favenc	northeast
1879	Thomson (1)	east (lakes)	A. Forrest (2)	northwest
1880	Thomson (1)	east (lakes)		
1881	Thomson (2)	east	Winnecke	northwest
1882				
1883	Thomson (3)	east (lakes)	Lindsay (1)	north
1884	Thomson (3)	east (lakes)		
1885				
1886				
1887	Stanley (3)	central		
1888	Stanley (3)	central		
1889	Stanley (3)	central	Tietkens	central
1890				
1891			Lindsay (2)	west
1892			Lindsay (2)	west
1893				
1894				
1895			Winnecke (2)	central
1896			Carnegie	west
1897			Carnegie	west
1898				
1899				

Notes

1. Continents

1. This was *Hints to Travellers,* 1st ed. (1854), and its predecessor, *Hints for Collecting Geographical Information* (1837). See Felix Driver, *Geography Militant* (Oxford, 2001), 56–67.

2. An exception of particular relevance is Norman Etherington, ed., *Mapping Colonial Conquest* (Crawley, 2007).

3. Robert I. Rotberg, "Introduction," in *Africa and Its Explorers* (Cambridge, Mass., 1970), 11. Much more recently, the African anthropologist Johannes Fabian's excellent

Out of Our Minds (Berkeley, 2000) adopts a similar stance. No comparable perspectives inform the scholarship on Australian exploration.

4. Robin Hallett, ed., *Records of the African Association, 1788–1831* (London, 1964), 42.

5. Alexander von Humboldt, *Personal Narrative of a Journey,* abridged ed. (Harmondsworth, 1996), introduction (unpaginated Kindle edition).

6. Joseph Conrad, "Geography and Some Explorers," in *Last Essays* [1926] (Freeport, N.Y., 1970), 10.

7. Charles W. J. Withers and David N. Livingstone, "Thinking Geographically about Nineteenth-Century Science," in *Geographies of Nineteenth-Century Science,* ed. David N. Livingstone and Charles W. J. Withers (Chicago, 2011), 2.

8. Martin W. Lewis and Kären E. Wigen, *The Myth of Continents* (Berkeley, 1997), 30.

9. Elizabeth Mancke, "Ocean Space and the Creation of a Global International System, 1450–1800," in *Maritime History as World History,* ed. Daniel Finamore (Gainesville, 2004), 149–166; Lauren Benton, *A Search for Sovereignty* (Cambridge, 2010).

10. I take issue here with James R. Akerman, ed., *The Imperial Map* (Chicago, 2009), especially the essay by Matthew H. Edney, "The Irony of Imperial Mapping" (11–45), which argues that it is possible to differentiate imperial from national cartography. The trigonometric methods used to map both spaces were the same, the surveys were launched at much the same time, and the state benefited from the resulting cartographic information about nation and colony in much the same way.

11. Richard Drayton, "Knowledge and Empire," in *The Oxford History of the British Empire,* vol. 2: *The Eighteenth Century,* ed. P. J. Marshall (Oxford, 1998), 246. See also Matthew H. Edney, *Mapping an Empire* (Chicago, 1997); Simon Berthon and Andrew Robinson, *The Shape of the World* (Chicago, 1991), ch. 6.

12. A point made by Thomas J. Bassett, "Cartography and Empire Building in Nineteenth-Century West Africa," *Geographical Review* 84, no. 3 (July 1994), esp. 322–325, 332–333; and Lucy P. Chester, "The Mapping of Empire," *Portuguese Studies* 16 (2000): 256–275.

13. These are the "implications of treating land as ocean" that are drawn by Martin Thomas, *The Artificial Horizon* (Carlton, Victoria, 2003), 117.

14. D. Graham Burnett, *Masters of All They Surveyed* (Chicago, 2000), 255.

15. Ibid., 104.

16. Introduction to James H. Tuckey and Christen Smith, *Narrative of an Expedition to Explore the River Zaire* (London, 1818), v; emphasis added. Barrow is identified as author of this anonymous introduction by Christopher Lloyd, *Mr. Barrow of the Admiralty* (London, 1970), 112.

17. On d'Anville, see Bassett, "Cartography," 322, and Chester, "Mapping," 257–258.

18. The analysis offered in this paragraph and the prior one on eighteenth-century maps of Africa is drawn from an examination of the historical maps digitized and displayed on the websites of the following: the University of Illinois at Urbana–Champaign Library (www.images.library.illinois.edu/projects/africanmaps/index.asp), along with the guide by Thomas J. Bassett and Yvette Scheven, *Maps of Africa to 1900* (Urbana-Champaign, 2000); the Northwestern University Library (http://digital.library.northwestern.edu/mapsofafrica); the Norman B. Leventhal Map Center at the Boston Public Library (http://maps.bpl.org); and the David Rumsey Map Collection (www

.davidrumsey.com), along with the catalogue of an exhibition at Princeton University Library by John Delaney, *To the Mountains of the Moon* (Princeton, 2007).

19. Joseph Conrad, "Heart of Darkness," in *Great Short Works of Joseph Conrad* (New York, 1966), 216.

20. See Thomas J. Bassett and Philip W. Porter, "'From the Best Authorities,'" *Journal of African History* 32, no. 3 (1991): 367–413.

21. This section draws on maps in the National Library of Australia's online map collection (mapsearch.nla.gov.au), the University of Melbourne Rare and Historical Maps Collection (www.lib.unimelb.edu.au/collections/maps/maps-historical.html), the David Rumsey Map Collection, and R. V. Tooley, *The Mapping of Australia* (London, 1979).

22. See Paul Carter, *The Road to Botany Bay* (London, 1987) and Simon Ryan, *The Cartographic Eye* (Cambridge, 1996).

23. Charles Sturt, *Two Expeditions into the Interior of Southern Australia* (London, 1833), 1:xii.

24. Philippa Mein Smith, "Mapping Australasia," *History Compass* 7, no. 4 (2009): 1099–1122.

25. They were drawing too on the influence of the sea on the British cultural imagination, as several scholars have recently shown. See Jonathan Scott, *When the Waves Ruled Britannia* (Cambridge, 2011); Margaret Cohen, *The Novel and the Sea* (Princeton, 2010); and Samuel Baker, *Written on the Water* (Charlottesville, 2010). "Water," observes a historian of colonial mapping in India, became "a metaphor for comprehending new territorial domains." Ian J. Barrow, *Making History, Drawing Territory* (New Delhi, 2003), 69.

26. Ryan, *Cartographic Eye*, 118.

27. T. L. Mitchell, *Three Expeditions into the Interior of Eastern Australia,* 2nd ed. (London, 1839), 1:221; T. L. Mitchell, "Memorandum respecting the Map of New South Wales" (1835), JMS 13/6, RGS.

28. Charles Sturt, *The Central Australian Expedition, 1844–1846,* ed. Richard C. Davis (London, 2002), 175.

29. D. A. Linacre, newspaper cutting #6 about the Western Australian Expedition of 1883, MS 39, NLA.

30. "Instructions to Dr. Andrew Smith . . . of the Expedition into Central Africa," *Journal of the Royal Geographical Society* 4 (1834): 365.

31. David Livingstone, *The Last Journals,* ed. Horace Waller (New York, 1875), 120.

32. Joseph Thomson to John Kirk, May 26, 1880, Joseph Thomson Correspondence, CB6/2173, RGS.

33. Ann Curthoys, "Indigenous Subjects," in *Australia's Empire,* ed. Deryck M. Schreuder and Stuart Ward (Oxford, 2008), 79.

2. Sciences

1. My discussion of Bruce draws mainly on Percy G. Adams, *Travelers and Travel Liars, 1660–1800* (Berkeley, 1962), 210–222, and Nigel Leask, *Curiosity and the Aesthetics of Travel Writing, 1770–1840* (Oxford, 2002), ch. 2.

2. Jonathan Swift, *Gulliver's Travels* [1735] (New York, 2003), 305.

3. Nicholas Thomas, *Cook* (New York, 2003).

4. Harry Liebersohn, *The Traveler's World* (Cambridge, Mass., 2006), 11.

5. Brian W. Richardson, *Longitude and Empire* (Vancouver, 2005), 6.

6. In addition to Richardson's *Longitude and Empire,* see J. C. Beaglehole, "Eighteenth Century Science and the Voyages of Discovery," *New Zealand Journal of History* 3, no. 2 (1969): 107–123, and Richard Sorrenson, "The Ship as a Scientific Instrument in the Eighteenth Century," *Osiris,* 2nd ser., 2 (1996): 221–236.

7. James Bruce, *Travels to Discover the Source of the Nile in the Years 1768, 1769, 1770, 1771, 1772, and 1773,* (Edinburgh, 1790), 1:lxvi. His account of the banquet appears in vol. 3, ch. 11.

8. Leask, *Curiosity,* 71.

9. Bruce, *Travels,* 1:i.

10. David Arnold, *The Tropics and the Traveling Gaze* (Seattle, 2006), 24. Also see Mary Louise Pratt, *Imperial Eyes* (London, 1992), and Simon Ryan, *The Cartographic Eye* (Cambridge, 1996).

11. Steven Shapin, *A Social History of Truth* (Chicago, 1994); Philip J. Stern, " 'Rescuing the Age from the Charge of Ignorance,' " in *A New Imperial History,* ed. Kathleen Wilson (Cambridge, 2004), 115–135.

12. Francis Bacon, "Of Travel," in *The Essays of Francis Bacon,* ed. Clark Sutherland Northrup (New York, 1908), 56.

13. See Felix Driver and Luciana Martins, "John Septimus Roe and the Art of Navigation, c. 1815–1830," *History Workshop Journal,* 54, no. 1 (2002): 144–161.

14. Robert Boyle, *General Heads for the Natural History of a Country, Great or Small; Drawn Out for the Use of Travellers and Navigators* (London, 1692); Roy Bridges, "Exploration and Travel outside Europe (1720–1914)," in *The Cambridge Companion to Travel Writing,* ed. Peter Hulme and Tim Youngs (Cambridge, 2002), 56–69; Marie-Noëlle Bourguet, "A Portable World," *Intellectual History Review* 20, no. 3 (2010): 377–400.

15. See Felipe Fernández-Armesto, *Pathfinders* (New York, 2006), 137, 141, 158, 246–247, 249, 280–281, 300, who notes how little use navigators made of instruments or maps before the seventeenth century. Readable introductions to the technical development of the compass and the chronometer can be found in Alan Gurney, *Compass* (New York, 2004), and Dava Sobel, *Longitude* (New York, 1996).

16. Michael T. Bravo, "Precision and Curiosity in Scientific Travel," in *Voyages and Visions,* ed. Jas Elsner and Joan-Pau Rubiés (London, 1999), 180.

17. John Kirk, *The Zambezi Journal and Letters,* ed. Reginald Foskett (Edinburgh, 1965), 1:195.

18. Marie-Noëlle Bourguet, Christian Licoppe, and H. Otto Siburn, "Introduction," in *Instruments, Travel and Science,* ed. Marie-Noëlle Bourguet, Christian Licoppe, and H. Otto Siburn (London, 2002), 8. The phrase "planetary consciousness" comes from Pratt, *Imperial Eyes.*

19. See Richard Drayton, *Nature's Government* (New Haven, 2000).

20. Drayton, *Nature's Government,* 67. See also Patricia Fara, *Sex, Botany and Empire* (Thirplow, Cambridge, 2004), and Richard Holmes, *The Age of Wonder* (New York, 2008), ch. 1.

21. David Mackay, *In the Wake of Cook* (New York, 1985), esp. 5.

22. See G. S. Ritchie, *The Admiralty Chart* (New York, 1967).

23. Mungo Park, *Travels in the Interior Districts of Africa* [1799] (Durham, N.C., 2000). James Rennell notes in an appendix to the volume (p. 338) that Park lost all of his instruments, maps, and astronomical readings. Another of Banks's protégés, Friedrich Hornemann, prepared for his association-sponsored expedition by studying geography, mineralogy, Arabic, and medicine, and he set out with a sextant, artificial horizon, telescope, thermometer, chronometer, and two compasses. He died of dysentery in the Saharan oasis of Murzuk. See "The Journals of Friedrich Hornemann's Travels," in *Missions to the Niger,* vol. 1, ed. E. W. Bovill (Cambridge, 1964), 10, 16.

24. Silvio A. Bedini, "The Scientific Instruments of the Lewis and Clark Expedition," in *Mapping the North American Plains,* ed. Frederick C. Luebke, Francis W. Kaye, and Gary E. Moulton (Norman, 1987), 93–110; Gary E. Moulton, ed., *The Lewis and Clark Journals* (Lincoln, 2003), introduction.

25. The case for romanticism's close relationship to science in this period is compellingly made by Holmes, *Age of Wonder.*

26. David Philip Miller, "Introduction," in *Visions of Empire,* ed. David Philip Miller and Pheter Hanns Reill (Cambridge, 1996), 11.

27. Darwin quoted in Jean Théodoridès, "Humboldt and England," *British Journal for the History of Science* 3, no. 9 (June 1966): 53.

28. Wallace quoted in Martin Fichman, *An Elusive Victorian* (Chicago, 2004), 23.

29. Hooker quoted in Arnold, *Tropics,* 190–191.

30. Ludwig Leichhardt, *Letters from Australia,* trans. L. L. Politzer (Melbourne, n.d.), 64.

31. Lyell quoted in Robert A. Stafford, "Annexing the Landscapes of the Past," in *Imperialism and the Natural World,* ed. John M. MacKenzie (Manchester, 1990), 85. The literature on Humboldt's influence is huge, but a good general introduction is Michael S. Reidy, Gary Kroll, and Erik M. Conway, eds., *Exploration and Science* (Santa Barbara, 2007), ch. 3. Also see W. H. Brock, "Humboldt and the British," *Annals of Science,* 50 (1993): 365–372; Michael Dettelbach, "The Stimulations of Travel," in *Tropical Visions in an Age of Empire,* ed. Felix Driver and Luciana Martins (Chicago, 2005), ch. 3; and an exceptional study of Humboldt's influence on American thought, Aaron Sachs, *The Humboldt Current* (New York, 2006).

32. This point is persuasively made by David N. Livingstone, *Putting Science in Its Place* (Chicago, 2003).

33. Jim Endersby, *Imperial Nature* (Chicago, 2008), 34.

34. See Stern, "'Rescuing the Age'"; Anthony Sattin, *The Gates of Africa* (New York, 2003); Robin Hallett, "Introduction," in *Records of the African Association, 1788–1831* (London, 1964).

35. Felix Driver, *Geography Militant* (Oxford, 2001), 25.

36. In addition to Driver, *Geography Militant,* ch. 2, see Robert A. Stafford, *Scientist of Empire* (Cambridge, 1989); Robert A. Stafford, "Scientific Exploration and Empire," in *The Oxford History of the British Empire,* vol. 3: *The Nineteenth Century,* ed. Andrew Porter (Oxford, 1999), 294–319; Max Jones, "Measuring the World," in

The Organization of Knowledge in Victorian Britain, ed. Martin Daunton (Oxford, 2005), 313–336; D. R. Stoddart, "The RGS and the 'New Geography,'" *Geographical Journal* 146, no. 2 (July 1980): 190–202; David N. Livingstone, *The Geographical Tradition* (Oxford, 1992), ch. 8. The two official histories of the RGS, neither of them very enlightening, are Clements R. Markham, *The Fifty Years' Work of the Royal Geographical Society* (London, 1881), and Ian Cameron, *To the Farthest Ends of the Earth* (London, 1980).

37. John M. MacKenzie, "The Provincial Geographical Societies in Britain, 1884–1914," in *Geography and Imperialism 1820–1940,* ed. Morag Bell, Robin Butlin, and Michael Heffernan (Manchester, 1995), 93–124; Saul Dubow, *A Commonwealth of Knowledge* (Oxford, 2006), ch. 1; Donal P. McCracken, *Gardens of Empire* (London, 1997), esp. 31; Glen McLaren, *Beyond Leichhardt* (South Fremantle, 1996), 135–136; Donald Malcolm Reid, "The Egyptian Geographical Society," *Poetics Today* 14, no. 3 (Autumn 1993): 539–572. Also see Annie E. Coombes, *Reinventing Africa* (New Haven, 1994); John M. MacKenzie, *Museums and Empire* (Manchester, 2009); Susan Sheets-Pyenson, *Cathedrals of Science* (Kingston, 1988); Tom Griffiths, *Hunters and Collectors* (Cambridge, 1996).

38. Adrian Desmond, "The Making of Institutional Zoology in London 1822–1836: Part 2," *History of Science* 23, no. 2 (September 1985): 229.

39. Record of correspondence, Horton, June 14 and June 21, 1825, CO 392/1/13 & 16, TNA.

40. "The Jolly Philosophers and Their Forthcoming Festival," *Melbourne Punch,* May 7, 1863, 323.

41. Lawrence S. Dritsas, "The Zambesi Expedition, 1858–64" (PhD diss., University of Edinburgh, 2005), published as *Zambesi* (London, 2010).

42. Richard F. Burton, "The Lake Regions of Central Equatorial Africa," *Journal of the Royal Geographical Society* 29 (1859): 20–21; James A. Grant, *A Walk across Africa* (Edinburgh, 1864), x; James A. Grant, "Botany of the Speke and Grant Expedition," *Transactions of the Linnean Society* 29 (1873–1875); Wendy Birman, *Gregory of Rainworth* (Nedlands, 1979), 159.

43. Anon., "Instructions to Dr. Andrew Smith . . . of the Expedition into Central Africa," *Journal of the Royal Geographical Society* 4 (1834): 369; Andrew Smith, *The Diary of Dr. Andrew Smith, 1834–1836* (Cape Town, 1939), 1:20, 53.

44. Stafford, *Scientist,* 216. A full list of the medal recipients can be found in Cameron, *To the Farthest Ends,* appendix II.

45. Endersby, *Imperial Nature,* 17 (quote), 137, 193, 201–202; Arnold, *Tropics,* 147, 169, 172; Stafford, *Scientist,* 194–195; John C. Waller, "Gentlemanly Men of Science," *Journal of the History of Biology* 34, no. 1 (2001): 83–114.

46. Bravo, "Precision and Curiosity," 176.

47. Jones, "Measuring the World," 322.

48. Galton referee report, May 4, 1862; Galton to ?, January 21, 1878, Francis Galton Correspondence Blocks 1861–1870 and 1871–1880, RGS.

49. Jones, "Measuring the World," 319–322. Another alumnus of that program was the Amazonian explorer Percy Fawcett, whose life and career are the subject of a fascinating book by David Grann, *The Lost City of Z* (New York, 2010).

50. Reports by C. George, curator of maps, and W. Ellis, computer at Greenwich, May 27, 1876, VLC 5/2, RGS. The term "computer" originally referred to individuals trained to carry out complex mathematical calculations. See David Alan Grier, *When Computers Were Human* (Princeton, 2005).

51. Thomson to Bates, September 20, 1880, CB6/2173, RGS.

52. Speke to Blackwood, January 30, [1864], Blackwood Papers, MS 4193, ff. 158–159, NLS.

53. Andrew C. Ross, *David Livingstone* (London, 2002), 67; David Livingstone, *The Last Journals of David Livingstone in Central Africa* (New York, 1875), 5.

54. Patrick White, *Voss* (Harmondsworth, 1960), 178.

55. Felix Driver, "Distance and Disturbance," *Transactions of the Royal Historical Society,* 6th ser., 14 (2004): 82. Also Driver, *Geography Militant,* ch. 3.

56. Markham, *Fifty Years' Work,* 39–44. I am grateful to Charles Withers for sharing his manuscript essay "Science, Method and Guides in Nineteenth-Century British Geography," which provides an illuminating analysis of the issues raised in this paragraph and the following one.

57. J. R. Jackson, "Hints on the Subject of Geographical Arrangement and Nomenclature," *Journal of the Royal Geographical Society* 4 (1834): 72–88; T. L. Mitchell, *Three Expeditions into the Interior of Eastern Australia* (London, 1839), 2:90.

58. J. R. Jackson, *What to Observe* (London, 1841), iv. The Victorians' preoccupation with the problem of observation and determination to resolve it is evident in various other publications with similar titles, such as H. T. De La Beche, *How to Observe: Geology,* 2nd ed. (London, 1836); Harriet Martineau, *How to Observe: Manners and Morals* (London, 1838); and Lonsdale Hale, *What to Observe and How to Report It,* 7th ed. (London, 1898).

59. Francis Galton, *The Art of Travel,* 2nd ed. (London, 1856); Jones, "Measuring the World," 321; Nicholas W. Gillham, *A Life of Sir Francis Galton* (New York, 2001), 98–99.

60. John F. W. Hirschel, ed., *A Manual of Scientific Enquiry,* 2nd ed. (London, 1851).

61. William B. Baikie, *Narrative of an Exploring Voyage up the Rivers Kwo'ra and Bi'nue* (London, 1856), 403; Dritsas, "Zambesi Expedition," 61; John Davis, *Tracks of McKinlay and Party across Australia* (London, 1863), 114; Henry M. Stanley, *Through the Dark Continent* [1899] (New York, 1988), 2; Dane Kennedy, *The Highly Civilized Man* (Cambridge, Mass., 2005), 97–98.

62. Speke to Blackwood, n.d. [c. 1863], Blackwood Papers, MS 4185, ff. 282–283, NLS.

63. For an excellent analysis of the substantive issues that divided explorers and armchair geographers, see Lawrence Dritsas, "Expeditionary Science," in *Geographies of Nineteenth-Century Science,* ed. David N. Livingstone and Charles W. J. Withers (Chicago, 2011), 255–277.

64. Stern, "'Rescuing the Age.'"

65. The seminal study of Murchison is Stafford, *Scientist.*

66. Barth to Cooley, April 13, 1851, Barth correspondence, Add. Ms. 32117E, ff. 15–17, BL.

67. Burton, "Lake Regions of Central Equatorial Africa," 3.

68. Richard F. Burton to Editor, *The Reader,* December 16, 1864, Sir Francis Galton Papers, 119/2, University College, London. He was responding to W. D. Cooley's

The Memoir on the Lake Regions of East Africa, Reviewed (London, 1864). Burton would continue to attack Cooley at every opportunity: see Kennedy, *Highly Civilized Man,* 103–104.

69. Dritsas, "Zambesi Expedition," 190–192.

70. Livingstone, *Last Journals,* 236.

71. Horace Waller quoted in Dorothy O. Helly, *Livingstone's Legacy* (Athens, Ohio, 1987), 147.

72. Speke to Blackwood, February 11, [1864], Blackwood Papers, MS 4193, ff. 164–165, NLS; Alexander Maitland, *Speke* (London, 1971), ch. 9.

73. Cooley to Macvey Napier, November 2, 1837, Napier Papers, Add. Ms. 34618, f. 326, BL.

74. Sir Thomas Mitchell, "Some Accounts of New South Wales," 1848, with reports by John Washington and John Arrowsmith, JMS 13/56, RGS. Someone—presumably one of the two reviewers—underlined Mitchell's remarks in red.

75. Quoted in Stuart McCook, " 'It May Be Truth, but It Is Not Evidence,' " *Osiris,* 2nd ser., no. 11 (1996): esp. 189, 190.

76. E. Cobham Brewer to Stanley, August 19, 1872, Stanley Archives, 2719, RAM. Also see Gillham, *Galton,* 131–135; Tim Jeal, *Stanley* (New Haven, 2007), 138–144.

77. William Farquhar, a Scottish sailor who accompanied the expedition, evidently knew the basic principles of navigation, but he soon died. Jeal, *Stanley,* 97.

78. Markham to Stanley, September 4, 1872, Stanley Archives, 2740, RAM.

79. Stanley to Markham, September 4, 1872, Galton Papers, 76, University College London.

80. Grant to Sir Henry Rawlinson, December 14, 1871, Grant Correspondence, 1871–1880, CB6/946, RGS.

81. Stanley quoted in James L. Newman, *Imperial Footprints* (Washington, D.C., 2004), 75, and subsequent preparations, 99, 101. Stanley's field notebooks are in the Stanley Archive, RAM.

82. Galton to Grant, November 24, 1864, Grant papers, MS 17909, ff. 93–94, NLS.

83. Edward Eyre, *Journals of Expeditions of Discovery into Central Australia* (London, 1845), 1:viii; Richard F. Burton, *The Lake Regions of Central Africa* [1860] (New York, 1995), vii; Livingstone, *Last Journals,* 331–332; Livingstone Search and Relief Expedition, *Report to the Subscribers by the Livingstone Search and Relief Committee* (London, 1882), 11, in VLC 1/1, RGS.

84. William D. Cooley, *The Negroland of the Arabs Examined and Explained* (London, 1841); Cooley to Napier, October 9, 1834, Napier Papers, Add. Ms. 34616, ff. 413–414, BL. Also see R. C. Bridges, "W. D. Cooley, the RGS and African Geography in the Nineteenth Century," part 2, *Geographical Journal* 142, no. 2 (July 1976): 274–286.

85. David Lambert, " 'Taken Captive by the Mystery of the Great River,' " *Journal of Historical Geography* 35 (2009): 44–65. Also see Charles W. J. Withers, "Mapping the Niger, 1798–1832," *Imago Mundi* 56, part 2 (2004): 170–193; and Adrian S. Wisnicki, "Charting the Frontier," *Victorian Studies* 51, no. 1 (Autumn 2008): 103–137.

86. Livingstone, *Last Journals,* 186; Burton, *Lake Regions,* 365n.

87. Adrian S. Wisnicki, "Cartographical Quandaries," *History in Africa* 35 (2008): 455–479; Wisnicki, "Charting the Frontier."

88. Francis Galton to Norton Shaw, June 11, 1859; Galton to Shaw, enclosure to letter headed "Count Lavaradio's Letter," May 17, 1860, both in Galton Correspondence Block 1851–1860, RGS. Galton used the same rationale to dismiss Portuguese claims of precedence.

89. John H. Speke, *Journal of the Discovery of the Source of the Nile* [1863] (London, 1937), 32–33.

90. Mitchell, *Three Expeditions.*

91. Ludwig Leichhardt, *Journal of an Overland Expedition in Australia* (London, 1847), 236.

92. D. J. Siddle, "David Livingstone," *Geographical Journal* 140, no. 1 (February 1974): 73.

93. W. Ellis, computer at Greenwich, report, May 27, 1876, VLC 5/2, RGS.

94. Memo on Grey and Lushington expedition, JMS 13/11j, RGS; Leichhardt, *Journal,* xiii–xiv. The photo of Speke is reproduced as the frontispiece of Maitland, *Speke.* It served as the basis for the famous posthumous portrait of Speke by James Watney Wilson, which is in the collection of the Royal Geographical Society. The scientific instruments taken by Speke and Grant are listed in Grant, *Walk across Africa,* appendix. It included three sextants, two artificial horizons, two chronometers, three lever watches, three prismatic compasses, two pocket compasses, six thermometers, and a telescope.

95. The list of items and their costs appear in CO 2/16/266 & 281a, TNA.

96. Jamie B. Lockhart and Paul E. Lovejoy, eds., *Hugh Clapperton into the Interior of Africa* (Leiden, 2005), 363–364, 369, 370.

97. Charles Sturt to Lord Stanley, March 16, 1843, and minute on Sturt's proposal by John Barrow, JMS 13/43/b & d, RGS; John Barrow, *An Autobiographical Memoir* (London, 1847), 143.

98. See James Ryan, *Picturing Empire* (Chicago, 1997), esp. ch. 1, and Leila Koivunen, *Visualizing Africa in Nineteenth-Century British Travel Accounts* (New York, 2009), 33–38.

99. No. 25, South Australia, *Northern Exploration* (c. 1858), 3. Paul Carter mistakenly claims that "in the first fifty years of photography, *not a single* [Australian] *expedition was photographed.*" Carter, "Invisible Journeys," in *Islands in the Stream,* ed. Paul Foss (Leichhardt, NSW, 1988), 48. In addition to Babbage, Alfred Howitt had "a Photographic apparatus" on his 1861–1862 expedition: Edwin Welch, diary, entries for December 6, 1861, and January 1, 1862, ML C322, ML. Although the expeditions that probed the deserts of central and western Australia in the 1860s and 1870s lacked the logistical means to carry bulky photographic equipment, many Australian expeditions from the 1880s on made use of photography, including W. H. Tietkens's 1889 expedition, the Elder Expedition of 1891, the Horn Scientific Expedition of 1894, and David Carnegie's 1896 expedition.

100. According to Speke, *Journal,* 50, the heat Grant "was subjected to in the little tent whilst preparing and fixing his plates would very soon have killed him." John Kirk

also makes reference to the challenges of wet plate photography and his experiments in other photographic processes. Kirk, *Zambezi Journal,* 1:50–51, 115, 215, 281; 2:535, with reproductions of some of his photographs. The photographs Grant took while in Zanzibar can be found in the Humphrey Winterton Collection of East African Photographs at Northwestern University. John Petherick's wife, Kate, mentions taking "a good photograph" and later being forced to abandon her photographic equipment during their explorations of southern Sudan in the early 1860s. Kate Petherick, diary, 90, 114, MSS 5788, Wellcome Library.

101. See the introduction by Mathilde Leduc-Grimaldi in *Africa in Images, Stanley I Presume?* (Brussels, 2007), which reproduces a number of Stanley's photographs.

102. Galton to Bates, November 10, 1880, Galton Correspondence Block, RGS.

103. Burchell quoted in John McAleer, *Representing Africa* (Manchester, 2010), 108.

104. Daniel G. Brock, *To the Desert with Sturt* (Adelaide, 1975), 1.

105. Oudney quoted by E. W. Bovill, "Introduction," in *Missions to the Niger,* vol. 2: *The Bornu Mission, 1822–25,* part 1, ed. E. W. Bovill (Cambridge, 1966), 49.

106. Heinrich Barth, *Travels and Discoveries in North and Central Africa* (London, 1965), 2:579.

107. Alexander Gordon Laing, "The Letters of Major Alexander Gordon Laing, 1824–26," in *Missions to the Niger,* vol. 1, ed. E. W. Bovill (Cambridge, 1964), 246. The Colonial Office grew impatient with his requests for new barometers to replace those "so easily destroyed by accidental circumstances." Hay to Laing, August 4, 1825, CO 392/3/23–24, TNA.

108. Hugh Clapperton, *Journal of a Second Expedition into the Interior of Africa* (Philadelphia, 1829), 70.

109. Richard F. Burton and J. H. Speke, "A Coasting Voyage from Mombasa to the Pangani River," *Journal of the Royal Geographical Society* 28 (1858): 221, 224.

110. John Oxley, "Journal of an Expedition into the Interior of New South Wales in the Year 1817," entries for August 5 (quote) and May 11, AJCP-M1923, SLV.

111. John McDouall Stuart, journal, March 15, 1860, JMS 13/109, RGS; S. Galland Briggs, journal kept during Favenc's expedition, August 1, 1878, C409, ML; Alan Moorehead, *Cooper's Creek* (New York, 1963), 97.

112. *Explorations by Mr. Hodgkinson* (Queensland, 1976), 19.

113. W. H. Hovell and Hamilton Hume, *Journey of Discovery to Port Phillip, New South Wales* (Sydney, 1831), iii.

114. William Landsborough, *Journal of Landsborough's Expedition from Carpentaria in Search of Burke & Wills* [1862] (Adelaide, 2000), 26.

115. Duncan Whyte, *Sketch of Exploration by the Late John M'Kinlay* (Glasgow, 1881), 27.

116. J. S. Roe, expedition journal for 1835, in Joanne Shoobert, ed., *Western Australian Exploration* (Carlisle, 2005), 467.

117. Eyre, *Journals,* 1:85–86.

118. Kirk, *Zambezi Journal,* 2:545.

119. R. Strachan to Captain C. George, May 31, 1876, Cameron Collection, VLC/7, RGS.

120. Livingstone, *Last Journals,* 410.

121. David Livingstone, *Missionary Travels and Researches in South Africa,* new ed. (London, 1899), 258–259.

122. Johannes Fabian, *Out of Our Minds* (Berkeley, 2000).

123. No. 19, South Australia, *Journal of Mr. Lewis's Lake Eyre Expedition, 1874–75* (1875), 12.

124. Charles Sturt, account of journey, 1838, MS 9025, MSB 450, SLV; Brock, *To the Desert,* 36, 144–145.

125. Stuart, journal entry for April 1, 1860, JMS 13/109, RGS.

126. William Carron, "Narrative of an Exploring Expedition," December 30, 1848, MS Q600, ML.

127. Kirk, *Zambezi Journal,* 1:298.

128. Leichhardt, *Journal,* 445.

129. See Iwan Morus, "Replacing Victoria's Scientific Culture," *19: Interdisciplinary Studies in the Long Nineteenth Century* 2 (2006), www.19.bbk.ac.uk; Bernard Lightman, *Victorian Popularizers of Science* (Chicago, 2007); Lightman, "Refashioning the Spaces of London Science," in *Geographies of Nineteenth Century Science,* ed. David N. Livingstone and Charles W. J. Withers (Chicago, 2011), 25–49.

3. Professionals

1. C. Coulthurst, August 10, 1832, CB1/15, RGS; Anon., "Failure of Another Expedition to Explore the Interior of Africa," *Journal of the Royal Geographical Society* 2 (1832): esp. 310, 305; CO 392/1/100–1, 127, TNA. Portions of Coulthurst's overwrought poem about Mungo Park appear in the *London Literary Gazette* 824 (November 3, 1832): 698.

2. Perhaps the most skilled and successful practitioner of this genre at present is Tim Jeal, whose latest books are *Stanley* (New Haven, 2007) and *Explorers of the Nile* (New Haven, 2011). For a critique of Jeal's biography of Stanley and a commentary on the limitations of popular biography, see A. G. Hopkins, "Explorers' Tales," *Journal of Imperial and Commonwealth History* 36, no. 4 (December 2008): 669–684. Felix Driver, "The Active Life," *Oxford Dictionary of National Biography,* online edition (May 2007), http://www.oxforddnb.com), offers thoughtful recommendations for overcoming these limitations.

3. See, for example, Christopher Hibbert, *Africa Explored* (Harmondsworth, 1984); Robert I. Rotberg, ed., *Africa and Its Explorers* (Cambridge, Mass., 1970); Tim Flannery, ed., *The Explorers* (New York, 1998).

4. A key text is Mary Louise Pratt's *Imperial Eyes* (London, 1992), which laid much of the groundwork for what is now a huge body of scholarship on travel writing.

5. Alison Blunt, *Travel, Gender, and Imperialism* (New York, 1994), 32.

6. Mary Kingsley to Mrs. Farquharson, November 26, 1899, CB7/52, RGS.

7. Unless otherwise indicated, the prosopographical analysis that follows derives from the biographical information in the *Oxford Dictionary of National Biography,* online edition (2004), http://www.oxforddnb.com, and the *Australian Dictionary of Biography,* online edition (2006), http://www.adb.online.anu.edu.au/biogs.

8. John McDouall Stuart, "Exploration in Australia," 2, JMS/13/125, RGS.

9. Randolph Cock, "Scientific Servicemen in the Royal Navy and the Professionalization of Science, 1816–55," in *Science and Beliefs,* ed. David M. Knight and Matthew
   D. Eddy (Aldershot, 2005), 95–111.

10. It also is worth noting that James Rennell, the man who oversaw many of the early
    expeditions sponsored by the African Association, made his reputation as a sur-
    veyor for the East India Company, producing important hydrographic surveys and
    the first map of India, the Bengal atlas of 1780.

11. Quoted in E. W. Bovill, "Introduction," in *Missions to the Niger,* vol. 2: *The Bornu
    Mission 1822–25,* part 1, ed. E. W. Bovill (Cambridge, 1966), 52.

12. D. R. Stoddart, "The RGS and the 'New Geography'," *Geographical Journal* 146,
    no. 2 (July 1980): 191.

13. Eric Leed, *Shores of Discovery* (New York, 1995), 221. The surplus of officers as an
    impetus for exploration after the Napoleonic Wars is also noted by Felipe Fernandez-
    Armesto, *Pathfinders* (New York, 2006), 345.

14. Bovill, "Introduction," 17; Lawrence S. Dritsas, "The Zambesi Expedition, 1858–
    64" (PhD diss., University of Edinburgh, 2005), 70; Andrew C. Ross, *David Liv-
    ingstone* (London, 2002), 67; A. Adu Boahen, *Britain, the Sahara, and the Western
    Sudan, 1788–1861* (Oxford, 1964), 182.

15. Harry Liebersohn, *The Traveler's World* (Cambridge, Mass., 2006), 125.

16. Tim Fulford, Debbie Lee, and Peter J. Kitson, *Literature, Science and Exploration
    in the Romantic Era* (Cambridge, 2004), ch. 6.

17. Cooley to Napier, May 9, 1835, Add. Ms. 34617, ff. 110–111, BL.

18. John M. MacKenzie, *Museums and Empire* (Manchester, 2009), 267–268.

19. Dr. G. Neumayer, "On the Scientific Exploration of Central Australia," *Proceedings
    of the Royal Society* 102 (1868): 347–363.

20. Becker, Beckler, and Henne all left written accounts of their experiences: Marjorie
    Tipping, ed., *Ludwig Becker* (Carlton, Victoria, 1979); Hermann Beckler, *A Journey
    to Cooper's Creek* (Carlton, Victoria, 1993); Diedrich Henne, journal, ML C407, ML.

21. Ludwig Leichardt, *Dr. Ludwig Leichhardt's Letters from Australia,* trans. L. L.
    Politzer (Melbourne, n.d.), 9, 26; Leichardt, *Journal of an Overland Expedition in
    Australia from Moreton Bay to Port Essington* (London, 1847), xiii.

22. Heinrich Barth, *Travels and Discoveries in North and Central Africa,* 3 vols. (Lon-
    don, 1965).

23. Anthony Kirk-Greene, "Heinrich Barth," in *Africa and Its Explorers,* ed. Robert I.
    Rotberg (Cambridge, Mass., 1970), 13–38; Major William Gray and Staff Surgeon
    Dochard, *Travels in Western Africa* (London, 1925), 4; British Parliamentary Pa-
    pers, Cd. 472 (1843), *Papers Relative to the Expedition to the River Niger,* 29; Boa-
    hen, *Britain,* 97, 197, 214. It is also worth noting that Dr. Ludwig Pappe of Hamburg
    became the first official botanist of the Cape Colony in 1858.

24. A point repeatedly made by Edgar Beale, *Sturt* (Sydney, 1979), 47, 61–62, 87.

25. George Grey, *Journals of Two Expeditions of Discovery in North-West and Western
    Australia* (London, 1841), 2:95.

26. Joseph R. Elsey, diary, September 14, 1855, MS25, NLA.

27. Alan Moorehead, *Cooper's Creek* (New York, 1963), 178–179, 191.

28. *The Burke and Wills Exploring Expedition* (Melbourne, 1861), 35.

29. Granville Stapylton, *Stapylton,* ed. Alan Andrews (Hobart, 1986), 72, 157, 179.
30. Daniel Brock, *To the Desert with Sturt,* ed. Kenneth Peake-Jones (Adelaide, 1975), 11, 117, 149, 172.
31. J. M. R. Cameron, Glen McLaren, and William Cooper, "Bushmanship," *Australian Geographer* 30, no. 3 (1999): 337–353. The last instance I have found of a convict involved in an expedition was the one John Forrest organized in 1869, which included David Morgan, a blacksmith who was a probationary prisoner. John Forrest, *Explorations in Australia* [1875] (New York, 1969), 24.
32. John Bailey, *Mr. Stuart's Track* (Sydney, 2007), 234.
33. Lt. Col. MacCarthy, n.d.; Major Peddie to Lord Bathurst, February 8, 1816; Capt. Campbell to Bathhurst, CO 2/5/14–15, 16–23, 62–69, TNA.
34. Andrew Smith, *The Diary of Dr. Andrew Smith, 1834–1836* (Cape Town, 1939), 1:35.
35. Francis Galton, *The Narrative of an Explorer in Tropical South Africa* (London, 1853), 52–53.
36. Jeal, *Stanley,* 97, 98, 159.
37. Quoted in Charles W. J. Withers and Innes M. Keighren, "Travels into Print," *Transactions of the Institute of British Geographers* 36, no. 4 (October 2011): 7.
38. Roy C. Bridges, "The Historical Role of British Explorers in East Africa," *Terrae Incognitae* 14 (1982): 10.
39. Quoted in Leila Koivunen, *Visualizing Africa in Nineteenth-Century British Travel Accounts* (New York, 2009), 32. The striking similarities between this passage (published in 1861) and the one in Burton's book (published in 1872) that opens this chapter leave little doubt that Burton plagiarized from Andersson.
40. Robert A. Stafford, *Scientist of Empire* (Cambridge, 1989), 216.
41. Lyon quote in Boahen, *Britain,* 53.
42. Kennedy to his father, February 27, 1848, T/2966/P/2/31, PRNI.
43. See No. 161, South Australia, *Cost of Exploring Expeditions* (1860); No. 128, South Australia, *Expenses of Exploring Expeditions* (1863); and entries on individual explorers in the *Australian Dictionary of Biography,* online edition (2006).
44. Anthony Sattin, *The Gates of Africa* (New York, 2003), 180.
45. Alexander Gordon Laing, "The Letters of Major Alexander Gordon Laing, 1824–26," in *Missions to the Niger,* vol. 1, ed. E. W. Bovill (Cambridge, 1964), 175.
46. Claire Pettitt, *Dr. Livingstone, I Presume?* (Cambridge, Mass., 2007), 32.
47. Kennedy to his mother, January 7, 1847, T/2966/P/2/24, PRNI; emphasis added.
48. John Frederick Mann, "Diary Kept during a Short Journey into the Interior in Company with Dr. Ludwig Leichhardt," entries for December 16, 1846 and January 13, 1847, ML B455, ML.
49. *Ernest Giles's Explorations, 1872–76* (Adelaide, 2000), 132.
50. Laing, "Letters," 1:280–281; also 1:267, 287.
51. John Kirk, *The Zambezi Journal and Letters of Dr. John Kirk, 1858–63* (Edinburgh, 1965), 1:226.
52. T. L. Mitchell, *Three Expeditions into the Interior of Eastern Australia* (London, 1839), 1:211, 219–220, 310, 316; 2:62–63.
53. Verney Lovett Cameron, expedition journals, June 13, June 19, and July 16, 1873, MSS 299(1) microfilm, NLS.

54. Stanley, field notebook, June 7?, 1876, Stanley Archives, 17, RAM.

55. David Livingstone, *The Last Journals of David Livingstone in Central Africa,* ed. Horace Waller (New York, 1875), 322–323, 428; Ross, *David Livingstone* (London, 2002), 215. The correspondence of James Grant is especially illuminating in this regard.

56. Bovill, "Introduction," 52, 65–71, quote on 66.

57. Charles Sturt, account of journey 1838, 126 (photocopy of original manuscript in Rhodes House Library), MS 9025, MSB 450, SLV; J. F. Hopkins to Andrew Mc-Crae, n.d., MS 12289, box 1829/7, SLV.

58. See W. B. Carnochan, *The Sad Story of Burton, Speke, and the Nile* (Stanford, 2006); Dane Kennedy, *The Highly Civilized Man* (Cambridge, Mass., 2005), ch. 4; Alexander Maitland, *Speke* (London, 1971), chs. 9–10.

59. John Empson, "A Study of the Origin and Significance of the Speke Memorial" (typescript, January 1994), RGS Correspondence Block, 1881–1900: Speke Memorial, RGS.

60. James Grant to Samuel Baker, June 26, 1890, M63d, Russell E. Train Africana Collection, Joseph Cullman Library, NMNH.

61. Salt in Robin Hallett, ed., *Records of the African Association 1788–1831* (London, 1964), 235.

62. Mitchell, *Three Expeditions,* 1:2.

63. W. H. Tietkens, "Reminiscences, 1859–87," PRG 1006/1, SLSA.

64. Galton, *Narrative,* 2.

65. John Davidson, *Notes Taken during Travels in Africa* (London, 1839), 163. See also Anon., "Extracts from the Correspondence of the Late Mr. Davidson, during his Residence in Morocco," *Journal of the Royal Geographical Society* 7 (1837): 144–172.

66. Quoted in Davidson, *Notes,* 207; Anon., "Annual Report of the Council," *Journal of the Royal Geographical Society* 7 (1837): v.

67. Cooley to Macvey Napier, July 26, 1833, Add. Ms. 34616, ff. 107–108, BL; Brock, *To the Desert,* 192.

68. I have found the following works especially illuminating: John Tosh, *Manliness and Masculinities in Nineteenth-Century Britain* (Harlow, 2005); Catherine Hall, *Civilising Subjects* (Chicago, 2002); Alan Lester and Fae Dussart, "Masculinity, 'Race,' and Family in the Colonies," *Gender, Place and Culture* 16, no. 1 (February 2009): 63–75.

69. David Livingstone, *Missionary Travels and Researches in South Africa,* new ed. (London, 1899), 266.

70. Kirk, *Zambezi Journal,* 2:525.

71. Gray and Dochard, *Travels,* 166; Macgregor Laird and R. A. K. Oldfield, *Narrative of an Expedition into the Interior of Africa* (London, 1837), 143, 408; Samuel Baker, *The Albert Nyanza* (London, 1866), 375.

72. Henry M. Stanley, *Through the Dark Continent* [1899] (New York, 1988), 1:80, 192.

73. Langer in Hugh Clapperton, *Journal of a Second Expedition into the Interior of Africa* (Philadelphia, 1829), 314; Jamie Bruce Lockhart and Paul E. Lovejoy, eds., *Hugh Clapperton into the Interior of Africa* (Leiden, 2005), 124.

74. Laing, "Letters," 302.

75. Peter Macinnis, *Australia's Pioneers, Heroes and Fools* (Miller Point, NSW, 2007), ch. 10.

76. S. Galland Briggs, journal of Favenc's expedition, 1878–1879, November 22, 1878, C409, ML; John Davis, *Tracks of McKinlay and Party across Australia* (London, 1863), 114. These claims should be viewed with some skepticism.

77. Davis, *Tracks of McKinlay,* 108–109, 248.

78. J. McDouall Stuart, journal entry for May 17, 1860, JMS 13/109, RGS.

79. Lockhart and Lovejoy, *Hugh Clapperton,* 402.

80. Clapperton, *Journal,* 326; Richard Lander, "Sockatoo, April 10th 1827," CO 2/16/8, TNA.

81. Clapperton, *Journal,* 328.

82. Peter Warburton, *Journey across the Western Interior of Australia* (London, 1875), 257, 258; Jackey Jackey's statement in John MacGillivray, *Narrative of the Voyage of H.M.S. Rattlesnake* (London, 1852), 1:164.

83. Dorinda Outram, "On Being Perseus," in *Geography and Enlightenment,* ed. David N. Livingstone and Charles W. J. Withers (Chicago, 1999), 290, 291.

84. David N. Livingstone, *Putting Science in Its Place* (Chicago, 2003), 152.

85. Michael Dettelbach, "The Stimulations of Travel," in *Tropical Visions in an Age of Empire,* ed. Felix Driver and Luciana Martins (Chicago, 2005): 43–58; Livingstone, *Putting Science in Its Place,* 74–75.

86. Roslynn D. Haynes, *Seeking the Centre* (Cambridge, 1998), 6.

4. Gateways

1. See printed instructions to B. H. Babbage, Commander of Northern Exploring Expedition, from Francis S. Dutton, Commissioner of Crown Lands, Adelaide, February 9, 1858, JMS 13/98/b, RGS; No. 25, South Australia, *Northern Exploration. Reports, &c., of Explorations into the Interior by Messrs. Babbage, Warburton, Geharty, and Parry* (1858); No. 128, South Australia, *Expenses of Exploring Expeditions* (1863).

2. Extract of dispatch from Governor R. G. Macdonnell to Sir E. B. Lytton, November 11, 1858, JMS 13/98/c, RGS.

3. No. 25, South Australia, *Northern Exploration. Further Correspondence Respecting the Exploring Party under Command of Mr. B. Herschel Babbage* (1858); *South Australian Advertiser,* November 10, 1858, clipping in JMS 13/98/c, RGS.

4. One exception is Peter Macinnis, *Australia's Pioneers, Heroes and Fools* (Miller Point, NSW, 2007), 95–99.

5. Sir R. G. Macdonnell to the Duke of Newcastle, September 27, 1861, JMS 13/124, RGS.

6. Robert A. Stafford, *Scientist of Empire* (Cambridge, 1989); James L. Newman, *Imperial Footprints* (Washington, D.C., 2004); Felix Driver, *Geography Militant* (Oxford, 2001). Driver's subtitle echoes an influential earlier work on American exploration: William Goetzmann, *Exploration and Empire* (New York, 1972).

7. George Grey, *Journals of Two Expeditions of Discovery in North-West and Western Australia* (London, 1841) 1:89; Report of RGS deputation to Colonial Secretary (1836?), JMS 13/11g, RGS.

8. British Parliamentary Papers, Cd. 2350 (1857–1858), *Papers Relating to an Expedition Recently Undertaken for the Purpose of Exploring the Northern Portion of Australia,* 2–4. Also see Augustus and Francis Gregory, *Journals of Australian Explorations* [1884] (New York, 1968), 99–194. Francis Gregory's expedition is detailed in Gregory, *Journals,* 52–98, and Francis Gregory, *Journal of the N.W. Australian Exploring Expedition* (n.p., n.d.).

9. J. McDouall Stuart journal, April 23, 1860, JMS 134/109, RGS.

10. Chris Cunningham, *Blue Mountains Rediscovered* (Kenthurst, NSW, 1996).

11. Sir George Bowen to Roderick Murchison, December 1, 1860, Murchison Papers, Add. MSS 46125, f. 201, BL.

12. See Joanne Shoobert, ed., *Western Australian Exploration,* vol. 1 (Carlisle, 2005), and Joseph Cross, ed., *Journals of Several Expeditions Made in Western Australia* (London, 1833).

13. Edward Eyre, *Journals of Expeditions of Discovery into Central Australia* (London, 1845), 1:10–11, 12, 16.

14. This background to the scramble is discussed in Jack Cross, *Great Central State* (Kent Town, South Australia, 2011), ch. 1.

15. "Exploration of the Interior," *South Australian Register,* January 5, 1858, in JMS 13/91, RGS.

16. Bessie Threadgill, *South Australian Land Exploration 1856 to 1880* (Adelaide, 1922), ch. 1.

17. Alfred Howitt, *Finding Burke and Wills* (Adelaide, 2007), 17; Threadgill, *South Australia,* 41.

18. Sir Richard Macdonnell to Roderick Murchison, October 26, 1860, Murchison Papers, Add. Mss 46127, ff. 142–43, BL.

19. The standard studies of the Burke and Wills expedition are Sarah Murgatroyd, *The Dig Tree* (Melbourne, 2002), and Alan Moorehead, *Cooper's Creek* (New York, 1963). For the official postmortem, see British Parliamentary Papers, Cd. 139 (1862), *Australian Exploring Expedition (Burke and Wills) Dispatches.* The description of Stuart comes from Macdonnell to Murchison (October 26, 1860), Add. Mss 46127, ff. 142–143, BL.

20. *Melbourne Punch,* December 8, 1860, 124.

21. No. 128, South Australia, *Expenses of Exploring Expeditions* (1863); Edward Stokes, *Across the Centre* (Sydney, 1996).

22. See John Davis, *Tracks of McKinlay and Party across Australia* (London, 1863).

23. Bowen to Murchison, December 1, 1860, Add. Mss 46125, f. 201, BL.

24. Gwen Trundle, "Landsborough, William (1825–1886)," *Australian Dictionary of Biography,* online edition (2006), http://www.adb.online.anu.edu.au/biogs.

25. Murgatroyd, *Dig Tree,* 199, 298.

26. Quoted in Stokes, *Across the Centre,* 141.

27. This story is vividly told by Cross, *Great Central State.*

28. See the damning account of the expedition by McKinlay's second-in-command, R. H. Edmunds, journals (4 vols., unpublished), Royal Geographical Society of South Australia, Adelaide.

29. No. 178, South Australia, *Northern Territory Exploration, 1867* (1867); No. 24, South Australia, *Exploration Northern Territory* (1868).

30. Geoffrey Blainey, *The Tyranny of Distance* (New York, 1968).

31. Western Australia, *Journal of Proceedings of the Western Australian Exploring Expedition* (Perth, 1875), 4.

32. Queensland Legislative Assembly, *Explorations by Mr. Hodgkinson,* 1876; John R. Bradford, journal of Cape York Expedition, 1883, A4054, ML; Alexander Forrest, *North-West Exploration* (Perth, 1880).

33. The phrase comes from Kathleen Fitzpatrick, "Introduction," in *Australian Explorers,* ed. Kathleen Fitzpatrick (London, 1958), 24.

34. Elder to Jess Young, June 15, 1876, in Ernest Giles, *The Journal of a Forgotten Expedition in 1875,* ed. James Bosanquet (Adelaide, 1979), 52.

35. Ernest Favenc, diary of a Queensland Transcontinental Expedition 1878–1879, B880–884, ML; James Henry Ricketson, journal of expedition to Cambridge Gulf, 1884–1885, ML MSS 1783, ML; J. G. Hill, *The Calvert Scientific Exploring Expedition* (London, 1905); David W. Carnegie, *Spinifex and Sand* (London, 1898).

36. Robin Hallett, ed., *Records of the African Association, 1788–1831* (London, 1964), 194.

37. Philip Curtin, *The Image of Africa* (Madison, 1964), 165–166, 296, 303.

38. See Kola Folayan, *Tripoli during the Reign of Yusuf Pash Qaramanli* (Ile-Ife, Nigeria, 1979), ch. 4.

39. This paragraph draws on the classic account of British expeditions in this region, A. Adu Boahen, *Britain, the Sahara, and the Western Sudan, 1788–1861* (Oxford, 1964), and Anthony Sattin, *The Gates of Africa* (New York, 2003).

40. Dixon Denham and Hugh Clapperton, *Narrative of Travels and Discoveries in Northern and Central Africa* (Boston, 1826), x.

41. Warrington quoted in E. W. Bovill, "Introduction," in *Missions to the Niger,* vol. 2: *The Bornu Mission 1822–25,* part 1, ed. E. W. Bovill (Cambridge, 1966), 10.

42. Bovill, "Introduction," 9n3.

43. Alexander Gordon Laing, "The Letters of Major Alexander Gordon Laing, 1824–26," in *Missions to the Niger,* vol. 1, ed. E. W. Bovill (Cambridge, 1964), 225. The Spanish dollar was the standard medium of exchange in Tripoli and much of the Mediterranean at this time.

44. Warrington was convinced that a prominent government minister had conspired with the French consul to murder Laing, his son-in-law. Folayan, *Tripoli,* 149–150.

45. Lisa Anderson, "Nineteenth-Century Reform in Ottoman Libya," *International Journal of Middle Eastern Studies* 16, no. 3 (August 1984): 328–335.

46. Muhammad S. Umar, "Islamic Discourses on European Visitors to Sokoto Caliphate in the Nineteenth Century," *Studia Islamica* 95 (2002): 135–159.

47. Heinrich Barth, *Travels and Discoveries in North and Central Africa,* 3 vols. [1857] (London, 1965).

48. Letter by Ahmad al-Bakayi ibn Sayyid Muhammed to Amir Ahmad, item 19 in Library of Congress exhibit, "Ancient Manuscripts from the Desert Libraries of Timbuktu," www.loc.gov/exhibits/mali/mali-exhibit.htm.

49. Dickson in Jamie Bruce Lockhart and Paul E. Lovejoy, eds., *Hugh Clapperton into the Interior of Africa* (Leiden, 2005), 421, quote on 427.

50. Hallett, *Records,* 57.

51. See Hassan Ahmed Ibrahim, "The Egyptian Empire, 1805–1885," in *The Cambridge History of Egypt,* vol. 2, ed. M. W. Daly (Cambridge, 1998), 198–216.

52. Eve M. Troutt Powell, *A Different Shade of Colonialism* (Berkeley, 2003).

53. See Scopas Poggo, "Zande Resistance to Foreign Penetration in the Southern Sudan, 1860–1890," in *White Nile, Black Blood,* ed. Jay Spaulding and Stephanie Beswick (Lawrenceville, N.J., 2000), 263–278.

54. McQueen to President, RGS, June 5, 1860, McQueen Correspondence Block 1851–1860, RGS.

55. Samuel Baker, *The Albert Nyanza* (London, 1866).

56. Samuel Baker to Roderick Murchison, March 8, 1867, M6a, Russell E. Train Africana Collection, Joseph Cullman Library, NMNH.

57. Samuel Baker, *Ismailia* (London, 1874), 1:7–8.

58. The fullest account of Baker's campaign of conquest is provided by Alice Moore-Harell, *Egypt's African Empire* (Brighton, 2010).

59. James Grant to Charles Gordon, March 14, 1874, Add. Ms. 51305, BL. David Livingstone also criticized Baker for exposing local peoples to Egyptian exploitation. David Livingstone, *The Last Journals of David Livingstone in Central Africa,* ed. Horace Waller (New York, 1875), 422.

60. Copy of written statement by Ismail Pasha, 28 Haj 1289, Verney Lovett Cameron Collection, VLC/6/1, RGS.

61. Donald Cumming, *The Gentleman Savage* (London, 1987), 128.

62. Dane Kennedy, *The Highly Civilized Man* (Cambridge, Mass., 2005), 87–88.

63. Jeremy Prestholdt, *Domesticating the World* (Berkeley, 2008), 72–77, 81–85, 91–93, 105–110.

64. Livingstone, *Last Journals,* 225.

65. James Grant, *A Walk across Africa* (Edinburgh, 1864), 19; Donald Simpson, *Dark Companions* (New York, 1976), 24. Grant, a hardened military man, insists that he was obliged to give the order for the decapitation of the condemned men because of the sultan's "effeminacy and timidity."

66. Abdul Sheriff, *Slaves, Spices and Ivory in Zanzibar* (Oxford, 1987), 172.

67. Cooley to Napier, March 23 and May 9, 1835, Macvey Napier Papers, Add. Ms. 34617, ff. 63, 110–111, BL; extract of letter from Cooley to Barth, March 1852, Heinrich Barth Papers, Add. Ms. 32117E, f. 19, BL.

68. Livingstone, *Last Journals,* 180, 208, 398. Also see Joseph Thomson, *Through Masai Land* (London, 1887), 106.

69. Richard F. Burton, *Zanzibar* (London, 1872), 2:292.

70. Quoted in Tim Jeal, *Stanley* (New Haven, 2007), 226.

71. Kirk to H. W. Bates, November 13, 1877, Sir John Kirk Correspondence, 1871–1880, CB6/1320, RGS.

72. A view influentially advanced by Ronald Robinson and John Gallagher with Alice Denny, *Africa and the Victorians* (Garden City, N.Y., 1968), 42–52.

73. Simpson, *Dark Companions,* 14.

74. Thomson to John Kirk, May 26, 1880, Joseph Thomson Correspondence, CB6/2173, RGS.

75. Norman Bennett, *Arab versus European* (New York, 1986), 116.

76. Hāmid ibn Muhammad, *Maisha Ya Hamed bin Muhammed el Murjebi Yaani Tippu Tip* (Nairobi, 1966), 109. Tip reports that he kept in constant communication with the sultan during his time in Stanley Fall (117).

77. John Barrow, *An Autobiographical Memoir* (London, 1847), 141.

78. "Expeditions into the Interior of South Africa," *Journal of the Royal Geographical Society* 4 (1834): 362–374; Andrew Smith, *Andrew Smith's Journal of His Expedition into the Interior of South Africa 1834–36* (Cape Town, 1975).

79. Francis Galton, *The Narrative of an Explorer in Tropical South Africa* (London, 1853), ch. 1.

80. Christopher Petrusic, "Violence as Masculinity," *International History Review* 26, no. 1 (March 2004): 20–55.

81. Andrew C. Ross, *David Livingstone* (London, 2002), 98.

82. Robinson and Gallagher, *Africa and the Victorians*.

83. On this point, see Durba Ghosh and Dane Kennedy, "Introduction," to *Decentring Empire*, ed. Ghosh and Kennedy (Hyderabad, 2006), 1–15; and Thomas R. Metcalf, *Imperial Connections* (Berkeley, 2008).

5. Logistics

1. Information about the expedition can be found in CO2/5 and CO2/7, TNA, which includes correspondence and the journals of Captain Thomas Campbell and Captain William Gray, who also co-authored a book about the expedition: Major William Gray and Staff Surgeon Dochard, *Travels in Western Africa* (London, 1825).

2. This stands in curious contrast to the high survival rate among the troops, which appears to have been due in no small part to the ministrations of "large Doses" of the "Bark" (quinine) by the expedition doctor. Dr. Dochard, report on diseases, January 19, 1817, CO2/5/90, TNA. Although the death toll among the African members of the expedition goes unreported, only four Europeans died, according to Lt. Stokoe, July 20, 1817, CO2/5/532–534 (though it is unclear whether this includes Major Peddie and his successor, Captain Campbell, both of whom died during the expedition). It is ironic that Dr. Dochard's apparent success in mitigating the effects of malaria with quinine seems to have passed largely unnoticed, probably because the expedition proved so disastrous in so many other respects.

3. Campbell, journal, CO2/7, ff. 230–231, 201–202, 30.

4. Gray, journal, CO2/7, f. 6.

5. Gray and Dochard, *Travels*, 263.

6. Banks quoted in Martin Thomas, *The Artificial Horizon* (Carlton, Victoria, 2003), 85–86.

7. G. S. Ritchie, *The Admiralty Chart* (New York, 1967), 82, 295; John D. Lines, *Australia on Paper* (Victoria, 1992), 19.

8. John Oxley, *Journals of Two Expeditions into the Interior of New South Wales* (London, 1820), appendix; Charles Sturt, *Two Expeditions into the Interior of Southern*

Australia (London, 1833); T. L. Mitchell, *Three Expeditions into the Interior of Eastern Australia* (London, 1839), 2:13.

9. George Grey, *Journals of Two Expeditions of Discovery in North-West and Western Australia* (London, 1841), 1:373.

10. Quoted in Alan Moorehead, *Cooper's Creek* (New York, 1963), 21.

11. Daniel G. Brock, *To the Desert with Sturt* (Adelaide, 1975), 100, 106. Also see Charles Sturt, *The Central Australian Expedition, 1844–1846* (London, 2002), 80, 160, 164.

12. British Parliamentary Papers, Cd. 2350 (1857–1858), *Papers Relating to an Expedition Recently Undertaken for the Purpose of Exploring the Northern Portion of Australia*, 3, 26.

13. Alexander Gordon Laing, "The Letters of Major Alexander Gordon Laing, 1824–26," in *Missions to the Niger*, vol. 1, ed. E. W. Bovill (Cambridge, 1964), 238, 295; E. W. Bovill, "Introduction," in *Missions to the Niger*, vol. 2: *The Bornu Mission, 1822–25*, part 1, ed. E. W. Bovill (Cambridge, 1966), 116; Heinrich Barth, *Travels and Discoveries in North and Central Africa* (London, 1965), 1:xxv.

14. James H. Tuckey and Christen Smith, *Narrative of an Expedition to Explore the River Zaire* (London, 1818); Christopher Lloyd, *Mr. Barrow of the Admiralty* (London, 1970), ch. 6.

15. MacGregor Laird and R. A. K. Oldfield, *Narrative of an Expedition into the Interior of Africa* (London, 1837).

16. Howard Temperley, *White Dreams, Black Africa* (New Haven, 1991), viii.

17. British Parliamentary Papers, Cd. 472 (1843), *Papers Relative to the Expedition to the River Niger;* William Simpson, *A Private Journal Kept during the Niger Expedition* (London, 1843); Temperley, *White Dreams*.

18. And reconfirming what Dr. Dochard had demonstrated during the otherwise disastrous Peddie/Campbell/Gray expedition discussed at the start of this chapter. See note 2.

19. William Balfour Baikie, *Narrative of an Exploring Voyage up the Rivers Kwo'ra and Bi'nue* (London, 1856), esp. 5.

20. See G. W. Clendennen and D. H. Simpson, "African Members of the Zambezi Expedition, 1861–64," *History in Africa* 12 (1985): 29–49.

21. Landeg White, *Magomero* (Cambridge, 1987), part 1.

22. John Kirk, *The Zambezi Journal and Letters of Dr. John Kirk* (Edinburgh, 1965), 2:475.

23. Lawrence S. Dritsas, "The Zambesi Expedition, 1858–64" (PhD diss., University of Edinburgh, 2005), 49. Also see Dritsas, *Zambesi* (London, 2010), ch. 1, for an excellent account of the expedition.

24. Dritsas, "Zambesi Expedition," 129.

25. Inga Clendinnen, *Dancing with Strangers* (Cambridge, 2005), 202–208; Glen McLaren, *Beyond Leichhardt* (South Fremantle, 1996), 29, 31.

26. William H. Hovell, journal, October 2, 1824, MS Q322, ML. Hovell contributed four bullocks, one horse, and a cart; Hume contributed one bullock, two horses, and a cart. According to Hovell's unpublished journal, the supplies included 640 pounds of flour, 200 pounds of pork, 100 pounds of sugar, 14 pounds of tea, 8 pounds of to-

bacco, and 12 pounds of soap. The figures for most of these items are nearly twice as high as those reported in W. H. Hovell and Hamilton Hume, *Journey of Discovery to Port Phillip, New South Wales* [1831] (Adelaide, 1965), appendix 1.

27. Oxley, *Journals,* appendix; Sturt, *Central Australian Expedition,* xxxiv–xxxvi; J. G. Steele, ed., *The Explorers of the Moreton Bay District 1770–1830* (St. Lucia, 1972), 255.

28. Joanne Shoobert, ed., *Western Australian Exploration* (Carlisle, 2005), 1:255–266, 376–383.

29. T. L. Mitchell, *Three Expeditions into the Interior of Eastern Australia* (London, 1839), 1:149–150; Granville W. C. Stapylton, *Stapylton* (Hobart, 1986), 64; J. H. L. Cumpston, *The Inland Sea and the Great River* (Sydney, 1964), 136.

30. McLaren, *Beyond Leichhardt,* ch. 4.

31. Sturt, *Central Australian Expedition,* xliv.

32. Sarah Murgatroyd, *The Dig Tree* (Melbourne, 2002), 69, 118.

33. Sturt, *Central Australian Expedition,* xlvii; Ludwig Leichhardt, *Dr. Ludwig Leich-hardt's Letters from Australia,* trans. L. L. Politzer (Melbourne, n.d.), 57; William Carron, "Narrative of an Exploring Expedition," MS Q600, ML; British Parliamentary Papers, Cd. 2350 (1857–1858), *Papers Relating to an Expedition Recently Undertaken for the Purpose of Exploring the Northern Portion of Australia,* 4–5; Murgatroyd, *Dig Tree,* 94–95; Moorehead, *Cooper's Creek,* 43.

34. Leichhardt, *Letters,* 58.

35. Edward Stokes, *Across the Centre* (Sydney, 1996), 140.

36. McLaren, *Beyond Leichhardt,* 245.

37. David Lindsay, "Contrasting Explorations in Australia between 1872 and 1891," D7743(L), SLSA.

38. Ernest Giles, *Ernest Giles's Explorations, 1872–76* (Adelaide, 2000), 232, 264.

39. John Forrest, *Explorations in Australia* (New York, 1969), 161; Alexander Forrest, *North-West Exploration* (Perth, 1880), 8.

40. Tom S. McKnight, *The Camel in Australia* (Carlton, Victoria, 1969), 17–18; Peter Macinnis, *Australia's Pioneers, Heroes and Fools* (Miller Point, NSW, 2007), 14.

41. "Note of the Proceedings of a Committee of the Royal Geographical Society Assembled to Consider the Subject of the Explorations in the Interior of Australia," May 30, 1853, SSC/113/2/1, RGS. This proposal did serve, however, as the impetus for what eventually became Augustus Gregory's 1855–1856 expedition to northern Australia.

42. British Parliamentary Papers, Cd. 139 (1862), *Australian Exploring Expedition (Burke and Wills) Dispatches,* 2.

43. Alfred Howitt's relief party had nine camels, John McKinlay's had four. Both parties, however, relied far more heavily on horses—forty-five and twenty-six, respectively.

44. Fayette Gosse, "Elder, Sir Thomas (1818–1897)," *Australian Dictionary of Biography,* online edition (2006), http://www.adb.anu.edu.au; Peter E. Warburton, *Journey across the Western Interior of Australia* (London, 1875).

45. Murgatroyd, *Dig Tree,* 83; Edwin James Welch, diary of Howitt expedition, January 3, 1862, ML C332, ML.

46. McKnight, *Camel,* 23–25. For a fascinating biography of one Australian cameleer who did come from Afghanistan, see Madeleine Brunato, *Hanji Mahomet Allum* (Leabrook, 1972).

47. Warburton, *Journey,* 139; No. 48, South Australia, *W. C. Gosse's Explorations, 1873* (1874), 1–2; No. 19, South Australia, *Journal of Mr. Lewis's Lake Eyre Expedition, 1874–75* (1875), 1; No. 67, South Australia, *Mr. J. Ross's Explorations, 1874* (1875), 4; Ernest Giles, *The Journal of a Forgotten Expedition in 1875* (Adelaide, 1979), 32; Giles, *Ernest Giles's Exploration,* 291.

48. Marjorie Tipping, ed., *Ludwig Becker* (Carlton, Victoria, 1979), 193, 194.

49. Murgatroyd, *Dig Tree,* 93; *W. C. Gosse's Explorations,* 6; *Journal of Mr. Lewis's Lake Eyre Expedition,* 27; Warburton, *Journey,* 261–262; Giles, *Journal,* 39, and Jess Young in Giles, 49.

50. Richard Barnes, ed., *The Elder Scientific Exploration Expedition, 1891–2* (North Adelaide, 2003), 101, 62, 12, 67, 98, 66.

51. McKnight, *Camel,* 66–71; H. M. Barker, *Camels and the Outback* (Melbourne, 1964), 88–91.

52. David W. Carnegie, *Spinifex and Sand* (London, 1898), 122; No. 39, South Australia, *Mr. Winnecke's Explorations during 1883* (1884); W. H. Tietkens, *Journal of the Central Australian Exploring Expedition, 1889* (Adelaide, 1891); Charles Winnecke, *Journal of the Horn Scientific Exploring Expedition, 1894* (Adelaide, 1897), 5–6; Valmal A. Hankel, "Bejah, Dervish (1862?–1957)," *Australian Dictionary of Biography,* online edition (2006), http://www.adb.anu.edu.au.

53. John MacKenzie, *The Empire of Nature* (Manchester, 1988), 131.

54. John Barrow, *An Autobiographical Memoir* (London, 1847), 143–144.

55. Andrew Smith, *Andrew Smith's Journal of His Expedition into the Interior of South Africa* (Cape Town, 1975), 10–11.

56. Francis Galton, *The Narrative of an Explorer in Tropical South Africa* (London, 1853), 13, 130–131, 198–199.

57. "The Journals of Friedrich Hornemann's Travels from Cairo to Murzuk," in *Missions to the Niger,* vol. 1, ed. E. W. Bovill (Cambridge, 1964), 55–56, 84; Laing, "Letters," 1:230.

58. Diary entry quoted in Tim Jeal, *Explorers of the Nile* (New Haven, 2011), 428. Regrettably, I was refused permission by the Baker family to quote directly from his diaries, which I have read in the Royal Geographical Society, where they are archived.

59. Samuel Baker, *The Albert Nyanza* (London, 1866), ch. 16. Also see Adrian S. Wisnicki, "Rewriting Agency," *Studies in Travel Writing* 14, no. 1 (February 2010): 1–27; Jeal, *Explorers,* ch. 16.

60. Catherine Coquery-Vidrovich and Paul E. Lovejoy, eds., *The Workers of African Trade* (Beverly Hills, 1985), esp. chs. 1 and 7; 'Deji Ogunremi, "Human Porterage in Nigeria in the Nineteenth Century," *Journal of the Historical Society of Nigeria* 8, no. 1 (December 1975): 37–59.

61. Richard Burton, *A Mission to Gelele King of Dahome* (London, 1966), 87–88; Ogunremi, "Human Porterage," 42.

62. Jamie Bruce Lockhart and Paul E. Lovejoy, eds., *Hugh Clapperton into the Interior of Africa* (Leiden, 2005), 395.

63. Stephen J. Rockel, *Carriers of Culture* (Portsmouth, N.H., 2006), from which the information in this paragraph is drawn.

64. Verney Lovett Cameron to John Kirk (?), March 18, 1873, VLC 2/14/3A, RGS.

65. David Livingstone, *The Last Journals* (New York, 1875), 196.

66. Joseph Thomson to John Kirk, May 26, 1880, Joseph Thomson Correspondence, CB6/2173, RGS.

67. John H. Speke, *Journal of the Discovery of the Source of the Nile* [1863] (London, 1937), 38.

68. James A. Grant, *A Walk across Africa* (Edinburgh, 1864), 22–23, 43 (quote).

69. Rockel, *Carriers,* 86–87; Richard F. Burton, *The Lake Regions of Central Africa* [1860] (New York, 1995), 22, 111; James L. Newman, *Imperial Footprints* (Washington, D.C., 2004), 40, 101; Verney Lovett Cameron, expedition journal, May 27, 1873, MSS 299(1), microfilm, NLS; Joseph Thomson, *Through Masai Land* (London, 1887), 31; Henry M. Stanley, *Through the Dark Continent* [1899] (New York, 1988), 1:51, 65. For the role of caravan women, see Stephen J. Rockel, "Enterprising Partners," *Canadian Journal of African Studies* 34, no. 3 (2000): 748–778.

70. Francis Galton, *The Art of Travel,* 2nd ed. (London, 1856), 81.

71. Cameron, expedition journal, April 14–September 25, 1875, 76, VLC 4/3, RGS.

72. Charles Gordon to Stanley, April 20, 1875, item 2921, Stanley Archives, RAM.

73. See Newman, *Imperial Footprints,* ch. 7.

74. G. W. Clendennen and D. H. Simpson, "African Members of the Zambezi Expedition, 1861–1864," *History in Africa* 12 (1985): 29–49.

75. McLaren, *Beyond Leichhardt,* 41–42; Macinnis, *Australia's Pioneers,* 106–107.

76. See William Cooper and Glen McLaren, "The Changing Dietary Habits of Nineteenth-Century Australian Explorers," *Australian Geographer* 28, no. 1 (1997): 97–105.

77. Richard Johnson, *The Search for the Inland Sea* (Melbourne, 2001), 57; Mitchell, *Three Expeditions,* 1:138. Strangely, Mitchell attributed the affliction's appearance among two men on his second expedition to one's association with degraded convicts and the other's consumption of rancid pork (316, 318).

78. Sturt initially misdiagnosed Poole's symptoms as rheumatism and expressed embarrassment when he realized his error. Sturt, *Central Australian Expedition,* 179, 188. As Davis notes (appendix C), the expedition's supplies included no antiscorbutic agents, which is puzzling given the fact that Sturt had brought lime juice and vinegar on an earlier expedition (McLaren, *Beyond Leichhardt,* 65).

79. There is some dispute about whether they succumbed to scurvy or beriberi, another disease caused by a vitamin deficiency. The expedition was stocked with preserved vegetables, which were intended to prevent scurvy, but the commission of inquiry found that they were not eaten because they were too hard to chew. Moorehead, *Cooper's Creek,* 194. In any case, at least some members of the expedition believed the disease could be warded off by consuming large quantities of fresh beef. Hermann Beckler, *A Journey to Cooper's Creek* (Carlton, Victoria, 1993), 11.

80. Stuart provides a harrowing description of scurvy's symptoms in his unpublished journal, entries May 15–21, 1860, JMS 13/109, RGS. Other accounts of outbreaks of scurvy include Warburton, *Journey,* 181, 185, 290; No. 209, South Australia, *Journal of Mr. Barclay's Exploration, 1878* (1878), 6–7; and No. 39, South Australia, *Mr. Winnecke's Explorations during 1883* (1884).

81. Baikie, *Narrative,* 221–222. Although Baikie was a medical doctor, his treatment of the Krumen raises doubts about his claim that he "thoroughly understood" the causes of scurvy. He dosed them with wine and regretted the fact that he had no rum to give them. Fortunately, he also increased their rations of rice, salt, and meat, which at least improved their caloric intake.

82. Samuel Baker diaries, entry for February 22, 1871, SWB/4, RGS.

83. Michael Adas, *Machines as the Measure of Men* (Ithaca, N.Y., 1989), esp. part 2.

84. "Balloon Exploration," *Melbourne Punch,* September 23, 1858, 71. The development of balloons as instruments of scientific discovery is discussed by Richard Holmes, *The Age of Wonder* (New York, 2008), ch. 3.

6. Intermediaries

1. Ludwig Leichhardt, *Journal of an Overland Expedition in Australia from Moreton Bay to Port Essington* (London, 1847), xv. Harry Brown was raised at the Lake Macquarie mission, according to Niel Gunson, "Biraban (fl. 1819–1842)," *Australian Dictionary of Biography,* online edition (2006), http://www.adb.anu.edu.au.

2. Leichhardt, *Journal,* 5, 14, 18, 144–145, 158–161.

3. John Murphy, journal of the Port Essington Expedition, entry for February 19, 1845, ML MSS 2193, ML.

4. Ludwig Leichhardt, *The Letters of F. W. Ludwig Leichhardt,* trans. M. Aurousseau (Cambridge, 1968), 3:844.

5. William Phillips, journal of the Port Essington Expedition with Leichhardt, p. 87, C 165, ML. When Charley and Harry fell out at a later point in the expedition, Leichhardt welcomed the development, noting that he "derived the greatest advantage from their animosity to each other, as each tried to outdo the other in readiness to serve me." Leichhardt, *Journal,* 232.

6. Leichhardt, *Letters,* 916. Charley was collecting birds for a Mr. Strange when Leichhardt organized this expedition (906).

7. John Frederick Mann, "Diary Kept during a Short Journey into the Interior in Company with Dr. Ludwig Leichhardt, 1 Oct. 1846–29 July 1847," entry for July 15, ML B455, ML.

8. Hovenden Hely, journal of the Leichhardt expedition, October 1, 1846–July 28, 1847, entries for July 2, 11, 15, C 264, ML. Hely went on to say that "L[eichhardt] is the worst Bushman I ever saw."

9. Hovenden Hely to Colonial Secretary, October 11, 1851, A1384, ML.

10. See Lowri M. Jones, "Local Knowledge and Indigenous Agency in the History of Exploration," (PhD diss., Geography Department, Royal Holloway University of London, 2010); Simon Schaffer, Lissa Roberts, Kapil Raj, and James Delbourgo,

eds., *The Brokered World* (Sagamore Beach, Mass., 2009); Felix Driver and Lowri Jones, *Hidden Histories of Exploration* (London, 2009); Benjamin N. Lawrance, Emily Lynn Osborne, and Richard L. Roberts, eds., *Intermediaries, Interpreters, and Clerks* (Madison, 2006); Stuart B. Schwartz, *Implicit Understandings* (Cambridge, 1994); Kapil Raj, "When Human Travellers Became Instruments," in *Instruments, Travel and Science,* ed. Marie Noëlle Bourguet, Christian Licoppe, and H. Otto Siburn (London, 2002), 156–188. The first important works to focus on the roles of intermediaries in African and Australian exploration were Donald Simpson, *Dark Companions* (New York, 1976), Henry Reynolds, *With the White People* (Ringwood, Victoria, 1990), and Henry Reynolds, "The Land, the Explorers and the Aborigines," *Historical Studies* 19, no. 75 (1980): 213–226.

11. Almost all of these firsthand accounts come from African intermediaries. They include James Henry Dorugu, "The Life and Travels of Dorugu," trans. and ed. Paul Newman, in *West African Travels and Adventures,* ed. Anthony Kirk-Greene (New Haven, 1971): 29–129; Selim Aga, "Incidents Connected with the Life of Selim Aga," in James McCarthy, *Selim Aga* (Edinburgh, 2006), 203–228; Jacob Wainwright, "'A Dangerous and Toilsome Journey,'" ed. and trans. R. C. Bridges, in *Four Travel Journals,* ed. Herbert K. Beals et al. (London, 2007), 329–384; and "Manuscript Translation of Testimony Given by Saleh Bin Osman, Regarding Stanley's Rear Guard in the Rescue of Emin Pasha," M55, Russell E. Train Africana Collection, Joseph Cullman Library, NMNH. The only verbatim testimony by an Aboriginal intermediary that I have found is that of Jackey Jackey, published in John MacGillivray, *Narrative of the Voyage of the H.M.S.* Rattlesnake (London, 1852).

12. Some friends who have read this chapter or heard presentations drawn from it have expressed unease with the term "deracinate," which means "to uproot." I recognize that it is not a commonly used term and that it can be erroneously assumed to carry racial connotations. But it effectively evokes the forces that ripped these individuals from their roots, unlike more fashionable terms such as "hybrid," "diasporic," and "liminal."

13. Inga Clendinnen, *Dancing with Strangers* (Cambridge, 2005), 97, 102, 141, 210–213, 266, 272; David Turnbull, "Boundary-Crossings, Cultural Encounters and Knowledge Spaces in Early Australia," in *Brokered World,* ed. Simon Schaffer et al. (Sagamore Beach, Mass., 2009), 399–401.

14. David W. Carnegie, *Spinifex and Sand* (London, 1989), 188–190, 231–235, 256, 258–267, 280–283, 380, 388, 390, 397–401, 407. Other cases appear in Peter Egerton Warburton, *Journey across the Western Interior of Australia* (London, 1875), 176–179, 206–208; Granville Stapylton, *Stapylton* (Hobart, 1986), 146; John Forrest, *Explorations in Australia* [1875] (New York, 1969), 214.

15. Francis Galton, *The Narrative of an Explorer in Tropical South Africa* (London, 1853), 155.

16. Edward John Eyre, *Journals of Expeditions of Discovery into Central Australia* (London, 1845), 1:102–104.

17. Neville Green, "Mokare (c. 1800–1831)," *Australian Dictionary of Biography,* online edition (2006), http://www.adb.anu.edu.au; Joanne Shoobert, ed., *Western Australian Exploration* (Carlisle, 2005), 1:4–5, 112, 242–252.

18. Robin Law, "Madiki Lemon, the 'English Captain' at Ouidah, 1843–1852," *History in Africa* 37 (2010): 107–123.

19. J. G. Steele, ed., *The Explorers of the Moreton Bay District, 1770–1830* (St. Lucia, 1972), 116, 240.

20. Henry Lefroy, "Diary and Journal of the Eastern Exploring Expedition," 7, ML MSS 1230, ML.

21. Joseph Ravenscroft Elsey, diary, October 25, 1855, MS 25, NLA. Also see the similar comment by Thomas Baines, journal, February 1, 1855, C 408, ML.

22. "The Journals of Friedrich Hornemann's Travels from Cairo to Murzuk," in E. W. Bovill, ed., *Missions to the Niger,* vol. 1 (Cambridge, 1964), 56; Robin Hallett, ed., *Records of the African Association, 1788–1831* (London, 1964), 225; Jason Thompson, "Osman Effendi," *Journal of World History* 5, no. 1 (1994): 99–123; Linda Colley, *Captives* (New York, 2002), part 1.

23. Mungo Park, *Travels in the Interior Districts of Africa* (Durham, N.C., 2000), ch. 3; James H. Tuckey and Christen Smith, *Narrative of an Expedition to Explore the River Zaire* (London, 1818), xxix–xxx, 261; John Davidson, *Notes Taken during Travels in Africa* (London, 1839); Abu Bekr, "Routes in North Africa," *Journal of the Royal Geographical Society* 6 (1836): 100–113.

24. British Parliamentary Papers, Cd. 472 (1843), *Papers Relative to the Expedition to the River Niger,* 24, 85; William Baikie, "Journal of Our Exploring Expedition up the River (Niger)," entry for July 26, 1854, Add. Ms. 32448, BL; William Baikie, *Narrative of an Exploring Voyage up the Rivers Kwo'ra and Bi'nua* (London, 1856), 16, 23; Samuel Crowther, *Journal of an Expedition up the Niger and Tshadda Rivers* (London, 1855), 49.

25. Baikie, *Narrative,* 30; Crowther, *Journal,* 18–20.

26. McCarthy, *Selim Aga.*

27. Richard and John Lander, *Journal of an Expedition to Explore the Course and Termination of the Niger* (New York, 1832), 1:118, 45. Also see Hugh Clapperton, *Journal of a Second Expedition into the Interior of Africa* (Philadelphia, 1829), xvii; Mac-Gregor Laird and R. A. K. Oldfield, *Narrative of an Expedition into the Interior of Africa* (London, 1837), 1:55, 260; Jamie Bruce Lockhart and Paul E. Lovejoy, eds., *Hugh Clapperton into the Interior of Africa* (Leiden, 2005), 27.

28. Simpson, *Dark Companions,* 191–198.

29. James A. Grant, *A Walk across Africa* (Edinburgh, 1864), 258, 272–273.

30. See Simpson, *Dark Companions;* Clare Pettitt, *Dr. Livingstone, I Presume?* (Cambridge, Mass., 2007), ch. 3.

31. Livingstone Search and Relief Expedition, *Report to the Subscribers by the Livingstone Search and Relief Committee* (London, 1882), 8, 17, Verney Lovett Cameron Collection, VLC1/1, RGS.

32. E. D. Young, *The Search after Livingstone* (London, 1868), 55, 256–257.

33. Henry M. Stanley, *My Kalulu* (New York, 1889).

34. Henry M. Stanley, *How I Found Livingstone* (London, 1872), 303; journal 7, entry for September 7, 1871, Stanley Archives, RAM. In the unpublished journal, Stanley gives Kalulu's original name as Dregum Ali; in his book, he refers to him as Ndugu M'hali.

35. James L. Newman, *Imperial Footprints* (Washington, D.C., 2004), 51, 199, 203, 293–294.

36. Robert Aldrich, *Colonialism and Homosexuality* (London, 2003), 41.

37. Dorugu, "Life and Travels," 49 (quote), 54.

38. Galton, *Narrative*, 13, 52.

39. Joseph Thomson, *Through Masai Land* (London, 1887), 7, 9.

40. Anthony Kirk-Greene and Paul Newman, "Introduction," in Dorugu, "Life and Travels."

41. See Ann McGrath, ed., *Contested Ground* (St. Leonards, NSW, 1995).

42. Reynolds, *With the White People,* ch. 5; Richard Broome, *Aboriginal Victorians* (Crows Nest, NSW, 2005), 60–62; Penelope Hetherington, *Settlers, Servants and Slaves* (Crawley, 2002), part 2.

43. Lefroy, "Diary," 7, ML MSS 1230, ML.

44. E. B. Kennedy, "Journal of Expedition to Central Australia," entries for April 22, November 17, and December 26, 1847, JMS 13/58, RGS.

45. Edward John Eyre, *Autobiographical Narrative of Residence and Exploration in Australia, 1832–1839* (London, 1984), 105, 124.

46. Francis Galton, *The Art of Travel* (London, 1856), 81.

47. No. 25, South Australia, *Northern Exploration* (c. 1858), 42.

48. A. W. Howitt, "An Episode in the History of Australian Exploration," in *Australian Association for the Advancement of Science* (pamphlet) (Melbourne, 1901), 292–293. For those rumors, see Duncan White, *Sketch of Exploration by the Late John M'Kinlay in the Interior of Australia, 1861–2* (Glasgow, 1881), 15–16.

49. John Davis, *Tracks of McKinlay and Party across Australia* (London, 1863), 110.

50. Eyre, *Journals,* 1:237–238; 2:138.

51. J. McDouall Stuart, journal, entry for June 25, 1860, JMS 13/109, RGS.

52. Leichhardt, *Journal,* 414.

53. Baikie, *Narrative,* 68–69.

54. John H. Speke, *Journal of the Discovery of the Source of the Nile* [1863] (London, 1937), 238–239, 242, 311, 327.

55. H. M. Stanley, "Speech or Preface Concerning the Rear Column" (undated ms.), 28, item 4710, Stanley Archives, RAM.

56. Charles Sturt, *Two Expeditions into the Interior of Southern Australia* (London, 1833), 1:18–19.

57. T. L. Mitchell, *Three Expeditions into the Interior of Eastern Australia,* 2nd ed. (London, 1839), 1:20.

58. John Forrest, *Explorations in Australia* [1875] (New York, 1969), 38; J. G. Hill, *The Calvert Scientific Exploring Expedition* (London, 1905), 35–36.

59. Peter Egerton Warburton, *Journey across the Western Interior of Australia* (London, 1875), 260.

60. Charles Sturt, *The Central Australian Expedition, 1844–1846* (London, 2002), 42.

61. Mitchell, *Three Expeditions,* 2:76.

62. Laird and Oldfield, *Narrative,* 1:94–95.

63. Simpson, *Dark Companions,* 10–11.

64. Richard F. Burton, *Zanzibar* (London, 1872), 2:179; John H. Speke, *My Second Expedition to Eastern Intertropical Africa* (pamphlet) (Cape Town, c. 1860), 16–17. Speke reiterated his praise in *What Led to the Discovery of the Source of the Nile* (Edinburgh, 1864), 186, 210.

65. Speke to Christopher Rigby, September 3, 1859, MS 17910, ff. 82–83, Grant Papers, NLS.

66. Speke, *Journal,* 158–159, 222; Simpson, *Dark Companions,* 38.

67. Grant to Sir Henry Rawlinson, December 14, 1871, James Grant Correspondence, CB 6/946, RGS.

68. H. M. Stanley, March 24, 1872, field notebook #10, Stanley Archives, RAM.

69. David Livingstone, *The Last Journals* (New York, 1875), 530.

70. V. L. Cameron, expedition journals, entry for June 29, 1873, MSS 299(1), microfilm, NLS; V. L. Cameron, journal (April 15–September 25, 1875), 17, 21, 48, VLC 4/3, RGS. Also V. L. Cameron, *Across Africa* (London, 1877), 1:9, 156.

71. Grant to Thomas Wakefield, May 19, 1876, M64, Russell E. Train Africana Collection, Joseph Cullman Library, NMNH.

72. Quoted in Robert Rotberg, *Joseph Thomson and the Exploration of Africa* (New York, 1971), 102.

73. Testimony of Adouiah Vallack, "Enquiry into the Death of E. B. C. Kennedy . . . ," New South Wales, Governor's Dispatches, vol. 60, March–April 1849, ML A1249, ML.

74. Davis, *Tracks of McKinlay,* 179.

75. Dorothy O. Helly, *Livingstone's Legacy* (Athens, Ohio, 1987), 163, 165, 169.

76. No. 24, South Australia, *Exploration Northern Territory* (1868), 14–15, 19; No. 178, South Australia, *Northern Territory Exploration, 1867* (1867), 3.

77. Ernest Giles, *The Journal of a Forgotten Expedition in 1875* (Adelaide, 1979), 40.

78. George Grey, *Journals of Two Expeditions of Discovery in North-West and Western Australia* (London, 1841), 2:58, 77, 86, 90–91.

79. Mitchell, *Three Expeditions,* 2:162.

80. Joseph Thomson to Secretary, RGS (July 19, 1880), CB6/2173, RGS.

81. Pettitt, *Dr. Livingstone,* 142.

82. Forrest, *Explorations,* 17, 145; F. K. Crowley, "Windich, Tommy (1840–1876)," *Australian Dictionary of Biography,* online edition (2006), http://www.adb.anu.edu.au; Tommy Pierre, another Aboriginal guide who accompanied several of the Forrest brothers' expeditions, was similarly honored for his contributions upon his death. See Alexander Forrest, *North-West Exploration* (Perth, 1880), preface.

83. Mitchell, *Three Expeditions,* 2:3, 339.

84. Edwin Welch, diary of Howitt expedition, June 26, 1861, ML C332, ML; Ray Ericksen, *Ernest Giles* (Melbourne, 1978), 108.

85. The Landers describe a revealing incident where their guide Pascoe was confronted by an ex-"wife," left behind during the previous Clapperton expedition, who demanded that he take custody of a child she claimed to be his. Lander, *Journal,* 1:103.

86. Granville Stapylton, *Stapylton* (Hobart, 1986), 113.

87. Wainwright, "'Dangerous and Toilsome Journey,'" 368, 372–373.

88. Mitchell, *Three Expeditions,* 1:50; emphasis added.

7. Encounters

1. The prevalence of slavery, and especially enslaved women, in Buganda at this time is detailed in Henri Médard and Shane Doyle, eds., *Slavery in the Great Lakes Region of East Africa* (Oxford, 2007). See especially the essays by Richard Reid, Holly Hanson, and Michael Tuck.

2. John Hanning Speke, *Journal of the Discovery of the Source of the Nile* [1863] (London, 1937), 296–299. Speke's biographer makes the unpersuasive argument that these remarks were a lame attempt at humor. Alexander Maitland, *Speke* (London, 1971), 158–159.

3. Richard Burton and James MacQueen, *The Nile Basin,* part II (London, 1864), 108, 147. This material was first published as a series of articles in the *Morning Advertiser.*

4. As pointed out in David Finkelstein's revealing analysis of the editorial process that turned Speke's often incoherent writings into a highly readable and successful book, "Unraveling Speke," *History in Africa* 30 (2003): 127.

5. John Hanning Speke, "Speke's Journal—First Print," MS 4872, f. 383, NLS.

6. Speke, MS 4872, ff. 367–368.

7. Speke, MS 4872, f. 383.

8. R. C. Bridges, "Europeans and East Africans in the Age of Exploration," *Geographical Journal* 139, no. 1 (June 1973): 229–230. Tim Jeal, who discusses Speke's Bugandan love affair in his *Explorers of the Nile* (New Haven, 2011), ch. 10, is skeptical of these rumors.

9. Richard and John Lander, *Journal of an Expedition to Explore the Course and Termination of the Niger* (New York, 1832), 1:173.

10. James Cook, *The Journals,* ed. Philip Edwards (London, 2003), 174.

11. T. L. Mitchell, *Three Expeditions into the Interior of Eastern Australia* (London, 1939), 1:171, 247–248; Granville Stapylton, *Stapylton* (Hobart, 1986), 64.

12. Edward J. Eyre, *Journals of Expeditions of Discovery into Central Australia* (London, 1845), 2:chs. 1–8; George Grey, *Journals of Two Expeditions of Discovery in North-West and Western Australia* (London, 1841), 2:chs. 9–18.

13. David Livingstone, *The Last Journals of David Livingstone in Central Africa,* ed. Horace Waller (New York, 1875), 370; Dorothy O. Helly, *Livingstone's Legacy* (Athens, Ohio, 1987), 140–141.

14. John Kirk, *The Zambezi Journal and Letters* (Edinburgh, 1965), 1:207, 209.

15. Dane Kennedy, *The Highly Civilized Man* (Cambridge, Mass., 2005), ch. 5; Speke, *Journal,* introduction; Francis Galton, *The Narrative of an Explorer in Tropical South Africa* (London, 1853), 123–124.

16. David W. Carnegie, *Spinifex and Sand* (London, 1898), 238.

17. Ernest Giles, *Ernest Giles's Expeditions, 1872–76* (Adelaide, 2000), 374.

18. Draft RGS recommendations for the exploring expedition, May 18, 1837, JMS 13/11/l, RGS. This passage appears to be a modified version of a generic circular published by the RGS a year earlier that includes much the same language about dealing with indigenous peoples. See Felix Driver and Lowri Jones, *Hidden Histories of Exploration* (London, 2009), 46.

19. Augustus and Francis Gregory, *Journals of Australian Explorations* [1884] (New York, 1968), 14.

20. John Forrest, *Explorations in Australia* [1875] (New York, 1969), 2.

21. Joanne Shoobert, ed., *Western Australian Exploration* (Carlisle, 2005), 1:376–383.

22. Edmund Kennedy to his father, December 18, 1845, and February 27, 1848, T/2966/P/2/18 & 31, PRNI.

23. E. B. Kennedy, "Journal of Expedition to Central Australia," September 21, 1847, JMS 13/58, RGS.

24. Mitchell, *Three Expeditions*, 1:247, 307, 274.

25. Daniel G. Brock, *To the Desert with Sturt* (Adelaide, 1975), 50–51.

26. Charles Sturt, account of journey, 1838 (photocopy), 126–127, MS 9025, MSB 450, SLV. Mitchell's account of this incident appears in *Three Expeditions*, 2:96–102.

27. Diedrich Henne, journal, December 13, 1862, ML C407, ML.

28. William Landsborough, *Journal of Landsborough's Expedition from Carpentaria* [1862] (Adelaide, 2000), 102.

29. R. H. Edmunds, journals, August 7, 1865, RGSSA.

30. Western Australia, *Journal of Proceedings of the Western Australian Exploring Expedition through the Centre of Australia* (Perth, 1875), 13 (quote), 25, 28; reprinted in Forrest, *Explorations*.

31. James Henry Ricketson, "Journal of an Expedition to Cambridge Gulf, 1884–85," November 1 and 2, December 6, 1884, ML MSS 1783, ML.

32. John McDouall Stuart, "Exploration in Australia," 2, JMS/13/125, RGS. An edited version of this journal was published as No. 119, South Australia, *Mr. Stuart's Exploration* (1858).

33. John Davis, *Tracks of McKinlay and Party across Australia* (London, 1863), 396.

34. Alexander Forrest, *North-West Exploration* (Perth, 1880), 12.

35. William Phillips, journal of Port Essington expedition, 6, C165, ML.

36. Captain John Bamber to J. S. Roe in Joanne Shoobert, ed., *Western Australian Exploration* (Carlisle, 2005), 1:130.

37. R. H. Edmunds, journal, entries for September 20, 1865, and March 24, 1866, RGSSA.

38. Alfred A. Turner, journal, entry for October 31, 1847, FM4/4179, ML.

39. W. H. Hovell and Hamilton Hume, *Journal of Discovery to Port Philip, New South Wales* (Sydney, 1831), 70; Mitchell, *Three Expeditions*, 2:277. The essay on mimicry appears in Homi K. Bhabha, *The Location of Culture* (London, 1994), ch. 4.

40. Daniel Bunce, "Journal of an Overland Expedition from Sydney . . . to Swan River," entry for December 12, 1846, B387, ML.

41. Gregory, *Journals,* 25.

42. Richard Broome, *Aboriginal Australians* (Crows Nest, NSW, 2002), 57. Numerous explorers' journals describe offers of women.

43. Sturt, *Central Australian Expedition,* 9 (quote), 317 (comments on Mitchell). At one stage in the expedition, a group of Aboriginal women were turned away from camp three nights in a row, causing Sturt to report that they were "quite indignant at having their favours rejected" (169).

44. Alfred A. Turner, journal, October 2 and 3, 1847, FM4/4179, ML.

45. Sturt, *Central Australian Expedition*, 79.

46. Kennedy, "Journal," October 8, 1847, JMS 13/58.

47. Carnegie, *Spinifex and Sand*, 263.

48. Giles, *Ernest Giles's Explorations*, 189.

49. Broome, *Aboriginal Australians*, 44.

50. Sturt, account of journey, MS 9025, MSB 450, 126, SLV.

51. Charles Sturt, memorandum, n.d., in papers relating to North Australia Expedition, SSC/133/2/3, RGS.

52. Sturt, *Central Australian Expedition*, 30, 31. Erroneous rumors of this sort affected other expeditions as well. See, for example, J. G. Hill, *The Calvert Scientific Exploring Expedition* (London, 1905), 28–31, 38–40.

53. Grey, *Journals*, 1:147–152; Mitchell, *Three Expeditions*, 1:appendix 1; Ray Ericksen, *Ernest Giles* (Melbourne, 1978), 33.

54. Mitchell, *Three Expeditions*, 1:113–115.

55. William Landsborough, field books, April 2 and 6, 1862, B1098, ML.

56. John F. Mann, "Diary Kept during a Short Journey into the Interior in the Company of Dr. Ludwig Leichhardt," January 4, 1846, ML B455, ML.

57. John Bailey, *Mr. Stuart's Track* (Sydney, 2007), 235, 240–241; Ericksen, *Ernest Giles*, 122–123.

58. Davis, *Tracks*, 119–120, 240 (quote).

59. Ludwig Leichhardt, *Journal of an Overland Expedition in Australia* (London, 1847), ch. 9; William Phillips, journal of Port Essington expedition with Leichhardt, C 156, 58, ML.

60. Hermann Beckler, *A Journey to Cooper's Creek* (Carlton, 1993), 154–176.

61. J. McDouall Stuart, journal, June 27, 1860, JMS 13/109, RGS.

62. Mary Louise Pratt observes that Park portrays himself in his narrative as "vulnerable, inept, limited in power and understanding," but she dismisses this as a mystification of imperial intentions. Pratt, "Travel Narrative and Imperialist Vision," in *Understanding Narrative*, ed. James Phelan and Peter J. Rabinowitz (Columbus, 1994), 199–221 (quote on 211).

63. Macgregor Laird and R. A. K. Oldfield, *Narrative of an Expedition into the Interior of Africa* (London, 1837), ch. 9.

64. James A. Grant, *A Walk across Africa* (Edinburgh, 1864), 121.

65. Samuel Baker to Charles Gordon, October 16, 1875, Add. Ms. 51305, ff. 75–77, BL.

66. Joseph Thomson to John Kirk, March 27, 1880, Thomson Correspondence, CB6/2173, RGS.

67. Mungo Park, *Travels in the Interior Districts of Africa* (Durham, N.C., 2000), 103, 154–155.

68. John Hanning Speke, *What Led to the Discovery of the Source of the Nile* (Edinburgh, 1864), 285.

69. Kirk, *Zambezi Journal*, 2:373.

70. Livingstone, *Last Journals*, 310.

71. Grant, *Walk*, 39, 41, 73–74 (quote).

72. Verney Lovett Cameron, journal, 40, 45, 93 (quote), Cameron Collection, VLC 4/3, RGS.

73. Joseph Thomson, *Through Masai Land* (London, 1887), 95; Thomson to John Kirk, March 27, 1880, Thomson correspondence, CB6/2173, RGS.

74. Anthony Sattin, *The Gates of Africa* (New York, 2003), 203.

75. Hornemann in Robin Hallett, ed., *Records of the African Association, 1788–1831* (London, 1964), 189; "Journals of Friedrich Hornemann's Travels from Cairo to Murzuk," in *Missions to the Niger,* vol. 1, ed. E. W. Bovill (Cambridge, 1964), 34.

76. Heinrich Barth, *Travels and Discoveries in North and Central Africa* (London, 1965), 1:xxxviii; Anthony Kirk-Greene, "Heinrich Barth," in Robert I. Rotberg, ed., *Africa and Its Explorers* (Cambridge, Mass., 1970), 31.

77. E. W. Bovill, "Introduction," in *Missions to the Niger,* vol. 2: *The Bornu Mission 1822–25,* part 1, ed. E. W. Bovill (Cambridge, 1966), 32.

78. Alexander Gordon Laing, "The Letters of Major Alexander Gordon Laing, 1824–26," in *Missions to the Niger,* vol. 1, ed. E. W. Bovill (Cambridge, 1964), 276 (quote), 284.

79. See, for example, Mary Louise Pratt, *Imperial Eyes* (London, 1992), and Simon Ryan, *The Cartographic Eye* (Cambridge, 1996).

80. Hugh Clapperton, *Journal of a Second Expedition into the Interior of Africa* (Philadelphia, 1829), 86–87, 320 (Lander quote).

81. Park, *Travels,* 277; David Livingstone, *Missionary Travels and Researches in South Africa* (London, 1899), 251; Richard Burton, *First Footsteps in East Africa* [1856] (New York, 1966), 64.

82. James H. Dorugu, "The Life and Travels of Dorugu," in *West African Travels and Adventures* (New Haven, 1971), 44.

83. John Davidson, *Notes Taken during Travels in Africa* (London, 1839), 150.

84. Jamie Bruce Lockhart and Paul E. Lovejoy, eds., *Hugh Clapperton into the Interior of Africa* (Leiden, 2005), 268, 293, 296.

85. Bovill, "Introduction," 91.

86. Dixon Denham and Hugh Clapperton, *Narrative of Travels and Discoveries in Northern and Central Africa* (Boston, 1826), 213.

87. Samuel W. Baker, *The Albert Nyanza* (London, 1866), 64; Galton, *Narrative of an Explorer,* 158, 173.

88. Barth, *Travels and Discoveries,* 2:58; Laird and Oldfield, *Narrative,* 8, 83–84; British Parliamentary Papers, Cd. 472 (1843), *Papers Relative to the Expedition to the River Niger,* 8; William B. Baikie, *Narrative of an Exploring Voyage up the Rivers Kwo'ra and Bi'nue* (London, 1856), 104, 403.

89. Kirk, *Zambezi Journal,* 2:358, 479, 1:180.

90. Samuel Baker to Charles Gordon, November 17, 1875, Gordon Papers, Add. Ms. 51305, ff. 79–82, BL.

91. The public controversy provoked by Stanley's dispatches is examined by Felix Driver, "Henry Morton Stanley and His Critics," *Past and Present* 133 (November 1991): 134–144; Felix Driver, *Geography Militant* (Oxford, 2001), ch. 6.

92. Stanley to Grant, February 10, 1880, Grant Papers, MS 17910, ff. 130–131, NLS.

93. Tim Jeal, *Stanley* (New Haven, 2007), 178–179.

94. Review of Cameron's "Across Africa," *Pall Mall Gazette,* January 31, 1877, 12, in clipping file, MSS 299(2), microfilm, NLS.

95. Verney Lovett Cameron, expedition journals, July 16, 1873, MSS 299(1), microfilm, NLS.

96. James L. Newman, *Imperial Footprints* (Washington, D.C., 2004), 101 (quote), 129, 292.

97. A. G. Hopkins, "Explorers' Tales," *Journal of Imperial and Commonwealth History* 36, no. 4 (December 2008): 672.

98. Johannes Fabian, *Out of Our Minds* (Berkeley, 2000), 25, 122.

99. Jeal himself notes that Stanley's Emin Pasha expedition included the following military supplies: two tons of gunpowder, 350,000 percussion caps, 100,000 rounds of Remington ammunition, 30,000 Gatling gun cartridges, 50,000 rounds of Winchester ammunition, and a Maxim gun. Jeal, *Stanley,* 322.

100. On this point, see David Cannadine, *Ornamentalism* (New York, 2002).

101. Galton, *Narrative of an Explorer,* 4 (quote), 220.

102. Cameron, expedition journal, June 29, 1873, MSS 299(1), NLS.

103. Captain William Allen, report, February 5, 1843, in British Parliamentary Papers, Cd. 472 (1843), *Papers Relative to the Expedition to the River Niger,* 136.

104. Henry M. Stanley, "African Royalties I Have Known," typescript, Stanley Archives, item 4712, RAM.

105. Henry M. Stanley, *Through the Dark Continent* [1899] (New York, 1988), 1:147, 153. In his field notebook, Stanley proclaimed Mutesa "the most intelligent African . . . I ever saw." Field notebook, November 8, 1875, Stanley Archives, item 15, RAM.

106. According to James Grant, Mutesa "imitated us in all we did, eating the same things, dressing . . . like us," and so on. Grant to Charles Gordon, March 14, 1874, Gordon Papers, Add. Ms. 51305, ff. 28–33, BL.

107. James H. Tuckey and Christen Smith, *Narrative of an Expedition to Explore the River Zaire* (London, 1818), 71, 108, 139, 294.

108. Denham and Clapperton, *Narratives of Travel,* xvi, xxviii, xix, lxi, 20, 28 (quote), 29, 36, 71, 113, 134, 162, 163, 182–183, 198–199, 216, 229, 230.

109. "Journals of Friedrich Hornemann," 105 (quote); Laing, "Letters," 281.

110. "Journal of Richard Lander," in Clapperton, *Journal,* 362.

111. Richard F. Burton, "The Lake Regions of Central Equatorial Africa," *Journal of the Royal Geographical Society* 29 (1859): 163.

112. The phrase is borrowed from Ann Laura Stoler, "Tense and Tender Ties," *Journal of American History* 88, no. 3 (December 2001): 829–865.

113. Davidson, *Notes,* 150.

114. Baker, *Albert Nyanza,* 237.

115. Donald Cumming, *The Gentleman Savage* (London, 1987), 89, 70, passim.

116. William Carron, "Narrative of an Exploring Expedition," June 14, 1848, MS Q600, ML.

117. Anon., *The Burke and Wills Exploring Expedition* (Melbourne, 1861), 3, 4, 30.

118. Edwin J. Welch, diary of Howitt expedition, September 15, 1861, ML C332, ML.

119. Ferdinand Mueller, "The Fate of Dr. Leichhardt, and a Proposed New Search for His Party," *Australian,* February 18, 1865 (reprinted as pamphlet); New South

Wales Legislative Council, *Dr. Leichhardt (Correspondence Respecting Proposed Expedition in Search Of)* (1865), 11; Duncan McIntyre, "The Leichhardt Expedition," unidentified newspaper clipping in Leichhardt Relief Expedition file, JMS/13/170, RGS.

120. Eccleston Du Faur, "Account of Andrew Hume's Story of a Survivor of Leichhardt's Expedition," JMS/13/208, RGS.

121. Giles, *Explorations,* 375. In his introduction to Giles's book (xx), Valmai Hankel raises the possibility that Giles fathered mixed-race children.

122. Bunce, "Journal of an Overland Expedition," entry for December 21, B387, ML.

123. Livingstone, *Missionary Travels,* 346.

124. See Thomas J. Bassett, "Indigenous Mapmaking in Intertropical Africa," and Peter Sutton, "Aboriginal Maps and Plans," both in *The History of Cartography,* vol. 2, book 3: *Cartography in the Traditional African, American, Arctic, Australian, and Pacific Societies,* ed. David Woodward and G. Malcolm Lewis (Chicago, 1998), 24–48 and 387–416.

125. Bassett, "Indigenous Mapmaking," 34. A number of these maps were collected by the armchair geographer William Desborough Cooley, who donated them to the Royal Geographical Society. Lockhart and Lovejoy, *Clapperton,* appendix V.

126. Adrian S. Wisnicki, "Charting the Frontier," *Victorian Studies* 51, no. 1 (Autumn 2008): 103–137; Adrian S. Wisnicki, "Cartographical Quandaries," *History in Africa* 35 (2008): 455–479.

127. Grey, *Journals of Two Expeditions,* 2:93.

128. Baker, *Lake Nyanza,* 170–171.

8. Celebrities

1. See Robert Clarke, ed., *Celebrity Colonialism* (Newcastle upon Tyne, 2009). Also relevant are John M. MacKenzie, "Heroic Myths of Empire," in *Popular Imperialism and the Military 1850–1950,* ed. John M. MacKenzie (Manchester, 1992), 109–138; Edward Berenson, *Heroes of Empire* (Berkeley, 2010).

2. The quotations and information in this paragraph and the following one come from Edwin James Welch's diary, entries for November 20–25, 1861, ML C322, ML. Also see Alan Moorehead, *Cooper's Creek* (New York, 1963), ch. 13, and Sarah Murgatroyd, *The Dig Tree* (Melbourne, 2002), ch. 18.

3. See Clare Pettitt, "Exploration in Print," in *Reassessing Exploration,* ed. Dane Kennedy (New York, forthcoming).

4. Quoted in Kenneth Lupton, *Mungo Park the African Traveler* (Oxford, 1979), 97. This subject is examined in Philip J. Stern, "'Rescuing the Age from the Charge of Ignorance,'" in *A New Imperial History,* ed. Kathleen Wilson (Cambridge, 2004), 115–135.

5. See Derek R. Peterson, ed., *Abolitionism and Imperialism in Britain, Africa, and the Atlantic* (Athens, Ohio, 2010).

6. See Howard Temperley, *White Dreams, Black Africa* (New Haven, 1991). The evangelical, antislavery agenda of the expedition is especially evident in the account given by William Simpson, *A Private Journal Kept during the Niger Expedition*

(London, 1843), though Seymour Drescher points out in "Emperors of the World," in Peterson, *Abolitionism and Imperialism in Britain, Africa, and the Atlantic,* 140–141, that the abolitionist community was divided about the wisdom of the expedition.

7. Edward Eyre, *Journals of Expeditions of Discovery into Central Australia* (London, 1845), 1:10–12. Eyre also insists that he spent £680 from his own pocket (16).

8. Charles Sturt to Charles Campbell, July 3, 1840, in Charles Sturt papers (microfilm of Rhodes House Library original), MAV/FM4/21, ML.

9. Eyre, *Journals,* 1:21.

10. Daniel Brock, *To the Desert with Sturt* (Adelaide, 1975), 2, 3.

11. Henry Maxwell Lefroy, "Diary and Journal of the Eastern Exploration Expedition Made in the Year 1863," 5, 6, ML MSS 1230, ML.

12. *Argus,* August 18, 20, and 21, 1860. These news reports and other information about the departure can be found at the Burke and Wills Web Online Digital Archive, www.burkeandwills.net.au.

13. Wendy Birman, *Gregory of Rainworth* (Nedlands, 1979), 193; William Landsborough, *Journal of Landsborough's Expedition from Carpentaria* [1862] (Adelaide, 2000), 120–128; Duncan White, *Sketch of Explorations by the Late John M'Kinlay in the Interior of Australia, 1861–62* (Glasgow, 1881), 37–431; Peter Warburton, *Journey across the Western Interior of Australia* (London, 1875), 293, 304–307.

14. This account comes from contemporary newspaper reports reproduced in John Forrest, *Explorations in Australia* [1875] (New York, 1969), ch. 6 (quotes on 275, 282). The Adelaide crowd estimate appears in Ray Ericksen, *Ernest Giles* (Melbourne, 1978), 180.

15. Ernest Giles, *Ernest Giles's Explorations, 1872–76* (Adelaide, 2000), 331, 332. Also see W. H. Tietkens, "Reminiscences, 1859–87," 70, PRG 1006/1, SLSA.

16. The 1876 census showed the population of Adelaide to be 91,408.

17. Roslynn Haynes, *Seeking the Centre* (Cambridge, 1998), 59, 115–122.

18. Ferdinand von Mueller to Governor Charles Darling, July 21, 1865, JMS/13/165, RGS. Also see New South Wales, Legislative Council, *Dr. Leichhardt (Correspondence Respecting Proposed Expedition in Search Of)* (1865). The expedition itself was a tragic disappointment, disbanding after the death from fever of its commander, Duncan McIntyre, and several members of his party. See the correspondence, clippings, and reports in JMS/13/170 & 175–178, RGS.

19. Tim Bonyhady, *Burke and Wills* (Canberra, 2002), 32.

20. J. G. Hill, *The Calvert Scientific Exploring Expedition* (London, 1905), 43 (quote), 44.

21. The RGS awarded gold medals to the following Australian explorers in the nineteenth century: Edward Eyre (1843), Count Strzelecki (1846), Charles Sturt and Ludwig Leichhardt (1847), Augustus Gregory (1857), John McDouall Stuart (1861), Robert O'Hara Burke (1862), Frank Gregory (1863), Peter Warburton (1874), John Forrest (1876), and Ernest Giles (1880). See Ian Cameron, *To the Farthest Ends of the Earth* (London, 1980), appendix 2.

22. Forrest, *Exploration,* 272.

23. Giles, *Ernest Giles's Explorations,* 311.

24. Andrew Smith, *The Diary of Dr. Andrew Smith, 1834–1836* (Cape Town, 1939), 1:40.

25. Tim Fulford, Debbie Lee, and Peter J. Kitson, *Literature, Science and Exploration in the Romantic Era* (Cambridge, 2004), ch. 4.

26. Tim Jeal, *Livingstone* (New York, 1973), 164. Also see Charles W. J. Withers, *Geography and Science in Britain, 1831–1939* (Manchester, 2010), 55, 85; Clare Pettitt, *Dr. Livingstone, I Presume?* (Cambridge, Mass., 2007), 36–37.

27. Pettitt, *Dr. Livingstone*, 36.

28. Charles W. J. Withers, "Scale and the Geographies of Civil Science," in *Geographies of Nineteenth-Century Science*, ed. David N. Livingstone and Charles W. J. Withers (Chicago, 2011), 113.

29. John Hanning Speke to William Blackwood, July 8, 1863, MS 4185, ff. 248–249, NLS.

30. *Times*, September 14 and 19, 1864.

31. Richard F. Burton, *Zanzibar* (London, 1872), 2:137; Galton quoted in Withers, *Geography and Science*, 85.

32. Ryan Johnson, "Tabloid Brand Medicine Chests," *Science as Culture* 17, no. 3 (September 2008): 249–268.

33. Pettitt, *Dr. Livingstone*, 12. Pettitt provides the fullest treatment of Stanley's mode of marketing his explorations, though James L. Newman, *Imperial Footprints* (Washington, D.C., 2004) also is informative. The controversy provoked by Stanley is treated in Felix Driver, *Geography Militant* (Oxford, 2001), ch. 6, and Tim Youngs, *Travellers in Africa* (Manchester, 1994), chs. 4 and 5.

34. There is a rich body of scholarship on this subject. See, in particular, Paul Carter, *The Road to Botany Bay* (London, 1987); Mary Louise Pratt, *Imperial Eyes* (London, 1992); Simon Ryan, *The Cartographic Eye* (Cambridge, 1996); Nigel Leask, *Curiosity and the Aesthetics of Travel Writing* (Oxford, 2002); Frederic Regard, ed., *British Narratives of Exploration* (London, 2009); and Youngs, *Travellers*.

35. See Kathryn Barrett-Gaines, "Travel Writing, Experiences, and Silences," *History in Africa* 24 (1997): 53–70; Haynes, *Seeking the Centre*, ch. 4; David Finkelstein, *The House of Blackwood* (University Park, 2002); Leila Koivunen, *Visualizing Africa in Nineteenth-Century British Travel Accounts* (New York, 2009); Adrian S. Wisnicki, "Interstitial Cartographer," *Victorian Literature and Culture* 37 (2009): 255–271; Charles W. J. Withers, "Geography, Enlightenment and the Book," in *Geographies of the Book*, ed. Miles Ogborn and Charles W. J. Withers (Farnham, Surrey, 2010), 191–220; Innes M. Keighren and Charles W. J. Withers, "Questions of Inscription and Epistemology in British Travelers' Accounts of Early Nineteenth-Century South America," *Annals of the Association of American Geographers* 101 (2011): 1–16; Charles W. J. Withers and Innes M. Keighren, "Travels into Print," *Transactions of the Institute of British Geographers* 36, no. 4 (October 2011): 1–12.

36. Cameron Collection, VLC 4/1 (diary), 4/2 (notebook), and 4/3 (journal), RGS. For an analysis of the rationale and practice of note taking by scientific travelers, see Marie-Noëlle Bourguet, "A Portable World," *Intellectual History Review* 20, no. 3 (2010): 377–400.

37. John Davis, *Tracks of McKinlay and Party across Australia* (London, 1863), 122.

38. Lord Bathurst, "Introduction," in Hugh Clapperton, *Journal of the Second Expedition into the Interior of Africa* (Philadelphia, 1829), xx.

39. Richard C. Davis, "Introduction," in Charles Sturt, *The Central Australian Expedition* (London, 2002), lvii.

40. Forrest, *Exploration,* 218.

41. Kennedy to his father, April 14, 1847, Edmund Kennedy letters, T/2966/P/2/30, PRNI.

42. Testimony of Jackey Jackey, "Enquiry Taken at Sydney . . . Relative to the Death of E. B. C. Kennedy . . . ," New South Wales, Governor's Dispatches, vol. 60, March–April 1849, ML A1249, ML.

43. Donald Cumming, *The Gentleman Savage* (London, 1987), 31; John Kirk, *The Zambezi Journal* (Edinburgh, 1965), 1:307.

44. George Grey, *Journals of Two Expeditions of Discovery in North-West and Western Australia* (London, 1841), 2:92.

45. Richard Lander, n.d., CO2/16/8; R. W. Hay, September 19, 1828, CO392/1/88; R. W. Hay, letter of instruction to Lander, December 31, 1829, CO392/1/106–109, TNA.

46. Ryan, *Cartographic Eye,* 44.

47. See Granville Stapylton, *Stapylton* (Hobart, 1986); John Murphy, journal of Leichhardt's Port Essington expedition, ML MSS 2193, ML; William Phillips, journal of Leichhardt's Port Essington expedition, C165, ML; John Frederick Mann, diary of Leichhardt's 1846–1847 expedition, ML B455, ML; Hovenden Hely, journal of the 1846–1847 expedition, C264, ML; and Daniel Bunce, journal of the 1846–1847 expedition, B387, ML, which was published as *Travels with Dr. Leichhardt in Australia* (Melbourne, 1859).

48. Brock, *To the Desert,* 22, 199; John Bailey, *Mr. Stuart's Track* (Sydney, 2007), 235.

49. Richard F. Burton, *First Footsteps in East Africa* (London, 1856), appendix. On Speke's resentment, see W. B. Carnochan, *The Sad Story of Burton, Speke, and the Nile* (Stanford, 2006), 19.

50. Contract signed by Grant and Speke, April 16, 1860, Grant papers, MS 17922, f.2, NLS.

51. Murchison to Grant, n.d. [1864], Grant papers, MS 17910, f. 1–2, NLS.

52. Newman, *Imperial Footprints,* 227. Similarly, Samuel Baker required his European assistants to sign a contract restricting publication of their accounts of the expedition to conquer Equatoria. Alice Moore-Harell, *Egypt's African Empire* (Brighton, 2010), 21.

53. Leask, *Curiosity,* 298, 296.

54. Mungo Park, *Travels in the Interior Districts of Africa* [1799] (Durham, N.C., 2000), 45.

55. Eyre, *Journals of Expeditions of Discovery,* 1:viii.

56. Richard and John Lander, *Journal of an Expedition to Explore the Course and Termination of the Niger* (New York, 1832), 1:x.

57. Giles, *Ernest Giles's Explorations,* 377.

58. *South Australian Advertiser,* October 10, 1874. See also the comments on Giles in Haynes, *Seeking the Centre,* 65.

59. Joseph Thomson, *Through Masai Land* (London, 1887), ix.

60. Stanley also wrote a work of adventure fiction, the dreadful young adult novel *My Kalulu* (New York, 1873).

61. Edward Marston to Stanley, August 14, 1878, Stanley Archives, 1551, RAM.

62. Keighren and Withers, "Questions of Inscription," 1.

63. Withers, "Geography, Enlightenment and the Book," 196. Also see Lupton, *Mungo Park,* 109.

64. Jeal, *Livingstone,* 163.

65. W. H. Hovell and Hamilton Hume, *Journey of Discovery to Port Phillip, New South Wales* [1831] (Adelaide, 1965), 1.

66. See, for example, *The Burke and Wills Exploring Expedition* (Melbourne, 1861); *Journal of Landsborough's Expedition from Carpentaria, in Search of Burke and Wills* (Melbourne, 1862); Thomas Foster, *Review of the Labours of Several Explorers of Australia* (Melbourne, 1863).

67. Koivunen, *Visualizing Africa,* 116, 117. The figures for Baker's advance come from Baker to Grant, February 10, 1866, Grant Papers, MS 17909, ff. 5–8, NLS.

68. See Beau Riffenburgh, *The Myth of the Explorer* (London, 1993), and Pettitt, *Dr. Livingstone, I Presume?*

69. Lupton, *Mungo Park,* 97 (quote), 98–99, 108.

70. Richard Lander to Colonial Office, June 22, 1829, CO2/16/25, TNA; Clapperton, *Journal.*

71. Lander, *Journal,* 1:42.

72. E. D. Young, *The Search after Livingstone* (London, 1868), v; Dorothy O. Helly, *Livingstone's Legacy* (Athens, Ohio, 1987).

73. Speke to Blackwood, November 5, 1859, Blackwood Papers, MS 4143, ff. 134–135, NLS.

74. Speke to Blackwood, April 1, 1860, M148, Russell E. Train Africana Collection, Joseph Cullman Library, NMNH.

75. Finkelstein, *House,* ch. 3; David Finkelstein, "Unraveling Speke," *History in Africa* 30 (2003): 121.

76. Blackwood quoted in Finkelstein, "Unraveling Speke," 121.

77. Finkelstein, *House,* 60.

78. Speke to Blackwood, July 25, [1864], Blackwood Papers, MS 4193, ff. 195–195, NLS.

Epilogue

1. Richard Barnes, ed., *The Elder Scientific Exploration Expedition, 1891–2* (North Adelaide, 2003), 63, 100.

2. Henry Morton Stanley, "Geographical Tasks for Future Explorers," n.d., 4, M184m, Russell E. Train Africana Collection, Joseph Cullman Library, NMNH.

3. See Edward Berenson, *Heroes of Empire* (Berkeley, 2011), and Berny Sèbe, "The Making of British and French Legends of Exploration, 1821–1914," in *Reinterpreting Exploration,* ed. Dane Kennedy (New York, forthcoming).

4. Samuel Baker to Mr. Craik, December 21, 1890, M6e, Train Collection, NMNH.

5. Tim Youngs, *Travellers in Africa* (Manchester, 1994), chs. 4–5, quote on 170; Felix Driver, *Geography Militant* (Oxford, 2001), ch. 6; James L. Newman, *Imperial Footprints* (Washington, D.C., 2004), 310–314. Saleh Bin Osmin, the African headman attached to the Rear Column, gave a revealing deposition about the moral disintegration of its British officers. See Edward Glave, "Manuscript Translation of Testimony Given by Saleh Bin Osman, Regarding Stanley's Rear Guard in the Rescue of Emin Pasha," November 12, 1890, M55, Train Collection, NMNH.

6. Stanley, "Geographical Tasks"; Peter Collier and Rob Inkpen, "The RGS, Exploration and Empire and the Contested Nature of Surveying," *Area* 34, no. 3 (September 2002): 273–283.

7. See, for example, Jack Cross, *Great Central State* (Kent Town, South Australia, 2011), 44–45, 143, 196–198.

8. Cheryl Frost, *The Last Explorer* (Townsville, 1983). On North, see William Beinart and Lotte Hughes, *Environment and Empire* (Oxford, 2007), 85–88. On women travelers more generally, see Dea Birkett, *Spinsters Abroad* (Oxford, 1989) and Cheryl McEwan, *Gender, Geography, and Empire* (Aldershot, 2000).

9. Stephanie Barczewski, *Antarctic Destinies* (London, 2007), is a good introduction to this subject.

10. Stephen J. Pyne, *Voyager* (New York, 2010), xviii. Also see Simon Naylor and James R. Ryan, eds., *New Spaces for Exploration* (London, 2010).

11. Dan Zak, "A Feckless Trek?," *Washington Post,* May 30, 2009. East African explorers bypassed Masai territory for several decades because of their fearsome reputations.

12. Tim Jeal, "Remembering Henry Stanley," *Telegraph,* March 16, 2011; Rebecca Lefort, "Row over Statue of 'Cruel' Explorer Henry Morton Stanley," *Telegraph,* July 25, 2010.

13. "Hendrik Coetzee," *Economist,* January 1, 2011, 78.

14. Christy Collis, "Walking in Your Footsteps," in Naylor and Ryan, *New Spaces for Exploration,* 232, 239.

Bibliography

Archival Sources

BRITISH LIBRARY, LONDON

Add. Ms. 32117E (Heinrich Barth correspondence)
Add. Ms. 32448 (William Baikie journal)
Add. Ms. 34616–34618 (Napier papers: William Desborough Cooley correspondence)
Add. Ms. 46125–46128 (Sir Roderick Murchison papers)
Add. Ms. 48226 (Morley papers: Samuel Baker correspondence)
Add. Ms. 51305 (Gordon papers: Samuel Baker correspondence)

JOSEPH CULLMAN LIBRARY, NATIONAL MUSEUM OF NATURAL HISTORY,
SMITHSONIAN MUSEUMS, WASHINGTON, D.C.

Russell E. Train Africana Collection

MITCHELL LIBRARY, SYDNEY, AUSTRALIA

A 1384 (Hely expedition correspondence)
A 2612 (William Landsborough travel diaries)
A 2625 (Frank Scarr papers)
A 3600 (William Dawson memorandum regarding North Australian Expedition)
A 4054 (John R. Bradford journal)
Ag 34/I (letter regarding North Australian Expedition)
B 387 (Daniel Bunce journal)
B 880–884 (Ernest Favenc diary)
B 1098 (William Landsborough field books)
C 165 (William Phillips journal of Port Essington expedition)

ML A1249 (New South Wales governor's dispatches regarding inquiry into death of
E. B. Kennedy)
ML B455 (John Frederick Mann diary)
ML C332 (Edwin James Welch diary)
ML C407 (Diedrich Henne journal)
ML MS 648 (letters of Sir Thomas Elder to Jesse Young)
ML MSS 683/1 (Ludwig Leichhardt exploration diary)
ML MSS 1230 (Henry Maxwell Lefroy diary and journal)
ML MSS 1783 (James Henry Ricketson journal)
ML MSS 2193 (John Murphy journal of Port Essington expedition)
MS Q322 (William Hilton Hovell journal)
MS Q600 (William Carron narrative of Kennedy expedition)

THE NATIONAL ARCHIVES, KEW

CO 2/1–17 (African exploration)
CO 325/48 (miscellaneous memoranda)
CO 392/1–3 (African exploration entry books)

NATIONAL LIBRARY OF AUSTRALIA, CANBERRA

MS 25 (Joseph Ravenscroft Elsey diary and papers)
MS 39 (D. A. Linacre diary and newspaper cuttings)
MS 334 (L. L. Politzer papers on Leichhardt)
MS 548 (John Howe diary extracts)

NATIONAL LIBRARY OF SCOTLAND, EDINBURGH

MS 4143, 4173, 4185, 4193 (Blackwood papers: John Hanning Speke letters)
MS 4181, 4190, 4198, 4209 (Blackwood papers: James Grant correspondence)
MS 4872–4873 (Blackwood papers: manuscript and page proofs of Speke's *Journal of Discovery*)
MS 17909–17910, 17922, 17931 (James Grant papers)
MS 20311 (various correspondence)

PUBLIC RECORDS OF NORTHERN IRELAND, BELFAST

T/2966/P/7 and P/2/1–39 (Edmund Kennedy diary and letters)

ROYAL GEOGRAPHICAL SOCIETY, LONDON

CB (Correspondence blocks: for Francis Galton, James Grant, Mary Kingsley, Sir John Kirk, James MacQueen, Joseph Thomson, others)
JMS/13/6–210 (papers on Australian exploration)

SSC (various exploration files)
SWB/1–4 (Samuel Baker diaries)
VLC/1–7 (Verney Lovett Cameron collection)

ROYAL GEOGRAPHICAL SOCIETY OF SOUTH AUSTRALIA, ADELAIDE

R. H. Edmunds journals

STANLEY ARCHIVES, ROYAL AFRICAN MUSEUM, TERVUREN, BELGIUM

Henry Morton Stanley manuscripts, journals, notebooks, correspondence

STATE LIBRARY OF SOUTH AUSTRALIA, ADELAIDE

D 7368(L) (Edward Coates journal)
D 7743(L) (David Lindsay notes)
PRG 1006/1–4 (W. H. Tietkens papers)

STATE LIBRARY OF VICTORIA, MELBOURNE

AJCP-M1923 (Manuscripts of Australian Explorers from the Foreign and Commonwealth
Office Library)
MS 6173, Box 216/1 (Benjamin Helpman papers)
MS 9025, MSB 450 (Charles Sturt account of 1838 journey)

UNIVERSITY COLLEGE ARCHIVES, LONDON

Sir Francis Galton papers

WELLCOME LIBRARY, LONDON

John and Kate Petherick journals and diaries

Government Reports

BRITISH PARLIAMENTARY PAPERS

Cd. 472 (1843), *Papers Relative to the Expedition to the River Niger*
Cd. 2350 (1857–1858), *Papers Relating to an Expedition Recently Undertaken for the
Purpose of Exploring the Northern Portion of Australia*
Cd. 139 (1862), *Australian Exploring Expedition (Burke and Wills) Dispatches*

NEW SOUTH WALES LEGISLATIVE COUNCIL PAPERS

Expedition in Search of Dr. Leichhardt (1858)
Dr. Leichhardt (Correspondence Respecting Proposed Expedition in Search Of) (1865)

QUEENSLAND LEGISLATIVE ASSEMBLY PAPERS

Explorations by Mr. Hodgkinson (1876)

SOUTH AUSTRALIAN HOUSE OF ASSEMBLY PAPERS

No. 156 (1857), *Explorations by Mr. S. Hack*
No. 189 (1857), *North-Western Explorations*

No. 25 (1858), *Northern Exploration. Reports, &c.*
No. 72 (1858), *Northern Exploration*
No. 119 (1858), *Mr. Stuart's Exploration*
No. 161 (1860), *Cost of Exploring Expeditions*
No. 128 (1863), *Expenses of Exploring Expeditions*
No. 178 (1867), *Northern Territory Exploration*
No. 24 (1868), *Exploration Northern Territory*
No. 48 (1874), *W. C. Gosse's Explorations, 1873*
No. 246 (1874), *Examination of Lake Eyre*
No. 19 (1875), *Journal of Mr. Lewis's Lake Eyre Expedition*
No. 67 (1875), *Mr. J. Ross's Explorations, 1874*
No. 114 (1875), *Report on the Lake Eyre Expedition*
No. 209 (1878), *Journal of Mr. Barclay's Exploration, 1878*
No. 39 (1884), *Mr. Winnecke's Explorations during 1883*
No. 45 (1893), *Journal of the Elder Exploring Expedition, 1891*

Serials

Australian Dictionary of Biography, online edition (http://www.adb.anu.edu.au)
Journal of the Royal Geographical Society
Oxford Dictionary of National Biography, online edition (http://www.oxforddnb.com)

Books and Articles

AFRICA

Africa in Images, Stanley I Presume? Brussels: King Baudouin Foundation, 2007.
Anderson, Lisa. "Nineteenth-Century Reform in Ottoman Libya." *International Journal of Middle Eastern Studies* 16, no. 3 (August 1984): 325–348.
Anon. "Annual Report of the Council." *Journal of the Royal Geographical Society* 7 (1837): v–xiii.
———. "Extracts from the Correspondence of the Late Mr. Davidson, during His Residence in Morocco." *Journal of the Royal Geographical Society* 7 (1837): 144–172.
———. "Failure of Another Expedition to Explore the Interior of Africa." *Journal of the Royal Geographical Society* 2 (1832): 305–312.
———. "Instructions to Dr. Andrew Smith . . of the Expedition into Central Africa." *Journal of the Royal Geographical Society* 4 (1834): 363–370.
———. *Prospectus of an Expedition into the Interior of South Africa from Dalagoa Bay.* London: Williams Clowes, n.d. [c. 1835].
Baikie, William Balfour. *Narrative of an Exploring Voyage up the Rivers Kwo'ra and Bi'nue (Commonly Known as the Niger and Tsádda) in 1854.* London: John Murray, 1856.
Baker, Samuel White. *The Albert Nyanza, the Great Basin of the Nile, and Explorations of the Nile Sources.* London: Macmillan, 1866.
———. *Ismailia: A Narrative of the Expedition to Central Africa for the Suppression of the Slave Trade.* 2 vols. London: Macmillan, 1874.

Barnett, Clive. "Impure and Worldly Geography: Africanist Discourse of the Royal Geographical Society, 1831–73." *Transactions of the Institute of British Geographers* 23, no. 2 (1998): 239–251.

Barrell, John. "Death on the Nile: Fantasy and the Literature of Tourism, 1840–60." In *Cultures of Empire,* ed. Catherine Hall. London: Routledge, 2000, 187–206.

Barrett-Gaines, Kathryn. "Travel Writing, Experiences, and Silences: What Is Left Out of European Travelers' Accounts—The Case of Richard D. Mohun." *History in Africa* 24 (1997): 53–70.

Barth, Heinrich. *Travels and Discoveries in North and Central Africa, Being a Journal of an Expedition Undertaken under the Auspices of H.B.M.'s Government in the Years 1849–1855.* 3 vols. London: Frank Cass, 1965.

Bassett, Thomas J. "Cartography and Empire Building in Nineteenth-Century West Africa." *Geographical Review* 84, no. 3 (July 1994): 316–335.

———. "Indigenous Mapmaking in Intertropical Africa." In *The History of Cartography,* vol. 2, book 3: *Cartography in the Traditional African, American, Arctic, Australian, and Pacific Societies,* ed. David Woodward and G. Malcolm Lewis. Chicago: University of Chicago Press, 1998, 24–48.

Bassett, Thomas J., and Philip W. Porter. "'From the Best Authorities': The Mountains of Kong in the Cartography of West Africa." *Journal of African History* 32, no. 3 (1991): 367–413.

Bassett, Thomas J., and Yvette Scheven. *Maps of Africa to 1900: A Checklist of Maps in Atlases and Geographical Journals in the Collections of the University of Illinois, Urbana-Champaign.* Urbana-Champaign: University of Illinois Library, 2000.

Bennett, Norman Robert. *Arab versus European: Diplomacy and War in Nineteenth-Century East Central Africa.* New York: Africana Publishing Co., 1986.

Berenson, Edward. *Heroes of Empire: Five Charismatic Men and the Conquest of Africa.* Berkeley: University of California Press, 2011.

Blunt, Alison. *Travel, Gender, and Imperialism: Mary Kingsley and West Africa.* New York: Guilford Press, 1994.

Boahen, A. Adu. *Britain, the Sahara, and the Western Sudan, 1788–1861.* Oxford: Clarendon Press, 1964.

Bovill, E. W. "Introduction." In *Missions to the Niger,* vol. 2: *The Bornu Mission, 1822–25,* part 1, ed. E. W. Bovill. Cambridge: Cambridge University Press, 1966, 3–117.

Bridges, R. C. "Europeans and East Africans in the Age of Exploration." *Geographical Journal* 139, no. 2 (June 1973): 220–232.

———. "The Historical Role of British Explorers in East Africa." *Terrae Incognitae* 14 (1982): 1–21.

———. *James Augustus Grant, 1827–1892: African Explorer and Illustrator.* Edinburgh: National Library of Scotland, 1982.

———. "The Sponsorship and Financing of Livingstone's Last Journey." *African Historical Studies* 1, no. 1 (1968): 79–104.

———. "W. D. Cooley, the RGS and African Geography in the Nineteenth Century." Part 1, *Geographical Journal* 142, no. 1 (March 1976): 27–47; part 2, *Geographical Journal* 142, no. 2 (July 1976): 274–286.

——. "William Desborough Cooley and the Foundation of the Hakluyt Society." In *Compassing the Vaste Globe of the Earth: Studies in the History of the Hakluyt Society*, ed. R. C. Bridges and P. E. H. Hair. London: Hakluyt Society, 1996, 51–78.

Brode, Heinrich. *Tippu Tip: The Story of His Career in Zanzibar and Central Africa.* Zanzibar: Gallery, 2000.

Bruce, James. *Travels to Discover the Source of the Nile in the Years 1768, 1769, 1770, 1771, 1772, and 1773.* 5 vols. Edinburgh: J. Ruthven, 1790.

Burton, Richard F. *First Footsteps in East Africa* [1856]. New York: Frederick A. Praeger, 1966.

——. *The Lake Regions of Central Africa* [1860]. New York: Dover, 1995.

——. "The Lake Regions of Central Equatorial Africa, with Notices of the Lunar Mountains and the Sources of the White Nile." *Journal of the Royal Geographical Society* 29 (1859): 1–454.

——. *A Mission to Gelele King of Dahome.* Ed. C. W. Newbury [1864]. London: Routledge and Kegan Paul, 1966.

——. *Zanzibar: City, Island, and Coast.* 2 vols. London: Tinsley Brothers, 1872.

Burton, Richard F., and James MacQueen. *The Nile Basin.* London: Tinsley Brothers, 1864.

Burton, Richard F., and J. H. Speke. "A Coasting Voyage from Mombasa to the Pangani River." *Journal of the Royal Geographical Society* 28 (1858): 188–226.

Cameron, Verney Lovett. *Across Africa.* 2 vols. London: Daldy, Isbister, 1877.

Carnochan, W. B. *The Sad Story of Burton, Speke, and the Nile; or, Was John Hanning Speke a Cad?* Stanford: Stanford University Press, 2006.

Clapperton, Hugh. *Journal of a Second Expedition into the Interior of Africa, from the Bight of Benin to Soccatoo.* Philadelphia: Carey, Lea, and Carey, 1829.

Clendennen, Gary W. "Historians Beware: You Can't Judge a Book by Its Critics; or, Problems with a Nineteenth-Century Exploration Record." *History in Africa* 21 (1994): 403–407.

Clendennen, Gary W., and D. H. Simpson. "African Members of the Zambezi Expedition, 1861–1864: A Prosopographical Foray." *History in Africa* 12 (1985): 29–49.

Cooley, William Desborough. *The Memoir on the Lake Regions of East Africa, Reviewed.* London: Edward Stanford, 1864.

——. *The Negroland of the Arabs Examined and Explained; or, an Inquiry into the Early History and Geography of Central Africa.* London: J. Arrowsmith, 1841.

Coombes, Annie E. *Reinventing Africa: Museums, Material Culture and Popular Imagination in Late Victorian and Edwardian England.* New Haven: Yale University Press, 1994.

Coquery-Vidrovitch, Catherine, and Paul E. Lovejoy, eds. *The Workers of African Trade.* Beverly Hills, Calif.: Sage, 1985.

Crowther, Samuel. *Journal of an Expedition up the Niger and Tshadda Rivers, Undertaken by MacGregor Laird Esq. in Connection with the British Government, in 1854.* London: Church Missionary House, 1855.

Cumming, Donald. *The Gentleman Savage: The Life of Mansfield Parkyns, 1823–1894.* London: Century, 1987.

Curtin, Philip D. *The Image of Africa: British Ideas and Action, 1780–1850.* Madison: University of Wisconsin Press, 1964.

Davidson, John. *Notes Taken during Travels in Africa.* London: J. L. Cox and Sons, 1839.

De Lacerda, D. José. *Reply to Dr. Livingstone's Accusations and Misrepresentations.* London: Edward Stanford, 1865.

Delaney, John. *To the Mountains of the Moon: Mapping African Exploration, 1541–1880.* Princeton: Princeton University Library, 2007.

Denham, Major Dixon, and Captain Hugh Clapperton. *Narrative of Travels and Discoveries in Northern and Central Africa in the Years 1822, 1823, and 1824, by Major Denham, Captain Clapperton, and the Late Dr. Oudney Extending across the Great Desert to the Tenth Degree of Northern Latitude, and from Konka in Bornou, to Sackatoo, the Capital of the Felatah Empire.* Boston: Cummings, Hilliard, 1826.

Dorugu, James Henry. "The Life and Travels of Dorugu." Trans. and ed. Paul Newman. In *West African Travels and Adventures: Two Autobiographical Narratives from Northern Nigeria*, ed. Anthony Kirk-Greene. New Haven: Yale University Press, 1971, 29–129.

Dritsas, Lawrence S. *Zambesi: David Livingstone and Expeditionary Science in Africa.* London: I. B. Tauris, 2010.

———. "The Zambesi Expedition, 1858–64: African Nature in the British Scientific Metropolis." PhD diss., University of Edinburgh, 2005.

Dubow, Saul. *A Commonwealth of Knowledge: Science, Sensibility, and White South Africa 1820–2000.* Oxford: Oxford University Press, 2006.

Fabian, Johannes. *Out of Our Minds: Reason and Madness in the Exploration of Central Africa.* Berkeley: University of California Press, 2000.

Finkelstein, David. *The House of Blackwood: Author-Publisher Relations in the Victorian Era.* University Park: Pennsylvania State University Press, 2002.

———. "Unraveling Speke: The Unknown Revision of an African Exploration Classic." *History in Africa* 30 (2003): 117–132.

Folayan, Kola. *Tripoli during the Reign of Yusuf Pasha Qaramanli.* Ile-Ife, Nigeria: University of Ife Press, 1979.

Frank, Katherine. *A Voyager Out: The Life of Mary Kingsley.* Boston: Houghton Mifflin, 1986.

Galton, Francis. *The Narrative of an Explorer in Tropical South Africa.* London: John Murray, 1853.

Grant, James Augustus. *A Walk across Africa, or Domestic Scenes from My Nile Journal.* Edinburgh: William Blackwood and Sons, 1864.

Gray, Major William, and Staff Surgeon Dochard. *Travels in Western Africa.* London: John Murray, 1825.

Hallett, Robin, ed. *Records of the African Association, 1788–1831.* London: Thomas Nelson, 1964.

Helly, Dorothy O. *Livingstone's Legacy: Horace Waller and Victorian Mythmaking.* Athens: Ohio University Press, 1987.

Hibbert, Christopher. *Africa Explored: Europeans in the Dark Continent, 1769–1889.* Harmondsworth: Penguin, 1984.

Hopkins, A. G. "Explorers' Tales: Stanley Presumes—Again." *Journal of Imperial and Commonwealth History* 36, no. 4 (December 2008): 669–684.

Hornemann, Friedrich. "The Journals of Friedrich Hornemann's Travels from Cairo to Murzuk in the Years 1797–98." In *Missions to the Niger,* vol. 1, ed. E. W. Bovill. Cambridge: Cambridge University Press, 1964, 3–122.

Jeal, Tim. *Explorers of the Nile: The Triumph and Tragedy of a Great Victorian Adventure.* New Haven: Yale University Press, 2011.

———. *Livingstone.* New York: G. P. Putnam's Sons, 1973.

———. *Stanley: The Impossible Life of Africa's Greatest Explorer.* New Haven: Yale University Press, 2007.

Kirby, Percival R. *Sir Andrew Smith, M.D., K.C.B.: His Life, Letters and Works.* Cape Town: A. A. Baikema, 1965.

Kirk, John. *The Zambezi Journal and Letters of Dr. John Kirk, 1858–63.* 2 vols. Ed. Reginald Foskett. Edinburgh: Oliver and Boyd, 1965.

Koivunen, Leila. *Visualizing Africa in Nineteenth-Century British Travel Accounts.* New York: Routledge, 2009.

Laing, Alexander Gordon. "The Letters of Major Alexander Gordon Laing, 1824–26." In *Missions to the Niger,* vol. 1, ed. E. W. Bovill. Cambridge: Cambridge University Press, 1964, 123–390.

Laird, Macgregor, and R. A. K. Oldfield. *Narrative of an Expedition into the Interior of Africa by the River Niger.* London: Richard Bentley, 1837.

Lambert, David. "'Taken Captive by the Mystery of the Great River': Towards an Historical Geography of British Geography and Atlantic Slavery." *Journal of Historical Geography* 35 (2009): 44–65.

Lander, Richard, and John Lander. *Journal of an Expedition to Explore the Course and Termination of the Niger.* 2 vols. New York: J. and J. Harper, 1832.

Law, Robin. "Madiki Lemon, the 'English Captain' at Ouidah, 1843–1852: An Exploration in Biography." *History in Africa* 37 (2010): 107–123.

Lawrance, Benjamin N., Emily Lynn Osborne, and Richard L. Roberts, eds. *Intermediaries, Interpreters, and Clerks: African Employees in the Making of Colonial Africa.* Madison: University of Wisconsin Press, 2006.

Livingstone, David. *The Last Journals of David Livingstone in Central Africa.* Ed. Horace Waller. New York: Harper and Brothers, 1875.

———. *Missionary Travels and Researches in South Africa.* New ed. London: John Murray, 1899.

Lockhart, Jamie Bruce, and Paul E. Lovejoy, eds. *Hugh Clapperton into the Interior of Africa: Records of the Second Expedition, 1825–1827.* Leiden: Brill, 2005.

Lupton, Kenneth. *Mungo Park the African Traveler.* Oxford: Oxford University Press, 1979.

MacKenzie, John M., ed. *David Livingstone and the Victorian Encounter with Africa.* London: National Portrait Gallery, 1996.

Maitland, Alexander. *Speke.* London: Constable, 1971.

McAleer, John. *Representing Africa: Landscape, Exploration and Empire in Southern Africa, 1780–1870.* Manchester: Manchester University Press, 2010.

McCarthy, James. *Selim Aga: A Slave's Odyssey*. Edinburgh: Luath Press, 2006.

McCook, Stuart. "'It May Be Truth, but It Is Not Evidence': Paul du Chaillu and the Legitimation of Evidence in the Field Sciences." *Osiris*, 2nd ser., 11, Science in the Field (1996): 177–197.

McEwan, Cheryl. *Gender, Geography, and Empire: Victorian Women Travellers in West Africa*. Aldershot: Ashgate, 2000.

Médard, Henri, and Shane Doyle, eds. *Slavery in the Great Lakes Region of East Africa*. Oxford: James Currey, 2007.

Moore-Havell, Alice. *Egypt's African Empire: Samuel Baker, Charles Gordon, and the Creation of Equatoria*. Brighton: Sussex Academic Press, 2010.

Muhammad, Haid ibn. *Maisha Ya Hamed bin Muhammed el Murjebi Yaani Tippu Tip*. Nairobi: East African Literature Bureau, 1966.

Newman, James L. *Imperial Footprints: Henry Morton Stanley's African Journeys*. Washington, D.C.: Potomac Books, 2004.

———. *Paths without Glory: Richard Francis Burton in Africa*. Washington, D.C.: Potomac Books, 2009.

Ogunremi, 'Deji. "Human Porterage in Nigeria in the Nineteenth Century—A Pillar of the Indigenous Economy." *Journal of the Historical Society of Nigeria* 8, no. 1 (December 1975): 37–59.

Park, Mungo. *Travels in the Interior Districts of Africa* [1799]. Ed. with intro. by Kate Ferguson Marsters. Durham, N.C.: Duke University Press, 2000.

Peterson, Derek R., ed. *Abolitionism and Imperialism in Britain, Africa, and the Atlantic*. Athens: Ohio University Press, 2010.

Petrusic, Christopher. "Violence as Masculinity: David Livingstone's Radical Racial Politics in the Cape Colony and the Transvaal, 1845–1852." *International History Review* 26, no. 1 (March 2004): 20–55.

Pettitt, Clare. *Dr. Livingstone, I Presume? Missionaries, Journalists, Explorers, and Empire*. Cambridge, Mass.: Harvard University Press, 2007.

Poggo, Scopas. "Zande Resistance to Foreign Penetration in the Southern Sudan, 1860–1890." In *White Nile, Black Blood: War, Leadership, and Ethnicity from Khartoum to Kampala*, ed. Jay Spaulding and Stephanie Beswick. Lawrenceville, N.J.: Red Sea Press, 2000, 263–278.

Powell, Eve M. Troutt. *A Different Shade of Colonialism: Egypt, Great Britain, and the Mastery of the Sudan*. Berkeley: University of California Press, 2003.

Prestholdt, Jeremy. *Domesticating the World: African Consumerism and the Genealogies of Globalization*. Berkeley: University of California Press, 2008.

Reid, Donald Malcolm. "The Egyptian Geographical Society: From Foreign Laymen's Society to Indigenous Professional Association." *Poetics Today* 14, no. 3 (Autumn 1993): 539–572.

Robinson, Ronald, and John Gallagher, with Alice Denny. *Africa and the Victorians: The Climax of Imperialism*. Garden City, N.Y.: Anchor Books, 1968.

Rockel, Stephen J. *Carriers of Culture: Labor on the Road in Nineteenth-Century East Africa*. Portsmouth, N.H.: Heinemann, 2006.

———. "Enterprising Partners: Caravan Women in Nineteenth-Century Tanzania." *Canadian Journal of African Studies* 34, no. 3 (2000): 748–778.

Ross, Andrew C. *David Livingstone: Mission and Empire*. London: Hambledon and London, 2002.

Rotberg, Robert I., ed. *Africa and Its Explorers: Motives, Methods, and Impact*. Cambridge, Mass.: Harvard University Press, 1970.

———. *Joseph Thomson and the Exploration of Africa*. New York: Oxford University Press, 1971.

Russell, Mrs. Charles E. B. *General Rigby, Zanzibar and the Slave Trade, with Journals, Dispatches, etc.* London: George Allen and Unwin, 1935.

Sattin, Anthony. *The Gates of Africa: Death, Discovery, and the Search for Timbuktu*. New York: St. Martin's, 2003.

Sheriff, Abdul. *Slaves, Spices and Ivory in Zanzibar*. Oxford: James Currey, 1987.

Siddle, D. J. "David Livingstone: A Mid-Victorian Field Scientist." *Geographical Journal* 140, no. 1 (February 1974): 72–79.

Simpson, Donald. *Dark Companions: The African Contribution to the European Exploration of East Africa*. New York: Barnes and Noble, 1976.

Simpson, William. *A Private Journal Kept during the Niger Expedition*. London: John F. Shaw, 1843.

Smith, Andrew. *Andrew Smith's Journal of His Expedition into the Interior of South Africa, 1834–36*. Ed. William F. Lye. Cape Town: A. A. Balkema, 1975.

———. *The Diary of Dr. Andrew Smith, 1834–1836*. 2 vols. Ed. Percival R. Kirby. Cape Town: Van Reibeeck Society, 1939.

Speke, John Hanning. *Journal of the Discovery of the Source of the Nile* [1863]. London: J. M. Dent, 1937.

———. *My Second Expedition to Eastern Intertropical Africa* (pamphlet). Cape Town: Saul Solomon [c. 1860].

———. *What Led to the Discovery of the Source of the Nile*. Edinburgh: William Blackwood and Sons, 1864.

Stanley, Henry M. *How I Found Livingstone: Travels, Adventures, and Discoveries in Central Africa*. London: Sampson, Low, Marston, Low, and Searle, 1872.

———. *My Kalulu: Prince, King, and Slave*. New York: Charles Scribner's Sons, 1889.

———. *Through the Dark Continent or, the Sources of the Nile Around the Great Lakes of Equatorial Africa and Down the Livingstone River to the Atlantic Ocean* [1899]. 2 vols. New York: Dover 1988.

Stern, Philip J. " 'Rescuing the Age from the Charge of Ignorance': Gentility, Knowledge, and the Exploration of Africa in the Late Eighteenth Century." In *A New Imperial History: Culture, Identity and Modernity in Britain and the Empire, 1660–1840*, ed. Kathleen Wilson. Cambridge: Cambridge University Press, 2004, 115–135.

Temperley, Howard. *White Dreams, Black Africa: The Antislavery Expedition to the River Niger*. New Haven: Yale University Press, 1991.

Thompson, Jason. "Osman Effendi: A Scottish Convert to Islam in Early Nineteenth-Century Egypt." *Journal of World History* 5, no. 1 (1994): 99–123.

Thomson, Joseph. *Through Masai Land: A Journey of Exploration among the Snowclad Volcanic Mountains and Strange Tribes of Eastern Equatorial Africa*. New and rev. ed. London: Sampson, Low, Marston, Searle, and Rivington, 1887.

Tuckey, James H., and Christen Smith. *Narrative of an Expedition to Explore the River Zaire.* London: John Murray, 1818.

Umar, Muhammed S. "Islamic Discourses on European Visitors to Sokoto Caliphate in the Nineteenth Century." *Studia Islamica* 95 (2002): 135–159.

White, Landeg, *Magomero: Portrait of an African Village.* Cambridge: Cambridge University Press, 1987.

Wisnicki, Adrian. "Cartographical Quandaries: The Limits of Knowledge Production in Burton's and Speke's Search for the Source of the Nile." *History in Africa* 35 (2008): 455–479.

———. "Charting the Frontier: Indigenous Geography, Arab-Nyamwezi Caravans, and the East African Expedition of 1856–59." *Victorian Studies* 51, no. 1 (Autumn 2006): 103–137.

———. "Interstitial Cartographer: David Livingstone and the Invention of South Central Africa." *Victorian Literature and Culture* 37 (2009): 255–271.

———. "Rewriting Agency: Samuel Baker, Bunyoro-Kitara and the Egyptian Slave Trade." *Studies in Travel Writing* 14, no. 1 (February 2010): 1–27.

Withers, Charles W. J. "Geography, Enlightenment and the Book: Authorship and Audience in Mungo Park's African Texts." In *Geographies of the Book,* ed. Miles Ogborn and Charles W. J. Withers. Farnham, Surrey: Ashgate, 2010, 191–220.

———. "Mapping the Niger, 1798–1832: Trust, Testimony and 'Ocular Demonstration' in the Late Enlightenment." *Imago Mundi* 56, part 2 (2004): 170–193.

Young, E. D. *The Search after Livingstone.* London: Letts, Son, 1868.

Youngs, Tim. *Travellers in Africa: British Travelogues, 1850–1900.* Manchester: Manchester University Press, 1994.

AUSTRALIA

Anon. *The Burke and Wills Exploring Expedition: An Account of the Crossing the Continent of Australia, from Cooper's Creek to Carpentaria, with Biographical Sketches of Robert O'Hara Burke and William John Wills.* Melbourne: Wilson and Mackinnon, 1861.

———. "The Search for Leichhardt." *Australian Monthly Magazine* 1 (September 1, 1865): 12–16.

Atkinson, Alan. *The Europeans in Australia: A History,* vol. 2. Melbourne: Oxford University Press, 2004.

Bailey, John. *Mr. Stuart's Track: The Forgotten Life of Australia's Greatest Explorer.* Sydney: Picador, 2007.

Barker, H. M. *Camels and the Outback.* Melbourne: Sir Isaac Pitman and Sons, 1964.

Barnes, Richard, ed. *The Elder Scientific Exploration Expedition, 1891–2: Confidential Report.* North Adelaide: Corkwood Press, 2003.

Beale, Edgar. *Sturt: The Chipped Idol.* Sydney: Sydney University Press, 1979.

Beckler, Hermann. *A Journey to Cooper's Creek.* Trans. Stephen Jeffries and Michael Kertesz. Carlton, Victoria: Melbourne University Press, 1992.

Birman, Wendy. *Gregory of Rainworth: A Man in His Time.* Nedlands: University of Western Australia Press, 1979.

Blainey, Geoffrey. *The Tyranny of Distance: How Distance Shaped Australia's History.* New York: St. Martin's Press, 1968.

Bonyhady, Tim. *Burke and Wills: From Melbourne to Myth.* Canberra: National Library of Australia, 2002.

Briggs, Hazel. *Exploring in Western Australia.* Perth: Western Australia Museum, 1997.

Brock, Daniel George. *To the Desert with Sturt: A Diary of the 1844 Expedition.* Ed. with intro. by Kenneth Peake-Jones. Adelaide: Royal Geographical Society of Australasia, 1975.

Broome, Richard. *Aboriginal Australians: Black Response to White Dominance, 1788–2001.* 3rd ed. Crows Nest, NSW: Allen and Unwin, 2002.

———. *Aboriginal Victorians: A History since 1800.* Crows Nest, NSW: Allen and Unwin, 2005.

Brunato, Madeleine. *Hanji Mahomet Allum: Afghan Camel-driver, Herbalist, and Healer.* Leabrook: Investigator Press, 1972.

Cameron, J. M. R. "Agents and Agencies in Geography and Empire: The Case of George Grey." In *Geography and Imperialism, 1820–1940,* ed. Morag Bell, Robin Butlin, and Michael Heffernan. Manchester: Manchester University Press, 1995, 13–35.

Cameron, J. M. R., Glen McLaren, and William Cooper. "Bushmanship: The Explorer's Silent Partner." *Australian Geographer* 30, no. 3 (1999): 337–353.

Carnegie, David W. *Spinifex and Sand: A Narrative of Five Years' Pioneering and Exploration in Western Australia.* London: C. Arthur Pearson, 1898.

Carter, Paul. "Invisible Journeys: Exploration and Photography in Australia 1839–1889." In *Island in the Stream: Myths of Place in Australian Culture,* ed. Paul Foss. Leichhardt, NSW: Pluto Press, 1988, 47–60.

———. *The Road to Botany Bay: An Essay in Spatial History.* London: Faber and Faber, 1987.

Clendinnen, Inga. *Dancing with Strangers: Europeans and Australians at First Contact.* Cambridge: Cambridge University Press, 2005.

Cooper, William, and Glen McLaren. "The Changing Dietary Habits of Nineteenth-Century Australian Explorers." *Australian Geographer* 28, no. 1 (1997): 97–105.

Cross, Jack. *Great Central State: The Foundation of the Northern Territory.* Kent Town, South Australia: Wakefield Press, 2011.

Cross, Joseph, ed. *Journals of Several Expeditions Made in Western Australia, during the Years 1829, 1830, 1831, and 1832.* London: J. Cross, 1833.

Cumpston, J. H. L. *The Inland Sea and the Great River: The Story of Australian Exploration.* Sydney: Angus and Robertson, 1964.

Cunningham, Chris. *Blue Mountains Rediscovered: Beyond the Myths of Early Australian Exploration.* Kenthurst, NSW: Kangaroo Press, 1996.

Curthoys, Ann. "Indigenous Subjects." In *Australia's Empire,* ed. Deryck M. Schreuder and Stuart Ward. Oxford: Oxford University Press, 2008, 78–102.

Davis, John. *Tracks of McKinlay and Party across Australia.* Ed. with intro. by William Westgarth. London: Sampson Low Son, 1863.

Day, Alan. *Historical Dictionary of the Discovery and Exploration of Australia.* Lanham, Md.: Scarecrow Press, 2003.

Ericksen, Ray. *Ernest Giles: Explorer and Traveller, 1835–1897.* Melbourne: Heinemann, 1978.

Evans, Julie. *Edward Eyre, Race and Colonial Governance.* Dunedin, New Zealand: University of Otago Press, 2005.

Eyre, Edward John. *Autobiographical Narrative of Residence and Exploration in Australia, 1832–1839.* Ed. with intro. and notes by Jill Waterhouse. London: Caliban Books, 1984.

———. *Journals of Expeditions of Discovery into Central Australia, and Overland from Adelaide to King George's Sound in the Years 1840–1.* 2 vols. London: T. and W. Boone, 1845.

Fitzpatrick, Kathleen, ed. *Australian Explorers: A Selection of Their Writings.* London: Oxford University Press, 1958.

Flannery, Tim, ed. *The Explorers: Stories of Discovery and Adventure from the Australian Frontier.* New York: Grove Press, 1998.

Forrest, Alexander. *North-West Exploration: Journal of Expedition from DeGrey to Port Darwin.* Perth: Government Printer, 1880.

Forrest, John. *Explorations in Australia: I.—Explorations in Search of Dr. Leichardt and Party. II.—From Perth to Adelaide around the Great Australian Bight. III.—From Champion Bay, across the Desert to the Telegraph and to Adelaide* [1875]. New York: Greenwood Press, 1969.

Frost, Cheryl. *The Last Explorer: The Life and Work of Ernest Favenc.* Townsville: Foundation for Australian Literary Studies, 1983.

Genoni, Paul. *Subverting the Empire: Explorers and Exploration in Australian Fiction.* Altona, Victoria: Common Ground, 2004.

Giles, Ernest. *Ernest Giles's Explorations, 1872–76: South Australian Parliamentary Papers, 1872–76.* Adelaide: Friends of the State Library of South Australia, 2000.

———. *The Journal of a Forgotten Expedition in 1875 by Ernest Giles.* Ed. James Bosanquet. Adelaide: Sullivan's Cove, 1979.

Gregory, Augustus Charles, and Francis T. Gregory. *Journals of Australian Explorations* [1884]. New York: Greenwood Press, 1968.

Gregory, Francis T. *Journal of the N. W. Australian Exploring Expedition under the Authority of H. M. Imperial and Local Governments, Aided by Private Contributions, under the Command of Francis T. Gregory, F.R.G.S., April to November, 1861.* N.p., n.d.

Grey, George. *Journals of Two Expeditions of Discovery in North-West and Western Australia, during the Years 1837, 38, and 39.* 2 vols. London: T. and W. Boone, 1841.

Griffiths, Tom. *Hunters and Collectors: The Antiquarian Imagination in Australia.* Cambridge: Cambridge University Press, 1996.

Haynes, Roslynn D. *Seeking the Centre: The Australian Desert in Literature, Art and Film.* Cambridge: Cambridge University Press, 1998.

Hetherington, Penelope. *Settlers, Servants and Slaves: Aboriginal and European Children in Nineteenth-Century Western Australia.* Crawley: University of Western Australia Press, 2002.

Hill, J. G. *The Calvert Scientific Exploring Expedition.* London: George Philip and Son, 1905.

Hovell, W. H., and Hamilton Hume. *Journey of Discovery to Port Phillip, New South Wales* [1831]. Adelaide: Libraries Board of South Australia, 1965.

Howitt, A. W. "An Episode in the History of Australian Exploration." In *Australian Association for the Advancement of Science* (pamphlet). Melbourne: McCarron, Bird, 1901, 291–296.

———. *Finding Burke and Wills: Personal Reminiscences of Central Australia and the Burke and Wills Expedition, with a Glance at Benjamin Herschel Babbage's 1858 Expedition.* Adelaide: Friends of the State Library of South Australia, 2007.

Johnson, Richard. *The Search for the Inland Sea: John Oxley, Explorer, 1783–1828.* Melbourne: University of Melbourne Press, 2001.

Landsborough, William. *Journal of Landsborough's Expedition from Carpentaria, in Search of Burke and Wills* [1862]. Adelaide: Friends of the State Library of South Australia, 2000.

Leichhardt, Ludwig. *Journal of an Overland Expedition in Australia from Moreton Bay to Port Essington.* London: T. and W. Boone, 1847.

———. *Lectures Delivered by Dr. Ludwig Leichhardt, at the Sydney School of Arts.* Sydney: W. Baker, 1846.

———. *Letters from Australia.* Trans. L. L. Politzer. Melbourne: Pan, n.d.

———. *The Letters of F. W. Ludwig Leichhardt.* 3 vols. Trans. M. Aurousseau. Cambridge: Cambridge University Press, 1968.

Lester, Alan, and Fae Dussart. "Masculinity, 'Race,' and Family in the Colonies: Protecting Aborigines in the Early Nineteenth Century." *Gender, Place and Culture* 16, no. 1 (February 2009): 63–75.

Lines, John D. *Australia on Paper: The Story of Australian Mapping.* Victoria: J. D. Lines, 1992.

Lines, William J. *Taming the Great South Land: A History of the Conquest of Nature in Australia.* Athens: University of Georgia Press, 1991.

Locke, John. *Remarkable Discoveries in Central Australia* (pamphlet). Dublin: Dublin University Press, 1862.

MacGillivray, John. *Narrative of the Voyage of H.M.S. Rattlesnake, Commanded by the Late Captain Owen Stanley, R.N., F.R.S., etc., during the Years 1846–1850.* 2 vols. London: T. and W. Boone, 1852.

Macinnis, Peter. *Australia's Pioneers, Heroes and Fools: The Trials, Tribulations and Tricks of the Trade of Australia's Colonial Explorers.* Miller Point, NSW: Pier 9, 2007.

McGrath, Ann, ed. *Contested Ground: Australian Aborigines under the British Crown.* St. Leonards, NSW: Allen and Unwin, 1995.

McKinlay, John. *John McKinlay's Northern Territory Explorations, 1866: South Australian Parliamentary Papers, 1865–66.* Adelaide: Friends of the State Library of South Australia, 1999.

McKnight, Tom L. *The Camel in Australia.* Carlton, Victoria: Melbourne University Press, 1969.

McLaren, Glen. *Beyond Leichhardt: Bushcraft and the Exploration of Australia.* South Freemantle: Fremantle Arts Centre Press, 1996.

Mitchell, T. L. *Three Expeditions into the Interior of Eastern Australia; with Descriptions of the Recently Explored Regions of Australia Felix, and of the Present Colony of New South Wales.* 2 vols. London: T. and W. Boone, 1839.

Moorehead, Alan. *Cooper's Creek.* New York: Dell, 1963.

Mueller, Ferdinand. *The Fate of Dr. Leichhardt, and a Proposed New Search for His Party* (pamphlet reprinted from the *Australian*, February 18, 1865).

Murgatroyd, Sarah. *The Dig Tree: The Story of Burke and Wills.* Melbourne: Text, 2002.

Neumayer, Dr. G. "On the Scientific Exploration of Central Australia." *Proceedings of the Royal Society* 102 (1868): 347–364.

Oxley, John. *Journals of Two Expeditions into the Interior of New South Wales.* London: John Murray, 1820.

Reynolds, Henry. "The Land, the Explorers and the Aborigines." *Historical Studies* 19, no. 75 (1980): 213–226.

———. *With the White People.* Ringwood, Victoria: Penguin Books, 1990.

Ryan, Simon. *The Cartographic Eye: How Explorers Saw Australia.* Cambridge: Cambridge University Press, 1996.

Scott, Ernest. "The Exploration of Australia, 1813–1865." In *The Cambridge History of the British Empire,* vol. 3, part 1: *Australia,* ed. J. Holland Rose, A. P. Newton, and E. A. Benians. Cambridge: Cambridge University Press, 1933, 121–145.

Shoobert, Joanne, ed. *Western Australian Exploration,* vol. 1: *December 1826–December 1835.* Carlisle: Hesperian Press, 2005.

Smith, Philippa Mein. "Mapping Australasia." *History Compass* 7, no. 4 (2009): 1099–1122.

Stapylton, Granville W. C. *Stapylton: With Major Mitchell's Australia Felix Expedition, 1836.* Ed. Alan E. J. Andrews. Hobart: Blubber Head Press, 1986.

Steele, J. G., ed. *The Explorers of the Moreton Bay District, 1770–1830.* St. Lucia: University of Queensland Press, 1972.

Stokes, Edward. *Across the Centre: John McDouall Stuart's Expeditions, 1860–62.* Sydney: Allen and Unwin, 1996.

Strong, Pauline Turner. "Fathoming the Primitive: Australian Aborigines in Four Explorers' Journals, 1697–1845." *Ethnohistory* 33, no. 2 (1986): 175–194.

Sturt, Charles. *The Central Australian Expedition, 1844–1846: The Journals of Charles Sturt.* Ed. Richard C. Davis. London: Hakluyt Society, 2002.

———. *Two Expeditions into the Interior of Southern Australia, during the Years 1828, 1829, 1830, and 1831.* 2 vols. London: Smith, Elder and Co., 1833.

Sutton, Peter. "Aboriginal Maps and Plans." In *The History of Cartography,* vol. 2, book 3: *Cartography in the Traditional African, American, Arctic, Australian, and Pacific Societies,* ed. David Woodward and G. Malcolm Lewis. Chicago: University of Chicago Press, 1998, 387–416.

Thomas, Martin. *The Artificial Horizon: Imagining the Blue Mountains.* Carlton, Victoria: Melbourne University Press, 2003.

Threadgill, Bessie. *South Australian Land Exploration, 1856 to 1880.* Adelaide: Board of Governors, 1922.

Tietkens, W. H. *Journal of the Central Australian Exploring Expedition, 1889.* Adelaide: C. E. Bristow, 1891.

Tipping, Marjorie, ed. *Ludwig Becker: Artist and Naturalist with the Burke and Wills Expedition.* Carlton, Victoria: Melbourne University Press, 1979.

Tooley, R. V. *The Mapping of Australia.* London: Holland Press, 1979.

Warburton, Peter Egerton. *Journey across the Western Interior of Australia.* London: Sampson Low, Marston, Low, and Searle, 1875.

Waterhouse, Richard. "Settling the Land." In *Australia's Empire: The Oxford History of the British Empire Companion Series,* ed. Deryck M. Schreuder and Stuart Ward. Oxford: Oxford University Press, 2008, 54–77.

White, Patrick. *Voss.* Harmondsworth: Penguin Books, 1960.

Whyte, Duncan. *Sketch of Exploration by the Late John M'Kinlay in the Interior of Australia, 1861–2.* Glasgow: Aird and Coghill, 1881.

Winneke, Charles. *Journal of the Horn Scientific Exploring Expedition, 1894.* Adelaide: Government Printer, 1897.

BRITAIN AND EXPLORATION: GENERAL

Adams, Percy G. *Travelers and Travel Liars, 1660–1800.* Berkeley: University of California Press, 1962.

Adas, Michael. *Machines as the Measure of Men: Science, Technology, and Ideologies of Western Dominance.* Ithaca, N.Y.: Cornell University Press, 1989.

Aldrich, Robert. *Colonialism and Homosexuality.* London: Routledge, 2003.

Arnold, David. *The Tropics and the Traveling Gaze: India, Landscape, and Science, 1800–1856.* Seattle: University of Washington Press, 2006.

Bacon, Francis. "Of Travel." In *The Essays of Francis Bacon.* New York: Houghton Mifflin, 1908, 56–58.

Baker, Samuel. *Written on the Water: British Romanticism and the Maritime Empire of Culture.* Charlottesville: University of Virginia Press, 2010.

Barczewski, Stephanie. *Antarctic Destinies: Scott, Shackleton and the Changing Face of Heroism.* London: Hambledon Continuum, 2007.

Barrow, Ian J. *Making History, Drawing Territory: British Mapping in India, c. 1756–1905.* New Delhi: Oxford University Press, 2003.

Barrow, Sir John. *An Autobiographical Memoir of Sir John Barrow, Bart., Late of the Admiralty; Including Reflections, Observations, and Reminiscences at Home and Abroad, from Early Life to Advanced Age.* London: John Murray, 1847.

Beaglehole, J. C. "Eighteenth Century Science and the Voyages of Discovery." *New Zealand Journal of History* 3, no. 2 (1969): 107–123.

Bedini, Silvio A. "The Scientific Instruments of the Lewis and Clark Expedition." In *Mapping the North American Plains: Essays in the History of Cartography,* ed. Frederick C. Luebke, Francis W. Kaye, and Gary E. Moulton. Norman: University of Oklahoma Press, 1987, 93–110.

Beinart, William, and Lotte Hughes. *Environment and Empire.* Oxford: Oxford University Press, 2007.

Belcher, Edward. *A Treatise on Nautical Surveying.* London: Pelham Richardson, 1835.

Benton, Lauren. *A Search for Sovereignty: Law and Geography in European Empires, 1400–1900.* Cambridge: Cambridge University Press, 2010.

Berthon, Simon, and Andrew Robinson. *The Shape of the World: The Mapping and Discovery of the Earth*. Chicago: Rand McNally, 1991.

Bhabha, Homi K. *The Location of Culture*. London: Routledge, 1994.

Birkett, Dea. *Spinsters Abroad: Victorian Lady Explorers*. Oxford: Blackwell, 1989.

Blyth, Robert J. *The Empire of the Raj: India, Eastern Africa and the Middle East, 1858–1947*. Houndsmill, Basingstoke: Palgrave Macmillan, 2003.

Bourguet, Marie-Noëlle. "A Portable World: The Notebooks of European Travellers (Eighteenth to Nineteenth Centuries)." *Intellectual History Review* 20, no. 3 (2010): 377–400.

Bourguet, Marie-Noëlle, Christian Licoppe, and H. Otto Siburn, eds. *Instruments, Travel and Science: Itineraries of Precision from the Seventeenth to the Twentieth Century*. London: Routledge, 2002.

Boyle, Robert. *General Heads for the Natural History of a Country, Great or Small; Drawn Out for the Use of Travellers and Navigators*. London: n.p., 1692.

Bridges, Roy. "Exploration and Travel Outside Europe (1720–1914)." In *The Cambridge Companion to Travel Writing*, ed. Peter Hulme and Tim Youngs. Cambridge: Cambridge University Press, 2002, 53–69.

Brock, W. H. "Humboldt and the British: A Note on the Character of British Science." *Annals of Science* 50 (1993): 365–372.

Burnett, D. Graham. *Masters of All They Surveyed: Exploration, Geography, and a British El Dorado*. Chicago: University of Chicago Press, 2000.

Butlin, Robin A. *Geographies of Empire: European Empires and Colonies, c. 1880–1960*. Cambridge: Cambridge University Press, 2004.

Cameron, Ian. *To the Farthest Ends of the Earth: The History of the Royal Geographical Society, 1830–1980*. London: Macdonald, 1980.

Cannadine, David. *Ornamentalism: How the British Saw Their Empire*. New York: Oxford University Press, 2002.

Chester, Lucy P. "The Mapping of Empire: French and British Cartographies of India in the Late Eighteenth Century." *Portuguese Studies* 16 (2000): 256–275.

Clarke, Robert, ed. *Celebrity Colonialism: Fame, Power and Representation in Colonial and Postcolonial Cultures*. Newcastle upon Tyne: Cambridge Scholars, 2009.

Cock, Randolph. "Scientific Servicemen in the Royal Navy and the Professionalization of Science, 1816–55." In *Science and Beliefs: From Natural Philosophy to Natural Science, 1700–1900*, ed. David M. Knight and Matthew D. Eddy. Aldershot: Ashgate, 2005, 95–111.

Cohen, Margaret. *The Novel and the Sea*. Princeton: Princeton University Press, 2010.

Colley, Linda. *Captives: Britain, Empire, and the World, 1600–1850*. New York: Pantheon, 2002.

Collier, Peter, and Rob Inkpen. "The RGS, Exploration and Empire and the Contested Nature of Surveying." *Area* 34, no. 3 (September 2002): 273–283.

Conrad, Joseph. "Geography and Some Explorers." In *Last Essays* [1926]. Freeport, N.Y.: Books for Libraries Press, 1970, 1–21.

———. "Heart of Darkness." In *Great Short Works of Joseph Conrad*. New York: Harper and Row, 1966.

Cook, James. *The Journals.* Ed. Philip Edwards. London: Penguin, 2003.

De La Beche, H. T. *How to Observe: Geology.* 2nd ed. London: Charles Knight, 1836.

Desmond, Adrian. "The Making of Institutional Zoology in London, 1822–1836." Part 1, *History of Science* (June 1985): 153–185; part 2, *History of Science* (September 1985): 223–250.

Drayton, Richard. "Knowledge and Empire." In *The Oxford History of the British Empire,* vol. 2: *The Eighteenth Century,* ed. P. J. Marshall. Oxford: Oxford University Press, 1998, 231–252.

———. *Nature's Government: Science, Imperial Britain, and the "Improvement" of the World.* New Haven: Yale University Press, 2000.

Driver, Felix. "The Active Life: The Explorer as Biographical Subject." *Oxford Dictionary of National Biography,* Oxford University Press online edition, May 2007, http://www.oxforddnb.com.

———. "Distance and Disturbance: Travel, Exploration and Knowledge in the Nineteenth Century." *Transactions of the Royal Historical Society,* 6th ser., 14 (2004): 73–92.

———. *Geography Militant: Cultures of Exploration and Empire.* Oxford: Blackwell, 2001.

———. "Henry Morton Stanley and His Critics: Geography, Exploration and Empire." *Past and Present* 133 (November 1991): 134–166.

Driver, Felix, and Lowri Jones. *Hidden Histories of Exploration: Researching the RGS-IBG Collections.* London: Royal Holloway, University of London, 2009.

Driver, Felix, and Luciana Martins. "John Septimus Roe and the Art of Navigation, c. 1815–1830." *History Workshop Journal* 54, no. 1 (2002): 144–161.

———, eds. *Tropical Visions in an Age of Empire.* Chicago: University of Chicago Press, 2005.

Edney, Matthew H. "The Irony of Imperial Mapping." In *The Imperial Map,* ed. James R. Akerman. Chicago: University of Chicago Press, 2009, 11–45.

———. *Mapping an Empire: The Geographical Construction of British India, 1765–1843.* Chicago: University of Chicago Press, 1997.

Elsner, Jás, and Joan-Pau Rubiés, eds. *Voyages and Visions: Towards a Cultural History of Travel.* London: Reaktion Books, 1999.

Emery, F. V. "Geography and Imperialism: The Role of Sir Bartle Frere (1815–84)." *Geographical Journal* 150, no. 3 (November 1984): 342–350.

Endersby, Jim. *Imperial Nature: Joseph Hooker and the Practices of Victorian Science.* Chicago: University of Chicago Press, 2008.

Etherington, Norman, ed. *Mapping Colonial Conquest: Australia and Southern Africa.* Crawley: University of Western Australia Press, 2007.

Fara, Patricia. *Sex, Botany and Empire: The Story of Carl Linnaeus and Joseph Banks.* Thirplow, Cambridge: Icon Books, 2004.

Fernández-Armesto, Felipe. *Pathfinders: A Global History of Exploration.* New York: W. W. Norton, 2006.

Fichman, Martin. *An Elusive Victorian: The Evolution of Alfred Russel Wallace.* Chicago: University of Chicago Press, 2004.

Finn, Margo. "Slaves Out of Context: Domestic Slavery and the Anglo-Indian Family, c. 1780–1830." *Transactions of the Royal Historical Society* 19 (2009): 181–203.

Fulford, Tim, Debbie Lee, and Peter J. Kitson. *Literature, Science and Exploration in the Romantic Era: Bodies of Knowledge.* Cambridge: Cambridge University Press, 2004.

Galton, Francis. *The Art of Travel; or, Shifts and Contrivances Available in Wild Countries.* 2nd ed. London: John Murray, 1856.

———. "The Exploration of Arid Countries." *Proceedings of the Royal Geographical Society of London* 2, no. 2 (1857–1858): 60–77.

Ghosh, Durba, and Dane Kennedy, eds. *Decentring Empire: Britain, India, and the Transcolonial World.* Hyderabad: Orient Longman, 2006.

Gillham, Nicholas W. *A Life of Sir Francis Galton: From African Exploration to the Birth of Eugenics.* New York: Oxford University Press, 2001.

Goetzmann, William. *Exploration and Empire: The Explorer and the Scientist in the Winning of the American West.* New York: Vintage, 1972.

Grann, David. *The Lost City of Z.* New York: Vintage Books, 2010.

Grier, David Alan. *When Computers Were Human.* Princeton: Princeton University Press, 2005.

Gurney, Alan. *Compass: A Story of Exploration and Innovation.* New York: W. W. Norton, 2004.

Hale, Lonsdale. *What to Observe and How to Report It.* 7th ed. London: Her Majesty's Stationery Office, 1898.

Hall, Catherine. *Civilising Subjects: Metropole and Colony in the English Imagination, 1830–1867.* Chicago: University of Chicago Press, 2002.

Harley, J. B. "New England Cartography and the Native Americans." In *The New Nature of Maps: Essays in the History of Cartography.* Baltimore: Johns Hopkins University Press, 2001, 169–195.

Hirschel, John F. W. *A Manual of Scientific Enquiry.* 2nd ed. London: John Murray, 1851.

Holmes, Richard, *The Age of Wonder: How the Romantic Generation Discovered the Beauty and Terror of Science.* New York: Pantheon, 2008.

Jackson, Col. J. R. "Hints on the Subject of Geographical Arrangement and Nomenclature." *Journal of the Royal Geographical Society* 4 (1834): 72–88.

———. "On Picturesque Description in Books of Travel." *Journal of the Royal Geographical Society* 5 (1835): 381–387.

———. *What to Observe; or, the Traveller's Remembrancer.* 2nd ed. London: Madden and Malcolm, 1845.

Jasanoff, Maya. *Edge of Empire: Lives, Culture, and Conquest in the East, 1750–1850.* New York: Alfred A. Knopf, 2005.

Johnson, Ryan. "Tabloid Brand Medicine Chests: Selling Health and Hygiene for the British Tropical Colonies." *Science as Culture* 17, no. 3 (September 2008): 249–268.

Jones, Lowri M. "Local Knowledge and Indigenous Agency in the History of Exploration: Studies from the RGS Collections." PhD diss., Royal Holloway University of London, 2010.

Jones, Max. "Measuring the World: Exploration, Empire and the Reform of the Royal Geographical Society c. 1874–93." In *The Organization of Knowledge in Victorian Britain,* ed. Martin Daunton. Oxford: Oxford University Press, 2005, 313–336.

Keighren, Innes M., and Charles W. J. Withers. "Questions of Inscription and Epistemology in British Travelers' Accounts of Early Nineteenth-Century South America." *Annals of the Association of American Geographers* 101 (2011): 1–16.

Kennedy, Dane. "British Exploration in the Nineteenth Century: A Historiographical Survey." *History Compass* 5, no. 6 (2007): 1879–1900.

———. "Exploration, Science and Cross-Cultural Intimacy." In *The British Empire and Its Contested Pasts*, ed. Robert J. Blyth and Keith Jeffery. Dublin: Irish Academic Press, 2009, 45–54.

———. *The Highly Civilized Man: Richard Burton and the Victorian World*. Cambridge, Mass.: Harvard University Press, 2005.

———, ed. *Reassessing Exploration: The West in the World*. New York: Oxford University Press, forthcoming.

Lamb, Jonathan. *Preserving the Self in the South Seas, 1680–1840*. Chicago: University of Chicago Press, 2001.

Lamb, Jonathan, Vanessa Smith, and Nicholas Thomas, eds. *Exploration and Exchange: A South Seas Anthology, 1680–1900*. Chicago: University of Chicago Press, 2000.

Leask, Nigel. *Curiosity and the Aesthetics of Travel Writing, 1770–1840*. Oxford: Oxford University Press, 2002.

Leed, Eric. *Shores of Discovery: How Expeditionaries Have Constructed the World*. New York: Basic Books, 1995.

Lewis, Martin W., and Kären E. Wigen. *The Myth of Continents: A Critique of Metageography*. Berkeley: University of California Press, 1997.

Liebersohn, Harry. "Scientific Ethnography and Travel, 1750–1850." In *The Cambridge History of Science*, vol. 7: *The Modern Social Sciences*, ed. Theodore M. Porter and Dorothy Rose. Cambridge: Cambridge University Press, 2003, 100–112.

———. *The Traveler's World: Europe to the Pacific*. Cambridge, Mass.: Harvard University Press, 2006.

Lightman, Bernard. *Victorian Popularizers of Science: Designing Nature for New Audiences*. Chicago: University of Chicago Press, 2007.

Livingstone, David N. *The Geographical Tradition: Episodes in the History of a Contested Enterprise*. Oxford: Blackwell, 1992.

———. *Putting Science in Its Place: Geographies of Scientific Knowledge*. Chicago: University of Chicago Press, 2003.

Livingstone, David N., and Charles W. J. Withers, eds. *Geographies of Nineteenth-Century Science*. Chicago: University of Chicago Press, 2011.

———, eds. *Geography and Enlightenment*. Chicago: University of Chicago Press, 1999.

Lloyd, Christopher. *Mr. Barrow of the Admiralty: A Life of Sir John Barrow, 1764–1848*. London: Collins, 1970.

Mackay, David. *In the Wake of Cook: Exploration, Science and Empire, 1780–1801*. New York: St. Martin's Press, 1985.

McCracken, Donal P. *Gardens of Empire: Botanical Institutions in the Victorian British Empire*. London: Leicester University Press, 1997.

MacKenzie, John M. *The Empire of Nature: Hunting, Conservation and British Imperialism*. Manchester: Manchester University Press, 1988.

———. "Heroic Myths of Empire." In *Popular Imperialism and the Military, 1850–1950.* Manchester: Manchester University Press, 1992, 109–138.

———. *Museums and Empire: Natural History, Human Cultures and Colonial Identity.* Manchester: Manchester University Press, 2009.

———. "The Provincial Geographical Societies in Britain, 1884–1914." In *Geography and Imperialism, 1820–1940,* ed. Morag Bell, Robin Butlin, and Michael Heffernan. Manchester: Manchester University Press, 1995, 93–124.

Mancke, Elizabeth. "Ocean Space and the Creation of a Global International System, 1450–1800." In *Maritime History as World History,* ed. Daniel Finamore. Gainesville: University Press of Florida, 2004, 149–166.

Markham, Clements R. *The Fifty Years' Work of the Royal Geographical Society.* London: John Murray, 1881.

Martineau, Harriet. *How to Observe: Manners and Morals.* London: Charles Knight, 1838.

Metcalf, Thomas R. *Imperial Connections: India in the Indian Ocean Arena, 1860–1920.* Berkeley: University of California Press, 2008.

Miller, David Philips. "Introduction." In *Visions of Empire: Voyages, Botany, and Representations of Nature,* ed. David Philips Miller and Peter Hanns Reill. Cambridge: Cambridge University Press, 1996, 1–18.

Morus, Iwan. "Replacing Victoria's Scientific Culture." *19: Interdisciplinary Studies in the Long Nineteenth Century* 2 (2006), www.19.bbk.ac.uk.

Moulton, Gary E., ed. *The Lewis and Clark Journals: An American Epic of Discovery.* Lincoln: University of Nebraska Press, 2003.

Naylor, Simon, and James R. Ryan, eds. *New Spaces for Exploration: Geographies of Discovery in the Twentieth Century.* London: I. B. Tauris, 2010.

Overton, J. D. "A Theory of Exploration." *Journal of Historical Geography* 7, no. 1 (January 1981): 53–70.

Pratt, Mary Louise. *Imperial Eyes: Travel Writing and Transculturation.* London: Routledge, 1992.

———. "Travel Narrative and Imperialist Vision." In *Understanding Narrative,* ed. James Phelan and Peter J. Rabinowitz. Columbus: Ohio State University Press, 1994, 199–221.

Pyne, Stephen J. *Voyager: Seeking Newer Worlds in the Third Great Age of Discovery.* New York: Viking, 2010.

Regard, Frederick, ed. *British Narratives of Exploration: Case Studies of the Self and Other.* London: Pickering and Chatto, 2009.

Reidy, Michael, Gary Kroll, and Erik M. Conway, eds. *Exploration and Science: Social Impact and Interaction.* Santa Barbara: ABC-CLIO, 2007.

Richardson, Brian W. *Longitude and Empire: How Captain Cook's Voyages Changed the World.* Vancouver: University of British Columbia Press, 2005.

Riffenburgh, Beau. *The Myth of the Explorer: The Press, Sensationalism, and Geographical Discovery.* London: Belhaven, 1993.

Ritchie, G. S. *The Admiralty Chart: British Naval Hydrography in the Nineteenth Century.* New York: American Elsevier, 1967.

Roberts, Jason. *A Sense of the World: How a Blind Man Became History's Greatest Traveler.* New York: HarperPerennial, 2007.

Rutherford, Jonathan. *Forever England: Reflections on Masculinity and Empire.* London: Lawrence and Wishart, 1997.

Ryan, James R. *Picturing Empire: Photography and the Visualization of the British Empire.* Chicago: University of Chicago Press, 1997.

Sachs, Aaron. *The Humboldt Current: Nineteenth-Century Exploration and the Roots of American Environmentalism.* New York: Penguin, 2006.

———. "The Ultimate 'Other': Post-Colonialism and Alexander von Humboldt's Ecological Relationship with Nature." *History and Theory* 42 (December 2003): 111–135.

Satia, Priya. *Spies in Arabia: The Great War and the Cultural Foundations of Britain's Covert Empire in the Middle East.* New York: Oxford University Press, 2008.

Schaffer, Simon, Lissa Roberts, Kapil Raj, and James Delbourgo, eds. *The Brokered World: Go-Betweens and Global Intelligence, 1770–1820.* Sagamore Beach, Mass.: Science History Publications, 2009.

Scott, Jonathan. *When the Waves Ruled Britannia: Geography and Political Identities, 1500–1800.* Cambridge: Cambridge University Press, 2011.

Shapin, Steven. *A Social History of Truth: Civility and Science in Seventeenth-Century England.* Chicago: University of Chicago Press, 1994.

Sheets-Pyenson, Susan. *Cathedrals of Science: The Development of Colonial Natural History Museums during the Late Nineteenth Century.* Kingston: McGill–Queen's University Press, 1988.

Smith, Bernard. *European Vision and the South Pacific.* 2nd ed. New Haven: Yale University Press, 1985.

———. *Imagining the Pacific in the Wake of Cook's Voyages.* New Haven: Yale University Press, 1992.

Sobel, Dava. *Longitude: The True Story of a Lone Genius Who Solved the Greatest Scientific Problem of His Time.* New York: Penguin, 1996.

Sorrenson, Richard, "The Ship as a Scientific Instrument in the Eighteenth Century." *Osiris,* 2nd ser., 2 (1996): 221–236.

Stafford, Robert A. "Annexing the Landscapes of the Past: British Imperial Geography in the Nineteenth Century." In *Imperialism and the Natural World,* ed. John M. MacKenzie. Manchester: Manchester University Press, 1990, 67–89.

———. "Scientific Exploration and Empire." In *The Oxford History of the British Empire,* vol. 3: *The Nineteenth Century,* ed. Andrew Porter. Oxford: Oxford University Press, 1999, 294–319.

———. *Scientist of Empire: Sir Roderick Murchison, Scientific Exploration and Victorian Imperialism.* Cambridge: Cambridge University Press, 1989.

Stoddart, D. R. "The RGS and the 'New Geography': Changing Aims and Changing Roles in Nineteenth Century Science." *Geographical Journal* 146, no. 2 (July 1980): 190–202.

Stoler, Ann Laura. "Tense and Tender Ties: The Politics of Comparison in North American History and (Post) Colonial Studies." *Journal of American History* 88, no. 3 (December 2001): 829–865.

Swift, Jonathan. *Gulliver's Travels* [1735]. New York: Barnes and Noble Classics, 2003.

Teltscher, Kate. *The High Road to China: George Bogle, the Panchen Lama, and the First British Expedition to Tibet.* New York: Farrar, Straus and Giroux, 2006.

Théodoridès, Jean. "Humboldt and England." *British Journal for the History of Science* 3, no. 9 (June 1966): 39–55.

Thomas, Nicholas. *Cook: The Extraordinary Voyages of Captain James Cook.* New York: Walker and Co., 2003.

Tosh, John. *Manliness and Masculinities in Nineteenth-Century Britain.* Harlow: Longman, 2005.

Trench, Richard. *Arabian Travellers.* London: Macmillan, 1986.

von Humboldt, Alexander. *Personal Narrative of a Journey to the Equinoctal Regions of the New Continent.* Abridged ed. Harmondsworth: Penguin, 1996.

Wainwright, Jacob. "'A Dangerous and Toilsome Journey': Jacob Wainwright's Diary of the Transportation of Dr. Livingstone's Body to the Coast, 4 May 1873–18 February 1874." Ed. and trans. R. C. Bridges. In *Four Travel Journals: The Americas, Antarctica and Africa, 1775–1874,* ed. Herbert K. Beals, et al. London: Hakluyt Society, 2007, 329–384.

Waller, John C. "Gentlemanly Men of Science: Sir Francis Galton and the Professionalization of the British Life-Sciences." *Journal of the History of Biology* 34, no. 1 (2001): 83–114.

Withers, Charles W. J. *Geography and Science in Britain, 1831–1939: A Study of the British Association for the Advancement of Science.* Manchester: Manchester University Press, 2010.

Withers, Charles W. J., and Innes M. Keighren. "Travels into Print: Authoring, Editing and Narratives of Travel and Exploration, c. 1815–c. 1857." *Transactions of the Institute of British Geographers* 36, no. 4 (October 2011): 1–12.

Acknowledgments

Doing this book was my kind of exploration—all pleasure, no pain. The only fever I experienced was archive fever, and, far from being debilitating, its effects were euphoric. My discoveries can't compare to those of the explorers I studied, but they were no less thrilling for me. I traveled to many new and wonderful places and met many wise and generous people. It's been a great trip.

I want to thank all of those individuals—new friends and old—who helped me bring this book to completion. I am especially grateful to Richard Broome, Lucy Chester, Tim Parsons, Richard Price, and Phil Stern, each of whom took the time and trouble to read and comment on one or more of my chapters. Their frank comments and helpful suggestions did much to improve the manuscript and save me from my own ignorance. So too did Harvard's two anonymous reviewers, whose exceptionally close and careful readings of the manuscript went far beyond the call of duty. And Joyce Seltzer was once again the ideal editor, encouraging but eagle-eyed in identifying those parts of the manuscript that needed work. Her assistant, Brian Distelberg, was indispensable as well.

I had the honor and good fortune to test some of my ideas and arguments in talks at the University of Calgary, Cambridge University, Harvard University, the University of Illinois at Urbana–Champaign, Kings College London, Latrobe

University, Leeds University, the National Humanities Center, Oxford University, Queens University Belfast, Royal Holloway College London, Seijo University, Sheffield University, West Virginia University, and the University of York. It is impossible to thank everyone whose questions and comments at these gatherings helped to improve this book, but the following deserve special note: Thomas Bassett, Liz Buettner, Antoinette Burton, Robin Butlin, Richard Drayton, Felix Driver, Peter Hansen, Joe Hodge, Will Jackson, Maya Jasanoff, Yoichi Kibata, Marilyn Lake, David Lambert, Alan Lester, Harry Liebersohn, John Lonsdale, Peter Mandler, Miles Ogborn, Doug Peers, Clare Pettitt, Ian Phimister, and Andrew Thompson. Additional advice, assistance, and insights came from Ann Curthoys and John Docker, Shane Doyle, Amelia Guckenberg, Mathilde Leduc-Grimaldi, Peter Macinnis, Mark McKenna, James Newman, Stephen Rockel, Priya Satia, Lewis Taylor, Lorenzo Veracini, Charles Withers, and Angela Woollacott. I also want to thank Elizabeth Shaw and Michael Wright, my always generous hosts in London. The book's two maps are the work of the skilled Bill Nelson.

Most of this manuscript was written at the National Humanities Center in the Research Triangle, North Carolina, where I was privileged to hold the John P. Birkelund Senior Fellowship in 2010–2011. Geoffrey Harpham and his remarkable staff have made the center an ideal environment for thinking and writing. I was surrounded by a wonderful group of fellows whose intellectual acumen and generosity gave new meaning to the trite phrase "a community of scholars." Special thanks go to the participants in two reading groups, who commented on early drafts of chapters: Suzanne Clark, Denise Davidson, Sabine Hake, Sharon Harley, Bayo Holsey, Luis Pares, Cynthia Radding, Eliza Richards, Leah Rosenberg, Marjorie Stone, Jay Straker, Miguel Tamen, Leslie Tuttle, and Katherine Zieman. I am also grateful during my year in residence at the center for the hospitality of David Gilmartin and Sandy Freitag, Phil and Kim Stern, Doug Zinn, and, above all, Jane and Martin Rody.

Could there be a more fitting way to celebrate the completion of this book than to open a bottle of excellent Australian shiraz named after the African explorer Mungo Park? The wine was a gift from my wife, Marty, who has been my essential companion on this adventure, as she has throughout my life. This book is dedicated to her and the rest of my family with love.

Index